DIVINING

*The art of searching for water, oil, minerals,
and other natural resources or anything
lost, missing or badly needed*

Christopher Bird

illustrations by Thomas Heston

A Raven Book

Macdonald and Jane's
London and Sydney

Copyright © 1979 by Christopher Bird

First published in Great Britain in 1980 by Macdonald General Books, Macdonald and Jane's Publishing Group, 8 Shepherdess Walk, London N.1.
A Raven Book published in association with Futura Publications

ISBN 354 043889

All uncredited photographs were taken by the author.

Designed by Winston Potter

CONTENTS

GRATITUDES

Works of nonfiction, like the fruits of any exploration, are cooperative efforts and this one is no exception.

In the late summer of 1967 at the recommendation of a friend living in Mexico I was about to call Peter Tompkins at his dairy barn home in Virginia when my telephone rang. "This is Peter Tompkins," gruffed a voice with an overtone of studied chilliness. "I understand we have a mutual friend in Cuernavaca who suggests we should get together. Why don't you come out now and get it over with?"

That invitation led to a series of adventures during which Peter introduced me to overlooked corners of the cosmos and to unsuspected crannies of English style. After a two-year stint as a correspondent in Yugoslavia, I entered into a collaboration with Peter that eventually led to our writing a book together.

In 1970, while pursuing research quarries, I was introduced on a Rockport, Maine, porch by another friend to Rexford Daniels who had spent a quarter century pioneering the study of what has come to be called "electromagnetic interference." Rex's huge files included investigations into undefined energies apparently unconnected to electromagnetism such as the "orgone" of the late Dr. Wilhelm Reich and an "X-force" which, hovering somewhere between the physical world and the realm of the psyche and with apparent roots in both, seemed to play a role in inexplicable actions by which living creatures, man included, relate to their fellows and to their environment.

In the fall of the same year, in the midst of tracking down more clues subtly dangled in front of me by Rex, I found myself talking with Dr. Bernard Grad of McGill University's Allan Memorial Institute of Psychiatry in Montreal, who suddenly asked: "What do you know about *dowsing?*"

The answer being "nothing whatsoever," Grad urged that on my drive down through New England I stop off at the convention of the American Society of Dowsers (ASD), held annually in the tiny village of Danville in Vermont's "Northeast Kingdom." To the ASD Board of Trustees, which I was subsequently invited to join, and to ASD members hailing from every state of the American Union and many foreign countries, *The Divining Hand* owes its principal inspiration, matched only by the constant encouragement and cooperation of all of this book's protagonists.

The way into a virtual Minotaur's lair of references to dowsing was provided by two compendious bibliographies. The first appeared in Arthur Jackson Ellis's *The Divining Rod: A History of Water Witching,* printed in 1917 as U.S. Geological Survey Water Supply Paper 416; the second appeared in a series of publications by Sir William Fletcher Barrett, physics professor at Dublin's Royal College of Science and a past president of London's famed Society for Psychical Research, and later collected in the volume *The Divining Rod: An Experimental and Psychological Investigation* (London, 1926). That classic would never have seen the light after Barrett's death without the perseverance of his younger collaborator, Theodore Besterman, who wrote in the preface: "Whether the results justify this [Barrett's] labor is for the reader to decide; but should it be agreed that the ability to find objects by other than normal means

IX

has been established, the question can hardly be answered otherwise than in the affirmative. For what scientific discovery could be of greater importance than that of a hitherto unknown human faculty?"

Taken together the two sources run to well over 1,500 titles, a large portion of which were examined at the Library of Congress in Washington, D.C., the Widener Library at Harvard, the Sterling Library at Yale, the Engineering Societies Library in New York City and the library of the Museum for Electricity in Life in Minneapolis, Minnesota. To the staffs of these five magnificent repositories of knowledge, and particularly to the heads of the Stack and Reader, and Loan, Divisions of the Library of Congress and to their courteous and helpful assistants, heartfelt thanks are expressed.

For dogged and detailed research I am indebted to George "Bud" Brainard whose diligence I hope I partly repaid by assisting him, in turn, with the production of his master's, and masterly, thesis on the pineal gland written for Goddard College and to Oliver Nichelson, Harvard divinity student turned budding inventor.

Translation from German sources by Reza Eghbal and Trudy (Mrs. John H.) Fisher were equaled in their expertise by English renderings from Latin by Gaby Christov; from Russian by George Petrov, Vadim Medish, Cyril Muromcew and David Chavchavadze; from Chinese by Jing Nuan Wu; and from Italian by Lisa Sergio. It was also Lisa's apt contribution that finally won the day among a plethora of titles suggested for this book.

In the Union of Soviet Socialist Republics, I am beholden to Dr. Alexander P. Dubrov, author of the recently published *The Geomagnetic Field and Life,* for his coordinating a review by himself and several colleagues of that portion of the text devoted to Soviet dowsing. In France, Maurice Plateau; Jerome Dumoulin, reporter at *L'Express;* and Jacques Richardson, editor of UNESCO's *Impact of Science on Society;* provided many courtesies. In Germany, Louis Bélanger, now writing and teaching in his native Quebec, was a more than able interpreter and a cordial host.

Enduring thanks to Thomas Heston, for his skillful illustrations turned out with great joy and dispatch under the trying circumstances of deadlines and to Dr. Andrija Puharich for opening my eyes to many marvels.

Finally, without the persistence of my wife, Lois Pengelly, and Rose McClark, the manuscript would never have gone through what seemed an innumerable number of typings and retypings, and without the judicious combination of knuckle-rapping and exhortation on the part of my editor, Bill Whitehead, the book would never have appeared.

CHRISTOPHER BIRD
Virginia Beach, Virginia
July 1978

> And I say unto you, Ask, and it shall be given you; seek, and ye shall find; knock, and it shall be opened unto you.
>
> For every one that asketh receiveth; and he that seeketh findeth; and to him that knocketh it shall be opened.
>
> Luke 11: 9–10

"Such was my debut in the art of discovering sources of water with the rod and, since that time, I have had many wells dug, all of which have furnished results predicted by it. The proverb: 'By working at the forge, one becomes a blacksmith' applies particularly to this phenomenon, for an attentive study of the subsoil has led me, time and again, to the determination of a veritable network of aquiferous sinuosities which, traced on a map, was the faithful reproduction of what occurs on the soil's surface: a network of streams, primary tributaries and secondary affluents.

"This subsoil reconnaissance has permitted me to effect with success the location of underground water to aliment the towns of Paimpol and Lannion and to augment the existing water-supply of Saint-Brieuc, all in Brittany.

"This method of proceeding unfortunately is opposed by two classes of detractors: the first being those in whose hands the dowsing rod remains motionless; the second, scientists who, unable to plausibly explain the phenomenon, find it easier either to negate it purely and simply by attributing it to charlatanry on the part of the operator or to include it among acts of simple suggestion. To the one, as to the other, class of such detractors we shall reply with our own experiments which we are willing to repeat at any time before unbelievers.

"Whatever the nature of the forces which cause the rod to move in the hands of those privileged to be adept in dowsing, to deny them is to demonstrate a closed mind and many times I have replied to persons who have remained stubbornly incredulous before such palpable results: 'Your negation of established facts matters little; it can have no value for those who practice dowsing and, through its use, benefit others.'

"It is not chimerical to hope that one day these phenomena will be explained when men of science will banish from their attitudes any idea of charlatanry or of suggestion and resolutely take up serious research like those who, in our time, have been led to the discovery of wireless telegraphy, the telephone and the phonograph."

Charles Carmejeanne, President of the North-West France Regional Society of Architects, in a letter to Henri Mager, expert dowser and author of several books including *Dowsers and Their Procedures*, Paris, 1913, from which the above is taken.

| INTRODUCTION | The Substance of Dowsing |

An Uncertain Etymology

To dowse is to search with the aid of a hand-held instrument such as a forked stick or a pendular bob on the end of a string—for *anything:* subterranean water flowing in a narrow underground fissure, a pool of oil or a vein of mineral ore, a buried sewer pipe or electrical cable, an airplane downed in a mountain wilderness, a disabled ship helplessly adrift in a gale, a lost wallet or dog, a missing person, perhaps a buried treasure.

When first introduced to this method of location that has long defied and continues to defy rational explanation, most people react with a knee-jerk response of rank disbelief—or, like primitives initially exposed to radio or TV receivers, with the same awe and amazement as small children witnessing a magic show. Yet just as radio and television have revolutionized human communication in the lifetime of still living grandparents, so dowsing, as one of a little recognized group of mental abilities called "psychic," promises no less a revolutionary advance in human communication with the cosmos surrounding us, of which we know so little.

Like expertise on the violin, figure skating, acrobatics, and other virtuosities seemingly inaccessible to the average citizen, it can be acquired by the open-minded and therefore especially by the young who have not yet developed a mind-set against the "obvious impossibility" of so uncanny a searching art.

No etymologist is sure of the origin of the verb which first made its appearance in print in a dry seventeenth-century essay, *Some Considerations of the Consequences of the Lowering of Interest,* by the English political philosopher, John Locke, who only half seriously referred to a *deusing* rod's purported ability to "divine," or discover, mines of gold and silver. His unorthodox spelling was likely an attempt to orthographize a local Somersetshire pronunciation of a word familiar to him since childhood. Even its present-day utterance is a matter of contention. While most Americans rhyme it with the noun, *house,* in other parts of the English-speaking world it is enunciated to be consonant with the verb, *browze.*

Despite Locke's literary pioneering, the word was nowhere found in any publication for more than a hundred years, the possible exception being a reference to miners in the Mendip

1

Hills *jowsing* for ore. It was not used in the *Mining Dictionary* of 1747 which otherwise provides a long description of the divining rod; or in William Borlase's *The Natural History of Cornwall* published in 1758 which refers to the same rod under its Latin name, *virgula divinatoria;* or in William Pryce's masterwork on Cornish mining that twenty years later extensively discussed divining for metals; or in 1770 and 1800 accounts of divining in the mines of Wales. Spelled as it is today, the word first appeared in an 1831 issue of *The Quarterly Mining Review* and eight years later in *Traditional Devonshire* by one Mrs. Gray who equated the whole process of dowsing to superstition.

Some have sought to relate *dowsing* to a proper name but it is probably only a curious coincidence that George Dowsing, a schoolmaster and necromancer at Saint Faith's near Norwich, was employed as a "hill-digger" by a certain Sir R. Curzon who had obtained a license to search for buried treasure during King Henry VIII's reign.

More likely is the supposition that *dowsing* is a loan word borrowed either from the miners of Cornwall, whose experience in digging out tin dates to the pre-Christian era, or from German mining parlance. The first derivation was suggested by the compiler of an 1887 *English-Cornish Dictionary,* Professor Frederick Jago. In Cornish, a now-dead language related to Gaelic and Welsh, "goddess" can be *dewsys* and "tree branch" *rhodl.*

2

Their combination, *dewsys rhodl,* is corruptible on an English tongue to "dowsing rod." On the other hand, because early German references mention forked sticks "striking" downward toward the ground, at least one etymological dictionary ties *dowsing* to the Middle English word *duschen* which also means "to strike." Another line of reasoning postulates its descent from the German *deuten,* an umbrella verb variously translatable as "to show," "to indicate," "to point out," "to explain," and even "to augur."

From Concrete to Abstract

A common cliché of dowsing is that of a rustic walking across a meadow with a forked stick in his hands, searching for a place to dig a water well. When the stick snaps downward toward the ground, instruction and experience indicate that there a bore will be successful. This "walk-around" method termed *field dowsing* has led to the justifiable assumption that something directly below a dowser's feet associated with the presence of flowing water affects either the dowser, the rod, or both, but it does not explain how dowsers are able to locate underground anomalies other than water.

At one point "walk-around" dowsers are usually told that they can save a lot of sole leather by first standing at one corner of the terrain they wish to survey and check *the direction* in which a potential well site might lie. Then they need only walk one traverse to pass over a water vein and confirm what they have detected remotely. *Remote dowsing,* like navigation, can also employ triangulation wherein lines from two known corners of a triangle are projected to an intersection that reveals its third corner, but, unlike field dowsing, it cannot easily be justified by reference to something beneath the dowser.

The effect of any physical cause in the earth acting to disturb dowsers is completely nullified when they resort to an almost incredible method known as *map dowsing* used to locate a well site not on the ground itself but on a map or a simple sketch of a terrain that can be hundreds or thousands of miles distant. Again, triangulation can be employed to pinpoint a drill site or a vertical

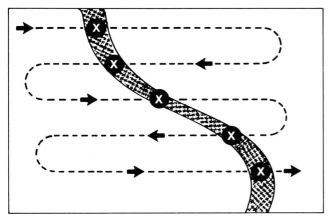

Location of an underground water course by field dowsing

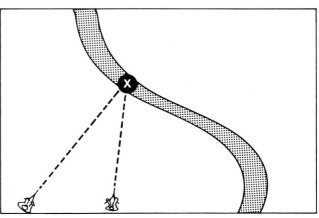

Location of an underground water course by remote dowsing

and horizontal grid-by-grid inspection undertaken. What is unbelievable to most people is that its representation on paper can substitute for a tangible portion of the earth on which a dowser can locate coordinates for a sought-for target.

No such representation is necessary in the case of *information dowsing* in which answers to yes-or-no questions are obtained. A simple "no" answer to the question: "Can a source of fresh water sufficient to the needs of its owners be drilled on this property?" tells a dowser that no more time need be spent on the problem. The concrete physical aspect of dowsing in the field involving bodily sensing of something underground has been replaced by a wholly abstract mental process.

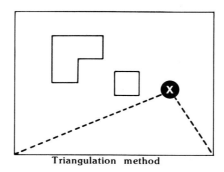

Triangulation method

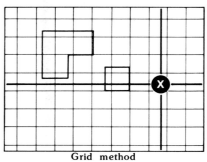

Grid method

Location of a potential well site by map dowsing

Garbage In, Garbage Out

More an art than a science, dowsing has never been adequately explained because of its intimate relationship to the unsolved *mind-body* problem, to which twelve pages are devoted in the eight-volume *Encyclopedia of Philosophy.*

In his theory on the evolution of consciousness entitled *The Reflexive Universe,* the inventor of the Bell helicopter, Arthur Middleton Young, holds that one of the simplest and most amazing examples of animal behavior is the motion of an amoeba, a single-celled living mass of clear colorless jelly, which can reach out by extending a pseudopod, devoid of any musculature, from any place in its body. What causes the projection, asks Young, if it is not attention and intent?

Like amoebas, dowsers project an "intent" to find, or a "request" for the location of, a given object or target. What is projected? A mental or psychic pseudopod of possibly infinite length? Whatever it is called, an answer to the request seems to be fed back via their bodies in the form of muscular movements which, because they are usually not consciously perceived, are called *involuntary.* The muscles cause the dowsing rod or pendulum to move, thereby objectifying the muscular action that, self-generated by the requester, cannot really be termed autonomic.

There are still many dowsers who adamantly maintain that not muscles but a mysterious external "force" moves a dowsing rod. Others invalidate the claim by pointing to the ability of particularly sensitive persons who, dispensing entirely with an instrument, can directly apprehend physiological changes in their

Jan Merta

hands, feet, stomach, throat, or other bodily organs. Proponents of a "force" also assert that it comes out of the ground to affect the rod when the dowsers move near or directly over objects they are seeking. How then does the "force" play a role when dowsers successfully locate targets many miles distant or come up with correct answers to abstract questions simply by tipping the balance of a rod held in equilibrium? If there is a "force" at play, it may be one related to pure intent or be operating on a frequency as yet undefined by science.

The mystery of whether a "force" affects a dowsing rod directly, or indirectly through the muscular movement of the dowser, may have been resolved by Dr. Jan Merta, a Czech-born physiologist, psychologist, gifted psychic, and professional deep sea diver now working on oil rigs in the North Sea.

During the autumn of 1970, Merta attended the convention of the American Society of Dowsers in Danville, Vermont, where he was particularly impressed by an extension, real or apparent, of the water dowser's art into the realm of the extrasensory, as illustrated by data presented on map dowsing, the location of lost children, and successful searches for missing objects.

From knowledge gained in his experimental work at McGill University in Montreal, Merta suspected that the movement of the dowsing device had to be directly connected to *muscular contraction* in the body—specifically in the arms or hands—of a dowser. He therefore reasoned that if he could build an apparatus that could simultaneously record both the movement of the dowsing device and any muscular contraction, he would be able unambiguously to determine which came first.

Merta constructed a measuring instrument called an accelerometer which, when attached to a pocket-sized Y-rod held in his hands in the dowsing mode, could record the rod's every movement through an extremely sensitive built-in crystal, including movements so slight or minimal that observers, unable to measure or detect them visually, believed that the rod was motionless. When the rod was under tension and moving in the hands of the dowser, its imperceptible motion was recorded on a strip chart as a wiggly line. When it lay still upon a table, the record on the chart flattened out into a perfectly straight line. This was clear proof to Jan that the dowser's muscular contraction could move the rod even before he went searching for a target.

Merta next reasoned that one of the principal muscles involved in the rod's movement might be the *carpi radialis flexor* in the wrist area of the forearm. To test this idea he electrically wired this muscle to his apparatus to allow any contraction in it to be recorded on the chart together with any motion in the rod.

He began his experiment by having a technician pass a vial of water in front of his face so that he could see it. This produced a reaction in both the muscle and the rod. The pen graph revealed clearly that the muscle contracted well before the rod responded to the same contraction. Since two squares on the tape's grid were the equivalent of a second of time, he concluded that the interval between the muscle's contraction and the rod's movement was about half a second.

5

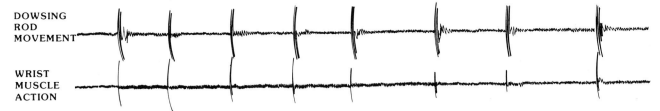

DOWSING
ROD
MOVEMENT

WRIST
MUSCLE
ACTION

Example of electronic measurement of the time of muscle action in the wrist of a dowser compared with the time of movement of the dowsing rod.   Data supplied by Dr. Jan Merta, Aberdeen, Scotland.

Dowsing device designed by Jan Merta. Balanced on a fingertip or even on a lath held in the hand (see photo of Merta), it consists of a heavy pendulum suspended from a thread attached to a bent metal rod. Two flanges are adjusted along the rod, one of them to act as a fulcrum. Both can be connected by wires to motion-recording instruments. A smaller light pendulum, hanging from the shorter arm of the rod, translates particularly weak signals into motion.

Merta was then blindfolded by the technician and the above experiment repeated with exactly the same result, the only difference being that he could not see the vial of water and thus had to be recording its presence in front of his line of sight extrasensorially.

As a result of these and many other tests, Merta believes he has unquestionably proven that dowsing devices react only after human beings operating them pick up a signal which stimulates a physiological reaction. He concluded that if the rod were only an amplifier magnifying a sensation, dowsers should be able to teach themselves to pick up such sensations without recourse to any dowsing device whatsoever by paying attention to otherwise unheeded nervous processes. His conclusion is strengthened by mounting evidence that through "bio-feedback" techniques humans can learn to recognize, and to *control,* so-called autonomic functions such as heartbeat or brain-wave emissions.

On the other hand, says Merta, everyone can learn to manipulate a dowsing device and respond to a signal, and to back up this allegation, he adds that he can teach anyone wishing to acquire the skill. Merta also is convinced that, ultimately, *all* forms of dowsing will be explained as clairvoyance, the ability to see at any given moment what is taking place elsewhere.

After listening with some amusement to assertions by various dowsers at Danville that their own particular dowsing devices were superior to all others, Merta while driving back to Montreal, began to design an instrument which he hoped might prove more sensitive and versatile than anything he had seen in Vermont. His brainchild, Merta asserts, allows him to pick up signals many times weaker than those which can be registered with an ordinary dowsing instrument. Gross movements of the heavy pendulum are amplified by a tiny lighter one, the changes in the speed and direction of which provide information. Merta readily admits that while it is *not* as good, or even very good at all, for ordinary field dowsing, it is excellent for a variety of other operations. One of these, demonstrated to many observers, enjoins a subject to sit behind Merta while flipping through the pages of a book or a magazine. From the actions of his smaller pendulum, Merta can tell when the subject is looking at or touching a page containing an illustration or a photograph. When the page contains only unillustrated text, the pendulum is quiescent.

The development of this instrument he regards only as a pure exercise in design. Highly skilled dowsers, he repeats, do not need his or any other device if they can teach themselves to react

Jan Merta's experiments proving the dowsing rod is moved by muscular contraction do not completely rule out the possibility of a "force" of some kind acting on the rod. Pictures taken of Gladys Chambers of Belcarra, Burrard Inlet, British Columbia, in February 1955, reveal a mysterious "energy" moving either upward out of "nowhere" to envelop the tip of the rod or downward out of the tip of the rod itself. The possibility remains that different effects are involved with different dowsers.

to a signal and know when they are reacting. The only reason many dowsers use a device, he believes, is because once they begin to get results with it they learn to "trust" and depend on it. For this reason, he says, it would be better to teach dowsing to neophytes without any device from the very beginning.

"It's all a question of being able to pick up a signal, a symbol, an idea, or a thought extrasensorially," he explains. "It doesn't matter in which form it's expressed. But it does require intensive training."

Merta has compared the process of dowsing to making a telephone call. If we dial a series of numbers correctly, we can chat almost instantly with a person in suburban Los Angeles, the outbacks of the Canadian north, or, with the aid of the latest satellite communications, correspondents in Europe or Japan. Let only one number be wrongly introduced into the series and we wind up talking to a stranger in a place we may not even be able to situate on a map.

A projected request for information in dowsing is analogous to the number selection, the bodily reaction to the workings of the vast telephone switching system, and the final muscular twitching or neural response to the ring of an appropriate telephone on the other end of the line. A successful search depends mainly on accurate formulation of the request. Otherwise, as computer specialists have it: "Garbage In, Garbage Out!"

Mind-Reach

In sixteenth-century Spain there lived a class of people known as *Zahoris*, after an Arabic word meaning "clear" or "enlightened" that is closely related to the Hebrew *Zohar*, a mystic cabalistic text. According to the Jesuit Martin del Rio, Zahoris were able "to see things hidden in the inward bowels of the earth, veins of water and treasures of metals and corpses placed within sarcophagi." The Mexican scholar, Alfonso Gutierrez of Vera Cruz, puzzled by the problem posed by the Zahoris, wrote: "There is no one who denies that there may be such an arrangement in a man's eyes, that he may be enabled to see at a great distance to which another man's eyes cannot reach . . . But I cannot conceive that anyone's sight can be so constructed that he can see an object behind a wall or any opaque substance."

Given his reluctance to conceive of the ability in terms other than that of visual perception, Gutierrez was right, as far as he went. But what if the Zahoris were somehow reaching out with their minds, like dowsers, to contact whatever they were seeking? Hard scientific evidence supporting the reality of the Zahoris' talent has only recently been provided in *Mind-Reach*, a compendium of experiments performed by two physicists, Harold Puthoff and Russell Targ, at the Stanford Research Institute in Menlo Park, California. The convincing data they offer on what they call *remote viewing* proves that humans have the capacity to locate and accurately describe scenes and objects hundreds and even millions of miles away. Given only its coordinates on the globe, one subject drew a recognizable sketch of Kerguelen Island in the south Indian ocean. Others "looked" at Mercury from afar to discover unknown features of the planet including a thin atmosphere, a weak magnetic field, and a cometlike tail of helium which, though contrary to the predictions of astronomers, were later verified by Mariner 10, the first space probe to reach Mercury's vicinity.

Peter Harmon in South Portland, Maine.

8

That remote viewing has little or nothing to do with ocular perception was made clear at the Frontiers of Physics Conference held in Reykjavik, Iceland, in November 1977. "We have done experiments with a man who lost his vision when he was five years old," stated Targ. "He functions as a blind person and describes things in nonvisual terms. For instance, he tracked a subject into a building far away from where he was located which he characterized as 'hot and crowded, the kind of place you'd like to get out of once you're in it.' The building was a police station."

Targ and Puthoff have found that, far from being limited to the gifted, remote viewing ability has been demonstrated by wholly inexperienced individuals, who were even skeptical or hostile to the whole notion, the very first time they tried it. It would seem that the repeated act of dowsing with an instrument also leads to the acquisition of the remote viewing talent. One example is the experience of Peter Harmon, a water dowser and driller living in Portland, Maine. One day, while telephoning a client in Oklahoma, Harmon suddenly "saw" the man's property in what has been fittingly termed his "mind's eye."

Harmon told his client: "You know, out in your back field you have a big dog house. Not far from its northwest corner there is a Coca-Cola bottle lying on the ground. Your best bet to spot a water well is going to be close to that bottle. Will you please go out and check to see if it's there?"

Taken aback, the man went outside and, northwest of the dog kennel, found the Coca-Cola bottle. Dashing back to the telephone, he shouted: "How in hell could you tell the bottle was there?" Unhampered by any scientific constraint, Harmon offhandedly replied: "Well, I can see it because *I'm there!*"

Strength of Attachment

To dispel any idea that dowsing or remote viewing abilities are unique to human beings, one has only to consider documented accounts of the many ways animals "home in" on targets.

Ruby-throated humming birds, all of three inches long, fly each year from Panama to the East Coast of the United States and back again. The Pacific golden plover makes a seasonal nonstop flight 3,000 miles from Alaska to the Hawaiian Islands with no landmarks to guide it. "As yet no one really knows how they find their way," states Chandler Robbins, head of the Migratory Non-Game Bird Studies section of the U.S. Bureau of Sport Fisheries and Wildlife. "We know some hawks travel overland by following mountain ridges and shore birds keep to the coastline." Experiments with other birds under artificially altered star maps tend to indicate that night fliers use a form of celestial navigation. It has been further established that birds can detect minute gradient changes in the earth's magnetic field which may help their orientation during migration. Other proposals ascribe to them a dependence on atmospheric infrasound waves inaudible to humans or electromagnetic microwaves to reach their destinations.

In his *Adventure of Birds,* Charles Ogburn tells of 411 golden-crowned and white-throated sparrows captured at San Jose, California, and shipped for release to Baton Rouge,

Louisiana. The following winter, seventy-two of the tiny birds were recaptured in San Jose, then flown across North America to Laurel, Maryland. Half a dozen of them made the long transit back to their California winter abode. "To those six little birds," wrote Ogburn, "frail and of indifferent powers of flight, that triumphed over such vast stretches of alien lands on the strength of attachment, one's heart goes out."

Equally poignant are countless tales of pet cats and dogs who mysteriously found their way home. When Walter Coleman, owner of a blue-eyed tomcat named Wahoo traveled from Seattle, Washington, to his summer home in Alaska, he decided to take his pet with him for company. In Gold Pan, British Columbia, 300 miles north of their starting point, Wahoo, startled by dogs, bolted from his owner's car and disappeared into the underbrush. Eleven months later the now bedraggled cat, his long hair matted and caked with filth, appeared on Coleman's Seattle porch.

Wahoo was aiming for a familiar location so his trek homeward might be explained by the same reasons put forward to account for bird migration. A more inexplicably fantastic journey was made by Clementine, a cat owned by Mrs. Robert Landmark, which traveled 1,600 miles across the great plains from Dunkirk, New York, to Denver, Colorado, to find her owner who had left her behind with friends when she moved west because the cat was about to produce kittens. After weaning her litter, Clementine hit the road and after four and a half months appeared on her mistress's doorstep. Mrs. Landmark was positive the cat was her Clementine because of the rare seven toes on each of her forepaws, two unmistakable white blotches on her stomach, and a scar on her left shoulder made by hot coals accidentally spilled on her. With no way of knowing where her owner was located, the cat was able to track her down simply by "dowsing" for her person.

It is disheartening that, instead of studying how an urge in animals leads them to their human friends, scientists mostly *explain away* such occurrences with the allegation that animal lovers, heartbroken at the loss of their pets, delude themselves into believing they have returned by adopting a look-alike facsimile. The only intensive effort to document the reality of animal *psi-trailing*—as the search for a person in an unfamiliar location has been called—was made at Duke University's Parapsychological Laboratory in North Carolina. There, rigorous criteria applied to eliminate doubtful or fraudulent cases established that at least twenty-eight dogs, twenty-two cats, and four birds had accomplished the feat.

A Famous Test

The charge of delusion was also applied to dowsing in a classic book, *Water Witching U.S.A.*, written by Ray Hyman, a magician turned social psychologist, and Evon Vogt, an anthropologist. Their feeble conclusion that dowsing was all superstition rested mainly on their irrelevant complaint that "no form of divination known to science can anticipate the future with 100 percent accuracy." No competent dowser would suggest any such infallibility. Even those with meager experience know that

10

virtuosity in their art, as in the mastery of a musical instrument, is either a natural gift or a combination of enthusiasm and assiduous practice. Most of us can scrape out "Turkey in the Straw" on a fiddle or play "Chopsticks" on a piano but few can equal the talent of a David Oistrakh or a Rudolf Serkin.

Tests of human dowsing ability have not been run, as they are for musicians, on the basis of competition. The usual approach has been to lump the results of a group of dowsers, with talents ranging from indifferent to exceptional, into an aggregate from which a conclusion is drawn; and, as in the case of Hyman and Vogt, the conclusion is usually that the whole searching art is worthless because it is not *always* effective.

One of the best tests of dowsers was made over sixty-five years ago by Armand Viré, a biologist who installed a laboratory in the catacombs beneath Paris's Jardin des Plantes to experiment on animals normally living in underground caverns. Viré described his initial attitude toward dowsing in a book, *How to Become a Dowser—What I've Seen and What I've Done:* "I was steeped in the exact sciences, particularly physics and biology and, out of habit, was used to imposing on any phenomenon the very limitations imposed on it by my venerable masters at the Sorbonne and the Museum of Natural History. Anything concerning dowsing seemed to me wholly cockeyed and unjustifiable. The art was practiced mostly by simple countrymen who operated on the basis of more or less unfathomable instructions which they ill-understood or seemed unwilling to explain."

While in this state of mind Viré was visited one evening in 1913 by a geographer, Henri Mager, whose chapter on dowsing in a book on methods to discover underground water Viré rated as "at best, mediocre." Mager explained that, in connection with the 2nd Congress on Experimental Psychology being held in Paris, several scientists were hoping that a test of the dowsing phenomenon could be organized. "It is expensive to establish proof of the dowsing phenomenon by drilling for water," he told Viré, "but as our country's leading expert in the study of subterranean caverns, we want to ask you if you will set up an experiment to test our ability to find them."

Viré's first reaction was to reject Mager's suggestion out of hand, but then he wondered whether a vast network of quarries dug under Paris and its environs from Roman times to the nineteenth century could not serve as a testing ground. Over the years they had been precisely illustrated at a scale of 1:1,000 on charts which, still unpublished, were kept under lock and key. Since there was no way in the world that any dowser could know about them, Viré felt that they might provide a means "to put an end, once and for all, to a superstitious fairy tale." Without telling Mager what he had in mind, he asked the geographer simply to have dowsers wishing to be tested assemble at Paris's Daumesnil Gate at eight o'clock the following Thursday morning.

The test area was covered by an extensive lawn, split by macadamized roads which revealed no trace of excavations ranging from 1.25 to 4 meters in height lying below it at depths

11

Dowsers under test by Armand Viré, Paris, 1913. (From Henri Mager, Les Sourciers et Leurs Procédés, *Paris, 1913.)*

between 16 to 20 meters. Viré's official report on the exercise to the Academy of Sciences, printed in *La Nature,* stated in part:

. . . Monsieur Pelaprat, a retired gendarme, discovered a void which I recognized as being at the border of the quarry. I asked him to follow its contours and, to my great astonishment, I saw him stake them out. I then had him come back to his point of departure and delimit the contours in the opposite direction which he did with precision. Monsieur Probst from Buglose in the Landes region, marked sixteen points on the ground which formed the borders of three squares and an elongated rectangle. Questioned as to their significance he told us that he sensed a solid mass within the confines of the outlined figures and voids outside them. My map immediately confirmed the correctness of his data. He had found columns put in place by the quarry-workers to obviate cave-ins. Monsieur Coursanges, of Cabrillan in the Drome region, indicated the presence of a well with galleries leading out from it in several directions which were found to be where he said they were.

All the dowsers also correctly maintained that the depths of the underground voids were in the 16 to 20-meter range.

Viré was no less impressed when, the following day, he took Father Alexis Mermet, a professional dowser from Savoy, to the Jardin des Plantes. Not only did the priest precisely locate a network of tunnels and other voids below it that were familiar to Viré, but discovered a completely unknown gallery. Mermet was

12

> *"The problem was to reconnoiter a water conduit the presence of which none of those present was aware but which was revealed the following day on a map belonging to the Water Works and subsequently verified by excavation performed by that company.*
>
> *"M. Probst uses both the rod and the pendulum as well as a little device he calls a "detector" the functioning of which he keeps secret and which he uses to determine distances.*
>
> *"We went along the Meudon road more than a kilometer in length. At a given point M. Probst installed his "detector," and said that the water conduit lay about 480 meters away. Measuring out the distance we came to a transverse alley.*
>
> *"Once there, Probst noted that his rod dipped and his pendulum moved. He situated the water conduit quite precisely under one of the alley's shoulders and that was exactly the one which was found there according to the verification made the next day. Then M. Probst followed the conduit to the Mail Alley which was quite correct.*
>
> *"This coincidence with what turned out to be the facts seems extremely remarkable to us."*
>
> From the report of the French Academy of Sciences' *Commission de la Baguette des Sourciers* (Commission on the Water Diviners' Rod), 1921.

also tested on his ability to determine whether or not water was flowing in a conduit nine meters below ground. Its faucet was opened and closed three times. Results showed that Mermet could pinpoint the exact moment when water started flowing but was late in saying when it stopped. Unsurprised by the slight error, Viré wrote: "Obviously, turning off the tap provokes eddies, gurgling and shockwaves in the pipe which extend the duration of the water's motion."

All of the tests impressed the scientist who wrote:

One can imagine how the precise data collected profoundly unsettled my skepticism. I admit it was not without great inner struggle that I gradually confronted the evidence which at first sorely vexed me. For convictions as firmly rooted as mine are not given up without excruciation. But the facts stared me in the face and I was forced to proclaim, *urbi et orbi,* that the dowsing ability was real and that there was just cause to take dowsers seriously and study the possibilities and the limitations of a phenomenon which they had so clearly revealed to us.

A dowser-prospector can inform us if there is source of water 10 meters, 100 meters or 2 kilometers in front of us. When the site is dug, the predicted water is often found. One may object that many dowsers can commit every kind of error. But are not many doctors insufficiently prepared to practice their art, or engineers of markedly inferior quality? Likewise, there are dowsers and there are dowsers.

Viré's opinions were shared by some of France's most eminent scientists, including Jacques d'Arsonval, who first proved the beneficial therapeutic action of high frequency electric currents; Daniel Berthelot, who used ultraviolet light to synthesize glucides; Edouard Branly, the inventor of a radio coherer used by Marconi, who became honorary president of the first French dowsing society; Henri Deslandres, developer of *spectroheliography* to study the chromosphere of the sun, who became president of the commission to study dowsers organized at the Academy of Sciences; and Charles Richet, a Nobel Laureate, whose own personal experience had led him to declare in print: "We must accept dowsing as fact. It is useless to work up experiments merely to prove its existence. It exists. What is needed is its development."

"Faith is the substance . . ."

To Viré's credit, he was aware that the dowsing talent could be easily disrupted by an overbearing insistence on objectivity on the part of experimenters who callously discount subjective feelings in dowsers under test. Rigorously avoided in the remote viewing experimentation at the Stanford Research Institute, overzealous testing has invariably produced unsatisfactory results. As the late world-famed anthropologist Margaret Mead commented in her introduction to *Mind-Reach*, it is senseless to put "subjects" through long, dull repetitive performances while treating them like rats in a maze or self-deluded oddities.

In the end, scientific scrutiny of the merits of dowsing may be putting the plow before the ox. If man can reveal truths about Mercury *before* his hardware can confirm them, then dowsing offers the opportunity to scrutinize other scientific imponderables. The English dowsing expert, Malcolm Rae, has pointedly observed that "physics is approaching very closely, in some directions, to the limits of observation achievable with *non-living* instruments." A key reason for this, Rae believes, is that something measurable requires a yardstick of comparable magnitude. No one would attempt to measure pond water with a teaspoon or set up a lathe to machine an accuracy of 1/1,000 of an inch with a foot rule. Even when compared with the highly miniaturized components of today's electronic instruments, the resonant circuit, which as far back as the 1920s the French researcher Georges Lakhovsky believed part of every living cell, would be microscopically small. This is why it appears logical to Rae that *living* detectors may always be required to measure patterns of energy emanating from or influencing life and that the dowsing faculty may become the foremost probe for penetrating the unknown in search of understanding and wisdom.

What has prevented the widespread adoption of this approach? Arthur Young provides one answer: "Empirical proof gathered to support the existence of a phenomenon does not guarantee that it will not be ignored or rejected. This is because *there is no theory to account for it* and existing theories apparently rule out its reality."

What causes our hands to reach out? To say it is the muscles or the action of nerves upon them avoids the issue. What activates the nerves? How does the muscleless amoeba extend a pseudopod? How does a cat walk across a continent to find its lost owner? How does dowsing work?

Are all these phenomena not related to *volition?* Are they

14

not made real by an investment? Investment of what? Young suggests an amusingly cogent answer. Greyhounds, bred to chase rabbits, can be induced to race around a track by a mechanical rabbit bounding along a rail in front of them. The fact the rabbit is not real makes no difference to the dogs. As long as they *believe* the object speeding in front of him is a rabbit, they run. Wherein for the dogs, asks Young, is the rabbit's substance? Young believes it may be some form of *condensed psychic energy* which Freud, in one of his more trenchant observations, equated to the German word *besetzung* meaning to "invest with a charge."

Is it the investment of charge, belief, anticipation, will, or faith that is the ultimate mysterious "force" that moves the dowsing rod at the appropriate moment? "Faith," wrote Paul to the Hebrews, "is the substance of things hoped for, the evidence of things not seen." If so, then faith may be the true substance of dowsing, the evidence for which follows.

Sebastian Münster in his Cosmographia Universalis *(Basel 1550) provided a charming mining scene including the first known clear illustration of a dowser holding his* virgula divina *or* glück rut *(lucky rod) while searching for ore above the mine works.*

Part One

Virgula diuina

UNEXPLAINED FACT

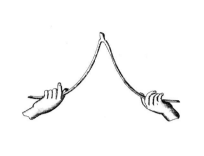

CHAPTER 1

Three Professionals

"Of the 'proper' ways to hold the rod, the first is the 'palms down' method . . ."

Dowsing East . . .

The Board of Governors of the sixty-year-old Misquamicut Club in Watch Hill, Rhode Island, was worried. For four years in a row a New England-wide drought had been causing its 187-acre golf course to deteriorate. An urgent request to the nearby town of Westerly to supply enough water to keep greens and fairways alive during summer months was flatly rejected, the town fathers gloomily complaining they hardly had sufficient water for their own needs.

The governors next asked Westerly to hire consultants in geophysics supposedly capable of determining whether an ample supply of underground water could be located anywhere on or near the club grounds. The consulting firm's verdict, costly to the town, was: "No major freshwater sources exist in the Watch Hill District."

Faced with the possible demise of their club, the governors appointed three local businessmen to report on how much water was needed to keep the golf course open. The men came to the conclusion that, if no rain fell during the summer ahead, 1½ million gallons—or enough water to fill seventy-five large swimming pools—would have to be sprinkled on the course each week.

Approached by the committee, a driller well known throughout Rhode Island was hardly encouraging. "No one can tell for sure where underground water is located," he said in the stock reply of his profession. "You just have to keep drilling test wells till you find it. The work will cost you $6 for each foot of depth drilled $9 if the well is cased."

Optimistic that the driller would find water, the committee opted for a cased well. In the late autumn of 1965, after another year of drought had turned the Misquamicut golf greens brown, a hole was drilled down to a solid rock shelf one hundred feet below ground and cased. The well was then sunk 130 feet deeper into the rock at which point water rose in the pipe, but elation turned to bitter disappointment when it was found to be too salty for irrigating grass.

After exhausting their budget by paying for more wells and professional advice, the Board of Governors met in New York City in April 1966, soberly concluding that, if water were not located by summertime, the golf course would have to close its

The drawings of dowsing devices and the manner of their utilization on this and following chapter heads were first illustrated in Johann Gottfried Zeidler's Pantomysterium, oder das Neue vom Jahre in der Wünschelrute als einem allgemeinen Werckzeuge menschlicher verborgenen Wissenschaft (Pantomysterium, or News of the Year Concerning the Divining Rod as a Universal Tool of Knowledge Hidden from Man), Halle in Magdeburg, 1700.

19

Much deeper water requires a hole to be bored into the ground as in drilling for oil. In days past the most common device of this kind was a "cable rig," so called because the boring instrument was hoisted on a cable and allowed to drop into porous earth like a pile driver before twisting to fill a long columnlike receptacle which could be pulled out and emptied. More modern devices are rotary drills—the giant equivalents of dentists' drills—which whir into the ground at much faster speeds than cable tools. Cooled by water, they eject "tailings," of anything that gets in the way. The newest ones are powered with air pressure and can penetrate hard rock such as granite at the rate of 25–60 feet per hour.

Probing for water can be accomplished in a variety of ways. If the source is shallow, a few minutes' or hours' work with a shovel will do the job. If somewhat deeper, a backhoe, clamshell bucket, or "bucket rig," such as the one shown above, will usually accomplish the task.

When water is found, the well-hole is "cased," or lined with tile or piping to prevent lateral cave-ins. A pump is then lowered into the hole and pushes, rather than pulls, the water out.

Water in a well will find a level in the pipe. If it gushes out of the ground (a rare occurrence), the well is said to "artesian"—a term borrowed from the name of the northern French province of Artois where the phenomenon was first discovered. When the water is pumped, the level drops in the well to a certain point, after which more pumping will be unable to lower it further unless a pump of unusual capacity is used. The difference between the original water level and that caused by the pumping is known as the "drawdown." A short drawdown indicates that the water below is under considerable pressure and a copious amount will be forthcoming. The amount of water a well can produce in gallons per minute (gpm) is determined by pumping under test conditions.

doors. At this juncture one of the club's governors, George Nichols, a New York financier who spent part of his summers in residence at the club, had an idea. After the meeting was adjourned he cornered Byron Hiscox, the water committee chairman. "Byron," he said, "I was hesitant to make this suggestion during the board meeting because many of the governors would not have understood it, but would you consider taking on a dowser to find you a supply of water for the golf course?"

Hiscox knew what Nichols was talking about. Born and reared in rural northeast Connecticut, across the Pawcatuck River from Rhode Island, he had often watched men with forked sticks walking the properties of his neighbors in search of a source of flowing water underground to supply both households and farm animals. Though completely mystified why a sudden snapping downward of a rod in a searcher's hands should indicate a spot to drill, he told Nichols that he could not recall any instance when the method had failed a client.

Encouraged by Hiscox's positive reaction, Nichols broached his idea to some of his fellow governors at lunch.

"How can you get in touch with the kind of water-finder you're talking about?" one of them inquired.

"You know Robert Plimpton, who owns a summer place across the road from the club, don't you?" replied Nichols. "Well, he's the president of a newly formed 'American Society of Dowsers.' If anyone can find us a good dowser, Bob can."

Plimpton's years-long interest in dowsing was first aroused when his father needed an additional water supply for fire protection at his home in Mansfield, in northeast Connecticut. The U.S. Soil Conservation Service agreed with the senior Plimpton's assessment that if a damp area on his property were deepened and widened, underground springs would fill it to provide a reservoir, and accordingly undertook to pay half the cost of its development. Equipment was moved in and a depression 120 feet deep dug out which, to everyone's surprise and disappointment, failed to fill with any water at all.

When the Plimptons learned that James W. Kidd, foreman of a dairy farm about a mile away, could reputedly locate subterranean water with a forked stick cut from a tree, in less than half an hour Kidd was walking around their hoped-for pond, with a forked apple branch gripped in both hands, its point sticking out like an antenna before him.

After circling around the dry pit, Kidd declared curtly: "Well, there's no water here, nothing. Let's go up the hillside and see what we get there."

About a hundred feet up from the pond's edge, the forked stick in Kidd's hands snapped down violently. Kidd took a wooden peg from his pocket and drove it into the ground between his feet to mark what he called a "vein of water" flowing in the ground below and told the Plimptons they would get water if a hole were drilled at the spot indicated.

"How deep do we need to go?" Kidd was asked.

Kidd backed away far enough so that he no longer could feel

any pull on his rod, then walked slowly and perpendicularly toward the water course. When he began to detect a slight downward tug on the rod, he stopped and put a second peg in the ground ten feet from the first.

"The water'll be ten feet down, or thereabouts," he stated flatly. "Same distance as from this peg to the other."

The following day a backhoe began digging into the rocky New England soil. A trench with straight vertical walls, measuring three feet across and ten feet long, began to take shape. As it grew deeper, tension mounted. Finally the big steel shovel was scraping earth and stones nearly ten feet down. The Plimptons and Kidd stared into the ditch. The shovel dragged its way along the bottom one more time and, as it rose with its load, a patch of water some 6–8 inches oozed out of the earth where one of the side walls of the trench met its bottom.

What began as a trickle soon became a flow. Diagonally across from the patch at the bottom of the trench wall, earth mixed with water fell away from the trench's opposite side into the water collecting at its bottom. Two watery holes, one on each side of the trench, marked places where an artery or vein of water flowing through the earth had been cut by the backhoe—much as a surgeon's scalpel would cut a blood vessel in a human body.

Since the vein of water was much higher uphill than the surface of the pond-to-be, it was only necessary for the backhoe to dig a communication channel from the site of the water to the surface level of the pond. This done, water began flowing down the hill behind the excavator and, when the channel was completed, started to fill the pond. To insure a clean flow of water, unmixed with earth or silt, the Plimptons neatly tiled the sides of their well and ran a six-inch underground pipe from its bottom into the pond, which, as Robert Plimpton was subsequently to write, "has been the delight of children and grandchildren ever since."

Thrilled by Kidd's performance, he decided to team with the dowser to form "Water Consulting Associates" which, advertising in *The New England Homestead* magazine, attracted so much attention that Plimpton finally had to rent a plane to fly all over southern New England with Kidd on intermittent dowsing jobs. Kidd's reputation as a water-finder grew so rapidly that he was able to quit dairy farming and take a job with an excavation contractor who, convinced of Kidd's prowess, offered his clients fixed-priced drilling contracts and guaranteed that they would produce water. Months later he reported to Plimpton that he *never once failed* to bring in a well at the precise location and depth predicted by his dowser.

Kidd's peculiar method for creating ponds became the butt of jokes in many New England counties. After first locating underground veins of flowing water on a given property, he would bulldoze the entire pond, including its dam and spillway, to the exact specifications required by a property owner, being careful to avoid disrupting any water veins detected by his dowsing rod. The dry cavities thus produced would usually elicit from friends and neighbors caustic comments about the

Jim W. Kidd (Photograph courtesy of his wife.)

"American Sahara" that Kidd's clients were paying for, but the hilarity would evaporate when Kidd, his excavation work completed, announced: "Okay, it's time to fill 'er up." By carefully digging out the water veins he had pinpointed with his bulldozer blade, he soon had the empty pond filled to overflowing.

It was a warm sunny day in May when Jim Kidd's truck pulled into the driveway of the Misquamicut Club. Within minutes after meeting with Plimpton and the committeemen, Kidd cut a forked stick from a nearby black cherry tree and set to work. Because of the considerable size of the club's acreage, this time Kidd simply stood at one spot, his dowsing rod pointing upward and asked out loud: "In which direction from here is the nearest underground vein of fresh flowing water?" He then began

23

slowly to turn in a circle where he was standing and, when he had rotated some 240 degrees, his rod began to move downward.

Raising the rod to its original position, Kidd then asked: "How far is it from where I am standing to the nearest vein?" He began to count: "Ten feet, twenty feet, thirty feet." No movement. He continued to count in increments of ten feet, all the way to 310 feet without the rod betraying the slightest motion. But when he intoned "320," it suddenly snapped downward.

Trailed by Plimpton and the astounded committeemen, Kidd moved off in the direction indicated, the rod held in the ready position, counting off his paces until he had reached a spot some 300 feet away from where he had started, several strides beyond which his rod again began a downward movement.

The rotation of the rod's branches in Kidd's hands was so forceful that, try as he would, he could not check it. So tightly did he squeeze the two forks that, as the rod twisted, Plimpton noticed the bark stripping away from the branches. When the rod finally pointed straight down toward the ground, Kidd made a mark with the heel of his boot in the hard-packed earth, walked some forty feet beyond the mark, about-faced and, his rod held upward once more, returned to it.

When he was three or four yards from his mark, the rod began afresh to tug at his hands, winning its fight when he was no more than a foot from it. Kidd heeled another mark into the ground where he stood.

"Center of the vein is right between 'em," he said gruffly.

Spitting on his hands, he grasped the rod again, moved fifty feet from the spot he had indicated, and began walking in a circle, the full circumference of which crossed the vein twice as indicated by a snap downward of his rod. Kidd marked the two points which, with the original spot, formed nearly a straight line. A stake was driven into each location.

"That's the direction of the water vein flowing underground," said Kidd matter-of-factly. "Now let's see how deep it is."

Returning to the spot he had first indicated to be the center of the vein, the dowser began to count: "1 foot, 2 feet, 3, 4, 5, 6 . . ." At 22 feet his rod began to move, at 23 feet it pointed straight downward, and at 24 it began to move back up.

"The vein is 23–24 feet deep at this point," affirmed Kidd.

One key question remained: How much water would the vein produce? Using the same countdown as for the depth, Kidd arrived at the same figure, 23–24, this time denoting gallons per minute. If Kidd was right, Misquamicut would get some 34,000 gallons a day to water its golf course with an expenditure of less than $250 for excavation.

But Kidd did not stop at this point. Raising his rod again, he asked: "Is this the *best* freshwater vein on the Misquamicut property?" The rod remained motionless.

"Seems like there are even better locations. Let's find 'em!" said Kidd.

Within an hour from the time he had arrived at the clubhouse, Jim Kidd, by following the same procedure as he had

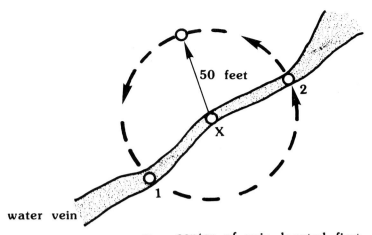

x — center of vein located first

1, 2 — points where vein was intercepted on circular walk

Kidd's technique.

used to find the first vein, had detected three more sources of fresh water with capacities equal to or larger than the first.

His work completed, Kidd accepted a fee for his services, climbed into his truck, and drove home.

The Misquamicut water committee decided to act on Kidd's suggestions. The first location was dug to a 20-foot level when the driller struck "ledge" or a shelf of solid rock normally considered unlikely to produce water.

Bitterly disappointed by the results, the committee telephoned Kidd. After consulting his rod at home, the dowser strongly recommended that the ledge be drilled to a depth of six feet.

Heartened by the new advice, the committee brought in a crane with a clamshell bucket with the help of which it was soon discovered that the supposed ledge was only an enormous boulder. This was removed and six more feet drilled below it to another equally large boulder at twenty-six feet. Drilling had now proceeded two feet below Kidd's predicted depth to water. Approached with the suggestion to scrap the whole effort, Committee Chairman Hiscox, though pessimistic, nevertheless suggested that the digger continue his excavation until midday.

Precisely at noon, Hiscox's phone rang again. On the other end of the wire a jubilant voice shouted at him: "Byron, drop whatever you're doing and get over here as fast as you can! We've got our first well! When the crane took out the boulder at twenty-six feet, the water gushed straight up in the air in a column as big as your forearm! I've never seen anything like it. The hole's got six feet of water in it already and it's still rising."

When a Massachusetts hydraulic engineering firm was called in to evaluate the find, its representative affirmed that the well should yield at least 100 gallons per minute, or more than half the amount originally estimated to fulfill the club's watering need.

The other half of the supply was assured when, precisely at twenty-eight feet, the clamshell bucket excavated a water source twice as prolific as the first. The club and Plimpton were overjoyed with Kidd's success and the city fathers of Westerly, Rhode Island, were forced to revise their conclusions about there being "no major sources of fresh water in the Water Hill District."

Ten years after the Misquamicut club began watering its golf course with its own water, its vice-president was able to state proudly: "The wells continue after a decade's operation to be capable of pumping at a rate of 80 gallons per minute each and keep our golf course well watered even in the driest years."

. . . and West

In the early part of 1977, the same year the club vice-president made his statement, Jack Livingston, a retired highway construction foreman, stood at the edge of a 2,000-acre rice farm in the foothills of the Sierra Nevada, the mountain range which runs for four hundred miles along California's eastern border. In his hands Jack held a virtually unbreakable plastic version of Kidd's forked fruit-tree branch.

The owner of the rice plantation, Francis Sargent, representing the fourth generation in a family who had pioneered the original farmstead, and his father, Charlie, were counting on Livingston's talent for their very survival. Like hundreds of farmers all over the state of California, they were faced with impending disaster. For two years running, the lack of rain and snowfall was turning their farmland slowly into desert. It was a drought the likes of which had not been seen for nearly fifty years.

Jack Livingston dowsing near Auburn, California, 1977, with a virtually unbreakable plastic rod that has all but supplanted the old forked stick cut from a tree. Jack employs the usual "palms up" method of holding the rod.

26

Well dowsed by Jack Livingston, supplying 2,000 gallons per minute. Left to right: Charles Sargent, Jack Livingston, Francis Sargent.

When Francis Sargent learned of Jack Livingston's water-finding exploits through a local newspaper, he drove over to Jack's small foothills cattle ranch to seek help. Just before the onset of the drought, he had drilled a deep well on his property some 400 feet down at a cost of more than twenty dollars per foot. This had netted him 250 gallons per minute (gpm) which, together with irrigation water supplied by the local water district, was enough to water his rice in any normal rainfall year.

Now, the water district had informed Sargent that he would get less than a quarter of his usual irrigation allotment during the hot, dry summer to come.

Of all crops, rice is the thirstiest. The rule of thumb for irrigating farmland is 500 gpm for one hundred acres. By applying that quantity steadily throughout the dry season, each acre is gradually afforded a total of 2½ to 3 feet of water which, week by week, soaks its way into the ground. Much more demanding than alfalfa, sugar beets, or wheat, rice requires up to 8 acre-feet of water during one season to make a decent crop.

In the heart of the rice country near Chico and Gridley, northwest of the Sargent spread, farmers were already in a panic. "I don't know what they're going to do up there this year," Charlie Sargent told Jack. "They're getting hardly any water up in that country. I was at a Rice Association meeting the other night where it was predicted that California may make only a third of its normal rice crop this year."

27

On Jack's recommendation, Sargent drilled two wells, one down to 240, the other to 250 feet. They both came up winners, the first producing 2,000 gpm, the second 800. In the meantime, Sargent's neighbor, who had sunk a well without the benefit of Jack's advice, obtained only 250 gpm after drilling 365 feet.

Like many water dowsers, Jack Livingston learned his art in childhood. When he had just turned seven, his Scots-born father decided to build a new house outside Victoria on Vancouver Island in British Columbia. The thorniest problem connected to this endeavor was the location of a good supply of underground water not too far from the site of the projected homestead.

Old John Livingston knew just how to solve the problem.

He drove over to the farm of one Wigglesworth, an immigrant from England then in his eighties, and asked him if he would come over the next morning and spot him a decent well. Wigglesworth said he would be along just after sunup.

After alighting from his horse and buggy, Wigglesworth took up a forked branch cut from a willow tree and began to rove over the Livingston acreage, holding the stick's forks in his hands, palms upward, with its point sticking out in front of him. Suddenly the point of the stick dipped downward with such force that the bark on the forked ends held by Wigglesworth's hands was stripped from the stick.

Wigglesworth shoved the point of the stick into the ground. "If you dig your well there," he said, "you'll have all the household water you need."

Little Jack, who had been following Wigglesworth's every move, was agape. "How does it work, Dad?" he asked his father. Before the senior Livingston could reply that he really did not know, Wigglesworth plucked the stick from the ground, showed the small boy how to hold it, and suggested he try to get a reaction over the site of the new well.

Jack backed off a few yards and advanced cautiously, his eyes glued to the tip of the stick which began to dip toward the ground a foot or so from the location Wigglesworth had pinpointed, finally coming to a vertical position when Jack's feet were over the place the stick had been inserted in the earth.

"You've got the real touch, son," Wigglesworth told the beaming Jack, "some day you'll make a fine water diviner."

How fine a water diviner Jack would become could be attested by hundreds of Californians, including G. W. Murphy, owner of a large cattle ranch stocked with prize Charolais, huge off-white beef cattle imported from France. At great expense, Murphy's land had been leveled to pool-table flatness in order to permit irrigation, so when water rationing threatened Murphy's alfalfa crop the rancher called Livingston to the rescue.

"The well-drillers who came over to Murphy's didn't even want to attempt to drill wells in this area," growled Jack as we drove into the ranch between two pastures flecked with Charolais yearlings. "They assured Murphy that there simply couldn't be any water that close to a well-known deposit of underground clay which has supplied the factory at Lincoln for so many years. They wanted to move his sites way down the valley nearly to the west

Jack Livingston teaching George Higbee how to dowse at Pine Grove, California, in 1977.

edge of his property. But I've got to give Murphy credit. He told 'em off. He said: 'That's where Jack said water's going to be and that's exactly where we're gonna drill one of our wells.'" That well plus two others pinpointed by Livingston, solved Murphy's problem.

Even in rainy times, lack of water has persistently plagued residents in California's mountains. Pine Grove, a small piedmont community lying across California State Route 88, ran out of water in 1964. By the following year, many of the settlement's 600 residents, tired of trucking water to their homes, were talking about moving elsewhere. Faced with the emergency, the city fathers called in a geologically trained civil engineer, who recommended that two wells be drilled near the little town. When sunk, they proved to be dry.

After Jack Livingston learned about Pine Grove's plight in a series of articles in the *Bee,* the Sacramento newspaper, he called the Pine Grove water authorities to offer his services as a water-finder and was immediately invited to drive down from Newcastle. The well he found has been serving Pine Grove ever since.

Curious to learn whether the 1977 drought was affecting Pine Grove's well, in March Jack again made the beautiful drive through the "Mother Lode" country made famous in American history by the miners of the 1849 gold rush (and also by Mark Twain, whose "Celebrated Jumping Frog" has given rise to an annual frog-jumping contest that takes place each year in Calaveras County, attracting croaking contestants from marshes and bogs as far away as Australia).

At two o'clock in the afternoon Jack pulled into Pine Grove to find that the local water district, as many California water supply agencies are called, had built a cabin-office over the same well he had brought in, thirteen years earlier. A minute or two later, a pick-up truck with two men rolled up alongside his car. Out of the driver's seat jumped Charles Widmer, secretary-manager of the water district. When Jack introduced himself, Widmer broke into a toothy grin. "I've read quite a bit about you, Jack. I've always wanted to meet the man who 'witched' us our water," he exulted.

Livingston asked shyly how the well was producing.

"Well, it just keeps going on and on, the son-of-a-bitch just keeps pumpin'," volunteered George Higbee, Widmer's assistant. "Right now, we're putting out about 45,000 gallons a day for a community of 750. During the summer we'll pump close to 150,000. But whatever we need, we just pump it."

"At the present time, Pine Grove is the only community out of some 250 around here that's not rationing water," added Widmer. "There was nothing in geology to suggest that any 100 gpm well would ever be brought in here in these mountains. But Jack got us a lot more than that. It's a hell of a well. I still can't hardly believe it."

"When they test pumped this well at seventy feet," reminisced Jack, "they couldn't get any more drawdown. It tested 209 gpm for one week straight. That's all the pump could pull. At

136 feet we hit even more water, more than they knew what to do with. But they asked if they could find still more deeper down. I told 'em to go on down to 220 feet and they'd pick up maybe another 100 gpm. The man who ran the test pump told me he thought that the well could make maybe 500 gpm at that depth if it were pumped to capacity but he didn't have the equipment for it."

Higbee frowned as if concerned. "Now that this well's been working as long as it has been," he queried Jack, "would we have any worry about the drought this coming summer or in future years?"

"To the best of my knowledge, no!" replied Jack decisively. "I've been locating wells for over thirty years in Placer and El Dorado counties, in other areas of California plus other Western states, and *I've never known any one of over 1,000 wells I've located to go dry yet.* I've watched a lot of 'em pretty close this past couple of years and they're showing no signs of diminishing. That's because I only locate on live water."

Jack Livingston's term, "live water," fits into a theory he developed over thirty years of dowsing in the hard rock country of the "Mother Lode." Just after World War II, when Jack moved to the Sierras from southern California, he was introduced to a dowser by the name of Vic Porter, then in his sixties. Like his father and grandfather, who had dowsed many wells for the Southern Pacific Railway, under construction from Arizona across the Mojave Desert to the coast, Vic was a well-driller by trade.

It was Porter who first suggested to Jack that there was plenty of water in the *very tops* of hills and mountains. It surged up into them from deep inside the earth to form enormous "domes" from which branched long "veins" in a manner akin to the tentacles extending from an octopus.

Jack dowsed one of the domes on the property of his neighbor, Bob Rich, to find thirteen veins coming out of it in nearly every direction all at levels only 4½ to 6 feet below the earth's surface. Like Kidd in Rhode Island, Rich dug into the ground with a backhoe and cut into five of them, then bulldozed a large hole in the ground to which he directed the water from the cut veins, which kept flowing down a ditch into the hole to create a pond. The veins, says Jack, were cut more than two years earlier and still produce the 15 gallons per minute, as they did when first opened, even after one of the driest years in California's history.

Asked on many occasions whether one could simply drill for water right into the center of a dome—between the eyes of the octopus, as it were—Jack has replied: "I don't think it'd work. In the first place, I never like to see a dome drilled into because I think this could affect a lot of wells that tap veins extending from it for several miles in all directions by breaking the vacuum pressure in the whole system and causing the water to drop far into the earth."

His conclusion rests on his belief that water in domes extends vertically downward into the earth. "A whole wide column of water," he says, "two or three miles or more high. Where it goes

30

Dowsing in an automobile. Nevada, 1977. Gaining confidence in his dowsing ability over the years, Jack Livingston can now detect water while riding in an automobile. His rod gives him an indication, not only of veins of water over which the automobile passes, but of the proper direction, or azimuth, in which to proceed in dry country to find water. As the car proceeds by a series of dry hills, Jack's rod, sweeping along them, dips only if there is an indication of water under a given hill. The practice has on occasion saved him a lot of time by eliminating the need for a more detailed search in an area where the grosser indication suggests it would be fruitless.

after that, I don't know. It's important not to confuse a dome, which is a really sizable amount of water, with a junction of two veins which may extend from two separate domes. I know of at least two domes on very high hills, one in Placer, the other in El Dorado, County, which to me indicate physical evidence of having actually *boiled out of the ground* at one time. Both of them have a dishlike depression and a big ring of rocks of various sizes all around their perimeters. They are still live domes but they no longer protrude above the ground. I've located several wells on veins coming from one of these domes—the veins can extend outward for several miles—and they're all still producing very well. I believe the domes constitute nature's own pumping system."

At Pine Grove, George Higbee still looked worried. "Up to last year," he went on, "the water in the standpipe here was up to nine feet below the surface of the ground. Now it's dropped. Shouldn't we be concerned about that?"

"Well, you might be losing a little pressure," offered Jack, "but that doesn't mean you'll lose any water. The source of your well could be a few miles up that mountain in a dome. I go on the theory that I've had for over twenty-five years—and a lot of us do—that a great deal of our water hasn't any connection with

31

LASSEN LAND C.

February 10, 1978

Mr. Jack Livingston
7168 Ridge Road
Newcastle, Ca. 95658

Dear Jack:

I thought you'd be interested in the well log data taken from the well which you dowsed for us in December. You've certainly made a believer out of me after watching your performance. The other three fellows with me — Carl Wiser, Steve Bogner, and Mike Wiser — also were very impressed.

I can understand how you can locate water, but it's beyond me how you are able to locate water depth. According to the well log, you missed the first water bearing strata by 40 or 50 feet, but hit the other two stratas perfectly. I suspect the upper strata didn't have much water as most wells in that vicinity that were less than 60 feet deep went dry last year.

According to the well driller the well test pumped at 3250 gallons per minute for two days. The water level before pumping was 52' and 110' during the pumping operation. This appears to be one of the best wells we have on the ranch.

We feel you saved us money by not having to dig a deep well. We followed your instructions and stopped at 280 feet. That compares with almost 500 feet for a well located 200 yards away in the same orchard. There we had a very difficult time finding gravel or sand stratas.

Jack, thanks again for your help. I'll be in touch with you when we get ready to dig another hole.

Sincerely,

Floyd Perry

FP/kd
Enclosure

The Wand or Bobbing Stick. Fallon, Nevada, 1977. Many dowsers, like Jack Livingston, left, use a long, straight, tapering stick, not unlike an oversized schoolroom pointer or a portion of a plastic fishing rod. This wand can be used, in lieu of a forked stick, to find water, but it is usually employed to ascertain its depth below ground.

Jack holds the wand at its thinner end and allows the thicker tip to come down a few inches from the ground. When it begins to move up and down, he counts the number of bobs, each one representing ten feet. When the tip of the wand stops bobbing and moves back and forth horizontally, he stops counting.

If water is, say, 194 feet below ground, the wand will bob nineteen times, each bob representing ten feet. Starting at 190, the dowser will resume counting, this time one foot per bob. If he is accurate, the bobbing should cease when he reaches four.

(LEFT) Reproduction of a letter of acknowledgment from the Lassen Land Company. Jack Livingston comments: "One reason a dowser might miss the water in the upper strata is that it often is 'dead' or accumulated water and that is the reason the wells at that depth went dry after two years of drought."

precipitation. It comes from deep subterranean sources that force their way up into the heights and then out into fractures in the rock where we find it. That's what I call 'live water.' And it's perpetual. As I said, *I've never seen one of my wells go dry yet. I think this well of yours will run indefinitely.* It's one of the best wells I've ever located at these high elevations. I've had some much bigger ones, but further out toward the valley.

"My experiences with these type of wells is that you can never hurt 'em by pumping if you keep 'em active, if you keep 'em comin' to you. One of the reasons this well is so good is that it's being constantly used. The harder you use a well, the better it'll develop as a rule. A lot of them increase their water flow because other little fractures or fissures get cleaned out on up the system and add to the production."

In his long dowsing career, Jack Livingston estimates he has brought in over 2,000 wells. If pumped steadily at an average rate of only 10 gpm, they would produce over 10 billion gallons of water every year or enough to supply the daily needs of a city of a quarter of a million people.

The loneliness of his work sometimes overpowers Jack, who has said: "Dowsing in the hard rock of the 'Mother Lode' is a heartbreaking task. It's not easy to go out on a man's property and tell him he has to drill maybe 400 feet in solid rock when

33

you know his bill may come to $10,000. You're all alone out there with no one but your conscience and perhaps your superconscious to guide you. It takes intestinal fortitude—a lot of guts—to do our thing in these earthquake-twisted mountains."

A Firm Professional Basis

In October 1970, *Ground Water Age*, a magazine specializing in water supply problems, featured a ninety-one-year-old Idahoan farmer who was successfully dowsing for water wells just as he had for over half a century. The publicity elicited an angry letter from Jay Lehr, Executive Director of the National Water Well Association (NWWA), a professional society for well-drillers.

"It was a severe shock to see you take three giant steps backward," Lehr castigated the magazine's editor-in-chief, James Tolman. "It is appalling that a major journal in the ground water industry is still capable of promoting water witching. Evidently, the job ahead of us in putting the water well industry on a firm professional basis is going to be harder than we expected, if people we *thought* to be intelligent and well read can continue to casually advertise the services of a water witch in Moscow, Idaho."

Lehr urged that the water well industry take a leaf from the book of the American Medical Association which, in his words, "had advanced its profession by clearly discrediting quack doctors and miracle medicines many of which have scientifically unverified histories of success equally as outstanding as your friendly water witchers. Until the water well industry can unite behind the efforts of the National Water Well Association in placing our work on a scientific rather than a superstitious level, we cannot hope to gain the respect presently commanded by our doctors, our lawyers, or our plumbers, electricians and bricklayers."

Tolman must have been chuckling when he calmly and pointedly replied to the indignant Lehr: "We had not thought our industry vulnerable to the charms of a ninety-one-year-old water witch. It has been our observation that water well contractors get about as much respect as they themselves earn. Some of our number even disagree with your scientifically demonstrated opinions about water witching. Where would Paul Bunyan and Pecos Pete be today if lumbermen and stockmen had hired PhD.s to label stories about them 'unscientific' and degrading to lumberjacks and cowboys?"

Only a few months later one member of the NWWA, Wayne Thompson, was sitting on a panel of water experts, including staffers from California's Department of Water Resources and independent consulting hydrologists, held to answer questions before a large public crowd concerned by the relentless drought.

After an NWWA-sponsored film, derisive of dowsing, entitled "The Water Witch Drowns in His Own Dry Hole" was shown, Thompson rose to declare that the movie just viewed was a distortion of fact. "Alone of this panel's members, I can prove this," he added quietly, "because we have used dowsing in our water-drilling business for the last twenty years and brought in good wells at a rate better than average than most of the drillers in our area. That's why our business has grown so fast. The word has spread to our benefit and today we're the biggest water-drilling operation in northern California."

The operation to which Thompson referred that evening is Weeks Drilling and Pump Company, located in the agricultural community of Sebastopol, east of Bodega Bay, of which Thompson is co-owner. Today practically every well the company puts down is dowsed beforehand either by Thompson, his son Greg, or one of three other dowsing employees.

In Thompson's home county of Sonoma, 85 percent of the wells drilled produce some water, no matter where they are located. The other 15 percent are dry holes. "We've beaten those figures," gloats Thompson. "Our dowsed wells come in successfully about 95 percent of the time. But where we really come out ahead with dowsing is in the *volume* and the *quality* of the water we produce. That's where we notice an enormous difference. We're not alone in this. Of the thirty-two drilling companies in Sonoma, the three which use dowsing all have a better success rate than average!"

Thompson, now fifty, was already twenty-seven years old when an amateur "witcher" stuck a forked stick in his hand for the first time. "It worked for me right off," he recalls; "it was scary at first, really spooky." For the next two years, Thompson checked his ability on wells that had already been successfully dowsed to gain experience. When he felt he was ready, he began to use his new skill professionally in the location of water for his clients. At first he performed his dowsing on the sly, because he did not want to open himself to the ridicule being heaped on dowsers, much of it by members of his own profession.

When he had proof that his company's drilling operations were achieving much greater production from wells found by dowsing than from those drilled on a conventional basis, he started, as he puts it, "witchin' in the open." During the 1977 California drought, Weeks Drilling was working almost around the clock with a dozen drills operating fourteen hours a day. Six phone lines in Thompson's office were constantly busy from 5:45 A.M. until late in the evening. In mid-March the dowser-driller had a backlog of 152 well-jobs which would take him eight to ten weeks to complete. One hundred twelve telephone messages littered his desk, appeals from people for a well survey of their properties, to which Thompson had not yet managed to reply.

The steep rise in business was accounted for mainly in neighboring Marin, just north of San Francisco's Golden Gate, which is northern California's most densely populated county. Thompson and his colleagues had worked in Marin for nearly eighteen years but, up to the time the drought set in, they had provided their services largely for farmers and home-owners who had no access to municipal water derived from reservoirs.

Even in early spring, a season normally blessed with bountiful rainfall, the reservoirs were showing their bottoms to the sun. "Most of Our Water's Gone!" screamed headlines on the cover of the Marin Municipal Water District flyer announcing a brand new

Wayne Thompson dowsing in Marin County, California, 1977. At 1/500 of a second, the picture captures the rod midway through its abrupt downward movement from the horizontal to the vertical. (Photograph by Dick Schmidt.)

stringent water-rationing program.

To maintain their way of life, residents were literally begging for Thompson's help. Jim Anderson, a seasoned *Sacramento Bee* reporter, was touring Marin County with Thompson and Jack Livingston to collect material for a feature story on dowsing when he heard one San Raphael businessman explain why he was going to the considerable expense of boring a well. "It's for my garden," he expostulated. "It's more important to me than my house and it's shot, nearly all burned up. Our lawn's nearly gone, too, as anyone can see. It's turning brown. We need water for the pool. We just have to have a well."

"Can you drill a well almost anywhere for water around here?" Anderson asked.

"The doctor across the street can answer that," came the reply. "He's just drilled down 175 feet and all he got was shale and sandstone, dry as a bone. Then his driller suggested another hole in the back of his house. It went down 140 feet with the same results as the first. He's spent $6,500 for nothing."

Thompson told Anderson that the abundance of new water-producing wells he was drilling was surprising many people because it had always been stated in official water resource circles that Marin County was dry. Geologists and well-drillers were skeptical that much water could be found under the Franciscan-type rock known to underlie the whole area. "A lot of them are astonished that we're coming up with good abundant water," Thompson added laughingly. "Of course we dowsers aren't too surprised."

In a water shortage, people can get along with little water by foregoing the pleasures of gardening, swimming in their own pools, constant showering, and unlimited operation of their clothes washers. For Marin County nurseryman Jim Egger, water was livelihood.

At Egger and Son Nurseries in Mill Valley, the plant salesman told Anderson: "I knew that the new allotment allowed us by the water district wouldn't take us through the dry season. They only gave us 51 percent of what we need to operate at minimum. Each of our three nurseries has an acre and a half of stock. We got Wayne Thompson to find us water at each of them. In Kentfield, we could only find 3½ gallons per minute so we put in a 4,300 gallon storage tank which the pump can fill in less than twenty-four hours and we use that. Under our Novato location, we got nearly 10 gallons per minute but, since we use much more water up there than here, we also put in a storage tank."

Egger added that he will never go back to using the municipal water system. "If I'd only drilled these wells years ago," he said wistfully, "think of the thousands of dollars I'd have saved."

Among agricultural clients satisfied with Thompson's dowsing is the Geyser Peak Winery in Alexander Valley near Geyserville, California, owned by the Schlitz Brewing Co., where Thompson's dowsing discovered what he calls an underground river 35–40 feet wide. He struck water at 205 feet in a hole two feet in diameter. When a 16-inch casing was put down and packed with

Wayne Thompson and Jim Egger in front of Egger Nursery in Mill Valley, California, 1977.

gravel, the well was pumped at the tremendous rate of 5,000 gallons per minute or enough to fill 300 large swimming pools every day. The water is used to irrigate Geyser Peak's extensive vineyards.

A year later, convinced that it could tap Thompson's subterranean river almost anywhere, the winery, without consulting the dowsing driller, sank a second well only 150 feet away from the large producer brought in by Weeks Drilling. To the wine producer's dismay, the well came up with only 1/50 of the amount of water in the dowsed well, or 100 gpm.

"Veins of water underground," says Thompson, "contrary to what the water experts teach, *seem to flow with water from independent sources.* Wells drilled in close proximity will thus often supply water without appearing to affect one another."

To illustrate this point, Thompson cites the case of a well drilled for another vineyard, in Dry Creek Valley near Healdsburg, desperate to find irrigation water for its grapes. His crew found that one of the vineyard's neighbors owned a well close to the common property line which pumped 12–15 gpm out of a hole some eighty feet deep.

"The neighbor was afraid that any well we drilled for the grape grower would affect his supply," said Thompson. "He told us in no uncertain terms that if the new well robbed water from his own well, Weeks Drilling would have to drill him a new well free of charge.

"I dowsed a well for the vineyard only fifteen feet away from the neighbor's well. We went down to about the same depth, eighty-four feet, and you can hardly believe it, but we struck 2,000 gpm in alluvial sand and gravel. The huge amount of water

37

we were pumping didn't affect the older well's supply at all. We were monitoring it very carefully. The only possible conclusion is that we hit a completely different and much larger source of water only fifteen feet distant from the other."

Thompson explained to the *Sacramento Bee* reporter that during the severe California drought, Marin County water supervisors, having relied on dammed water for years, were being forced to look underground in 1977.

"The county is even being compelled to reactivate unused wells drilled years ago and they're talking about drilling a whole series of new wells for pumping into their dried-out reservoirs. We know of several good spots that we've dowsed years ago but abandoned. Just the other day we test pumped some of them and they put out 100–150 gallons per minute steadily."

When Anderson asked to see wells on a rocky height such as Thompson was describing, the driller took him and his companions to a mountaintop near the village of Ross where he had dowsed and drilled a well for two neighbors. A prior geological report on the area prepared by Eugene Boudreau,

The saga of how a retired livestock and vegetable farmer from the Mahoning Valley in Lehighton, Pennsylvania, found water for a mission hospital in Haiti's Arbonite Valley is only one of many hundred tributes to man's dowsing ability. Guy Snyder, 72, who up to January 1, 1979, had dowsed 834 wells (140 of them in 1978 alone) was asked by the Green Walks Trout Hatchery in nearby Bangor to find water about ten years ago. His dowsing produced a 300 gpm artesian well. In 1976, the hatchery recommended Snyder's services to the Rolling Rock Club at Ligonier outside Pittsburgh, which stocks a stream for its wealthy members with trout raised in its own hatchery near the crest of a small mountain.

California Registered Geologist No. 3000, had stated that it was unlikely that any water would be found. Entitled "Geology and Ground Water Potential of the Denicke Property in Ross, Marin County," the report specifically declared that "the search for ground water is the search for permeable rock below the water table. It is impossible to predict in advance of drilling just how much usable water will be found . . . The most practical exploration technique that can be used in finding ground water is to try to drill into the most potentially permeable rock available and to avoid drilling in obviously impermeable rocks . . . As the known geologic conditions are so unfavorable for finding usable amounts of ground water due to a lack of potentially permeable rock, I must recommend that no drilling be done. If the owners still wish to gamble on finding water, then they should drill down 200 to 300 feet in order to give the rock a better chance to change for the better."

Thompson relied, not on the geologist's report, but on his dowsing rod. He told Dr. E. W. Denicke, one of the property owners, he would find water if he put down a well close to the

(LEFT) Rig built by Levi Mast of Weatherford, Oklahoma, used to drill well dowsed by Guy Synder at Tercilia's Bakery, Mahon, Haiti. Good water struck at 100 feet.

Guy Snyder

"Springs supplying 125–150 gpm for the hatchery began to dry up," related hatchery manager Horace Stiff. "When they dwindled to only 18–25 pgm, we were in real trouble." Called to the rescue, Snyder recommended a well be drilled at a spot 40 feet higher than the hatchery and 200 feet from it. A local driller doubted any water could be found at the spot underlain with hard blue stone. Confident that Snyder knew what he was about, Stiff insisted a well be drilled at the spot marked by the dowser.

"We struck bed rock at 32 feet," says Stiff, "and went on down into the blue stone to a depth of 365 feet. We hit a large fissure and the drill bit dropped six inches. The result was an artesian well producing 210 gpm that has been flowing around the clock ever since."

Snyder's dowsing attracted the attention of club member Dr. Murray F. McCaslin, an eye specialist who arranged with Pittsburgh's Grant Foundation for Snyder to travel to Haiti and locate water for the 200-bed Albert Schweitzer Hospital it operates at Deschappels together with a vocational training center and a farm.

Snyder recommended a well be drilled back of the hospital's power house, then went on successfully to locate four more wells for villages in an area thirty miles around the hospital inhabited by 100,000 people.

Dr. William Larimer Mellon, head of the mission hospital, wrote to Snyder on May 11, 1977: "Since we began drilling in February, we've broughtin four good wells . . . So far your average is 100% with me."

Introduced by hospital staffers to their adolescent son, Gerard Frédériqui Jr., Snyder taught the young Haitian to dowse. By 1979 Frédériqui had used his dowsing rod to find potable water for over a dozen more villages throughout the area.

edge of a ravine where the property fell off steeply into the valley below.

A water source was struck in hard, gray *impermeable* rock admixed with a little clay at 151 feet below the surface of the ground. When tested by bailing, it produced 4½ gallons per minute of cool, fresh water which, stored in a redwood tank, has been used by the joint owners ever since to irrigate their extensive gardens.

Thompson has dowsed successful wells for California's Division of Beaches and Parks, one of them in a redwood grove nearly halfway up the side of Marin County's 2,571-foot Mount Tamalpais, the region's highest peak, held sacred in former times by local Indians. The new source was needed to supply drinking and toilet flushing water for thousands of tourists who annually visit the grove in buses and private vehicles. When he announced his location to his client, geologists were doubtful that he could produce water at so high an altitude.

"They claimed that, normally, it should be found only much lower down," reported Thompson, "but we've had a lot better success drilling into the hard rocky mountaintops around here than at points further down. I'd say we struck a lot more water than when we tried at lower elevations."

The existence of water on the summit of mountains and hills, though completely illogical from the viewpoint of academic hydrology, has been repeatedly demonstrated by the dowsing of Thompson and his associates. A typical example of discovery of water atop a mountain came on property owned by the Great Western Savings and Loan Company on Sonoma Mountain from which San Francisco and the Golden Gate Bridge can easily be seen on a clear day.

The company was seeking sufficient water for a future housing development commanding the spectacular view. In 1976, Thompson dowsed a spot only forty-five feet from the very top. It produced 12 gpm at a depth of 120 feet and has been flowing ever since.

On the same mountain the well for an already existing subdivision was going dry. One of the world's largest geological consulting firms, with an office in San Raphael, was hired to find a new well site. The locations it recommended were drilled, one deeper than 400 feet, but came up bone dry. Finally, the owners of the subdivision turned to Weeks Drilling. Less than 250 feet from one of the dry holes and 300 feet from the existing well that was fast drying up, Thompson spotted a potential well location. Drilled to 380 feet, it gushed forth with 110 gpm and has now been pumping the same amount for nearly five years.

Near Santa Rosa, last home of Luther Burbank, the world famous plant breeder, Thompson drilled a well found with his dowsing rod on the top of Parker Hill. When water came out of a 453-foot deep fracture in hard volcanic rock, surprised geologists claimed he must have made a lucky strike on a source of water that had percolated as rain into the hill itself.

"But the water keeps on pumping," says Thompson. "It's as if the supply is endless."

40

CHAPTER 2

The Non-Subject

". . . then, the 'palms up' method with the arms crossed or uncrossed . . ."

Denial at the USGS

In 1966, the United States Geological Survey, a branch of the United States Department of Interior, published a 14-page brochure entitled "Water Witching," the main aim of which was to serve as a standard reply to anyone inquiring about the merits of dowsing for locating water. The brochure was hardly equivocal. "A truly astonishing number of books and pamphlets," it stated, "have been written on the subject of water witching, but as far as scientists are concerned, the subject is wholly discredited." To back up this categorical assertion, the USGS also referred readers to its half-century-old Water Supply Paper No. 416, *The Divining Rod: A History of Water Witching,* which labeled dowsing a "curious superstition" that was "practically useless."

The unmitigated contempt of dowsing as a means for finding water evidenced in the USGS brochure aroused the indignation of Raymond Willey, secretary of the American Society of Dowsers, a group organized in 1960 when a few experienced New England dowsers informally gathered in Danville, Vermont, some forty miles south of the United States-Canadian border, to exchange experiences and swap stories during a two-day meeting. Today society membership, numbering nearly 2,000, is represented by all the states in the American Union and by some fifteen foreign countries.

Willey himself estimated that his dowsing skill has brought in hundreds of wells including one for the General Electric Company in Schenectady, New York, which produced 400 gallons per minute, twenty-four hours a day, seven days a week, for several years, saving the giant company a potentially enormous water bill.

Writing to USGS Director William Pecora in October 1967, Willey accused the survey of intending, through the issuance of its new brochure, to discredit the value of dowsing and to cast doubt on the validity of the process itself and added that so authoritative a position taken by a department of the federal government should be supported with better evidence.

This thrust by a private citizen at a governmental behemoth was met only by a weak parry in the form of a letter which, in support of the brochure, tiresomely quoted from the fifty-year-old

Paper No. 416. Sensing sluggishness and potential uncertainty in his adversary, Willey pressed his attack with a two-dozen page report on the "why" and "how" of dowsing, bluntly noting that he hoped it would be sufficient for the USGS to start a reconsideration of its position on the subject. As a final barb, Willey noted that inasmuch as the U.S. Internal Revenue Service had recognized the "scientific and educational purpose of the ASD," at least one important branch of the American bureaucracy did not consider the subject as silly as the USGS.

When he obtained no satisfactory rejoinder from the Survey,

"*The literally millions of water wells located by dowsing around the world since before history was first recorded, and those being added every day, continue to challenge geologists and hydrologists. The facts of these wells cannot be disregarded or swept under the rug forever.*

"*As the need for conserving our water resources becomes more compelling, the responsibility of the USGS to become acquainted with the facts of those water sources which supply a good percentage of our citizens becomes no less compelling. It is time to drop the controversial attitude and to inquire, to conduct research, to evaluate reliable evidence and to become informed.*"

Raymond C. Willey
Editor, *The American Dowser*;
Secretary, the American Society
of Dowsers, Danville, Vermont,
May 1977

"*The pages of the* Water Well Journal *have long remained silent on the age-old controversy of water witching. Now with the national water crisis finally bringing ground water the attention it deserves, the time has come to face up to our industry's albatross . . . Whether you believe in water witches or not (and I realize that there is still an element among us who does) we have the water witches to thank for the predicament of a grossly underdeveloped ground water resource in a period of critical water shortage . . .*

"*Thus, I think the time has come to stop laughing at these renaissance retards who have obstructed the growth of our industry. It is time to take a firm stand on behalf of the high level of competence our industry exhibits in dealing with a scientific discipline every bit as sophisticated as the more accepted fields of electronics, engineering, space physics, and the like . . .*

"*Palmistry and tea leaf reading have now become largely a part of our past. America would be far better off if water witches followed suit.*"

Jay Lehr, Editor
Water Well Journal, 1978

at the beginning of 1968 Willey decided to have done with niceties. In a sharply worded missive, he stated that because the Geological Survey's position was "completely unsubstantial and inadequate," he now felt compelled to request that all USGS publications on dowsing which could "be taken to make the government of the United States of America authoritative on the value of dowsing" *be withdrawn*.

Like a ram bested by his rival at the mating season, Pecora declined any further head-on confrontations. Admitting that "our exchange has reached the point of diminishing returns," he

Raymond C. Willey. (Photograph by Edward Kanzelmyer.)

submitted to Willey what he termed the "final summary of our points of view":

The Geological Survey specializes in earth sciences. The study of underground water systems constitutes a considerable part of our effort. Together with other hydrologists throughout the world, we have kept up to date on developments and techniques thought to be useful in ground water exploration. Some years ago, our Survey scientists concluded that dowsing is not the best method for determining where water is, or is not, located in an unexplored area. Their reports, like other technical writings, are permanent parts of the scientific record. We have seen no evidence in recent years to invalidate their conclusions.

Determining where ground water is, or is not, likely to be found is a relatively simple matter for a professional geologist who is more concerned with the quantity of water available and the effect of long-term use upon it. For these reasons dowsing would have little value in our work regardless of the layman who lacks such capability. Public interest and curiosity in this subject have resulted in our stating the Survey's position from time to time.

The unctuous tone of Pecora's reply did not reveal to Willey that he had won, if not the whole of the fight, at least a crucial round, for unbeknownst to him, Pecora sent a memorandum to his information officer ordering that the controversial brochure "be removed from our list of popular publications and our regional information offices" until it could be rewritten in a "more objective" style.

Seemingly laid to rest, the issue of the brochure was reanimated at the USGS in the spring of 1970 when the District Chief of Survey's Water Resources Division in Portland, Oregon, plaintively inquired of his boss C. L. McGuinness, head of the Groundwater Branch in Washington, D.C., why it was no longer available to his staff members who were constantly besieged with inquiries about dowsing.

McGuinness could only reply to his underling that a "marathon exchange of letters" between Willey and Pecora had led to the USGS Director's "backing off" from the fight, a decision with which he, McGuinness, who "had enjoyed battles with water witches over the years," did not concur.

The next complaint about the brochure came in a letter to the USGS Assistant Chief Hydrologist for Scientific Publications and Data Management from its Water Resources Development field representative in Lincoln, Nebraska. During his official travels in the high plains, he was constantly bombarded, he wrote, with questions about the USGS stance on water witching. By far the easiest way of responding to them had been the brochure which now was no longer available for distribution because "someone" had decided that the subject of dowsing was too controversial.

Even more alarming to USGS bureaucrats was the revelation that the Bureau of Land Management and the National Parks Service had utilized the services of water witches. "Perhaps the defunct brochure could at least be distributed to our sister agencies in the Department of Interior," one urged. "I think they need help." The plea earned the immediate support of Gerald Meyer, Chief of the Ground Water Branch, who recommended that, because the old brochure was clearly and concisely written and palatable to both believers and doubters, it be reissued with only minor revisions.

By the end of 1975, it was obvious that no consensus had been reached as to which revisions should be made or even whether a revised brochure should or should not be made available to the public. Opinions ranged all the way from "too sensitive a subject, no formal issuance" to "petition for approval of the leaflet as written, if fail, try again when climate improves."

In the meantime, dowsing was afforded new publicity when, in May 1976, the widely circulated *Reader's Digest* published an article, "The Forked Stick Phenomenon," supporting the notion that a centuries-old mysterious way of locating subterranean riches was productive enough to warrant serious investigation. Hardly had the issue been delivered to newsstands when NWWA president Jay Lehr shot off a letter to the USGS complaining that "it seems such stories will go on plaguing us forever and it is particularly disturbing because we can do without 18 million believers in water witching."

Lehr unsuccessfully insisted that the USGS send a letter to the *Reader's Digest* protesting the promotion of a dubious water-seeking technique. However, he failed to add that none of the publications issued by his own association made clear how reliably water-drillers went about locating places to put down wells. Clearly, the idea that dowsers could do the job efficiently and cheaply meant that water-drillers might be deprived of thousands of drilling dollars paid by exasperated clients for nothing but dry holes.

In 1977 the USGS, reconciling the divergent opinions of its workers, finally printed a new brochure "Water Dowsing" to replace the one taken out of circulation by Pecora but giving no explanation for the policy reversal.

The tireless Willey, refusing to let the USGS off the hook, now wrote to Pecora's replacement, V. E. McKelvey, to accuse the survey of a "breach of faith": Referring to the energy crisis in the United States, Willey affirmed that dowsing could substantially assist the nation to prospect for water, oil, and mineral ores where normal methods of search were helpless to find them and to help in the inspection of earth-fill dams across the country, many of which were suspected to be in a near leaky and therefore dangerous condition.

Far from accepting the challenge, the USGS only reasserted its position that the new brochure was "objective, noncritical and accurate." That this was far from the case was obvious from the brochure excerpt quoted in an article in *Science Digest* published in March 1978. "The natural explanation of 'successful' water dowsing is that in many areas water would be hard to miss," read the excerpt. "The dowser commonly implies that the spot indicated by the rod is the *only* one where water could be found, but this is not necessarily true. In a region of adequate rainfall and favorable geology, it is difficult *not* to drill and find water." All of which was tantamount to saying that if circumstances were right, the Misquamicut Club would not have needed a Kidd, the town of Pine Grove a Livingston, or the Weeks Drilling Company

> *"Since we are talking geology, we must note, alas, that it has become the fashion among dowsers, who have not the slightest knowledge of this science, to hold it in utter contempt and to declare that geologists are powerless to disclose water courses or mineral deposits of any kind.*
>
> *"Geology is a science of observation which has already attained a high degree of perfection. With its findings one can forecast the existence of layers of water enclosed within permeable and impermeable geological strata, know whether this water will or will not spurt out of the ground and whether it will or will not be mineralized.*
>
> *"I have myself been able, before I knew anything about the methods of dowsers, to identify, solely by geological means, the existence of underground waters and bring them to light.*
>
> *"But when it comes to determining the actual presence and precise location of subterranean water courses or hydric networks, caverns and hollows, and metallic veins in certain— and particularly in calcareous—terrain, the geologist is stymied.*
>
> *"It is at this point that the dowser can be called in significantly to add to geological findings.*
>
> *"The dowser is able to discover whether there really are sources of water or metallic substances in a given area, determine their precise location as well as the width and breadth of such bodies and, to a certain extent, their depth.*
>
> *"It is thus as puerile as it is unjust to seek to oppose these two methods. Instead of slandering and anathematizing one another, geologists and dowsers share the self-serving interest of joining hands."*
>
> Armand Viré, *Docteur ès Sciences*, Honorary Laboratory Director at the National Museum of Natural History, Paris, in *How to Become a Dowser—What I Have Seen and What I Have Done*, Paris, 1948.

four dowsers that gave them the edge over their competitors.

More disturbing to Willey was the same excerpt's unsupported assertion that "scientifically controlled experiments" reported in books on dowsing had led the USGS to conclude that the "expense of testing dowsers was not justified."

By the spring of 1978, having received no satisfactory reply from the USGS, Willey wrote to the Secretary of the Interior, Cecil Andrus, to complain that by issuing a new pamphlet, the USGS had unilaterally broken the earlier understanding made between USGS Director Pecora and the American Society of Dowsers. "The Federal Government," he stated, "is put in the position of officially denying the value of dowsing and questioning the credibility of a large number of dowsers, who have been and still are contributing to the welfare of their fellow citizens through their effort. No other government, to my knowledge, has seen fit to take such a position."

Once more, Willey raised the question of the USGS's lack of integrity and its refusal to furnish "responsible answers to legitimate questions." Noting that the "human rights" of dowsers were being violated, he hinted that dowsers, with track records of hundreds, in some cases, thousands of wells behind them, might find in the wording of the USGS pamphlet a personal basis for legal action in court or for seeking an injunction against the pamphlet unless the USGS could come up with proof of certain statements and implications in its text.

"As I see it," he concluded, "the question of theories about the nature of underground water occurrence is not a factor in this discussion. Dowsers were locating water wells centuries before there were any such subjects as geology and hydrology. Very few contemporary dowsers worry about theories. They find water where it is. And very often they find it in places where hydrologists say there shouldn't be any. The fact is, as I have concluded, if hydrologists had followed the work of water dowsers and the drilling of wells after the locations were made, as they have followed the drilling for oil and gas, the data accumulated would have compelled a much broader look at underground water conditions."

Silence at the Soil Conservation Service

No one would chuckle more readily over the USGS's bureaucratic discomfiture than Francis Lindsay, a former grass seed farmer, former owner of plum and pear orchards, former representative of ten eastern California counties in the state legislature, and a water dowser who knows from first-hand experience how deep prejudice and fear about dowsing can run.

Today, with forty years of locating wells behind him, Lindsay can boast: "Whenever I'm asked to find water, I never tell people they are sure to get it. A lot of times it won't be there under their land. What I can and do say is that, *whenever I've had a positive indication of water with my rod, drilling has always corroborated it.*"

After he joined the United States Forest Service in 1936 as a Junior Range Examiner, Lindsay, together with forty colleagues, attended a training session on a ranch high in the rolling hills south of Livermore, California. As the rancher showed off his acreage, he complained that a beautiful spring near the top of one of the hills had dried up completely after an earthquake had closed off its source of underground water. One of the senior forest rangers present chimed in: "What you need is a good water witch to find you a well."

The suggestion caught fire and soon all the trainees were trying their luck with four forked sticks cut from a nearby willow tree. The old ranger, who told Lindsay he had successfully dowsed wells for years, showed his younger colleague how to manipulate the stick. What happened next Lindsay related as follows:

"I was walking along with the fork in my hands and suddenly the damn thing went down and scared me almost to death. I couldn't believe it. Trying not to look ridiculous, I turned my back on the crowd and started back over the same terrain and

Francis Lindsay and his divining rod. (Photograph courtesy of Mike Durant.)

down it went again. Well, this time the old ranger was watching me, and he hollered: 'Hey, look at that! Maybe he's found something!' So all the others swarmed up to where I was and I went back and forth, and each time I passed over this one spot, down the rod would go. So, then, they blindfolded me, and turned me round and round and walked me all over that hill. But the fork never dipped until I came over that one zone and when I passed beyond it, the fork would come up again. The zone was a narrow one, not more than four feet wide."

Lindsay traced the vein down the hill to a place where he could no longer get any reaction from his fork. The rancher turned to his foreman and ordered him to put a stake in the ground where Lindsay had experienced the last pull of the rod. During a festive lunch-hour barbecue held for the trainees, the same foreman excitedly drove up in his truck and announced to the surprised crowd: "Well, Lindsay was right! We found it!"

In Lindsay's words: "Everybody jumped in their cars and went back up the hill. The ranch hands had dug a deep ditch across the zone and, sure enough, there was a nice stream of water running in a gravel bed, maybe four to five feet wide. It flowed along until it came to a two-inch crack in rock and went straight down into the earth."

Lindsay was the hero of the day. He had found water by dowsing on his very first attempt.

A few years later Lindsay, now an employee of the United States Conservation Service, was observing a well being drilled for a forest ranger headquarters at Capitan in New Mexico's Sacramento Mountains. Out of curiosity he cut a forked stick and, after checking the drill site for water, bluntly asked the driller: "What on earth are you drilling here for?"

Obviously flustered, the driller testily replied: "Because that's where the engineers planning this project told me to drill."

Lindsay shook his head. "You won't find any water here," he said gloomily.

To Lindsay's surprise, the driller concurred. "Yeah, I know that," he admitted, then foxily added: "Say, you must be a 'water witch.' Why don't you see if you can find some water around here?"

By this time, Lindsay had mislaid his dowsing stick, so he headed toward a tree to cut another. The driller stopped him with the admonition: "If you can witch, you can witch with anything. Here, take this piece of baling wire and curve it over like this."

As Lindsay recalled: "That was the first time I'd tried anything except a willow switch. I started walking with the baling wire and, over in one corner, within 150 feet of where the drilling was taking place, the darn thing snapped down. So I came back and told him: 'The wire went wild over there in that corner.' "

"Exactly where?" the driller inquired.

"Right over the spot where that white rock lies on the ground," replied Lindsay.

The driller's eyes widened. "Well, I'm the one that put the rock down there," he confessed. "I didn't tell you before, but I witched a vein of water at that very spot a few hours ago. My dad, he's been an expert witcher for years. He taught me how to do it. He's coming up here tonight and he'll check this place out, too."

At the construction site the following morning Lindsay learned that the driller's father arrived well after dark and, with only his truck's headlights to illuminate his way, dowsed over the whole area. In less than ten minutes he picked up the rock put down by his son as a marker and put a piece of paper under it, then told his son to drill in the middle of the paper. Three dowsers had come to the same conclusion without any of them telling the other two about the spot they had located.

A few days later, the forester in charge of the region came down from Albuquerque and, after talking to the dowsers, told his driller: "Okay, if all three of you think there's water to be had at that place, that's where we'll try next." It was only then that Lindsay learned that the U.S. Forest Service had already drilled a 180-foot well for its new headquarters which, as Lindsay sardonically commented, "was just as dry on the bottom as it was on the top."

The forester took Lindsay aside out of earshot of the other two dowsers and ominously warned: "Francis, there had better be water down there because, if there isn't, and it gets around that we acted on the recommendation of water witches, we are going to be the laughing stock of every U.S. government agency in New Mexico."

Unabashed, Lindsay retorted: "Look, nobody's paying me a dime for this. If there's no water there, that's tough. But at least, you have a chance. There's no chance at all anywhere else."

On the results of the drilling, Lindsay could brag: "At eighty-five feet they got a couple of gallons a minute. Then they went on down to between 105 and 110 feet and struck at least another five gallons of water, more than was needed. When chemically analyzed, it turned out to be the best ever found in Capitan. The word got out all over the region that the driller and I were both good water witches. We began dowsing more wells and *we never missed!* It got to a point where the driller would tell a rancher: 'We'll drill you a well and we'll tell you how deep your water lies.' And he'd give him a price and promise him: No water, No pay! And boy, from that time on, that well-driller had orders to keep him busy round the clock. He never stopped."

Aware of his special talents, Lindsay's conservation service supervisors now began to assign him to water location jobs all over the southern half of New Mexico. "They'd get a phone call from a man hard up for water," he remembers, "and they'd call me in and say: 'Francis, here's your official travel orders for two or three days. You go to such-and-such a town and look up a rancher named so-and-so and see if you can solve his problem.' That's all they'd say. They always left it up to the rancher to tell me his problem even though they knew exactly what it was. So I'd drive maybe one or two hundred miles and meet the ranchers. The problem was always finding them a well. And I solved all the problems."

Over three years Lindsay brought in at least fifty wells. The dowser-driller, able to spend full time on the work, found many more. Throughout the period none of Lindsay's superiors ever mentioned or reported on his dowsing ability.

"I get a real kick out of the fact," laughs Lindsay, "that none of them would ever admit that the U.S. Soil Conservation Service had anything to do with finding water by dowsing. In fact, I don't think news of my special talent ever was allowed to spread beyond my own Range Management Section, with the possible exception of a couple of specialists in Engineering who heard about it and became fascinated. Every time they'd call me in to assign me to a water-finding job, they'd simply say this or that rancher had 'a problem' and wanted to see me. I knew damn well what they were talking about. But they would never never breathe a word about dowsing. It was a non-subject."

The "Unscientific Method"

If the general bureaucratic pattern has been a lack of courage to admit the usefulness of a method which, though "scientifically" unfathomable, *works* in practically every instance it is put to test, then the exception is the pragmatic attitude of two Swiss business executives who have unerringly employed dowsing to locate water for one of the world's largest industrial companies.

"Without chemistry, no pharmaceutical industry. Without water, no chemistry." So begins an article, "The Unexplainable is Nevertheless Fact," published in the 1972–73 issue of *Roche-Zeitung,* a German-language in-house journal of the multinational pharmaceutical firm, Hoffman-La Roche, headquartered in the Swiss city of Basel.

Because water in enormous quantities is needed by its factories for purposes of cooling, sanitation, and chemical processing, Roche (as the company is known for short) first asks, before undertaking the construction of any manufacturing installation, "Is there enough water on the proposed site?"

To answer this urgent query the company, in the words of the *Roche-Zeitung* editor, "though itself based on science, does not search for its water using methods based on science, but— with a dowsing rod! And the amazing thing is that, with this unscientific method, Roche has been 100 percent *successful* in places where it has sought water all over the world."

The dowsers sent abroad on Roche's water-finding missions were Dr. Peter Treadwell, Director of Roche's vitamin plant at Sisseln, Switzerland, and Rudolph Rupp, a senior engineer at the company's headquarters. Before joining Roche, Treadwell learned the art of dowsing from his father, who was employed as an engineer for the city water works in Zürich. His father relied on his rod to find underground pipes of all kinds, thus saving hours of needless excavation. Employed by Roche in 1944, Treadwell kept practicing his new skill but had no way of proving whether water really existed below ground at places where his rod indicated it to be.

In 1952, realizing that the Roche installation in Basel was seeking underground water for cooling purposes (a supply which has since been supplanted by direct tapping of the Rhine river), Treadwell gathered sufficient courage to suggest to his boss that

(LEFT) Dr. Peter Treadwell and (RIGHT) Rudolph Rupp in action with huge circle-shaped aluminum dowsing rods. (Photograph by Hoffman-La Roche, Basel, Switzerland.)

he might be able to spot a few wells. Asked how he intended to find them, Treadwell boldly explained that he was a dowser.

Far from turning him down, his superior suggested to Treadwell that he first submit to a test. When he gladly accepted, he was taken out onto the Roche grounds, and asked to mark on the pavement areas where pipes were known to be located. After successfully passing the test, he went on to stake drilling points for wells between the Schwarzwaldallee and the railway embankment.

"Trial borings and pumping tests that followed got us wells producing from 600-900 gpm," he told the *Roche-Zeitung* editor. "We also charted a series of potentially productive holes near the 'Bierburg' where the Institute of Immunology stands today."

So fruitful was Treadwell's water-finding that Roche began sending him on trips to foreign countries wherever the company was considering the installation of a plant. In Australia Treadwell discovered a large supply of water under sand dunes close to the seashore in a suburb of Sydney but, for a variety of reasons unconnected to the find, his company did not purchase the site.

On his way home he stopped to dowse for water in India where a factory site had been proposed at Thana, near Bombay. As Treadwell recalled during the interview: "Just imagine the following scene. You're in the middle of a dusty plain. Everything is flat, with red sand as far as you can see. It's appallingly hot and, for the life of you, you haven't the wildest notion where water might be found in such a wasteland. Then, only with the aid of your dowsing rod you finally locate a thin strip no more than a meter and a half wide under which a vein of water is indicated."

Treadwell's feat at Thana so impressed Rupp, at the time the technical manager for Roche in India, that, despite his initial engineer's skeptical disbelief, he asked his colleague to teach him how to manipulate a rod. As soon as he tried it, it worked perfectly, and he was able independently to confirm other prospective water veins located by Treadwell, some of them for

(RIGHT) Treadwell teaching a Hoffman-La Roche employee to dowse. When the employee held the huge dowsing rod alone, he could get no reaction. But when he held one handle and Treadwell held the other, plus the employee's hand, the rod responded as if Treadwell were manipulating the rod by himself. (Courtesy of Hoffman-La Roche, Basel, Switzerland.)

other Swiss firms such as Ciba-Geigy and Sandoz.

"Of all the challenges I ever faced as a water dowser," said Rupp during the interview, "India was without question the most difficult. Where we were dowsing, subterranean veins of water existed only in 1 to 10 centimeter-wide cracks in solid rock. On one well we could drill no more than three feet or so each day. After ten weeks we reached a depth of 200 to 230 feet and struck a water-bearing fissure right on the button! Our dowsing had to be that accurate. Some companies using water-detecting instruments had missed narrow veins by 24, 28, and 40 inches or more."

Treadwell explained that because he had been introduced to it by his father, he preferred a slender, straight branch of green wood bent into a hoop shape and held palms downward. When he used such a device to dowse a Roche-planned industrial site in the Philippines, he met a Catholic priest who was equally successful with a forked stick. "The only difference between us was that when I came across a vein, my hoop-shaped stick rose upward," reported Treadwell, "but the priest's forked stick snapped downward. Don't ask me why."

Both Treadwell and Rupp then surprised the *Roche-Zeitung* editor by showing him enormous hoop-shaped dowsing devices made of aluminum. "We have found," said Rupp, "that by using lightweight aluminum instruments, we become less fatigued when dowsing over a long period. We have used these rods in Indonesia where in early September 1972 we found two economically worthwhile sources of water near Jakarta. We drilled through various layers of rock and hit an underground stream delivering approximately 45 gpm. Without this source we would not have been able to build a Roche factory as there was no piped water anywhere nearby. In Indonesia one easily locates water almost anywhere at about thirteen feet of depth but it is stagnant surface runoff water useless for our purposes."

"My most recent search was at Village-Neuf in the French province of Alsace," added Treadwell, "where Roche has now just opened a new vitamin plant. Alsace, too, so abounds in water sources that one can practically drill anywhere and hit them. What we were after were the zones of high porosity. We determined drilling points and came up with yields far greater than local French geologists had expected. Our predictions were not just for the 'presence of water or not' but for 'more water here, less water there.'"

At the interview's end, the magazine editor asked a final question: "How is it that Roche, a company based on science, uses a nonscientific method to find water? Isn't this a bit weird on the surface of it?"

"That problem has bothered me for a long time," Treadwell sighed, "but the plain truth is that we keep finding water for our company with a method that neither physics nor physiology nor psychology have even begun to explain. To directly answer your heretical question: *Roche uses methods that are profitable, whether they are scientifically explainable or not. The dowsing method pays off. It is 100 percent reliable!"*

A Lake Restored

If Treadwell's pragmatic and positive statement had been heeded instead of the jibes of geological and engineering authorities, Verne Cameron might have been saved a twenty-year fight to bring one of southern California's largest bodies of water back to life.

In 1927, construction began on the Railroad Canyon Dam across the San Jacinto River which fed beautiful six-mile long Lake Elsinore some twenty miles due south of Riverside. When the dam was completed, the reservoir's water behind it was diverted to the Temescal Water District for sale to the city of Corona twenty-two miles to the northwest. Only a small portion of the river's normal flow reached the lake.

Within months, citizens who had enjoyed swimming and boating were appalled to see the level of their lake gradually falling. In ensuing years its surface continued to drop at a rate of about 4½ feet, or 50 billion gallons, a year. Sulphur gas and other effluvia belched up through the fast-evaporating water killing many fish, and, reputedly, even a few swimmers. By the summer of 1951, Lake Elsinore, except for a tiny fetid puddle at its western end, was bone dry.

During the next two decades, Elsinore's townspeople all but uninterruptedly looked out on the dusty lake bottom occasionally alleviated when rare heavy rains would partially fill the lake cavity. When the rain water receded, swarms of mosquitoes and eye gnats, proliferating in thousands of stagnant puddles, blanketed Elsinore as did clouds of dust blown from the lake bed by the prevailing southwest wind. The smell of rotting algae wafted continually over the town.

Elsinore's elected officials, anxious to restore the beauty of the lake that had made their community so exceptional, proposed in 1949 to donate the lake bottom to the State of California as a park, in hopes that governmental authorities in Sacramento would recreate the no longer existing body of water. The state turned their offer down cold.

At this point an Elsinore resident named Verne Cameron entered the picture. Cameron had had extensive experience as a water dowser ever since his grandmother taught him the technique and had even invented a special dowsing device of his own design. His dowsing had convinced Cameron that an abundant supply of water flowing in deep earthquake faults that had originally formed the lake could be tapped by drilling. Only three wells were necessary, said Cameron, to supply 6,000 gallons of pure fresh water per minute, or 8,640,000 gallons per day, a flow which he calculated was sufficient to fill the lake within six to eight months.

His announcement was immediately ridiculed by one Max Bookman, a California State geologist, as well as by a host of Bookman's colleagues and a cohort of state engineers. Flying in the face of the experts' pronouncements, and what turned out to be fruitless efforts to bring the lake's level back to normal, Cameron teamed with Bill Cox, a newspaperman, to form "The Water for Lake Elsinore Committee" which, by popular subscription, collected $5,700 to pay a driller to sink a well in what Cameron considered to be a choice location above the lake's northern end.

A test hole six inches in diameter drilled to a depth of 658 feet more than proved Cameron's contention since, when water was brought in, it rose in the hole higher than the surface of the lake when full. It looked as if the well could easily produce 2,500 gallons per minute if properly completed, meaning that the hole required reaming out to 20-inch diameter, as well as proper casing and gravel-packing, all at an additional cost of $5,000.

Plans to raise the money went awry when a proposal was made that the town purchase the lakesite and donate it to the state. Believing that this deal would finally commit the state to develop a park and fill the lake, Elsinore citizens were shocked to discover that California had not the slightest intention of doing either. Particularly bitter were those who owned segments of the former lake's shoreline.

54

Verne Cameron. (Courtesy of Borderland Sciences Research Association, Vista, California.)

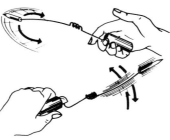

THE CAMERON "AURAMETER." *In his book, Aquavideo, published after his death in 1969, Cameron describes a dowsing device designed by himself which many dowsers consider to be particularly sensitive. The idea of using a spring came to Cameron when he saw a contractor using a T-bar, the longer arm of which was supported in midair by a light coil spring, the other end of which was held in his teeth. The contractor maintained that the depth of an object underground could be gauged by the amount of "pull" on the spring.*

Many devices utilize a spring such as the Adjustable Sensitivity Detector manufactured in Antwerp, Belgium. The spring can be telescoped into the tubelike handle when not in use.

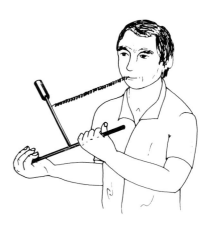

Cameron's instrument seems to embody the quality of action of four dowsing devices. Like a Y-shaped rod it will dip earthward. Like an L-shaped rod it will move sideways. Like a wand it will bob up and down. Like a pendulum it will rotate. Because Cameron's friend, Max Freedom Long, who spent decades researching magical practices of Hawaiian shaman-priests called kahunas, considered the new instrument capable of detecting a field emitted by living organisms called an "aura," he christened it, not entirely appropriately, an aurameter. The name stuck and is applied to it today by its several manufacturers.

In 1957, the Elsinore city administration began a campaign to persuade property owners to approve the laying of a $2,700,000 pipeline to Lake Elsinore through which water purchased from the Metropolitan District, a multibillion dollar corporation, was to be pumped. Like the bulk of southern California's water, it was to come all the way from the Colorado River backed up behind Parker Dam on the Arizona-California border through a more than 250-mile-long aqueduct terminating in Lake Mathews in Riverside County.

According to the United States Salinity Bureau, Colorado River water contained more than a ton of salt for each acre-foot—enough to cover one acre of land with a foot of water and equal to 325,000 gallons—and had such high corrosive action that it rapidly ate up pipes and other plumbing fixtures. Nevertheless, the District had induced most southern California towns to buy expensively transported water rather than develop their own resources from underground.

The approved plan initially seemed successful for, by March 1964, 30,000 acre-feet of water had flowed into the lake to restore it to its pristine state. But to the dismay of Elsinore taxpayers, the solution proved only temporary. The costly water began to evaporate anew. At public debates held to decide what should be done, citizens' tempers flared as hotly as their opinions were divided.

A thoroughly discouraged Cameron, who had vowed he would have no more to do either with Elsinore or its people, at last caught the ear of two ranchers, one of whom was also an experienced water engineer and well-driller. He took them on a tour of the lake bottom showing them the course of the principal fault which had originally split the Elsinore valley and pointing out the exact spot where he believed another well, if put down, would produce 3,000 gallons per minute. Cameron won further support when Cox dug up an old log of a dry oil well drilled into the lake bottom which clearly revealed that water had been struck at 1,800 feet and unearthed a long-forgotten lake basin study by a maverick hydrologist that concurred with Cameron's theory.

Armed with this evidence, the two ranchers insisted that the local park board spend $5,000 to create a test hole down to 1,800 feet at a spot as close as possible to the defunct oil well. With support from the California State Parks System, which shared expenses with the board, the hole was at last drilled in the summer of 1965. Extensive testing, completed by October, proved that an underground water-bearing formation had been encountered.

Helped by pressure from Congressman Gordon Cologne of Indio, but still opposed by state geological authorities, Cameron and his allies finally persuaded the state to put up 25,000 additional dollars to see if water could finally be brought up from under Lake Elsinore. The well was reamed out to a diameter of 26 inches and cased. When tested, it easily pumped 5,100 gallons per minute.

Right up to the time of testing, engineers and geologists continued to insist that the well was a waste of money. Now they claimed that the driller had only hit a "pocket of trapped water that would pump dry within two or three days, or, at most, a week." When the well continued to pump water, $200,000 was appropriated for two more wells. Drilled to 1,776 feet, the second well tested 5,600 gallons per minute, the limit of the pump's capacity, with only a 50-foot drawdown, a combination practically unheard of in the drilling industry. The third well was as productive as the second.

At the dedication of the wells, California Governor Edmund "Pat" Brown met Verne Cameron at the ceremony but could not officially congratulate the dowser for saving Lake Elsinore. According to Riley Crabb, Director of Borderland Sciences Research Association in Vista, California, this was because "state geologists were so green with envy that official recognition could not be given to Mr. Cameron for his work. To have given him such recognition would have been politically embarrassing to Governor Brown, and a black eye to the uninspired textbook professors of geology at State Universities."

Another lake restored by dowsing. From Comment Devinir Sourcier, Ce Que J'ai Vu—Ce Que J'ai Fait *(How to Become a Dowser, What I've Seen and What I've Done), by Armand Viré.*

"Lake Bouvante. In the mid-1920s in the Vercors region of France a dam was built to supply electric power at a cost of 30,000,000 gold francs. The project completed, it was found that the impounded water instead of rising to the top of the dam was dropping at an alarming rate. Desperate to find a solution, the power company turned to dowsers including Armand Viré who made a survey. When the lake was drained, bouys left by the dowsers to mark each hole in the lake's bottom through which they believed water to be draining landed squarely on top of the holes themselves. The drainage holes and the fissures into which they led were blocked with cement until losses were reduced from 300 gallons per second to an insignificant 12 gallons per second."

Armand Viré

Part Two

THAVMATVRGVS
PHYSICVS,
Siue
MAGIÆ VNIVERSALIS
Naturæ et artis
pars IV.
Auctore P. GASPARE SCHOTTO
E Soc Iesu

ORIGINS

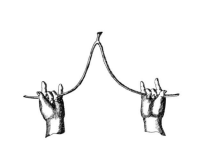

CHAPTER 3

From Divination to Dowsing

"The rod can be held with all four fingers, or with two . . ."

Divine or Diabolic

The unconcealed hostility toward dowsing exhibited by bureaucratic lethargy, academic incredulity, political squeamishness, and professional envy is a twentieth century repetition of earlier "scientific" prejudice against any form of divination, or "knowing through hidden senses," with which dowsers have had repeatedly to contend.

Throughout the ages men and women have developed practices, indeed arts, regarded as divine or demonic to seek by means other than reason the answers to questions reason could not provide. Through divination they foretold events, received revelation, discovered hidden essentials, and controlled natural forces by invoking a world of the spirit ridiculed by materialists as imaginary.

Soothsayers, seers, and shamans, witch doctors, wisemen, and wizards, are only a few of the many names for practitioners of divining which, like most professions, was regularly infiltrated by charlatans who cast doubt on its benign intent and efficacy, thus causing its popularity to decline with cyclic regularity.

In the Christian era divination has been considered either a devilish or sublime practice, depending, as the Roman statesman Cicero noted, whether it is traced to the classical Greek *mantike*, from which the English word *mania* and the suffix *-mancy* are derived, or the Latin nouns *divinus*, meaning "one inspired by the gods," and *divus*, "divine or godlike." "It cannot be gainsaid," Cicero affirmed, "that there is no nation, whether the most learned and enlightened or the most grossly barbarous, that does not believe that the future can be revealed and does not recognize in certain people the power of foretelling it."

Divining has taken many forms and many names. In ancient Rome it was called *augury* and practiced by professionals, their number first limited to three, then gradually expanded until, in the time of Julius Caesar, who was one of them, it totaled sixteen. Their function was to prophesy, portend, and predict what was in store for individuals or groups and advise them how to prepare for it.

Astrology, the study of the position of planets in the firmament, from which the word *consideration*—originally meaning "the study of the stars"—derives, was another ancient form of divination whose popularity has endured for centuries

61

"Clay model of an animal liver with Babylonian cuneiform inscriptions used in haruspicy, the art of divination through the inspections of the bowels of animals."

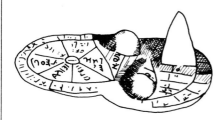

"Bronze liver found in 1877 at Piacenza in Italy. The whole surface is divided in irregular sections in which the names of divinities are written. This type of divination, known as heptascopy, was quite different from the Babylonian and indicates a fusion of this kind of divining art with astrology."

From G. Contenau
La Divination Chez les Assyriens et les Babyloniens

and is growing today, as facts are collected that go far to shore up its assertions, despite organized efforts on the part of "official" science to proclaim it a useless superstition.

Though some types of divination occur spontaneously (as in the much-heralded woman's "intuition," the all but indefinable business "acumen," the "second sight" of the clairvoyant, and the "I gotta hunch" of almost anybody), diviners have usually made use of external physical instrumentalities to assist them in penetrating the veil. Some have been enlightened through the observation of anomalies in the bones or entrails of freshly slaughtered animals, candle flames, the trails made by creeping snakes, the movement of delicately balanced objects such as axes, or the grains selected by a hungry rooster. Others have been fascinated by their own or their client's reactions to shapes formed by oil or molten wax on the surface of or within water into which they were dropped. A latter-day descendant of this kind of divining is the "ink-blot" test designed by Hermann Rorschach to assess a person's emotional and intellectual integration with the cosmos and used in clinical psychology and psychotherapy, both modern forms of the divinatory art.

Though widely ridiculed over the centuries divination has won the deep respect of those who became convinced of its effectiveness. Thus, Canon Callaway, who spent long years in the South African province of Natal, could write of Zulu divination: "It appears to me one of the most unwise things to pooh-pooh it as a system of mere imposture and deceit practiced by intelligent men on the credulity of the ignorant."

Aeromancy—	by atmospheric phenomena	Cleromancy—	by dice or lots
Alectromancy—	by a rooster picking up a grain	Coscinomancy—	by sieves and shears
Amniomancy—	by a caul, the membrane surrounding the human fetus	Crystallomancy—	by a crystal
		Dactylomancy—	by a finger ring
Arithmancy—	by numbers; today's numerology	Geomancy—	by dots on paper, or marks on the earth of particles of soil
Austromancy—	by the winds		
Axinomancy—	by a balanced axe, or a stone on a red-hot axe	Gyromancy—	by whirling until dizziness causes a fall
Belomancy—	by arrows	Halomancy—	by salt
Bibliomancy—	by random passages in books	Haruspicy—	by the entrails of animals
Botanomancy—	by herbs	Hepatoscopy—	by the entrails or livers of animals
Capnomancy—	by smoke		
Cartomancy—	by cards; today's fortune-telling	Hydromancy—	by water
		Icthyomancy—	by fishes
Catoptromancy—	by mirrors	Lampadomancy—	by the flame of a candle or torch
Ceromancy—	by molten wax dropped in water	Leconomancy—	by the shape taken by oil poured on water
Cheiromancy—	by the hands; today's palmistry	Lithomancy—	by stones
		Margaritomancy—	by pearls
Cledonomancy—	by chance remarks or events	Moleosophy—	by moles on the body

Myomancy—	by the movements of mice
Oenomancy—	by the appearance of wine poured in libation
Omphalomancy—	by the shape of a navel
Oneiromancy—	by dreams
Onomancy—	by letters of a name
Onychomancy—	by fingernails
Ophiomancy—	by the behavior of snakes
Pegomancy—	by fountains
Rhabdomancy—	by a wand
Scapulomancy—	by the shoulder blades of animals
Spedomancy—	by ashes
Stichomancy—	by random passages in books
Theomancy—	by oracles or by persons inspired of the gods
Uremancy—	by urine
Xylomancy—	by dry sticks
Zoomancy—	by the behavior of animals

Rods

No mark of holy, or wicked, superhuman power has been more widely diffused than a *rod*, from time immemorial associated with the aura of authority or the mystery of supernatural power. As a *pointing stick*, it traces back to the mists of the Stone Age and in this century was being used by the Arunta, an aboriginal tribe of central Australia, to avenge crimes committed by sorcery.

In Malaysia the pointing stick became a *dagger* that was "sung to" before its use and thus endowed with *mana*, a force or energy inherent in sacred objects. This energy, recognized throughout the Pacific basin as far east as the Hawaiian archipelago, where its manipulation by *kahuna*-priests was studied in this century over half a lifetime by Max Freedom

Pointing sticks used by the Arunta, an Aboriginal tribe in Australia as illustrated in The Arunta, *by Sir Baldwin Spencer and Francis James Gillen, London, 1927.*

64

Long, is recognized by a special word in practically every primitive language on earth.

As a *scepter* it was, and is, the mark of chieftains, going back at least to the Mycenean king, Agamemnon, whose own scepter was considered so powerful that it was itself worshiped as a god. Scepters of great magnificence, held in the hands of Etruscan rulers and illustrated in paintings on the walls of their enormous circular tombs in Italian Tuscany, were later surmounted by an eagle to become the *scipio,* borne by consuls and chief magistrates of the Roman Republic. This, in turn, evolved in the Middle Ages into the Christian Church's *crozier,* a long rod carried before bishops and abbots and curved, like a shepherd's *crook,* to symbolize the loving care of a pastor for his flock.

A *club,* the simplest weapon of an aggressor or defender, evolved into a mark of ceremonial authority among the American Indians, such as the Hopi of the Arizona mesas and the pueblo-dwelling Zuñi of New Mexico, whose leaders bore clublike rods made from the stalks of the agave plant. Rod-shaped *arrows* have also been favored as insignia of rank and, in belomancy, as divinatory artifacts to predict the fortunes of a warring party or the outcome of a battle by the manner in which they fell from their quivers onto the ground.

In the Bible the prophet Ezekiel reports that King Nebuchadnezzar of Babylon, standing with his army at a crossroads, was uncertain whether to attack Jerusalem, capital of Judah—the Israel of his day—or Rabbah of the Ammonites. His diviners used belomancy—backed up by consultation with teraphim, small images or idols, and the inspection of the liver of a sacrificed animal—to come up with the answer that Jerusalem was the likeliest target, which led to its seizure and to the half-century "Babylonian captivity" of the Jews.

During their enslavement, the Israelites adopted customs of their captors, including the art of divination, which angered the prophet Hosea to write: "Old wine and new deprive my people of understanding. They *consult their piece of wood and their wand makes pronouncements for them.* For the spirit of harlotry has led them astray."*

A *wand* is associated with supernatural beings in human form who, like Atropos, Clotho, and Lachesis, the three fates of Greek and Roman mythology, often appeared to be governors of human destiny. Homer refers to the rod in Greek as *rhabdos,* from which the word *rhabdomancy*—or "divining by a rod"—is derived and still used in Italy as *rhabdomanzia* to denote dowsing. The poet relates that, with her wand, the golden-haired Circe, daughter of Helios, the sun god, after being exiled to the isle of Aeaea for poisoning her husband, changed unwary visitors into a troop of wild beasts who served her as attendants.

The New American Bible, Hosea, Chapter 4, verse 12. The Living Bible, Paraphrased has: "Wine, women and song have robbed my people of their brains. For they are *asking a piece of wood to tell them what to do.* 'Divine Truth' comes to them through tea leaves. Longing after idols has made them foolish." More archaically and poetically, the King James translation provides: "Whoredom and wine and new wine take away the heart. My people *ask counsel at their stocks, and their staff declareth unto them.* For the spirit of whoredoms hath caused them to err."

Bishop's crozier, a staff with a hook, like the shepherd's crook, symbolizes the loving care of a pastor for his flock. It is thought to be derived from the rod of the Roman Augur.

As the stalk of the broom plant, or *broomstick,* with a bunch of leaves at its head, rods were specially linked to witches, who were popularly believed able to fly up chimneys and through the air with them. Before their employment they were thought to be greased with magic ointment. In 1477, a witch in Savoy confessed that the devil himself had given her a stick eighteen inches long which she would grease before putting it between her legs. After uttering: "In the Devil's name, Go!" she would be carried through the air to a witches' sabbath.

The sexual connotations surrounding the broomstick are not hard to imagine, especially when one considers that for centuries any virgin who stepped over a kitchen or house broom was believed to have become impregnated against her will and forced to bear an illegitimate child. Even the crime of traveling by broomstick was abolished in England only in the eighteenth century when a judge, Lord Mansfield, ruled in his courtroom that he knew of no law that prohibited flying and that, in his view, anyone was free to do so with any means at their disposal. This verdict in no way could atone for several centuries of sickening cruelty on the part of self-righteous clerical and secular authorities toward women or men accused of witchcraft.

Rods are still used today as symbols of power. As *batons* they are wielded by drum majorettes, military officers, and orchestra leaders. In the argot of the underworld a rod is a gun, in that of sexuality a *phallus,* a word tracing back to an old Sanskrit root meaning *to swell.* The same root migrated into Scandinavian to denote "the trunk of a tree" which swells with sap at given times of the year, and it may be that the earliest divining rods were cut from trees exactly because of the oracular, or divinatory, power attributed to them.

At Dodona, the ancient sanctuary near Epirus dedicated to Zeus, sounds of leaves rustling in a grove of oaks, and water gurgling from under their roots, were interpreted by priestesses to provide enigmatic guidance to supplicants. Equally renowned was the Delphic oracular cult, though it has almost been forgotten that its tutelary demon, Python—a serpent as wily as the victimizer of Adam and Eve—was considered by many philosophers, including Moses Maimonides, twelfth century rabbi of Cairo, to be the original initiator of the divining art.

Maimonides subtly recommended excommunication of anyone using divination *with knowledge of its cause.* Describing some of the wiles of Python, he commented: "There is one which consists of an offering of a certain perfume while holding in one's hand a rod of wood and pronouncing certain words. The rod holder crouches as if he would consult someone under the ground who replies in so low a voice that one can only understand the answers in one's mind without hearing anything distinctly."

This extraordinary observation with its allusion to the subterranean world giving up secrets, and to answers being received purely "psychically," anticipated the wide use of divining for underground water and minerals, which has been practiced throughout the centuries following Maimonides's death, as well as the modern opinion that the real essence of the dowsing art is an inexplicable tuning of the dowser's being to a sought-for target.

Further ties between serpent-power and a magic rod were made when Apollo handed over a wand to Mercury—or Hermes, as he was called in Greek. Homer's *Odyssey* records how Hermes's rod could send men's souls to Hades or bring them back again to unleash winds and tempests. Called a *caduceus,* it is generally represented as being entwined with snakes and was passed in turn to Aesculapius, god of healing, to become the symbol of modern medicine.

Young girl accused of witchcraft bound hand and foot and thrown into a pond. If she floated, she was innocent; if she sank and drowned, guilty. Taken from Eberhard David Hauber's **Bibliotheka Acta et Scripta Magica,** *1738.*

"Witchcraft and heresy were primarily maladies of Christian theology, a projection of the problem of evil which could not be explained or contained in a despotic church authority which substituted absolute power for simple faith, class division and privilege for universal brotherhood, and sexual anxiety for normal secular pleasure. The combination of rigid authority and repressed sexual energy was, in itself, a kind of Black Magic of Christianity, a paranoid fantasy which brought to life the diabolical conspiracies and sorceries of its own disordered imagination."

Leslie Shepard in introduction to *Demonolatry* by Nicholas Remy, University Books, Secaucas, New Jersey.

Is there a mysterious and forgotten connection between a rod, the serpent, and a bird—or the power of flight—that may have been common knowledge all over the world? Is Mercury's wand with its bird wings and snakes a more sophisticated version of the rod, bird, and snake carved by Indians into rocks at the Yonan Pass along the River Jejetepeque in Peru? Illustrated in Thomas J. Hutchinson's Two Years in Peru, *London, 1873.*

In Norse mythology the "world tree," *Ygdrassil*, supporting the universe was a giant *ash.* At its base were three wells, one of which was a source of divinatory wisdom so powerful that for its water Odin, lord of all gods, sacrificed one of his eyes. Mythologists have maintained that trees erected at the winter solstice in honor of Ygdrassil and its mysteries later became Christmas trees. The ash was long the favorite tree from which to cut dowsing rods in Scandinavia.

As far back as the fifth century, B.C., the "father of history," Herodotus, wrote of the use of *willow* divining rods among the Scyths, a nomadic Iranian people who roved the prairies of what is now southern Russia. Eight hundred years later Ammianus Marcellinus, who provided a 31-volume Roman history, reported the willow in use among the Alains, invaders of Scythian territory, as well as among the Illyrians, settlers of a region comprising part of today's Yugoslavia, and the Huns, Asiatic nomads who were to overrun large parts of Europe two centuries after Marcellinus's death.

According to Saint Jerome, translator of the Bible into the Latin vulgate in the fourth century, and to Saint Cyril who, in the ninth century, converted the Slavs to Christianity and invented the Cyrillic alphabet, the divining staffs so dramatically denounced by Hosea were cut from *myrtle,* an aromatic shrub with pink-white flowers and blue-black berries.

On the other side of the world, the New Zealand Maori, in addition to arrow divination, also sought advice from short thin sticks of *mahoe* wood or, more specifically, from a spirit called *Korohaha Tu* believed to reside in them and, in the not-far-distant Banks Islands of the New Hebrides, *bamboo* poles were employed to evoke spirits of the departed.

Of all trees imbued with divining power none have been so widely celebrated in Indo-European languages as the *hazel,* extensively distributed in the Northern Hemisphere. Vedic sources offer that rods cut from the hazel were carried by the priestly caste of ancient India called *Brahman,* a title equivalent to "essential divine reality of the universe" or "eternal spirit from which all being originates and to which all returns."

Divinatory use of the hazel as well as other nut and fruit trees by Germanic tribes along the Roman frontier was described in the first century A.D. by the Roman historian, Cornelius Tacitus, in his *De Origine et Situ Germanorum,* the first work to combine ethnographic description with geopolitics. Tacitus also referred to what he called a *Virga Mercurialis,* a term which harked back to the *cadaceus* but embodied a specific, if undescribed, use. In medieval manuscripts the noun was retained but the adjective changed to produce *Virga Divinatoria* or "Divining Rod."

So-called "Mercurial" rods made their first appearance in German literature one millennium after Tacitus when a monk named Notker, from the Swiss province of Saint Gallen, noted in a manuscript that they could be characterized as "volatile," meaning that they were strangely animated and even had the power to vaporize and disappear.

68

It was sometime shortly after the year 1000 A.D. that the magical aspect of rods and their ability to fulfill wishes combined in the German-speaking lands in the coining of a new term, "wishing rod." Old High German, a language indigenously spoken and written until the end of the eleventh century, had *uunschiligarta* and *uunskilgartel*—"wishing" plus "thin stick"—and other variants, and also the term, *hasilriuta*—"hazel" plus "rod"—in its lexicon.

The "wishing" part of the word was later transformed into *wunschel*, when the poet Conrad of Wurzburg described Helen of Troy as "coming, straight and tall, lovely as a *wunschelgerta*." The rod in today's German is *rute*, and a dowsing rod, *wünschelrute*, while a dowser is a *rutenganger*, "one who goes, or walks, with the rod."

The Rod Forks

First known illustration of a forked *stick*, ancestor of the Y-shaped dowsing rod.

"*The evening prior to the great enterprise, you shall go and find a rod or verge of wild hazel which has never been touched and which is precisely similar to the one illustrated, said rod being forked. You shall touch it only with your eyes, waiting until the morrow, the day of action, when you shall go and cut it at sunrise. You shall remove all the leaves and small branches from it, if it has any, with a steel blade that has been used to cut the throat of a sacrificial animal. Begin your cut when the sun emerges, while uttering the following words: 'I ask you, o great Adonay, Elohim, Ariel and Jehovah, to give this rod the force and virtue of those of Jacob, Moses and the great Joshua.'*"

From *Le Dragon Rouge ou L'Art de Commander les Esprits*, first published in 1521.

All early references to divining or "wishing" rods describe them only as straight, with a slight bend or crook at the top. In the thirteenth century, however, Neidhart von Reuenthal, a Bavarian lyricist provided the first clue that the *forked* dowsing rod of today had been invented when he proposed the analogy "*split like the stem of a wunsciligerta.*" In 1521 this splitting was first illustrated in *Le Dragon Rouge*, a French grimoire, one of many "how to" directories setting forth procedures for relating to the occult world.

Variations of the Red Dragon's instructions on how to cut rods fill the archives of nearly every European country. One German formula insisted that the cutter approach a hazel bush backward and pull a branch through his legs, cutting it off in front of him, which may have related the whole performance to the ancient mystery of self-castration. As late as the nineteenth century such precepts with accompanying incantations were in current use in central Europe, including Hungary, where folklorists were avidly collecting them. In the late nineteenth century an old Hungarian widow was observed to hang the corpse of a black hen on a hazel tree from which she then cut a dowsing rod at a single stroke while uttering a prayer. The rod was then taken home, stripped before sunrise on New Year's day, and moistened with blood from her left arm and leg. During this procedure the woman intoned: "I give blood to the rod. She gives me its bark which I consume: in this way we are bound to each other, betrothed as it were, and when the moment is come when my strength has reached the time when it must break out, then the rod must show me exactly where is hidden the treasure which I am appointed to raise."

Instructions on the use of rods, as detailed as they are obscure, were left in his last testament by Basil Valentine, a Benedictine monk and alchemist said to have lived in the Saxon city of Erfurt in the late 1300s and credited with the discovery of antimony, an element used today in the manufacture of paints, semiconductors, and ceramics. When Valentine found that traces of the new metal put in the food of hogs remarkably accelerated their fattening, he next tried it on his fellow monks who had

69

become emaciated through prolonged fasting. Unlike the swine, the monks did not gain weight, but died, which supposedly led Valentine to labeling the element *antimonium* or "anti-monk."

In a hermetic vocabulary difficult to translate, Valentine wrote of six kinds of divining rods and their use in the detection of etheric forces, or atmospheres, wafting into the earth from above its surface and out of it from its depths, and intimately

MOSAIC FLOOR IN THE NAVE OF AN ANCIENT SYNAGOGUE. *Discovered at Bet Alfa in the eastern end of Israel's Jezreel Valley in 1929, it reveals a zodiac. One of its signs, Aquarius, appears to be holding what some have believed to be a forked dowsing rod. Archaeologist Hannah Katzenstein of Jerusalem writes: "It is difficult to say with certainty what the Aquarius figure holds in his hands. The excavator, the late Professor Sukenik, wrote at the time in his publication on the ancient synagogue (1932) that Aquarius, in Hebrew called* deli *meaning pail, is mostly represented by a young man pouring water from a vessel which he holds in his hand, while in the Bet Alfa Zodiac it is treated differently: here a man stands near a well and draws water from it by means of a bag or pail, which he holds by a rope with both his hands." Many dowsers have claimed that dowsing rods have been depicted even earlier, notably in paintings on cave walls at Tassili, Algeria, dating to neolithic times, but examination of the paintings suggests a high degree of wishful thinking.*

Six Rods Described in Basil Valentine's Last Testament		
Latin	*German*	*English*
Lucente Virgula	Feuer Ruthen	Fire Rod
Virgula Candente	Brandt Ruthen	Burning Rod
Salia Virgula	Spring Ruthen	Springing Rod
Fucilla	Schlag Ruthen	Striking Rod
Virgula Trepidante	Hebe Ruthen	Lifting Rod
Virgula Cadente	Unter Ruthen	Lower Rod

related to the genesis and "life" of certain metals.

Valentine's assertion that seven rods could help to locate metals underground seems to moderns as strange as ancient Chinese statements that gifted diviners, using rodlike instruments, were able to detect subterranean water and even start it from the ground. The Emperor Ta Yü, founder of the Hsia Dynasty who was born 2,205 years before Christ, and who was most famous for his hydrological flair, was reputed to learn the secrets of underground water by "inspecting the earth" ' 相地 *(siang ti)*. An extended meaning for *siang* is "to look at in order to *divine* that which is hidden under an apparent reality." Since the same character also means "mutual," its use together with "earth" could imply a sort of "resonating frequency with what is below ground."

Yü has been represented in a bas-relief holding a double branched instrument, which some Europeans have taken to represent the earliest example of the forked dowsing rod of today. Since the device is not only held in one hand, but also carried in such a way that the forked end points forward, this is an evident impossibility. A better analogy for the instrument would be a tuning fork.

Ancient Chinese manuscripts refer to army generals plunging swords into the ground only to pull them out again and reveal a source of water for a potential encampment. The swords' magical properties were matched by those of tin canes carried by Buddhist monks which had the power of scattering venomous reptiles from the trail ahead or repelling vicious dogs, bulls, and wild animals. The canes were driven into the ground not only to find an enduring supply of water but also to mark the establishment of a new monastery. Thus, by extension, the Chinese expression "to plant one's tin," written as 錫丑 *(chu hsi),* came to mean "to stop" and to refer, especially in geographical works, to certain monasteries and the water wells that supplied them. One part of the character for "tin" can also be written separately as 易 (*i,* "to change" or "easy"). It is also drawn to represent the first word in 易經 the *I Ching,* or *Book of Changes,* perhaps the sole extensive document of divinatory practices still extant.

Years of study of the *I Ching* by Jing Nuan Wu, a Harvard-trained engineer turned acupuncturist, has convinced him that divination is closely tied with the perception of water movement and the time needed for its fulfillment. That the *I* of *I Ching* is "in accordance with heaven and the earth's water

71

Han Dynasty Bas Relief in Shantung Province, China, shows Emperor Yü holding instrument similar to a tuning fork. The inscription reads: "Yü of the Hsia Dynasty was a master in the science of the earth and in those matters concerning water veins and springs; he was well acquainted with the Yin principle and, when required, built dams." (Photograph from the Freer Gallery, Washington, D.C.)

levels," as the appendix to the document states, is, in Wu's understanding, the earliest recognition of forces expressed metaphorically in many languages as the "tides of the times" and which is most forcefully conveyed in the English proverb: "Time and tide wait for no man."

Wu notes that the character 易 *(i)* is further subdividable into two parts, one 日 *(jih,* "the sun" or "light"), the other 勿 *(wu,* "the absence of light," at least in one interpretation). Because, in the China of old, markings on river banks served the purpose of measuring both the level of water *and* the movement of light and shadow during the course of a day, it is not surprising that in the character 晷 *(kui,* "dial" as in sundial) the component parts, taken separately, can be represented to mean 处, "to go one's way" after 口, "hearing" advice from 卜, "a divination," while under 日, "the sun," the chief regulator of all our notions of time.

It is only fortuitous that the simple two-stroke character 卜

72

might be construed to have the shape of a forked divining rod. It carries the spiritual meaning implied in the whole divining art because it seems to have been derived from the practice of scapulamancy, or divining from the shoulder blades of sheep and oxen. In 1899 bones of this type were excavated by a peasant digging a new garden plot in the village of Hsiao-tun—formerly the site of the ancient capital of the Shang Yin Dynasty (1700–1100 B.C.). To the surprise of scholars, they were found to be incised with the oldest forms of Chinese characters ever discovered. The sensational disclosure caused such bones, which up to then had been ground to powder by Chinese pharmacists, to be carefully scrutinized for traces of more characters.

Decades of study revealed that the inscriptions themselves recorded questions about sacrifice, harvests, weather conditions, the location of game, travel, the fortune of a given evening or fortnight, and many other dilemmas of life. Answers to the questions were inscribed on the bones along with the name of the diviner and information as to whether the divination had been successful. Despite their careful dating and meticulous deciphering, the whole remarkable story of the inscriptions has yet to be fully told in the Western world. The scapulamancers first carefully chiseled one side of an animal shoulder blade. When the resultant hollow was cauterized, cracks appeared in the other side, usually in the variation of a shaped form, the meaning of which a diviner would interpret.

It is Jing Nuan Wu's proposition that the cracks were

Oracle bone with four cauteries. The cracks caused by heating (enlarged, A-D) were interpreted by Chinese scapulomancers. From the characteristic forked splitting the Chinese character, ⼘ , "to divine," was derived. (Drawing adapted from the Menzies Collection of Shang Dynasty Oracle Bones, *Toronto, 1972.)*

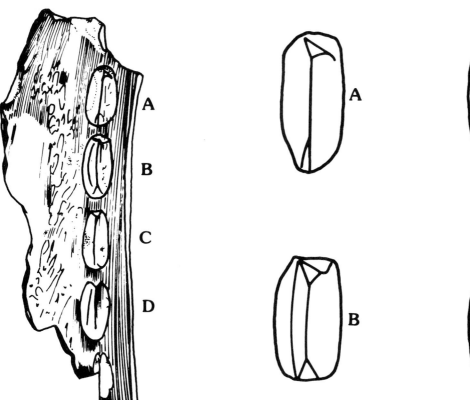

interpreted both with respect to the direction of their alignment on the bones as well as the sequence of their appearance. This would accord with the time and space parameters judged by Roman augurs from birds flying across arbitrarily chosen rectangular patches of sky. "Many practical problems need direction in their solving," asserts Wu. "Which way to go? The hunt, a primary pursuit of early Chinese society, had forcibly to have direction. Closely associated with this type of problem solving were the requirements for troop movements in wartime, and travel in peacetime."

According to Wu, the heat in cautery was applied with a red-hot metallic probe. "The sexual symbolism of the moment of conception seems clear," he adds, "especially since the hollows carved in many bones resemble the female sexual opening and also the under side of cowrie shells, the currency used to pay for a diviner's services." Written 貝 *(pei)* in Chinese, the cowrie shell ideogrammatically combines with 卜 to form 貞 *(chen)* which also means "to divine."

It was also believed by the ancient Chinese that water flowed in subterranean courses called "veins of the dragon." Passing to and fro out of sight, the hidden veins of water served, like the bloodstream of animals, to remove impurities from the body of the earth, considered not a pile of rock but a living being, and to deposit curative minerals, often in hardly detectable trace quantities, within it. The earth's circulatory system was matched by an ever-undulating network of currents in the atmosphere.

To quote Chen Ssu-Hsiao, who died in 1332 A.D.: "In the subterranean regions there are alternate layers of earth and rock and flowing spring waters. These strata rest upon thousands of vapours which are distributed in tens of thousands of branches, veins and threadlike openings . . . The body of the earth is like that of a human being . . . Ordinary people, not being able to see the veins and vessels which are disposed in order within the body of man, think that it is no more than a lump of solid flesh. Likewise, not being able to see the veins and vessels which are disposed in order under the ground, they think that the earth is just a homogenous mass."

The currents, running through 經 *(ching)*, or "channels," carried the vapors or "vital cosmic breath," 氣 *(ch'i)*, the equivalent of the *pneuma,* or "vital spirit," of the Greeks. The connection, in Chinese cosmology, between these breath-bearing channels and the divinatory arts can at once be understood from the fact that the character for the "channels," 經 , is also the second ideogram in the title of the *I Ching*, the diviner's guide, though in this case it means "book."

Channels of vital energy analogous to those detected in the earth's macrocosm were also discovered by supersensitive Chinese medical practitioners in the microcosm of the human body as well as those of animals, long before modern instrumentation was available to prove them correct, as it is today.

The diviner-doctors charted tiny spots distributed from head to toe all over the flesh. Known as "holes," they are linked by "channels," also called meridians. In acupuncture, these provide

Dwin Gordon demonstrating his technique of diverting a water vein. The ropes on the lawn represent edges of an underground vein running toward the foundation of a house in the background. Gordon first pounds a crowbar with T-shaped handle into the earth with a maul. He then strikes the crowbar at ground level. The vein turns at a right angle and begins to flow in the direction of the maul's pounding. Photos by Bob Ater.

An unfathomable proclivity of underground water veins to change the direction of their flow in response to percussion has apparently been discovered by Dwin Gordon, trustee of the American Society of Dowsers, who has put it to practical use.

A resident of Portland, Maine, Gordon has been engaged in water-proofing basements for nearly a decade. Through his dowsing skill, he affirms that he has found that many basements were constantly wet from water oozing into them from veins 5½ to 6 feet below ground or the same average depth of the basements themselves.

Says Gordon: "The vein'll seep under the basement floor and, creating hydrostatic pressure, the water generally either forces its way up through a crack in the floor or "weeps" into the basement where the floor joins the wall."

Gordon had been using a huge crowbar with a T-shaped handle to make holes into which bentonite, a clay that swells when water is added to it, is poured to seal up channels into which water intruded.

"One day," he recounts, "we pounded a bar down outside a house and were having an ungodly time trying to twist it out again. So I grabbed an 8-pound maul and began whaling the daylights out of it to loosen it. Then—I don't quite know why—I grabbed my angle rods to check the vein running towards the house's basement and I couldn't find any trace of it between the point where the bar was stuck and the house itself."

"I remembered I'd done all the pounding against the bar in a direction at a right angle to the vein's flow. So, dowsing around the bar, I found the vein had turned at a right angle and was now flowing alongside, rather than toward, the house. So I said to myself then and there, 'what's the use of trying to seal off veins if we can turn 'em?' "

Gordon has used his new-found method many times not only to divert water veins around a house basement but also to divert them towards a well gone dry, or to "cut" and turn a vein away from a source of pollution rendering its water impotable.

"To cite one example," he relates, "I dowsed a vein flowing about 6 gpm that was running right past a well gone almost dry. By putting my T-bar directly into a spot over its center and pounding the bar at ground level in a direction leading to the well, I was able to direct the flow of the vein into the well itself. You could stand over the well with a flashlight and see the water flowing in and filling up the well. That was five years ago in April and that well has produced ever since although before she'd always gone dry during one part of the year even when there was no serious drought.

"I've had 90–95% success diverting water into dry wells and the method I use is really helpful to some poor devil who's got $3–4,000 dollars tied up in wells that aren't giving him a drop of water."

the basis for a whole new philosophical approach to medicine based on energy fields and their balancing rather than on the prescription of drugs.

Written off as witchcraft or quackery by the American medical profession—until it was used as local anesthesia during an appendicitis operation performed in Peking on James Reston who reported it in his paper, the *New York Times*—acupuncture may be one of the world's earliest divining arts. This is because, as Wu so succinctly puts it, "its main use is as a *preventive* therapeutic, both to forestall and forestay any disbalancing influence, or disease, in the body." Like other forms of divination, it is predictive.

The notion that the earth and the living creatures upon it were related through energy fields common to both, was accepted in ancient times in Eastern and Western cultures. That acceptance was grounded in knowledge obtained, not in scientific laboratories, but through a spiritual, or supersensory, awareness that later fell into desuetude, but which is now becoming the object of renewed inquiry.

In the West, this special awareness has for at least 500 years been kept alive by dowsing which, as practiced today, seems to have had its origin in the mines of central Europe.

CHAPTER 4

The Dawn of Dowsing

". . . or even by the fingertips . . ."

Dowsing for Ore in the Erzgebirge

In 1912, *The Mining Magazine* in London published the first translation into English of a massive Latin opus on mining and metallurgy that had appeared 356 years earlier. It was so all-encompassing that, chained to church altars and translated by the priests to miners between religious services, it was not to be superseded as a textbook for eighteen decades. The translators were a professional mining engineer, Herbert Clark Hoover, soon to become the thirty-first president of the United States, and his wife, Lou Henry. They had lugged the manuscript all over the world, working on it whenever they had a free evening or weekend.

The object of the Hoovers' attention was *De Re Metallica (On Metals)* by a German physician turned mining scholar, Georg Bauer, whose professors during his student days had latinized his family name, which in English means "peasant," to Agricola.

Georgius Agricola, as illustrated in Agricola on Metals *by Bern Dibner. (Courtesy Burndy Library, Norwalk, Connecticut.)*

At the age of thirty-three, Georgius Agricola was appointed medical practitioner in Joachimsthal, a mining camp on the southeast slopes of the Erzgebirge, or Ore Mountains, where he became increasingly fascinated with the rough-and-tumble life in a boom town that had already produced the silver Joachimsthaler, first ancestor of the dollar.

For three years Agricola spent his nights reading every Greek and Latin text on mining he could acquire and long days with a mining expert, Lorenz Berman, who lectured to him on every facet of the industry. Berman introduced him to ways minerals could be found by skill, one of which was to observe water bubbling from natural springs which, as Agricola put it, "cannot be very far from the veins because the source of the water is from them." This may be the first reference linking a vein of metal with water and could explain how the term "vein of water" came into the present-day vocabulary of dowsing.

Plants, too, Agricola found, could provide important clues. During hoarfrosts, he wrote, "all herbage is whitened except that growing over the veins, because the veins emit a warm and dry exhalation which hinders the freezing of the moisture."

The exhalation, so similar to the *ch'i* of the Chinese classics, was early thought to explain the attraction of a dowsing rod in a miner's hands to the metallic vein being sought. As the centuries passed, this explanation would give way first to generalized "sympathetic attractions" between specific minerals and rods cut from certain trees; then to an "emanation of corpuscles"; next to "magnetic and electrical influences" on both dowsers and their rods; and finally to "radiations" or "waves" equivalent or akin to electromagnetic waves emitted by a radio or television station.

In 1530, Agricola published a catechism on mineralogy, mining terms, and mining lore entitled *Bermannus* in honor of his friend and teacher. The same year he was able to translate his academic knowledge into financial opportunity when a poor peasant digging a trench for storing and cooling milk accidentally uncovered an outcropping of the purest silver. Overjoyed that the *bergmeister,* an official empowered to award mining rights,

78

allowed him to stake a claim, he reverently named what he hoped was a nascent mine *Gottsgab,* or "God's Gift."

Lacking sufficient capital for the enterprise, he set about its development by selling shares. As owner of one of the shares, Agricola was to write: "Then this mine yielded such a quantity of pure silver as no other mine that has existed in our town or our fathers' memories with the exception of the Saint George at Schneeberg. We, as a shareholder, through the goodness of God, have enjoyed the proceeds of this 'God's Gift' since the very time when the mine began to bestow such riches."

His fortune made, Agricola moved to Chemnitz where he was appointed mayor and solicited as a consultant by mining magnates of the day, including Duke Henry of Braunschweig who was seeking advice on how to work new mines in the Harz Mountains. While in the Harz, Agricola heard a centuries-old tale about how the first rich silver mine in Germany was discovered on the 636-meter-high Rammelsberg, a mountain at Goslar, in 936 A.D.

The mine, wrote Agricola in his *De Veteribus et Novis Metallis,* was found by a stallion named Rammel which, tied by his noble owner to a tree growing on the mountain, pawed the earth in his boredom. One of the horse's shoes uncovered a hidden vein of lead, not unlike the winged Pegasus who, as Agricola recalled, "in poetic legend opened a spring when he beat the rock with his hoof."

Based on other evidence, Mikhail Lomonosov, the renowned Russian scientist and poet who studied for a time at Saxony's Freiburg Mining Academy, claimed that the name Rammel applied not to the horse but to its rider, a huntsman to Otto I, Goslar's suzerain. In our day, a Soviet geologist and mining engineer, M. M. Maksimov, discovered that one of Otto's

One-and-a-half-ounce silver coin struck to commemorate the discovery of a mine on Rammelsberg, a mountain near Goslar, Germany, in 936 A.D. "The coin is a memorial to the history and mine-working of the day," writes Soviet mineralogist M. M. Maksimov in his article "Thousand-Year-Old Discoveries" published in the Russian journal, Geology of Ore Deposits. "On it can be seen a panorama of the mine, a line for the levered transmission of energy from a place beyond the edge of the coin to the right, a grinding wheel, chunks of ore, subterranean structures, a system of mining works in cross-section, and various methods of prospecting, surveying, and exploitation. Even a non-specialist glancing at the coin will above all notice that on the left side of the ore deposit a figure is walking while searching with a 'witching' rod, and that on the right side, at a spot indicated by the 'dowser,' a hole is already being dug. The deposit is revealed as a mine with a system of horizontal galleries and blind shafts which differ very little from those of today." (Photograph courtesy of the Smithsonian Institution, Washington, D.C.)

descendants, Ernst August, Duke of Braunschweig-Luneburg, grateful for the riches produced by the Rammelsberg find, decided that coins should be struck in its memory.

If, as is supposed, the relief on the coin depicts mining as actually performed at the end of the first millennium, the clear illustration of a dowser on the coin's left side may indicate that the dowsing art was used to locate metals in Germany at least 1,000 years ago.*

*Rammelsberg is still extremely productive. According to contemporary encyclopedic sources it produced, in 1970, 30,000 tons of lead and 800,000 tons of zinc concentrates as well as 40,000 tons of by-products. The haul represented a quarter of the West German and nearly 10 percent of the European Common Market production of lead. For zinc the corresponding figures were 35 percent and 14 percent. The same sources state opaquely that iron ore deposits at Rammelsberg are "controversial, and probably of complicated origin."

(LEFT) Woodcut from Agricola's *De Re Metallica*, illustrating a dowsing rod being cut from a tree (center top) and two rods being employed (A) to locate places (B) where miners should dig for ore. The dowser in the background holds his rod with an unusual "palms downward" method while the dowser in the foreground grips his rod with one palm facing downward, the other upward. This may attest to inattention or lack of interest in detail on the part of the illustrator or to insufficient data. Close examination also suggests that the rods were split into their forked shape with a knife rather than cut forked from a tree, the usual later practice.

During a quarter of a century of toil on his *magnus opus*, Agricola expended great sums on woodcuts to illustrate his text lest his descriptions, as he put it, "which are conveyed by words should either not be understood by men of our own times or should cause difficulty to posterity." It is due to this precaution, which delayed the publication of *De Re Metallica* until a year after Agricola's death, that we can today see miners typical of the late fifteenth and early sixteenth centuries using forked sticks cut from hazel trees to find ore underground.

To the woodcut Agricola apposed the first lengthy description and commentary on dowsing used to detect subterranean metallic ores. His very first observation on the subject indicates that there was no more consensus on the rod's efficacy in his day than in ours: "There are many great contentions between miners concerning the forked twig, for some say that it is of the greatest use in discovering veins, and others deny it."

Agricola informs his readers that many dowsers preferred forked sticks cut from a hazel bush, especially one growing above a metallic vein. This implied that the hazel wood, itself impregnated by the mysterious "exhalation" of the metal, would consequently react when over a similar deposit. Other miners used a different kind of wood for each metal, hazel for silver, ash for copper, pitch pine for lead and tin. For gold and silver, rods made not of wood but of iron were fancied. Dowsers, wrote Agricola in the first recorded description of field dowsing, "wander hither and thither at random through mountainous regions. It is said that the moment they place their feet on a vein the twig immediately turns and twists, and so by its action discloses the vein; when they move their feet away again and go away from that spot the twig becomes once more immobile."

For an explanation of *why* a rod should turn, Agricola merely repeated the assertions of some dowsers that "power" in the veins moved the rod and that an exceptionally "powerful" vein could even cause branches of trees growing nearby to deflect in its direction. Others, deriding the notion, maintained that if "power" resided in the veins of metal themselves, then it should be able to cause a rod to turn in anyone's hands, and that because the rod did not turn for everybody, then only those who employed mysterious incantation and other forms of witchcraft could employ it successfully.

Agricola would have sided with the USGS of his day for, in his treatise, he concluded that "a miner, since we think he ought to be a good and serious man, should *not* make use of an enchanted twig." This was because "if he is prudent and skilled in the natural signs"—today one would substitute *scientific methodology*—"he understands that a forked stick is no use to him."

Agricola may have been influenced in his opinion by the statement of his predecessor, Paracelsus, the Swiss physician and alchemist who had written in his *Metallographia:* "Therefore, care is sedulously to be taken that ye suffer not yourselves to be seduced by the divinations of uncertain arts. For they are vain and frivolous, especially the Divinatory Rods, which have deceived many miners. For if they once show anything rightly, they on the contrary deceive ten times. In like manner, we are not at all to trust to other fraudulent signs of the Devil, which are done and appear against nature upon the night, and at inconvenient time, as apparitions, visions and the like."

Whatever the case, the final pronouncement by Germany's leading mining scholar was no more effective in banishing dowsing than those of geological authorities today, even though it was soon to be buttressed by the ecclesiastical opinion of stern Martin Luther, himself a miner's son, who in a book of maxims attacked mining superstitions. His condemnation of dowsing as the work of the devil was to be repeated by both Protestant and Catholic clerics in succeeding centuries.

Other scholars of the day supported the use of the dowsing rod, including the brilliant Phillip Melanchton, appointed at age twenty-one to become the first professor of Greek at the University of Wittenberg, newly founded by Luther. Melanchton allowed favorable references to the hazel rod's being attracted to metal to creep into his *Discourse on Sympathy* in the 1550s as did his son-in-law, Gaspard Peucer, whose comprehensive work, *The Diviners,* came out in 1553. Perhaps because of such support, dowsing for minerals, far from succumbing to its critics, began to spread and by the end of the sixteenth century migrated for the first time to the English kingdom.

Dowsing Crosses the Channel

Just over a decade after the publication of Agricola's *De Re Metallica,* Elizabeth the First ascended the throne of England at the age of twenty-three. The "Virgin Queen" was dismayed to find that her kingdom had not kept abreast of technical advances which the Renaissance was bestowing upon the rest of Europe. Nowhere was this lag more evident than in mining.

Her secretary and principal advisor, Sir William Cecil, was aware of his country's backwardness in the production of brass, an alloy of copper and zinc, indispensable to the manufacture of weapons, particularly cannons needed by the navy. To counteract this state of affairs he decided to import mining know-how from Germany. To this end, preliminary negotiations were opened in 1561 with one Marcus Steinberger, a mining expert from Augsburg, to form a company to explore for copper and open mines in England's scenic Lake District.

From the start it became obvious that the Germans were not going to part easily with their knowledge or their hardware. Steinberger wrote a clause into the contract that, in the event of the new company's dissolution, all mining equipment brought across the channel was to be repatriated. William Humphry, Assay Master of the English Mint, complained that, despite his best allurements, the Germans were refusing to import certain items of "the art of battery," as metal-working was called at the time, essential to the production of weapons.

Undaunted by early setbacks, the English continued to press their case with other German mining masters. One may imagine the excitement at court when one of them, Daniel Hochstetter, revealed to Humphry that, during a short prospecting trip in the

Whatever the opinions expressed by learned professors and their students about dowsing, we can be sure that the method was producing wealth in Germany in the mid-seventeenth century, or otherwise it is hardly likely that it would have been honored on a huge silver mining pitcher, or stein, made in 1652 for the upper Harz Mining and Smelting Works in Clausthal . . .

. . . or by a Meissen porcelain by Kändler in 1750 . . .

(All photographs courtesy of the Bergbaumuseum in Bochum, German Federal Republic.)

. . . or even in a scene of Christ's nativity carved in ivory in the Erzgebirge.

west of England, he had discovered a large quantity of calamine, an important zinc ore.

Although well known in Germany, calamine had up to the moment of Hochstetter's announcement not been discovered in any useful quantity within the English realm. When the German, presumably hoping to extort a considerable emolument for his search, refused to say exactly where the newly found zinc ore was located, the clever Humphry brought over from the Erzgebirge still another German metals specialist, Christopher Schutz, to look for it.

His almost instant success was recognized, after his death, in a charter granted to the Mines Royal Society by the queen's brother, King James I, which characterized Schutz as a man "of great cunning and experience, as well in the finding of the Calamine Stone, called in Latin *Lapis Calaminaris,* and in the right and proper use of the commodity called 'Laten,' and in reducing it to be soft and malleable, and also in orpting, mannering, and working the same for and into all sorts of battery wares, cast work, and wire, and also in the mollifying and mannering of iron and steel, and drawing and forging of the same into wire and plates, as well as convenient and necessary for the making of armor, and also for divers other needful and profitable uses."

Schutz found important calamine deposits in the Mendips, a low range of hills in Somersetshire. We cannot be sure that the ore was located by dowsing since, as J. W. Gough relates in his *The Mines of Mendip,* "In some places the ore was so thickly distributed that often in prospecting from a mine a man would simply dig a trench forward through the ground until he came upon a vein." But the same author also states that "great faith was placed in the virtues of the divining rod." Its continued use in the west of England may therefore have been Schutz's greatest legacy.

The Schutz accomplishment opened the door to an agreement between English and Germans, as confirmed on October 10, 1564, by letters patent issued to Daniel Hochstetter, whose services must have been sufficiently valued to excuse his earlier secretiveness, and to his compatriot, Thomas Thurland, a former clerk of chaplains and Master of the Hospital of Savoy. To these two miners and their heirs were granted "full power, license and authority to search, dig, open, roast, melt, stamp and wash, drain or convey waters, or otherwise work for all manner of mines within the counties of York, Lancaster, Cumberland, Westmoreland, Cornwall, Devon, Gloucester and Worcester and within the principality of Wales."

The following year Schutz himself found his reward when, together with the faithful Humphry, he was granted by the Queen the right to develop "all mines, minerals and subterranean treasures which should be found in all other parts of England and within the English pale in Ireland."

Hardly had the ink dried on the two documents than whole "colonies" of German miners began to emigrate to England. Within a few years the Keswick Works near the Derwent Water

(LEFT) A "mountain-knight" or miner, carrying 1. raw ore; 2. multe, or basket; 3. the insignia of a privileged mining official; 4. scales; 5. a "lucky," or dowsing, rod; 6. mountain pick carried by mining initiates; 7. molten metal in the scales; 8. chisel; 9. sieve for molten ore; 10. basket in which the molten ore is weighed; 11. trough with which the ore is pulled out of the mine; 12. smelter; 13. coat of arms of the electorate prince, prince, or mine owner; 14. garter; 15. bellows. (From a copper etching by Martin Engelbrecht, 1730.)

(RIGHT) Dowser Holding a Forked Rod to Search for Veins. (From Chr. Weigel's Berg-Kostümbuch, 1721.)

"Let a two-forked rod be cut of one year's growth, of hazel or oak, whose forks or two twigs must be equal, and without fault. This being done, let the two ends be taken into the opposite hands, the fingers compressed upwards toward Heaven; to wit, that on both sides the ends of the twigs of the divided branch, or fork, may extend forth out of the hands at both the thumbs pressed to the hands. But the root of the forked branch must bend outwardly between the two hands. Which if any having silver buttons fixed to his doublet, that cut end of the foot, although with all thine endeavor thou compress the rod in both hands, will make a circle by moving by itself, and will turn itself, inwardly toward thy doublet, even to the buttons. But if, having no metal at all about thee, then lay silver or gold upon the earth; then holding it fast, and being unwilling, the cut part of the foot will bend outwardly, until with a strong motion, it smite the metal."

Ralph Eglin, *Treatise on the Helian Art*, Marburg, 1608, as first translated by John Webster in London in 1671.

in Cumberland was growing into what was soon to be the largest copper-smelting operation in Europe. Twenty years after its formation, its German mining manager, Ulrich Frosse, who was also Overseer of Mineral Works at Perranzabuloe on the north Cornish coast and Metal Master at the Neath Mines in Wales, could write with half-boasting reverence: "As to melting twenty-four hundred weight of ore every day with one furnance, God be thanked." New mines opened by the "Dutch"—as the English, and after them, the Americans, termed immigrants from Germany—were given typically Saxon names in anglicized versions. Thus, namesakes for the Joachimstal "God's Gift" mine, which had enriched Agricola, turned up both at Saint Austel in Cornwall and at Newlands in Cumberland.

First Attempts at a Scientific Explanation

At the start of the seventeenth century German controversy continued to surround dowsing for minerals in spite of its having been successfully exported to England. To one author, Percis Heliopolis, a pseudonym for Ralph Eglin, we owe the first written description of how to hold a dowsing rod as well as the first notion that metal worn on one's person could adversely affect the instrument.

Learned Jesuits, too, added to the persisting altercations on dowsing. In yet another huge book on mineralogy written in Latin, Father Bernard Caesius in 1636 began to wrestle with the problem of, not whether, but *why* the rod should turn at all. He came to the conclusion that the rod did not move of itself but was somehow moved by the dowser. It is to Caesius's fellow Jesuit, Father Athanasius Kircher, that the first attempt to solve the dowsing problem by experiment can be credited. Kircher, who struggled with the problem for nearly half a century, has been characterized by a twentieth century member of his order, Conor Reilly, S.J., professor at the University of Lusaka in Zambia, as "one of the most knowledgeable and hard-working scholars ever to be produced by the Society of Jesus."

During a lifetime of study and teaching all over western Europe, from Wurzburg to Sicily and Avignon to Vienna, Kircher turned out a shelf of books devoted to subjects as varied as Roman antiquities, optics, the nature of water, Egyptian hieroglyphics, and the first European analysis of the Coptic language. Eschewing the "arm-chair philosophizing" and tendentious moralizing dear to natural philosophers and religious writers of his time, Kircher sought, above all, to "see for himself." After listening, while in Naples, to endless speculations about the nature of the earth's interior, he climbed to the top of Vesuvius and had himself lowered by a burly peasant into its crater, remaining there long enough to take accurate notes of his surroundings.

As one of the first proponents of experimental science, Kircher, helped by the patronage of dukes and princes, set up one of the finest laboratories in Europe where he produced a series of inventions including the magic lantern used to project the enlarged image of a picture.

When it came to studying dowsing, the Jesuit scholar, hoping

Athanasius Kircher (Reproduced from the collection of the Library of Congress.)

"*Make a little rod one span (twelve digits) long from a piece of fossil salt and join it to any wood such that the wooden part is joined to the salt rod. When it is set on a pivot and balanced, or hung from a thread, it moves freely. Place this wood-salt rod above a pot with a fire under it. Let the salt water or brine boil and you will adhere to the salty rod by magnetic influence as to a body like themselves. So, weighed down by saline corpuscles, the rod will gradually bend down towards the pot. I believe the same motion will take place if a similar instrument were placed over a salt mine in the ground.*"

Translated from the Latin
in Athanasius Kircher, *Mundus Subterraneus,*
Amsterdam, 1665, Book 10, Section 2, page 182.

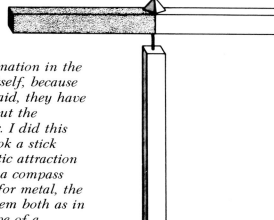

"*I judge unlikely the notion that this ability of divination in the rods comes from any magnetic force in the wood itself, because if we place the rods next to metals to which, it is said, they have special affinity, even if balanced exactly and without the slightest pressure, we get no inclination whatsoever. I did this experiment many times without any result . . . I took a stick from those trees which are believed to have magnetic attraction to different metals. Then I made a needle (not like a compass needle) from different woods, one with an affinity for metal, the other from any kind of dried out wood. Uniting them both as in the illustration, I let them form a unity in the shape of a pointed cap. Upon the point on the vertical stick let the two joined sticks be perfectly balanced. This done, if you wish to experience the moving power, go to a place located on top of a vein with this instrument and that half of the stick which has affinity to that metal should necessarily incline itself if full of motile force.*"

Translated from the Latin in Athanasius Kircher, *Magnes sive de Arte Magnetica,* Cologne, 1643, Book 3, Part 5, Chapter 3, pp. 635–663.

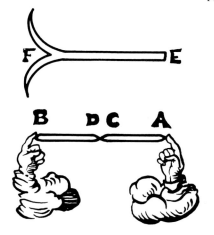

The divining rod, or metalloscope, is particularly used to search for metals. I'll give the reason for that. First, a stick of hazel wood which they judged apt to find veins they cut with a knife. It is in fact necessary to compress the fingers and look at the sky and lift the rod by its horns. In Germany they also take a very thick fork of hazel wood without knots, and, dividing it into two parts, they dig out *the end of one part and the end of the other they sharpen into a point such that it may be fitted into the concavity of the other.*

Translated from the Latin in Athanasius Kircher, *Magnes sive de Arte Magnetica,* Cologne, 1643, Book 3, Part 5, Chapter 3, pp. 635-663.

Illustration showing two dowsers from **Magia Universalis** *by Gasper Schott, S.J. The man in the foreground holds the rod palms upward, the dowser in the background palms downward.*

to remove all taint of mysticism from the *virgula divinatoria,* renamed it *virgula metalloscopia*—or metal-seeking rod—and thus was the first of many savants extending into the twentieth century to try to make dowsing scientifically more respectable simply by altering its vocabulary. His terminology disposed of, Kircher made experiments with, and watched others operate, dowsing devices. Early in his study he believed that a rod might be attracted to vapors from a mine, at least from one harboring salt, and set up a test to prove it. His experiments later convinced him that "affinity" between a rod and metal could not play any role in its action, so he proposed a special dowsing device with which dowsers could prove this assertion for themselves.

Both Caesius and Kircher were among the first to state that seemingly *involuntary* muscular action on the part of a dowser causes their dowsing instruments to move. To quote Kircher's seventeenth century opinion in full:

No reason can be given why a two-pronged rod grasped firmly by either branch, even with every consideration of magic excluded, could still experience so great an impetuous movement from metallic vapors, that they should draw it down. Certainly for my part I often undertook an experiment on this phenomenon in regard to bodies of gold and silver, and was always disappointed in my hope. And I clearly noticed that it was a manifest illusion not of the devil but of the person handling the rod, since he is *duped by the power of his own imagination* and thinks that the rod dips of its own accord towards the metal though he himself is inadvertently twisting it . . . I do not think that it can happen that hidden metals impress on a rod, that is not balanced but violently twisted, so great and sudden a force that the rod is spontaneously caused to bend down even to the ground.

Far from laying the matter to rest, Caesius's and Kircher's arguments were attacked by supporters of the ancient theory of *atomism,* first developed in classical Greece by Democritus and Epicurus. One of these was the French Epicurean philosopher and intellectual foe of Descartes, Pierre Gassend, who wrote copiously on scientific subjects and was the first to observe a planetary transit, that of Mercury. As a partisan of atomism, he taught that because the whole universe was made up of tiny particles called atoms, which in Greek means "uncuttable" and thus "indivisible," it was these bodies that somehow radiated from various metals to affect the rods directly and cause them to react *independently* of the dowser. Others, such as the German didactic versifier, George Phillip Harsdorfer, referred to this unseen, and therefore unprovable, phenomenon more poetically as "streaming of metals."

Kircher's attempt to keep moralistic judgment out of any consideration of dowsing was no more successful than Agricola's recommendation that its use in mining be abandoned. Gaspar Schott, S.J., who had studied physics and become fast friends with Kircher in Rome, first ascribed Satanic power to the rod:

Some pretend that the hazel rod moves through the effect of a warped imagination. Others, of severer mein, abruptly decide that the whole thing is a sleight of hand executed by an adroit swindler who causes the rod to move. Still others have been found who have not hesitated to say that, at the very least, the thing was linked to an implicit pact with the Devil; this is why they warned me not to use this rod without previously renouncing any such pact, and without their having preliminarily stuck holy wax to the ends of the rod and even pronounced exorcisms while it turned in my hands.

He changed his opinion only when he received a letter from a "pious and God-fearing" clerk who, referring for the first time in print to the dowsing rod's potential for seeking out water, wrote to the priest:

To your Reverence, I would state frankly what several experiences of the most indubitable nature have taught me: the thickness and size of the rod is of no consequence and, as I absolutely deny that one need observe either the time of day or the weather, or the calendar when setting out to cut a rod, I have always laughed at those who stand on superstitious ceremony in this connection. The rod is considered to work better if the forked branch comes out of the ground almost from the roots themselves. This rod indicates not only all kinds of metals, but there are even those who hold that it is used to discover sources of water which run in the earth, something I have not had occasion to put to test. The effect of the rod is most natural. Nevertheless, I would not wish to assure anyone that it is impossible to be mistaken with this simple instrument: this is because the sympathy of the hazel is thus far not entirely known to us.

Two dowsers indicate the strike of a metallic vein which a miner marks with stakes. From Balthazar Rössler's Speculum Metallurgiae Politissimum, Dresden, 1700.

Rod designed by Johann Rudolf Glauber. "This is the work of the Art, if anyone conjoining metals in the fire under a certain constellation melt them into an electrum and make of them a little ball, perforated in the middle, wherein a wand of hazel of one year's growth wanting little boughs is to be implanted, which carry straight out before thee where thou conjecturest metals to be, when the little ball bows the rod and bends toward the ground it is without doubt that thereunder are metals, and that the labor undertaken about them will not be in vain. This testimony, proceeding from the natural and infallible foundation of philosophy, is deservedly to be preferred before all other arts concerning the finding out of metals." **The Works of the Highly Experienced and Famous Chemist, John Rudolph Glauber: Containing Great Variety of Choice Secrets in Medicine and Alchemy in the Working of Metallic Mines and the Separation of Metals,** *translated into English and Published for the Publick Good by the Labor, Care and Charge of Christopher Packe, Philo-Chymico-Medicus, London, MDCLXXXIX.*

On the strength of this testimony Schott, in his "Thaumaturgus Physicus" the third volume of his massive *The Magic of Nature and Art, or Occult Science of Natural and Artificial Things,* came down positively on the side of dowsing.

Shortly after Kircher lent his prestige to the subject of dowsing, it began to spawn a series of academic dissertations. Two scholars at Wittenberg University, Jacob Klein and Johann Sperling, came to the conclusion in 1658 that no occult force was necessary to explain the rod's movement because it usually could be attributed to pure fraud on the part of the dowsers or, if genuine, to an implicit pact with the devil. More positive was another doctoral aspirant, John Praetorius of Leipzig, who admitted in 1667 that "while the divining rod often correctly locates *something,* and thus cannot be pure charlatanry, if one relies on it like a blindman his cane, this could prove stupid and even harmful." Five years later Matthias Willenius in Jena put forward a third thesis, justifying the dowsing rod's use and maintaining that the influence of the stars under which dowsers were born contributed importantly to their success in locating specific metals.

It was during this period that the Saxon, Balthazar Rössler, was writing his *Mirror of Metallurgy* which was to appear in 1700, more than a quarter century after his death. His comments on dowsing are worth more than any of the speculative essays written in the universities, largely because in a long mining career Rössler won the title of *Bergmeister,* the highest rank in the German mining service.

In his precise instructions on how to dowse for ore Rössler came to grips with the dowsing controversy by stating that, based on his own practical experience, "dowsing works from the *nature in man* however much some would like to attribute it to the rods." Avoiding long-winded theories, he offered the following solidly practical advice: "He who wishes to use a dowsing rod should know of what he is capable and study how the rod deflects for him, whether over a vein or a rock, in all cases of success or failure. Though dowsers seek to know whether a vein will be productive or what kind of ore it carries, their attempts to discern this information with the rod will sometimes not work."

Rössler's practical approach to dowsing, relying on experience rather than book-learning, was also adopted by prominent natural scientists in the mid-seventeenth century. Chemist and alchemist Johann Rudolf Glauber, best known for his discovery of "Glauber's salts" used in paper and glass manufacturing and as a cathartic in medicine, designed his own dowsing rod. He used it successfully to find underground metals whose formation in the

Rod designed by Gabriel Plattes.

earth he ascribed, like Basil Valentine, to astrological influence.

The English "Doctor of Physick," Robert Fludd, a cabalist and Rosicrucian, whose theories that living things are affected by the positions of heavenly bodies anticipated recent twentieth century findings, witnessed German dowsers at work in Wales. In his *Mosaicall Philosophy Grounded Upon the Essential Truth or Eternal Sapience* that appeared in London in 1659, he stirringly concluded:

Moreover, to express the exceeding sympathetical relation, which is between the vegetable nature and the mineral, let us but mark diligently the occult property of the hazel-tree. For if at certain times there be forked twigs cut from it, and each twig of the forked branch held in each hand, so that the forked place where they join stand directly upward, and, as it were, perpendicularly: and with this kind of posture of the stick, the party that holdeth it pass over a mountain, that hath in its bowels some rich mineral, or mattaline vein, when as the man walketh right over the place of the mine, the perpendicular twist will forcibly, and that whether the bearer will or no, bow downward towards the earth; but if there be no mine or vein, it will not move.

Lord, what a stir would the enemy of the weapon-salve make, to behold such a fight. What! An unsensible branch of a tree consisting of two twigs only, to discover hidden metal, and to penetrate with his invisible beams about five hundred fathom in the solid earth, and that quite through craggy rocks and stony veins.

Such will their censures be, I know, who are apt to judge before the case be known, when in verity it is that proportioned harmony in all these lower creatures by which they do correspond unto the celestial bodies, or rather to the divine influences in them, which spring from one capital, catholic and all eternal emanation, which infuseth immediately his verrous beams, as well of sympathy as antipathy, into this elementary world, causing a harmonious and symphonical consent betwixt both regions. It is therefore certain, that the metallic beams concurring in their ascent with the beamy influences of the forked rod, do cause that portion in the hazel rod's twist, to move downwards, no otherwise than the loadstone is noted to draw iron, or another loadstone, most strongly by the pole.

I know it will seem strange unto these kind of men to hear that metallic substances in their veins should send forth beams; but if they were as well conversant with the lively natures of the minerals, as the mineral men of Tirol, in Germany and in Hungary are, they would be assured by occult experience, that at times they send forth thunder and lightning in the earth, which appeareth most dangerous unto the workmen, so that except they get out of the mine when they observe the signs, they suffer.

Gabriel Plattes, an agricultural experimentalist and author of *Treatise on Husbandry,* one of the best works on the state of seventeenth century English agriculture, developed his own form

91

of dowsing rod and went out into the mountains to see if he could find a vein of lead ore. Working with an assistant, he found one before the morning ended. Though his unique version of a dowsing instrument was not adopted by others, there is no reason to suppose that it would not work just as effectively today as it had before its designer was found dead and destitute in the streets of London.

Nor was dowsing beneath the scrutiny of one of the most eminent of English scientists, Robert Boyle, who had founded the "Invisible College," predecessor of Great Britain's prestigious Royal Society of London for Improving Natural Knowledge. Originator of the law which states that "the volume of gas varies inversely with the pressure" and coiner of the term "chemical analysis" for the technique he developed to detect ingredients in mixtures and compounds, Boyle sought all his life to be "provided of experiments" in his search for scientific truth. This approach did not shake his alchemist's view that metals were transmutable. He was so sure that some day he would make gold and silver from base metals that, after years of lobbying, he finally won the repeal of Henry IV's statute against multiplying them.

In his "Second Essay on Unsucceeding Experiments," part of a large collection published in 1661, Boyle dealt with dowsing as tolerantly and broad-mindedly as any scientist before or since— and far more unprejudicially than the majority of his successors. After confessing that he had unsuccessfully tried more than once to obtain a dowsing reaction over pieces of metal resting on top of the ground and over ores within it, he nevertheless acknowledged that the dowsing rod appeared to be effective in the hands of certain persons and judiciously concluded: "I must content myself to say what I am wont to do when my opinion is asked of those things which I dare not peremptorily reject, and yet am not convinced of: namely, that they that have seen them can much more reasonably believe them than they that have not."

If Boyle's "seeing is believing" attitude which cuts to the heart of the dowsing controversy had been universally adopted, good dowsers today would find themselves welcomed instead of rejected by scientific pundits, and politicians responsible for the development of resources. Unfortunately their experience is all too often similar to that of an extraordinary couple who, in seventeenth century France, made a dowsing survey for the mineral wealth of an entire country.

CHAPTER 5

Sorciers or Sourciers?

". . . a small wire finger rod, properly manipulated, will rotate through a complete circle and return to its original position . . ."

Dowsing Surveys on an Entire Country

In 1629, a carriage coming from the northeast drove into the small French provincial town of Chateau Thierry, soon to become famous as the birthplace of Jean de la Fontaine, who ranks with Aesop as a fabulist. Stopping before the Fleur de Lys, a local hostelry, it disgorged a striking middle-aged lady who requested a room where her teen-age son might rest for a few days to recover from an affliction acquired during the course of their incessant travels.

While the lad slept away his illness, Martine de Bertereau unpacked from one of her traveling cases a series of strange instruments, including seven different dowsing rods, and proceeded to rove the neighborhood in a continuation of her twenty-year-long exploration for sources of water and minerals.

Her wanderings had taken her not only to many regions of her native France but to other European countries and even to the high Andes of Bolivia. There she had descended into what she described as "galleries and shafts of horrendous depth" in the fabulously rich gold mines of Monte Cerro de Potosi where its curate, Alonzo Barba, was, like Agricola, studying mining and writing his *Art of Metals* in which he, too, refers to the dowsing rod.

Guided by her instruments, she returned to the courtyard of her lodging. After a careful survey, she announced that under the ground on which she was standing ran a course of water with excellent curative properties.

Noting that the townspeople crowding into the courtyard appeared as doubtful of her declaration as they seemed distrustful of her methods—which at one point led to her "setting a mysterious astrolabe in its hinge"—the earliest female dowser on record, and one of the most illustrious of either sex, demanded the immediate formation of a committee, composed of legal officers, apothecaries, and physicians, to verify her statement on the hidden presence of the mineral water and its specific quality. The water, said the diviner, having run through deposits of gold and green vitriol—today called ferrous sulfate—was rich in trace elements of these minerals and, consequently, was particularly effective for obstructions of the liver and gall bladder, kidney stones, dysentery, and other ills.

93

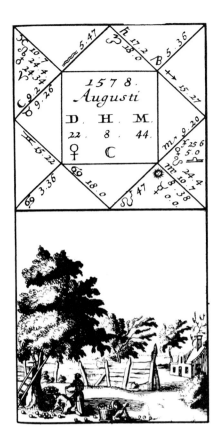

Astrological data on this and the opposite page provided by Baron and Baroness de Beausoleil in connection with the proper times to cut dowsing rods.

One of the medical doctors present, Claude Galien, was inspired to record what he had seen. In his book, *The Discovery of the Mineral Waters of Chateau Thierry and Their Properties,* he acclaimed the gentlewoman's finds but attributed them, not to what he considered to be her "magical" practices, but to her astute observations of how underground currents of mineral-rich waters had stained cobblestones on the ground above them.

Martine de Bertereau's life is a clear reflection of the inherent success of the dowsing art and the calumny unkindly hurled upon it by officialdom. While still in her teens, and already fluent in three foreign languages, she married Jean de Chastelet, some twenty years her senior, who had been born Baron of Beausoleil and Auffenbach during the late 1570s in the Brabant, a former duchy, now part of the Netherlands and Belgium. In an age when most of his aristocractic peers opted for a career at arms, the baron had taught himself the budding sciences of mineralogy and mining engineering and, by the age of twenty-five, was an expert in both. The year following his marriage, he was invited by his countryman, Pierre de Beringhen, first valet to France's King Henry VI whom he also served as controller-general of mines, to reconnoiter mining rights in southwestern France which de Beringhen had acquired through his connections at court.

His survey for de Beringhen finished, the Baron de Beausoleil and his newly wedded wife embarked on journeys as mining consultants which took them all over Germany, Silesia, Moravia, Poland, Switzerland, Italy, Spain, Scotland, and England. The baron served two Holy Roman Emperors as Commissioner General for Mines in Hungary, the Austrian Archduke Leopold as Director of Mines in the Tyrol and Trentino, and the Holy See as mining advisor in the Papal States. In 1626, he was again summoned to France, this time by Antoine de Ruzé, Marquis d'Effiat, superintendant for mines and ore deposits under Louis XIII, and offered a commission to reconnoiter the length and breadth of the kingdom for its potential mineral wealth.

Arriving with a team of sixty mine-workers recruited in Germany and Hungary, the Beausoleils spent a year in the southern sun-drenched provinces of Languedoc and Provence where they discovered over forty mines and wrote a strange treatise, *Explication of the True Philosophy Concerning the Primary Matter of Minerals,* filled with astrological and alchemical recipes for the prospection of mineral ores. Now as lost to memory as the practices detailed in its pages, the document teemed with arcane knowledge of the same stamp as that set down by Basil Valentine and other alchemists. Even the names of dowsing rods recorded by Valentine were listed in it, this time in Italian since the couple had first heard their names pronounced in Alpine mines south of today's Italo-Austrian frontier. These the Beausoleils used in conjunction with sixteen separate instruments—including a compass with seven angles; a mineral astrolabe, dial-plate, and geometer; and a metallic rake—all at astrologically propitious times.

The couple next proceeded to the Duchy of Brittany where they first encountered signs of organized opposition to their

94

endeavors. While on an expedition to examine a mine in the Buisson-Rochemares forest near Morlaix, their personal effects were ransacked by provincial officials who, under the pretext of investigating the de Beausoleils for the use of "black arts" in their work, helped themselves to 100,000 *ecus* worth of silver and precious stones and to a large collection of mining samples, reports, and detailed maps of surveyed mines. Though the suspected culprits were able to convince higher authority that their official mission for the French crown included no pacts with the devil, their demand that the erring functionaries be punished and their property returned to them was not met, an injustice that was to foreshadow worse to come.

Because they had as yet not received a cent's worth of recompense from the French royal house for their extensive mineral survey of the kingdom, the baroness wrote a memoir to the French mining superintendant setting forth what they had accomplished. Her declaration quickly produced another commission to the Beausoleils from d'Effiat's successor, de la Porte de la Meilleraye, who gratefully acknowledged the couple's work "done with such love and diligence." The new assignment, however, was matched neither by repayment of the fantastically large sum of 600,000 *ecus* spent in maintaining a work force to reconnoiter France's mineral wealth nor by any salary. The Beausoleils's hope that a concession to mine certain claims of their own might at last be forthcoming was dashed when a councillor to the king who had drawn up documents to implement it suddenly and mysteriously retired.

Driven to desperation, the baroness again took up her pen and prepared a long report, *The Restitution of Pluto,* which set forth an account of all discoveries of mines and mineral deposits made by herself and her husband in France from 1602 to 1640. The title obviously referred, with neoclassical sentiment so appreciated at the time, to an ancient Greek god who, as ruler of the underworld, was dubbed, cautiously and euphemistically, "The Unseen," and the "Giver of Wealth," attributes which could as easily apply to subterranean natural resources.

This time the new work was dedicated, not to Louis XIII but to France's sickly, diplomatically crafty, and ruthless prime minister—and real king—"His Ementissimus, Cardinal, the Duke of Richelieu." One of the most imposing accounts of prospecting exploits ever put to print, it assured the cardinal that, if the mines discovered were worked, the finances of His Majesty would be far more ample than those of any other Christian prince and that his subjects would be the most fortunate of all peoples.

Martine de Beausoleil boldly asserted that she and her husband had come to France neither as "mining apprentices" nor because they were "constrained by necessity" and added that they had traveled "nine long years" to bring solid proof to the court of France's underground treasure. She also recommended to Richelieu the establishment of a mining administration made up of a council of engineers headquartered in Paris with branches in each province, a suggestion so good that it was ignored for more than a century and a half until acted upon by Napoleon.

Backing up her claim, the baroness listed over 150 mines

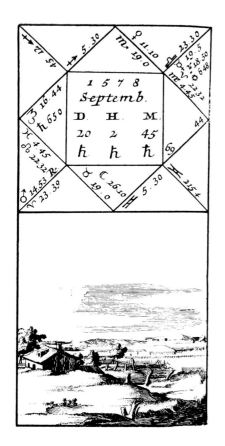

95

LA
RESTITVTION
DE PLVTON.
A MONSEIGNEVR
l' Eminentissimè Cardinal,
DVC DE RICHE-LIEV.

Oeuure auquel il est amplement traitté
des Mines , & minieres de France,
cachées , & detenuës iusqu'à present
au ventre de la terre , par le moyen
desquelles les Finances de sa Majesté
serôt beaucoupplus grades, que celles
de tous les Princes Chrestiés, & ses su-
jects plus heureux de tous les Peuples.

Ln'importe pas de qui l'on
soit conseillé , pomueu
que le conseil soit bon.
On en doit premierement faire

A

First spread of Martine de Bertereau is **The Restitution of Pluto,** *dedicated to Monseigneur, the most eminent Cardinal, the Duke of Richelieu. "A work in which is amply treated the mines and mineral deposits of France hidden and held up to now in the bowels of the earth by means of which the finances of his Majesty will become much larger than those of all Christian Princes and his subjects the happiest of all peoples." The first sentence reads: "It makes no difference by whom one is advised as long as the advice is good."*

discovered all over France, many of which were checked a century later by a scholar of mineralogy, Nicolas Gobet, who assembled ancient documents on the subject in his *Former Mineralogists of France,* and found to be exactly where the baron and his wife said they were.

So encouraging a report on the extent of France's mineral riches should have pleased any primate of the Catholic Church. In light of Richelieu's subsequent reaction, it can be concluded that details provided by the baroness on *how* mineral deposits were found were less to his liking. In her new oeuvre she openly avowed that dowsing rods, both wooden and metallic, had been key prospecting tools and took pains to note that such instruments had been successfully used long before the seventeenth century.

"The ancients," she candidly explained, "that is to say our ancestors, used any available forked stick from hazel or other nut trees which, by a virtue, inclines and dips over those places where sources of water or metals are located, whether beneath earth or water." As if to underscore her own particular talent, not easy to equal, she added: "Not everyone can use the rod."

To the baroness's supplication, the cardinal responded with peremptory cruelty. He issued orders for her incarceration together with one of her daughters to whom she was teaching mineralogical sciences, in the castle of Vincennes, a former royal residence converted into a prison. The Baron de Beausoleil, taken simultaneously, was remanded to the Bastille, a fortress in the heart of Paris used for the first time in its centuries-old existence as a dungeon, not for common criminals, but for persons who in some way were held to be dangerous to the security of the state or its sovereign. When one of his young sons had the temerity to try to visit his father, the boy, too, was locked away. Separated from each other, the forlorn parents both died behind bars.

Ethics of Dowsing Debated

Not quite half a century after the de Beausoleil's demise, a vintner and his wife were hacked to death with a butcher's cleaver in their wine cellar at Place Neuve-Saint-Jean in the French silk-producing city of Lyon. Searching for a motive, gendarmes found a rifled strongbox in the couple's private apartment. Informed that 130 *ecus,* 8 gold *louis,* and a treasured silver belt were missing from the box, they attributed the crime to panicky thieves but were unable to find a single trace of the malefactors.

The sheer brutality of the slaughter was not lost on the populace. Alarmed that one of their number might soon face similar disposition at the hands of desperados ostensibly still at large, it angrily pressed the police for a solution to the crime. Reduced to grasping at straws, the law officers eagerly accepted the suggestion, implausible on the face of it, that a rich peasant living in the neighboring province of Dauphiné could, through some uncanny ability, track criminals to their hiding places. Part of the Alpine piedmont, the Dauphiné was and is famous for its dowsers—known in French vernacular as *sourciers,* finders of *sources,* or springs of underground water. With the elimination of a single letter the word becomes *sorciers,* meaning sorcerers or witches, and thus may offer another explanation for the connection between "dowsing" and "witching" in English.

Acting on the tip, the king's procurator summoned Jacques Aymar Vernay from Saint Marcellin, his native village, to Lyon where he was forthwith taken to the scene of the mayhem. To the stupefaction of police agents, the man took a forked stick from his jacket pocket and began nervously walking back and forth in the cellar, trembling violently and sweating profusely. The stick twisted in his hands when he stood over two locations which one policeman observed were precisely where the two corpses of the victims had lain.

Taking off like a bloodhound on the trace of an escaped convict, Aymar, as he was usually known, led a party of curious onlookers through the streets. Almost trotting, he skirted the archbishop's residence to arrive at one of the city gates leading to a bridge over the Rhone River, only to find the gate padlocked for the night.

Next morning Aymar and three police officials crossed the bridge and, guided by the rod's indications, turned downstream along the bank. When they came upon a gardener's house, Aymar checked momentarily, then went in the front door. Spying an

This drawing of a dowser reacting to "corpuscles," published by the Abbé de Vallemont in Occult Physics, *has been taken to represent Jacques Aymar.*

empty wine bottle on the table he put it under his right foot and saw the rod in his hands give a violent twist, as it did when held over the three chairs and the table itself. From this evidence, the dowser declared to his companions that the sought-for fugitives, three in number, had paused in their flight to consume a liter of wine.

When questioned for corroboration, the gardener's two small children, at first terror-stricken that they would be punished by their father for having left the door to the house unlocked during his absence and therefore unwilling to speak a word, finally admitted that three men had suddenly appeared the day before and hastily drained the wine from its bottle before disappearing downriver at a run.

His finding confirmed, Aymar at once renewed the chase. The trail led all the way to Beaucaire, a small town lying against the base of an enormous rocky cliff from the top of which the Camargue, as the delta of the Rhone is called, could be viewed in the distance. Here Aymar's search with the rod took him to the gates of the local prison. A cooperative warden ordered a line-up of thirteen recently arrested prisoners. Passing in front of each man with his rod at the ready, Aymar observed it to dip only when he stood before a lame ruffian who had been jailed an hour previously for petty larceny. The dowser stated flatly that the man targeted by his rod had played a role, though not the leading one, in the crime.

The limping suspect was returned to Lyon where he vigorously denied having ever set foot in the city. When taken over the same route traveled by Aymar, and confronted by people who recognized and identified him, he broke down and admitted that, while Aymar had been correct in all details, he had not actually committed murder but had been paid by the real slayers, a pair of Provencal-speaking southerners, to assist them in carrying their spoils.

The culprit's confession encouraged the procurator to assign the dowser, now supported by a troop of archers, to continue his search. His dipping rod led the armed troop to Toulon, a port on the Mediterranean coast, where Aymar discovered that the fugitives had supped at an inn the previous evening before embarking in a small boat to carry them to refuge in the Italian city of Genoa. Since the searching party was not empowered to go beyond the confines of the French kingdom, the chase was broken off.

In Lyon, the lame confessor, revealed as a pirate from Toulon, was condemned by a solemn panel of thirty judges to be broken alive on the wheel before a huge crowd at Terreaux Square. On his way to his final agony, preordained by the action of a dowsing rod, his sentence was publicly read in front of the wine cellar where the murder victims had met their bloody fate.

Moral Qualms and Occult Physics

When Aymar's feat at Lyon was repeated by him in other police jurisdictions and other criminals successfully apprehended, misgivings began to be expressed by members of the French clergy perspicacious enough to see that, if practiced widely, dowsing to determine questions of guilt and innocence could lead to gross injustice.

Even before the news of Aymar's exploits began to leak out to the public, Pierre Lebrun, a priest of the Oratory, had written to Father Nicolas Malebranche, the famous Cartesian philosopher, about experiments conducted in Paris involving "a strange practice that seemed to have taken over nearly the whole population of Grenoble and the Dauphiné." This involved the use of a forked rod not only to search for metals and water in the earth, but to track criminals to their hiding places and correctly establish property boundaries, even if they had been altered surreptitiously by former owners. Most startling to Lebrun was

Title page of Occult Physics *by Abbé de Vallemont.*

99

1ᵉ Manierᵉ de tenir la Baguette.

2ᵉ Manierᵉ de tenir la Baguette.

3ᵉ Manierᵉ de tenir la Baguette

"The most common way of using a divining rod is to take a forked hazel branch, or one from a nut tree, a foot and a half long, thick as a finger and no more than a year's growth, as far as possible. One holds the two branches, A and B, in the hands without squeezing them too much, such that the back of the hands are turned toward the earth and the point C of the rod projects forward and is parallel to the horizon. Then one walks slowly along in those places where water or minerals are suspected to lie, or hidden money. One should not walk too fast for otherwise one will scatter the volume of vapors and exhalations which arise from the place where these things lie and which impregnate the rod, causing it to turn."

"There are those who hold the rod in another way. The method of Monsieur Royer is to hold it on the back of an outstretched hand in balance. This is how he describes his method: "In order to find water, one should take a forked branch cut either from a hazel, elm, oak or apple tree about one foot in length and thick as a finger so that the wind cannot easily move it. One should place it on one of the hands as much in balance as is possible, then walk slowly and when one passes above a course of water it will turn.""

"The Jesuit Father Kircher says that he saw this kind of divination practice in Germany in an entirely different manner. One takes a straight hazel sprout without knots and cuts it into two pieces of equal length; one carves the end of one piece into the form of a tiny basin and the end of the other into a point, such that the tip of one stick can enter into the tip of the other. One holds this combination before one between the two index fingers as the figure shows. When one passes over water the pieces move and incline."

4e Maniere de tenir la Baguette

"*There is another way which I have seen used only by a few persons who practice the water-seeking art. They take a long sprout of hazel, or any other wood straight and smooth, like an ordinary cane. They hold its ends in their hands bending it slightly into an arc. They carry it parallel to the horizon, and when they pass over a water source, the rod turns and the arc twists toward the ground.*"

from Abbé Vallemont's *Occult Physics or Treatise on the Divining Rod*, Paris, 1693.

the incredible assertion he had heard many times to the effect that a dowsing rod would turn *only over something which the dowsers specifically wished to find.* If they sought water, it would not move when they crossed over metal, and vice versa.

Malebranche replied to Lebrun that, while he had heard of a rod being used to find water and metals, he had never come across its employ to resolve moral issues. Trying to sort out the two distinct types of problem for his colleague he reasoned that because material bodies usually affected one another only through impact, the only explanation for the dowsing rod's movement over matter such as water and minerals was its attraction by subtle, invisible corpuscular bodies emitted by them as proposed by Descartes. To Malebranche this kind of reaction depended on causes which, having neither "intelligence nor liberty," had necessarily to produce the same results under similar circumstances.

When it came to settling boundary lines or adjudicating felonies, the disinterested repeatable causes could not apply. If the rod were effective in such cases, then the causes had to be *intelligent, moral,* and *supernatural.* Because God and angels could not be expected to be concerned with the outcome of every human squabble, the causes necessarily were the work of infernal spirits. Malebranche concluded that dowsing rods should be used neither to find material objects nor to decide moral questions.

Lebrun countered that the purely physical relation between matter sought and the rod should allow its use in hunting for metals or water. He even provided an escape clause for dowsers by saying that it appeared to work best in the hands of "simple" men and even children. In the ensuing debate, Malebranche's opinion was echoed by a well-known Cistercian, Armand Jean de la Rance, who publicly sermonized that no priest of the faith should even consider dowsing. The chancellor of the University of Paris, Abbé Pirot, went further and stated that priests should not only abstain from using the divining rod but prohibit their parishioners from doing so.

Widening press coverage of Aymar's doings and the private debate between Lebrun and his fellow ecclesiastics began to unleash a furious public controversy. Aymar's dowsing ability was put to test in Lyon on September 3, 1692, before a number of distinguished witnesses, including a respected physician, Pierre Garnier, who published the results of the trials in a 108-page report: *Philosophical Treatise in the Form of a Letter to Monsieur de Sève, Seigneur de Flechères, in Which it is Proved that the Extraordinary Faculties by Which Jacques Aymar, with a Divining Rod, Followed Murderers and Robbers, Discovered Water and Buried Silver, Re-established Landmarks, etc., Depended on a Very Ordinary Natural Cause.*

Leaning directly on the Cartesian corpuscular theory to account for Aymar's ability to track humans, Garnier held that corpuscles exhaled by the sweat of the murderers *at the moment they perpetrated their crime* were of a different pattern than those they would normally emit. It was these crime-connected

101

particles, said Garnier, that acted upon Aymar by penetrating his skin to cause a "fermentation" in his blood, an increase in his heartbeat and perspiration, and the onset of convulsions. The corpuscles did not affect the rod directly but passed from the dowser's hand into its pores, exerting a pressure on it and causing it to twist.

Because Descartes's corpuscles or "subtile matter" was also termed "magnetic matter"—thus anticipating what is today called a magnetic field—by analogy, Garnier coined two new terms for the particles detected by Aymar at the scene of the crime: "murderous matter" and "felonious matter."

Garnier was supported by another medical expert, Dr. Pierre Chauvin, who had also witnessed the Aymar tests. In a *Letter to Madame La Marquise de Senozan on the Means to Discover the Accomplices in an Assassination Committed at Lyons on 5 July 1692*, he added the extraordinary observation that, because of their infinitessimal size and hardness, the corpuscles could remain in the air where they had been exhaled, no matter how much that air might have been agitated by wind or any other cause.

Chauvin disagreed with his colleague about the corpuscles directly affecting a dowser, affirming instead that, his "animal instincts stimulated" by them, Aymar unconsciously moved the rod by flexing the muscles of his little and ring fingers. He also astutely concluded that the dowsing reaction permitted no judgement whatsoever about a dowser's proficiency, which had to be measured *solely on the basis of successful results*.

The controversy continued to swirl in the pages of the *Mercure Galant*, France's most popular weekly, which in January 1693, printed one of a series of anonymous letters combating the corpuscular theory as nonsense. A month later, it was followed by another, affirming that there was nothing supernatural or magical about the movement of a dowsing rod and that physicists had better get busy and explain how the rod really worked, since Drs. Garnier and Chauvin certainly had not.

This challenge was taken up the same year in a spirited defense of dowsing not inappropriately entitled *Occult Physics*. A "Treatise on the Divining Rod and its Utility for the Discovery of Sources of Water, Mineral Ores, Etc.," by yet another French savant-priest, Pierre le Lorrain, Abbé de Vallemont, a numismatic expert and part-time physicist, it was written down, set in type, and rushed into print in less than seven months, and opened with a sentence that could easily serve to introduce the subject of dowsing today: "Since men have been philosophizing, no subject more curious or important has been given their attention than the one treated in this work."

De Vallemont took issue with Malebranche's idea that the action of a dowsing rod was obviously due solely to nonmagnetic corpuscles just as a compass was commonly believed to respond to magnetic corpuscles, and that it was absurd to credit it to dowsers' particular temperaments, peculiar senses, or special gifts. Admitting that a magnetized compass certainly sought a northerly direction no matter who held it, he offered that this was because the *total cause* for its movement was inherent in the compass itself, whereas the movement of the rod was due to the *combination* of corpuscles emitted from water veins and minerals *and* the disposition of the dowser. If vapors rising from the earth alone affected the rod, then it should turn in anyone's hands.

Since certain persons were gifted with exceptional acuity of sight or hearing, why wouldn't it be possible, asked the priest, for human sensory organs connected to dowsing, whatever they were, also to be of varying sensitivity? Rare spirits, he wrote, could "accustom their bodies to do extraordinary things" like the priest mentioned by Saint Augustine in *The City of God*, who, similar to a fakir, was able to fall into an apparently unconscious state wherein he could be pinched, pricked with needles, or even burned without feeling any pain and at the same time be aware of whispered conversations around him. Perhaps, he suggested, the dowsing faculty lay entirely within dowsers themselves and that, therefore, the rod served only as its extension, just as a microscope or telescope served to extend one's range of vision.

Whatever the scientific explanation might turn out to be, de Vallemont was adamant that dowsing could be a boon to humankind. "The method of searching for water with the divining rod," he concluded, "is a discovery that cannot be overestimated, since it is surer and faster than all other methods practiced to this day. One must be a real enemy of public utility to decry so natural and noble a practice from which society can take so many advantages. One should concentrate on the cultivation of this gift and on developing persons whom Nature has favored with it instead of applying oneself to embarrassing them and to obfuscating a subject the secret natural mechanism of which is already difficult enough to explain."

Prohibition Fails

The appearance of de Vallemont's book with illustrations of dowsers practicing their art caused such a sensation in Parisian society that some of its leading lights decided to bring Aymar from the Dauphiné to the capital to see if what had been reported about him was true. The experimenters dug six holes in a garden, filling four of them, each with a different kind of metal, the fifth with gravel, and leaving the sixth empty. Grass sod was carefully replaced over the tops of the holes. Asked to hold his rod over the holes, Aymar found that it turned only over the gravel and the void but not over the metals.

The dowser was apparently equally unsuccessful in tracing criminals. A letter written by the procurator of the king to the deputy priest-general of the Oratory reported that in the Rue Saint Denis, where an archer sentry had been killed a few days before by fifteen thrusts with a sword, Aymar's rod would not turn over the exact spot upon which the victim had fallen. By way of an alibi the embarrassed Aymar offered that his rod would not move if the swordsman had been drunk or angry at the time of his assault or if he had already confessed his crime.

Aymar's reputation was further held up to question when, in answer to de Vallemont, Father Lebrun brought out his own long book, *Letters which Lay Bare the Illusion of Philosophers and Destroy Their Systems,* in which he provided a whole series of documented accounts of errors committed by the dowser. Some

103

of these had been communicated to Lebrun by his superior, Cardinal le Camus of Grenoble, who was adamant against the use of dowsing to decide moral questions and issued a *Mandamus* against this use of the rod on February 24, 1690.

Le Camus recounted how easily the affable Aymar could be inveigled into an awkward situation. A number of persons had persuaded him to walk along the streets of villages and towns and tell, by means of his art, whether the ladies of any house, wives or daughters, had "soiled their honor." The result of this dowsing-voyeurism, wrote Lebrun, "soon spread through the town, causing so much slander and calumny and creating such an uproar in several families, that the devil had good cause to rejoice."

Accepting Malebranche's "free and intelligent" cause for the rod's movement, Lebrun also asked why Aymar's instrument could turn in his hands at certain times but not at others. To him the only possible answer was that it *would move only in response to something the dowser himself wished to locate or determine.* If the rod had a "special intelligence," then corpuscles would no longer be necessary to its movement. His conclusion, said Lebrun, was justified by his experience with a young girl who, because she had heard dowsing was linked to the devil, was racked with scruples and doubts about her own dowsing skill. Lebrun admonished her to pray to God to preempt the rod's working for her if she felt the devil played any part in her success. After a two-day retreat in seclusion, the device would no longer respond for hers, indicating to Lebrun that "the *cause* which made the rod move could be accommodated to the desires of men and comply with their intentions."

The following year another priest, Claude-Francois Menestrier, entered the debate with an essay on dowsing appended to his book, *The Philosophy of Enigmatic Images.* Like Lebrun, Menestrier solicited considerable correspondence from anyone who could enlighten him about how, and to what end, dowsing was practiced. After putting questions to dowsers on every subject he could think of, Menestrier concluded that there was no question to which the rod could not provide an answer. It could evaluate the talents and capacities of individuals, their wealth, known or unknown, their sins and their number. While it was infallible for the present or past circumstances, it was less reliable in predicting the future.

His experiences persuaded Menestrier that the cause of the rod's movement could have nothing to do with the physical world as he knew it, and that dowsing was therefore to be rejected as being linked with realms infernal. The prelate was particularly horrified that the art should be used to determine innocence or guilt and wrote a reasoned and powerfully worded objection to this practice:

Let none say that this is a wise disposition of Providence and of God's justice to prevent certain crimes from remaining unpunished. For it is not permitted to justice to utilize directly or indirectly such indications either to absolve or to condemn, inasmuch as they are subject to great error and bad faith on the part of persons who claim they have such a talent. By dowsing with their rods, they can thus render false opinions

104

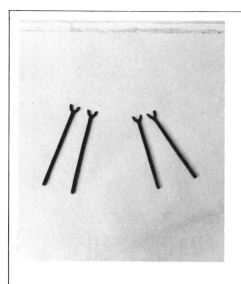

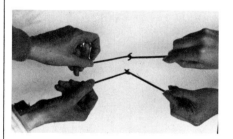

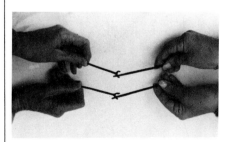

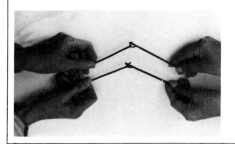

Lebrun referred to a strange dowsing practice involving the simultaneous use of four forked rods by two persons as described, albeit insufficiently, in Giambatista della Porta's compendium, Natural Magic, *that had come out in 1569. The method was supposed to be particularly advantageous in seeking out buried treasure.*

No way of illustrating this bizzare practice would have been possible had it not been for the author's fortuitous encounter with Cherie Andrade, a Mexican student, in Washington, D.C. During a conversation on dowsing, Cherie, who up to then had never discussed or heard of the subject while in the United States, exclaimed excitedly that her grandmother, Señora Maria Esther Audrade, a native of Nayarit Province in west-central Mexico, had a set of four forked rods made of steel which, when not in use, she always kept tied together with a skein of crimson wool. When Señora Andrade visited the American capital in December 1976, she brought the dowsing rods with her and, together with her granddaughter, demonstrated how to operate them.

The only known dowsing method utilizing the cooperation of two individuals requires some practice before one is able to move with one's partner together over the ground while keeping the rods, called "Spanish needles," in contact with one another. Successfully manipulated, the rods will move to left or right, up or down, to indicate the direction of the treasure sought. Señora Andrade believed that the rods pictured here had been handed down in her family for more than 400 years, indicating that at least one use of dowsing entered the North American continent shortly after the publication of della Porta's book. Today "Spanish" needles are known mostly in parts of the American West first colonized by Spaniards.

about individuals they seek to harm. When it is a question of the life, property or honor of persons, one must have proof and testimony.

Despite Menestrier's caution and Cardinal le Camus's order, dowsing spread like wildfire in France at the end of the seventeenth century. Aspirant dowsers had access to a textbook, first of its kind, on the subject, *Jacob's Rod, The Art of Finding Treasures, Springs, Boundaries, Metals, Mines and Other Hidden Things Through the Use of the Forked Stick.* Flatly stating that dowsing rods would "react over *anything* hidden, whatever their nature," it provided instructions on how to locate sources of underground water, metal pipes, with or without water flowing through them, buried objects of all kinds, and boundaries between adjacent parcels of land that had become effaced with the passage of time.

Dismayed by the popularity of the new instruction manual, Father Lebrun worked assiduously during the next decade to bring out another entire book against dowsing and its proponents, *Critical History of Superstitious Practices Which have Seduced Lay Persons and Embarrassed Savants,* published in 1702. The book included accolades by several theologians of note, including the Professor Royal of Philosophy at the University of Paris, and, in official science's first debut as a dowsing opponent, a solemn judgment by the secretary of the French Academy that praised Lebrun for combating practices that were "pure impostures or had causes unconnected to the physical world."

The approval given to Father Lebrun's tome, and the subsequent placement of de Vallemont's on the *Index Librorum Prohibitorum* by the Inquisition on October 26, 1701, should have made certain that dowsing would thenceforth be prohibited to Catholics. This was not the case. In the eighteenth century an enormous number of priors, abbots, curates, and even the Bishop of Grenoble not only approved and studied dowsing but used the art themselves, and the fortuitous discovery of electricity offered new hope that it might at last be scientifically explained.

CHAPTER 6

Dowsers Tested—
By Skeptics and Electricity

". . . and an even smaller one can be held by a mounted dowser . . ."

"Rare Articles"

By the beginning of the eighteenth century it was clear that a line had been drawn between two schools of thought concerning the dowsing mystery; already in print were many descriptions, interpretations, and contradictions about the action of a dowsing rod and the cause of its behavior that are still current today.

On one side of the controversy stood proponents of a *physical influence* directly affecting either dowsers or their rods; on the other, advocates of a purely *mental cause* that activated rods through its translation into bodily movement in the hands and arms.

Neither of the two camps were unanimous in what they thought dowsing could accomplish. Some believed the method capable of finding anything concealed or missing or of answering the most abstract question. Others considered the whole dowsing method at best uncertain, largely because it could not be explained and seemed to be within the purview of only a talented minority. At the same time, a clash continued between those holding that rod-divined replies came from a benevolent, though otherworldly, source, and those who attributed them to infernal realms skilled not only in meting out gross injustice to innocent victims but in exposing dowsers, however unwittingly, to metaphysical self-abuse.

In 1700, a thick German book written by Johann Gottfried Zeidler appeared, its very title, *Pantomysterium or News of the Year Concerning the Dowsing Rod as a Universal Tool of Knowledge Hidden from Man,* underscoring the enigmatic character of the searching art. Supporters of dowsing and naysayers alike could take comfort in its contents. On the one hand, it provided drawings and descriptions of most of the ways to hold a dowsing rod and many household objects which could be substituted for a forked stick. On the other, it sarcastically noted that everything written in Lebrun's *Illusions of Philosophers* about dowsing "fitted the whole subject as a fist fits an eye."

Hard on the heels of Zeidler came Theophil Albinus, whose book, *The Exposed Idol of the Dowsing Rod, or a Thorough Examination as to What has Happened to it Historically, If it is Physically Founded in Nature, and According to What Rules it Should be Used—From Love of Truth and as a Warning Against*

Frontispiece of Johann Gottfried Zeidler's Pantomysterium. *The illustration shows in the background the head of a dragon disgorging rods to waiting dowsers; in the midground, a dowser at work being driven by a tiny representation of the devil; to the right, a priest trying to exorcise a dowser while having his nose tweaked in return. In the foreground, a dowser holds a tray containing various implements suitable for dowsing, also described in the text, while at the same time tweaking the nose of "God's City," symbolically represented by a three-eyed globe. In the sky are represented a whip and a swarm of locusts, both potential scourges of the dowsing abomination.*

Flippancy, was published in Dresden with the approval of the Protestant Theological Faculty of Leipzig University. Its very first page, illustrating a clergyman in the act of unmasking a dowser to reveal him as the devil, forewarned readers of its censorious contents: "Let human temerity rest in peace, let it not search for what is not, let it not find that which is."

Unfazed by these schoolmen's opinions, miners, presumably in the best position to know its worth, continued to champion the utility of the dowsing rod. Abraham von Schonberg, whose post of *oberberghauptmann* in the mining hierarchy was at least equivalent to the military rank of colonel, issued a decree proclaiming that "because they were a 'rare article,' dowsers should be kept well-provided for so they might live for a long time." At the same time the fear was growing that a proliferation of unskilled neophytes—or worse, charlatans—was endangering the reputation of skilled dowsers. This fear prompted two of them to send a formal recommendation in 1738 to the Saxon Mining Directorate in Freiberg urging it to "enlist only the proficient and eschew the talentless who too often failed at their tasks." The warning was echoed in 1747 by J. G. Kiessling in his *Documented*

Account of Mining and Smelting in the Principality of Mannsfield, which insisted that "dowsing is well known in European mining circles and there is no better means of finding ore," but also cautioned: "One can safely depend on it only if it is practiced by an experienced man."

The troublesome problem remained of why dowsing for ore should work at all. In an attempt to resolve this, dowsers were increasingly put to test. In 1713, one thirty-eight-year old Freiberger, Hans Wolff, subjected to hours of scrutiny, startled his examiners with his ability to locate veins of metal simply by stretching forth his right arm, with its hand balled into a fist in front of him. When he approached a vein, his arm shook violently and when he came directly over it, the trembling extended to his whole body. "If you tremble so much near a vein," he was asked, "how can you work in mines where veins surround you at all times?"

Wolff's incisive answer, years ahead of its time, might have

With the approbation of both the Theological and Philosophical faculties in Leipzig, presented by Theophil Albinus, Dresden, Johann Jakob Winkler, 1704. The illustration shows a priest unmasking a dowser to reveal him as the devil.

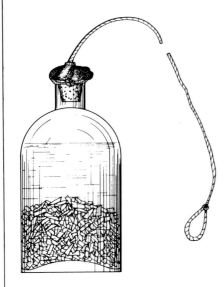

JONATHAN SMITH'S DOWSING ROD. *The "purselike" bag likely contained whatever material was being sought. The practice relied on the idea that the sample reacted or "bore witness" to the target object and thus was indispensable to the dowsing process. In 1889 Samuel Adams Goodman, Jr., of Smith County, Texas, applied in England for a patent on an "Improved Means of Detecting the Presence of Gold and Silver Underground." Reproduced in full-size below, its object as reported in the specification was to "enable precious metals to be discovered by a process commonly known as divination and it consists in a composition which has a strong attraction and affinity for gold and silver, the attraction resembling somewhat that of magnetism. If there are any precious metals in the immediate neighborhood, the flask will be attracted by such metals, and will move toward them at first, and will then vibrate, thus indicating the presence of the metal sought for." Such samples or "witnesses" are today attached to or incorporated in dowsing instruments or simply held in a dowser's hand. Modern theory holds that they help the dowser to "attune" to or "program the mind" for a searched-for object.*

gone far to clear up the mystery surrounding the dowsing art had it not been ignored for more than 250 years. "If I do not *orient my thoughts* specifically to finding a vein of ore," he said, "I get no reaction when I cross over a vein or work near one." This conclusion completely escaped the physicist J. G. Kruger of Helmsted in eastern Germany who, when Wolff was nearly seventy years old, performed his own experiments with a dowsing rod and concluded that the motion was attributable simply to a movement of the dowser's muscles and "if one adds superstition and outright cheating, the art is perfected."

Certain English mining experts remained no less confounded by the dowsing enigma than Kruger. The Derbyshire miner, William Hooson, solemnly related in his *Miner's Dictionary* that he had "been informed that the dignified author of this invention was a *German* and that, at last, he was deservedly hanged as a cheat." Still, he was not sure that the dowsing rod should be ruled out in prospecting, as he had also been told that a certain Jonathan Smith, living in the Low Peak near Worksworth, was "the most famous of any in my time for the instrument he had wherewith he pretended to discover mines." Smith possessed a rod of steel at the upper end of which a silk string was fastened. Tied to the other end of the string was a "small bag or purse with something therein, but what it was none knew but himself, for this was the chief secret."

Like Robert Boyle, whose opinion he quoted in full, Hooson finally decided that he had to have more convincing proof before reporting the divining rod as useful in prospecting for ore. "I am inclined much to the negative," he concluded, " 'til by a clear and plain experiment I shall be better informed."

Had Hooson ever met her, he might finally have been converted by an English noblewoman, Lady Milbanke, whose activities with the rod so irritated her son-in-law, the famous poet Lord Byron, that, following her death, he wrote acrimoniously that she had "at last gone to a place where she could no longer dowse." In 1772, while sojourning in southern France, she heard a popular tale of a well having been discovered generations previously by a boy who cried out in pain each time he passed over water flowing underground. "This was held by myself," Lady Milbanke wrote, "and the family I was with in utter contempt and believed as much as the tradition in England that Saint Dustan's head rolled to the spot where Durham Abbey was to be built and dedicated to him."

Later she visited the Marquis D'Ansouis, owner of a chateau in a tract of mountainous country north of Durance, who was building an aqueduct to convey water to his home from a spring half a league away. The spring would never have been discovered, said the marquis, were it not for a local who knew how to dowse. Because his guests chortled at the idea, he arranged for a demonstration. As Lady Milbanke described it: "The man, quite a peasant in manners and appearance, produced some twigs of different sizes and strength cut from a hazel. He held the ends of the twigs between each forefinger and thumb, with the vertex pointing downwards. Standing where there was no water, the baguette remained motionless; walking gradually to the spot where the spring was underground, the twig was sensibly affected; and as he approached the spot, began to turn round."

Excited by the demonstration, the witnesses all tried the dowsing rod to see if they could get a reaction but only Lady Milbanke was successful. "No sooner," she wrote, "did I hold the twig as directed, than it began to move as with him, which startled me so much that I dropped it, and felt considerably agitated. I was, however, induced to resume the experiment and found the effect perfect."

Lady Milbanke's conversion to dowsing is only known through her correspondence with Charles Hutton, the learned editor of the Royal Society's *Transactions* who in 1803 translated a 4-volume French work, *Recreations in Mathematics and Natural Philosophy*, which held that dowsing was a fraud beneath contempt. Challenged by Lady Milbanke to witness a demonstration of her ability, Hutton invited her to his house on Woolwich Common where, as Hutton related: "In the places where I had good reason to know that no water was to be found, the rod was always quiescent; but in the other places, where I knew there was water below the surface, the rod turned slowly and regularly."

111

As a result of his observations and his own subsequent experimentation Hutton, in an 1814 edition of the *Recreations*, set the record straight:

Notwithstanding the incredulity above expressed relative to the indication of springs by the motion of the baguette, or divining rod; there appears to exist such evidences of the reality of that motion as it seems next to impossible to be questioned. The editor of this edition, in common with many other persons, notwithstanding the numerous accounts of that motion which have been published to the world, and attested by multitudes of eye-witnesses, was still incredulous, and remained satisfied that there must have been some trick, used in making the experiment, by which spectators might be deceived, and imposed on. Such evidence of the motion in question has now been exhibited as leaves little or no doubt on the minds of all the spectators as to the reality of that motion.

In her correspondence with Hutton, Lady Milbanke, aware of the scholar's inability to offer any explanation for the dowsing reaction, sympathized: "I lament you can throw no light on this extraordinary circumstance, which has ever strongly excited my curiosity as to the cause of it, but hitherto I have met with none who have gone beyond a vague conjecture. A very sensible and well-informed physician *imagined* it might be occasioned by some singular effect of electricity on my frame, but could not satisfy himself of the certainty of his conjecture."

The Beginnings of an Electrical Theory

The physician to whom she referred could well have been an extraordinary Frenchman, Pierre Thouvenel, who before reaching thirty had carved so excellent a reputation as a practitioner in Paris that he numbered among his patients many distinguished personages at court and in society. A good decade before the discovery of electrical current, Thouvenel had become convinced that dowsing was somehow connected with a subterranean electrical phenomenon associated with flowing water.

In 1780, the doctor began to study Barthelemy Bléton, a young herdsman and water-diviner who (like so many dowsers)

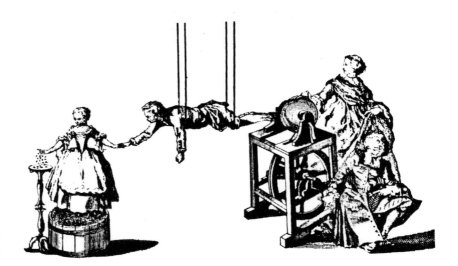

Rendering of old engraving of an experiment with "human electricity." (Source unknown)

The "Bishop's Rule"

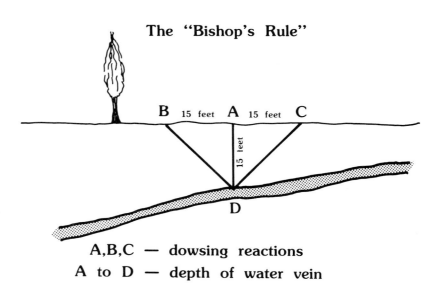

B 15 feet A 15 feet C

15 feet

D

A,B,C — dowsing reactions
A to D — depth of water vein

Illustration of how Bléton held his rod. From La Verge du Jacob, *1693. This rod was in use in Germany before that date since a letter written by a "distinguished physician" to Dr. Pierre Thouvenel states that "some in Germany use a simple rod placed across the back of the hand or, like Bléton, on the two index fingers."*

hailed from the Dauphiné, where he performed countless tests for the Bishop of Grenoble, some of them while perched atop a high ladder. The churchman purported to have discovered that Bléton would get a dowsing reaction not only while standing directly over a water vein but at a given distance on either side of it that seemingly corresponded to the vein's depth below ground. Though the observation applied only to a small minority of wells dug under the bishop's supervision, its apparent simplicity was so appealing that ever since it has been incorporated into dowsing annals as the "Bishop's Rule."

It was only in deference to local custom and to those who wished to put his talent to a test, that Bléton, perfectly capable since early childhood of detecting flowing water through the unpleasant effects it produced in his body, used a dowsing instrument of an unusual configuration. To the common forked stick, he preferred a straight rod barely bent into a slight arc and placed on the tops of his two outstretched index fingers. Over the flowing water the rod would rotate on its axis from thirty to eighty times per minute depending, as Bléton surmised, upon the rate of flow.

Thouvenel convinced himself of Bléton's dowsing ability by eliciting his assistance in locating the still famous mineral waters near Contrexéville, at the foot of the Vosges Mountains. Overnight the discovery turned the sleepy little town into a tourist resort for the wealthy and led to the doctor's appointment by the crown as Inspector General for Mineral Waters, charged with writing a history of their past and of assuring their future development.

In his research with Bléton, Thouvenel was joined by Dr. Nicolas Jadelot who, only in his twenties, already had a chair at the University of Nancy Medical School and was writing an 8-volume compendium on inexpensive medicines, *Pharmacopoeia for the Poor.* The two physicians sought to get to the bottom of the supposed electrical tie to dowsing by touching Bléton with "recently electrified magnetic compositions" to see if they could "short circuit" the rotation of the rod or his fingers and the

113

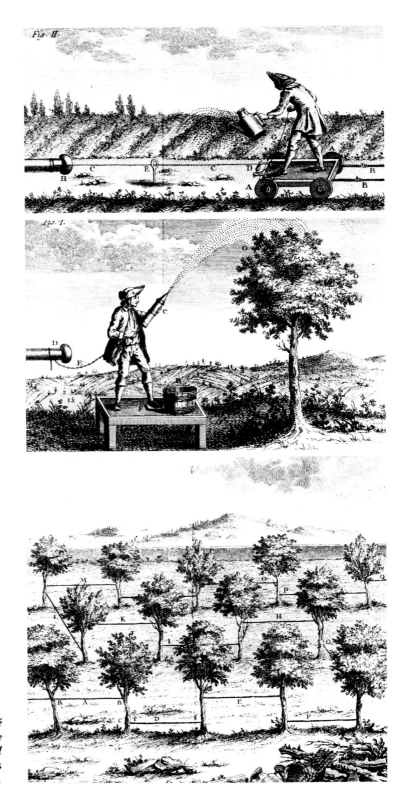

Experiments by the Abbé Bertholon to electrically stimulate the growth of trees, as illustrated in his book De L'Eléctricité des Végétaux, *Lyon, 1783.*

convulsions in his body. In this they were successful but, like many subsequent investigators, they overlooked the role potentially played by the power of suggestion to which Malebranche had so clearly called attention a century before. Thus they did not take into account the fact that Bléton could have just as easily responded to the experimenters' innuendo as to any physical effects produced by the taction.

Inasmuch as the study of electricity and magnetism and their effect on living things was a new scientific passion of the day, the doctors' explanation for the dowsing mystery was natural. Abbé Bertholon was soon to publish his *De L'Electricité des Vegetaux* in which he claimed to have invented an electrovegetometer and to be able to spur the growth of crops and trees by watering them while he was electrified but isolated from the ground. At the same time the Viennese medical genius, Franz Anton Mesmer, was startling Paris with his *baquet*, a huge wooden tub filled with "magnetized" water that, properly oriented, purported to alleviate and even cure a host of illnesses. Their research may have encouraged Thouvenel. At any rate, he became so impressed with Bléton's ingenuously assured skill and with his fellow researcher's conversion from total skepticism to complete certainty about dowsing that, in 1781, he published a 304-page book: *Physical and Medicinal Memoir Showing the Evident*

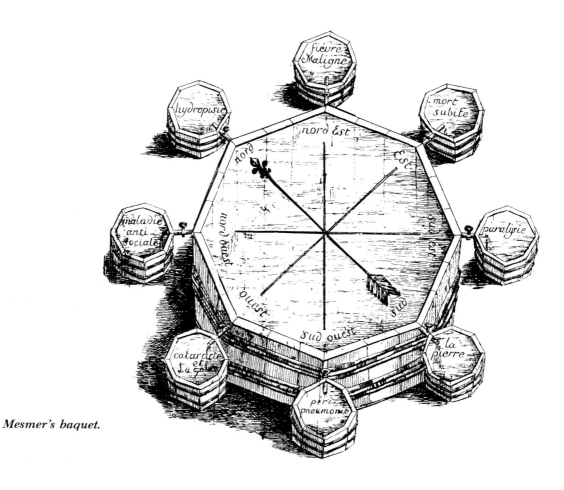

Mesmer's baquet.

115

Connections Between Phenomena of the Dowsing Rod, Magnetism and Electricity.

In this work, Thouvenel for the first time replaced the *sympathetic attraction* and *corpuscles* of earlier theorists with *effluvia of an electric nature* as the prime cause of the dowsing rod's movement. Their electromotive power must affect dowsers in air, said Thouvenel, just as they would be affected in water by Surinam torpedo-fish or electric eels. The appearance of his book once more startled the learned world in Paris and resulted in the formation of a study commission composed of five academics (including Guillotin, the doctor who suggested the use of an instrument of decapitation which was ultimately put to work at his own, and all subsequent, French executions).

On May 25, 1782, a member of the commission led the blindfolded Bléton along an alley in a garden off the Faubourg Saint Denis, under which ran a lead pipe that conducted water to a small fountain. While Bléton accurately followed the course of the pipe, the observers were amazed to see his slightly arced rod spinning crazily on his fingers.

The commission's was only one of a score of tests to which Bléton was submitted while in Paris. In another, reported in the *Journal de Paris* and carried out in the Luxembourg Gardens under the aegis of the king's Intendant General for Buildings, Bléton easily traced the winding course of an underground aqueduct far out into the countryside. The intendant general declared that, were official charts of this aqueduct with its 15,000 separate bends ever to be lost, it could be accurately recharted solely on the basis of Bléton's almost mathematically perfect indications.

The commission resubmitted the dowser, this time blindfolded, to the same test before a crowd of 500 onlookers, including ministers of government, ambassadors of foreign powers, clerics, scientists, and jurists. Impressed, one newspaper commented: "Bléton has been submitted to the most rigorous examination that incredulity, even prejudice, can devise and it has only produced more amazement, and stimulated more conviction, about his ability."

As in the past, other authorities, loathe to admit the potential of dowsing, were determined to prove him wrong. One of them, the Abbé Mongez, subjected Bléton to a series of public trials the atmosphere of which was so pervaded with ill will that a reporter for the *Paris Monthly Review* felt compelled to write: "It is certainly possible that even honest zeal for the discovery of imposture or enthusiasm may be exerted in a manner not perfectly adapted to the discovery of truth. It is observed by all that Bléton is uncommonly timorous and easily disconcerted, even so far as to suspend his impressions. This we can well conceive, be his talent ever so real. The very talent seems to announce a sensibility of nerves that may render him peculiarly susceptible of perturbation. Who has not seen schoolboys of the most retentive memories lose the remembrance of the best learned lesson by being intimidated."

As usual, physicists could come to no agreement on Bléton's capacities. Sigaud de la Fond affirmed that, from his examination

of the evidence, Bléton was no charlatan. On the other hand,
Jacques-Alexandre-César Charles who, with his brothers, was
building a hydrogen balloon in which they were to rise more than
a mile above the earth the following year, devised another
experiment. Eager to demonstrate that Thouvenel's electrical
theory was nonsense, they had Bléton stand above a source of
flowing water on a platform electrically isolated from the ground.
Bléton's rod would not turn. Without informing the dowser,
Charles connected the platform by wire to the ground and, when
the rod still would not turn, Charles told assembled spectators
that the whole of dowsing was nothing but hocus-pocus. What
escaped Charles's attention, just as much as Thouvenel's before
him, was the power of suggestion. Atop the platform Bléton could
easily have *believed* his dowsing talent to be blocked by his
isolation.

It was left not to skeptical priests or physicists to dispose of
Thouvenel and Bléton but to Joseph-Jerome de Lalande whose
discovery, at the age of twenty-one, of the earth's distance from
the moon had already won him admission to the Berlin Academy
of Sciences and a post as adjunct astronomer at the Paris
Academy. In a letter to the *Journal des Savants,* a publication
well known for the arrogant tone of its criticism, he opined:
"Thouvenel was not sufficiently calm to admit the reasoning of his
adversaries or even to observe a tawdry charlatanry of which he
was the dupe. He was completely seduced by Bléton's skill in
causing a piece of curved metal to turn in his hands, not
perceiving that this movement has a simple mechanical cause.
For if one places on two fingers a rod of metal curved into an arc
in such a way that the summit of the arc is lower than its two
extremities, but that the whole is in near equilibrium, the
slightest drawing together of the fingers, were it a distance no
longer than one *ligne,* would suffice for the extremities, in turn,
to move and for the summit of the arc to come to the top. If one
separates them, the summit will instantly descend and, with a
similar alteration, the movement can continue as long as one
might judge it fitting. To accomplish this, a practiced individual
needs only the slightest trembling movement which is hardly to
be perceived if one is not warned about it." Lalande sarcastically
ridiculed Thouvenel's opinions on the dowsing rod and purported
to show how Bléton could have artfully manipulated it as easily as
any magician.

Lalande nowhere addressed the crucial question as to
whether this trembling was voluntary or involuntary. Because
blinking one's eyes is usually an involuntary action, this does not
mean that one cannot blink them on purpose. As in the 1700s,
dowsers today, aware that they can *cause* a reaction in a dowsing
instrument, take special pains *not to cause* any motion in the rod,
but wait until the motion occurs nonvolitionally.

As so often in the history of science, Thouvenel's spirit of
sincere inquiry did not carry the day against "authority." The
astronomer's verdict on the dowsing rod was all that one author,
Henri Decremps, needed to include a chapter on dowsing in his
book, *White Magic Unveiled,* giving precise instructions how
anyone at all could duplicate Bléton's feat with prestidigitation.

117

Decremps's allegations and scathing conclusion were eagerly read the following year in England when the same book appeared under the title *The Conjurer Unmasked, with Directions for the Tricks of the Divining Rod.*

So bitter were the attacks on Thouvenel that his closest friends begged him to break off all research on dowsing. Convinced of the importance of a question that cried out for solution and fervently hoping that a new laboratory instrument would soon be invented that could prove his idea that electrical effluvia came straight out of the ground, he rebuffed their advice.

First to conceive of the dowsing phenomenon as a new branch of science, Thouvenel wrote: "The whole phenomenon of the rotation of the rod on the fingers of a 'turner' is the most inconceivable of the whole of this marvelous physics. Will it one day become calculable through geometric procedure and susceptible of rigorous demonstration?"

Despite his being named Inspector General for Military Hospitals, and thus, before the age of forty, having attained nearly every distinction with which a French physician of his day could expect to be honored, Thouvenel decided he had to find an atmosphere more receptive to his research. The bloody horror of the French Revolution which took the lives of several of his intimate friends reinforced his decision and during its inexorable progress he emigrated to Italy.

Italian Scientists For and Against the Rod

With the help of Bléton who had accompanied him into exile and died soon after, Thouvenel discovered still another dowser from the Dauphiné by the name of Pennet, who used a dowsing instrument identical to that of his countryman. After performing successful experiments with the new man, Thouvenel sought to persuade distinguished Italian scientists of the day to repeat his own observations.

He first addressed Alberto Fortis, an Augustinian abbot who had given up monastery life for the more worldly pursuits of natural science that were to lead to his appointment as permanent secretary of the National Institute of Italy founded by Napoleon Bonaparte. At first Fortis's attitude toward the possibility of dowsing as expressed in a series of letters to Thouvenel was, much to the French researcher's exasperation, one of unreserved hilarity. One evening Fortis was invited to dinner in Naples where, to his great surprise, Thouvenel was the guest of honor. When the company began to question the Frenchman about the marvels of his human mineral and water-finder, Thouvenel could not help noticing Fortis's embarrassment.

"I know perfectly well that you are hardly my coreligionist in this matter," he half-jestingly told the abbot.

"My religion, Sir, has always been that of proven truths," replied Fortis quietly. "If you can prove to me the reality of Pennet's strange ability, then you can count on my becoming a proselyte because, at that point, my habitual prejudice will no longer prevent me from discussing this truth with other incredulous brethren."

118

The dowser Pennet, subject of Dr. Pierre Thouvenel in Italy, as depicted in Della Raddomanzia Ossia Electrometria Animale *by Carlo Amoretti, Milano, 1808.*

When Thouvenel accepted the challenge, the abbot requested Vincenzo Comi, a young physicist, to go to Chiaja, near Naples, and bury a small sack of silver coins called *carlini* in the garden of Fortis's home. After Pennet unerringly located the money, Fortis was deeply moved. As he recalled: "I confess that this experiment done with all imaginable caution to prevent cheating so convinced me that I reddened when I recalled that I previously mocked something about which I knew nothing."

Fortis, whose account of an extended journey taken with Thouvenel and Pennet throughout southern Italy makes just as entertaining a tale today as when it was written, was so repeatedly offered proof of Pennet's dowsing ability that he came to three important conclusions about dowsing tests.

The first was embodied in his criticism of Thouvenel for "too readily consenting to experiments on small isolated deposits of metals which may fail because of the limited volume of substances buried." This was particularly true if linked to his second conclusion that sudden variations in atmospheric conditions appeared markedly to affect Pennet's ability. Third and importantly, Fortis felt strongly that Pennet was affected by the "moral climate" in which he worked. The attitudes of experimenters were of the greatest importance to the success or failure of the experiments, the abbot maintained, and added that Pennet succeeded best when he was tested in a lighthearted fashion rather than under conditions of great solemnity.

"Finally," concluded Fortis, "if the facts here reported are insufficient irrevocably to establish Monsieur Thouvenel's theory, they should at least be sufficient to enable anyone wishing to be called a sensible man to stop mocking such experiments, for derision will never help in the development of true knowledge."

Thouvenel also turned to one of Europe's most renowned biologists, Lazzaro Spallanzani, a professor at the University of Pavia, whose innovative work in culturing microscopic organisms paved the way for Henri Pasteur in the nineteenth century. Because Thouvenel knew that Spallanzani had referred to Pennet's dowsing feats as "the dreams of a sick mind and fantasies of a bad novel," he had Pennet hand deliver a letter to the professor so he could talk to the dowser in person.

As a result of his meeting with Pennet, Spallanzani, reconsidering his hasty opinion, took the dowser to places in Pavia where known currents of water flowed below the city and was surprised when Pennet found their exact locations. At the orphanage, and in the courtyard of the Botta mansion, Spallanzani first saw Pennet seized with strong convulsions. "His pulse more than doubled," he recounted, "his pupils dilated and his curved rod moved on his fingers as if animated by a subtle force."

Spallanzani was sufficiently impressed with Pennet's initial efforts to organize a public examination. At his orders four anvils weighing more than 1,000 Italian pounds were lashed together and buried one foot deep in the courtyard of the Leano palace by three workmen sworn to secrecy. Led into the 250-foot-square courtyard at 10:30 the next morning, Pennet walked slowly toward an area where earth had been disturbed. As he moved

119

across it, his rod made not the slightest motion. Some yards further on he got a reaction, checked the location twice more, then sat down on a low wall as if lost in thought. At a wave from Spallanzani, one of the workmen dug a hole at the spot where Pennet had been standing and immediately struck the anvils which were hauled out of the earth to the amazement of all present.

At this point, one might have thought that Pennet would have deserved a rousing cheer. Instead, a man in the crowd shouted coarsely: "It's all trickery! He finds the anvils because he's hidden a magnet in his clothing!" In answer, the dowser removed everything but his underdrawers and requested that his garments be scrupulously inspected to see if any magnet had been concealed within them. None was found. As Spallanzani confessed: "His aplomb made the greatest impact on my spirit." Even after several more successful public tests, Spallanzani had to

Dowsing rods illustrated by Carlo Amoretti in his Della Raddomanzia Ossia Electrometria Ammale. *Some of the rods seem to be related to those of the Swiss dowsers, Treadwell and Rupp, and to the Soviet rod illustrated on page* 232.

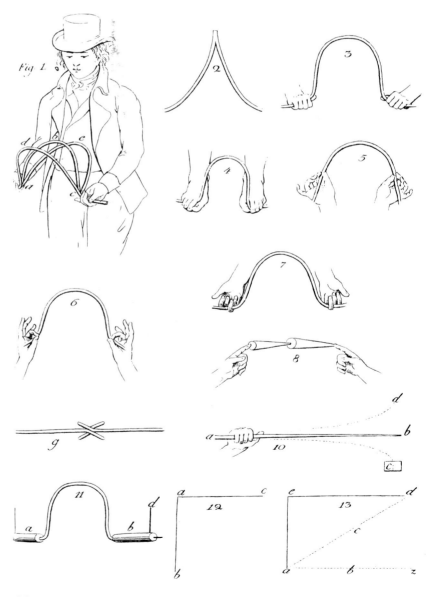

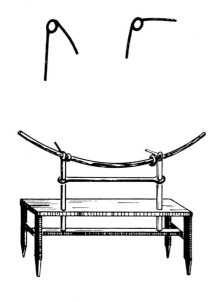

Device used by Father Stella to test Pennet. Two glass rods were embedded in a table. A third was tied to them with silk ribbons to help keep them stable. Two loops of iron wire were stuck into the tips of the vertical rods to serve as a support for the curved dowsing rod which was notched at the points of contact to prevent all but a rotary motion.

report a continued and ugly skepticism on the part of many persons who observed them. "Despite every precaution," he noted, "it was alleged that he'd been at the test site beforehand, that he'd bribed the workers for information, that he'd used sign language or some other secret signal to communicate with them, that his convulsions were artificially produced. One of the doubters was so ferocious in his opinion that he even heatedly refused my invitation to witness any future tests."

Whether the negative opinions finally held sway with Spallanzani himself is not known but, in the summer of 1791, he somewhat unaccountably wrote to Fortis that, his great astonishment at what he had witnessed notwithstanding, he was still not ready to consider the experiments entirely convincing. Nor is it known why, a short time later, Spallanzani finally harshly declared himself against the reality of "hydroscopes," as he termed dowsers, without providing any reason. Fortis who published the letter in which Spallanzani expressed his irrevocable opinion, added in a supplementary note that he could hardly believe the professor's "awful diatribe which has done the greatest wrong, in the minds of honest and intelligent persons, to the celebrated Pavia professor, while proving nothing about the ever honest procedures of the French scientist, Thouvenel."

A key link in the chain of dowsing research spanning the end of the eighteenth and beginning of the nineteenth centuries was provided by Carlo Amoretti, conservator of the Ambrosian Library in Milan and editor of a leading journal in natural science. Amoretti, whose own father had been a dowser, devoted part of his life to researching the phenomenon that culminated in his enormous volume, *Rhabdomancy or Animal Electrometry.*

When he learned of Thouvenel's theory, he suggested that Pennet be sent to Udine on Italy's northeast frontier, where a Father Stella was using a machine that could electrify objects and even human beings, to see if the priest could detect anything electrically peculiar about the dowser. A forerunner of the machine developed in the nineteenth century by James Wimshurst, the generator, when manually activated, built up an electrical charge collected on a brass cylinder which could be relayed by means of two brass chains eight feet long to the hands of a subject to be electrified.

Aware that Pennet, like Bléton, had been accused of sleight-of-hand, Stella wondered whether the dowser's power to move the rod, based on a supposed electricity produced in his body, could be demonstrated when the rod was not in direct contact with his fingers. Pennet was ordered to touch the protruding ends of wire loops holding a dowsing rod on a special support built partly of glass rods to isolate it from the ground. A few seconds after electricity was generated and transferred to Pennet's body, the rod was seen to turn upon itself as many as forty times in succession. Somehow Pennet could cause the rod to move simply by touching the metal with which it was in contact.

Amoretti, observing the procedure, related that the rod would also sometimes raise itself a quarter of a turn and more and, apparently defying the laws of gravity, remain suspended in the air. When the rod was in motion, Pennet was simultaneously

121

afflicted, just as over a dowsing zone, by a racing pulse, an excess of body heat, twitching muscles, and dilated pupils as verified on numerous occasions by physicians in attendance. Inexplicably, when chains linking him to the generator were held in Pennet's hands, or attached to his feet, the rod would turn in one direction; when put on his head in the shape of a crown, in the other.

It seems that, while the electrified Pennet was able to produce a rotatory motion in the rod, other subjects could not duplicate the feat. Several skeptics, insisting that the motion effected by Pennet could be caused by his bending the vertical glass rods with pressure, actually grew so desperate in their efforts to prove their assertion that they broke them. Especially puzzling to the experimenters was the fact that Pennet's ability to move the rod varied according to weather conditions.

The pioneering efforts of Thouvenel to relate the dowsing faculty to electricity, though not conclusive, renewed consideration about some kind of natural energy in the body that the "animal magnetism" of Franz Anton Mesmer and the "animal electricity" of Luigi Galvani had already anticipated. Thouvenel's own name for it was "organo-electricity" and it was to become the focus of attention by several dowsing researchers in the nineteenth century.

Galvani's experiments with frog legs and electricity. From Abbé Bertholon, De l'Electricité des Végétaux, *Lyon, 1783.*

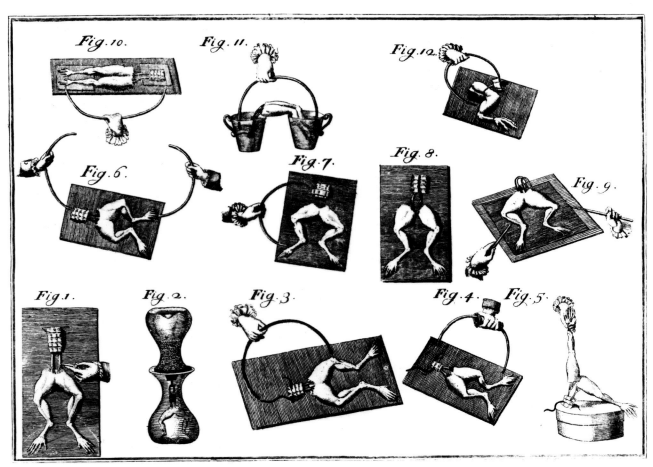

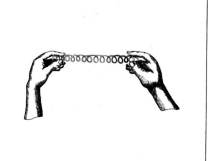

CHAPTER 7

Physical or Sidereal:
A Pendular Question

". . . a coiled spring held between the forefingers and the thumbs . . ."

A Dangerous Frontier

While sojourning with the dowser Pennet in the Appenine village of Gualdo, Abbot Fortis was introduced for the first time to a practice that was as new to him as it was strange. A man secretly hid a handful of silver coins under a heavy blanket. One of his friends then appeared holding a cube of pyrite hanging on a silken string between his thumb and his index finger. As he moved it over the blanket, at one spot it began to swing in a tight elliptical pattern. When he retracted it, the motion ceased. The blanket was then stripped back to reveal the money lying directly at the spot over which the pendulum had been in motion.

When he returned home, Fortis, seeking an explanation for what he had seen, began experimenting and was surprised that his own "stone of the Incas," as pyrite was known, seemed to be affected not only by silver but by a variety of metals each of which would cause it to swing in a peculiar pattern.

When Fortis drew the phenomenon to the attention of a clerical colleague, the priest recalled that as far back as the first century A.D., the Roman writer, Marcellinus, had referred to a tripod, ornately decorated with snakes and other animals symbolic of divination, from which hung a ring on a thread. Used in conjunction with a circle showing the letters of the Latin alphabet on the circumference of the tripod, the ring was said to swing toward one letter or another in succession and thus spell out answers to questions whenever the thoughts of certain people were ritually focused on it.

That the practice had survived into the Middle Ages was also evident to Fortis from a bull issued in 1326 by Pope John the 22nd against the "use of a ring to obtain answers in the manner of the Devil," and a 1553 description of a peasant holding a threaded ring over a vessel half full of water and carrying them across country as an alternative to a dowsing rod.

Why, wondered Fortis, did a pendulum on the one hand appear to respond to emanation from a *physical* body such as a metallic substance or an underground water vein and, on the other, to a simple act of mentation, an effort of the mind, or *psyche,* as the soul was known in Greek?

At the beginning of the nineteenth century the problem came to the attention of Johann Wilhelm Ritter, a younger

123

Roman divinatory device with ring-pendulum as illustrated in a Ph.D. dissertation, "On the History and Theory of the Sideric Pendulum," by Father Andreas Resch, Innsbruck, Austria, 1967.

member of the Bavarian Academy of Sciences, who today is recognized as the father of electrochemistry, the discoverer of ultraviolet light, and the inventor of the dry cell battery. In 1806 Ritter, whose enthusiasm for dangerous laboratory work cost him one eye, one ear, and part of his nose, received a letter from a fellow scientist traveling in Italy revealing that one Francesco Campetti living near Lago di Garda appeared to possess a wholly inexplicable power to find water and minerals under the earth's surface.

Excited by the report of what to him was a completely unheard-of phenomenon, Ritter immediately applied for a Bavarian Royal Government travel order to proceed to Italy and study Campetti's ability. His request, stressing the potential importance of his research mission for physics, was supported by the romantic philosopher and superintendent of the Bavarian Mines, Francis Xavier von Baader who, like Hegel and Goethe, was to become fascinated with Ritter's new research project.

On November 21, 1806, Ritter set forth to Italy where, working with an Italian scientist, Cannella, who had performed many successful experiments with the "second Pennet," he became convinced that Campetti could do all that was claimed for him. After watching Campetti put to test by Abbé Fortis, Ritter felt that "having seen everything I was looking for, I was faced with a whole new world in physics." The experience was for him one of "fulfilling wonder: actually seeing for oneself something that cannot equate to hearsay however many times it may be reported."

In Como, Ritter was received by Volta with great warmth and hospitality. Though he was impressed with the Italian professor's "childlike vitality," he could not arouse Volta's interest in the dowsing feats of Campetti or get him to say anything about the subject of dowsing. This he reported in a series of letters to his close friend Karl von Hardenberg, brother of the philosopher and romantic poet, Novalis.

Ritter obtained permission from the dowser's parents to take him back to Munich for study. Elated, he felt this accomplishment to be "a triumph for science over prejudice and a new advance in the study of Dr. Thouvenel's 'subterranean electrometry.'" On his way home the scientist detoured to Milan where Amoretti introduced him to a series of seemingly inexplicable effects produced by inert substances and living matter on a number of delicately fashioned pendular devices, some supported by solid dowels, rather than threads, held between two digits of one hand.

To avoid exposing Campetti to the Munich public, Ritter installed the dowser in his own home where, before an audience of intrigued companions, he began to work out how dowsing rods or pendulums reacted to materials. In vain Ritter tried to get the same reactions as his experimental subject from the two instruments, succeeding only when, one day, Campetti suddenly grasped his shoulder. Subsequently, he was able to get dowsing responses unaided and became the first to record that the dowsing gift could apparently be communicated by touch.

The fact that pendulums nearly always swung in a specific

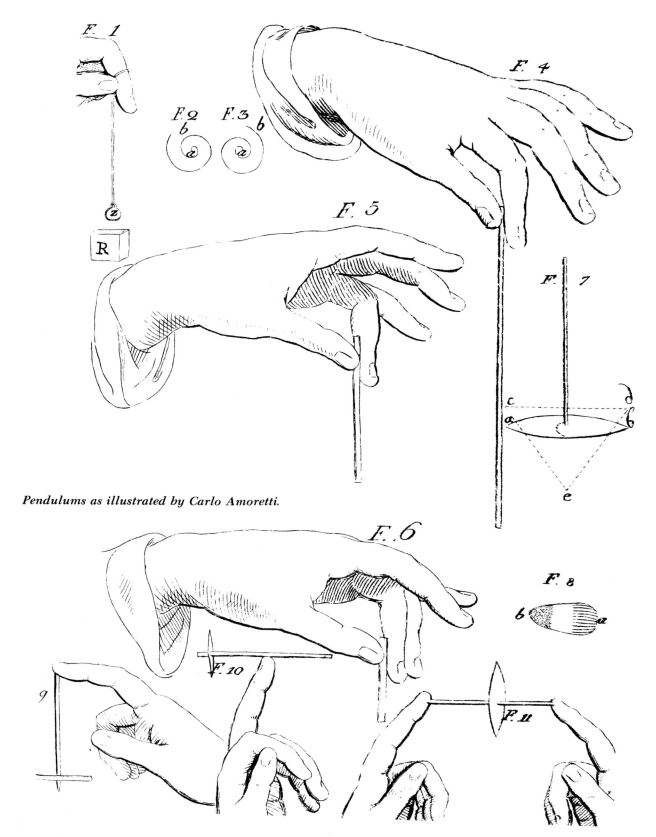

Pendulums as illustrated by Carlo Amoretti.

125

pattern over given substances suggested to Ritter that each kind of matter contained within it energy of a special signature detectable by the simple instrument. Over the north pole of a magnet the pendulum would begin to describe an elliptical clockwise motion which, as it speeded up, became circular, as it would when held over a piece of zinc or tin, near the obtuse end of an egg, the stem end of a fruit, and various parts of the human body including the palm of the hand. The south pole of the same magnet a piece of copper or aluminum, the tapering end of an egg, the side of a fruit opposite the stem, and the back of a hand would cause a counterclockwise rotation. Other substances provoked more complicated patterns of movement or a series of backward and forward swings which, when they had attained a specific number, would inexplicably cease.

Believing he had encountered a new property in the human body, Ritter used the pendulum to examine its every part. Salacious academic gossip in Munich had it that, at the Ritter residence, the pendulum swung far into the night over "the delicate parts of nubile and naked females," to quote one reporter who harshly attacked Ritter's work in a vitriolic book, *Conspiracy Against Common Sense.*

Because various parts of the organic bodies produced pendular movements in opposing directions, Ritter, likening them to magnets, now began to refer to their *polar* nature. In coming to this conclusion he was influenced by Baader's friend, the philosopher Frederich Wilhelm Joseph von Schelling, who insisted that the fundamental aim of science was not to study matter by mechanically breaking it apart and reducing it to its smallest indivisible units but intuitively to grasp the essence of natural functions and interpret how they fit into the universe as a whole. There was, said Schelling, a "force" in nature that could be revealed mechanically, chemically, electrically, magnetically, and also *vitally.* The pendulum, he believed, was able through the sensitivity of its operator to detect how this force expressed

"Swing configuration of the pendulum as an expression of musical intervals. The top row illustrates unison intervals, the middle row, octaves, and the lower row, fifths. These patterns are also of material significance in the use of the sidereal pendulum." From Count Carl von Klinckowstroem's Die Wünschelrute (see Bibliography).

126

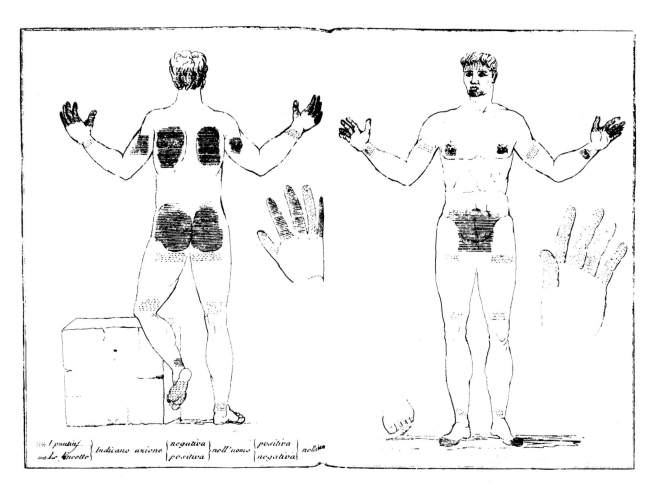

l puntini. } *Indicano azione* { *negativa* } *nell'uomo* { *positiva* } *nella*
Le linette. } { *positiva* } { *negativa* }

Polarities in the body as first visually illustrated by Carlo Amoretti.

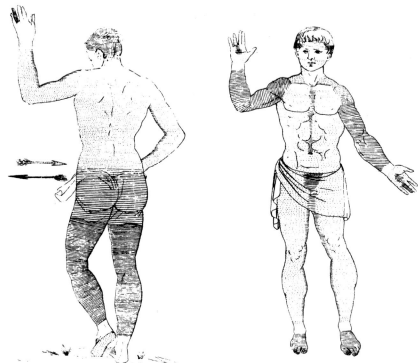

127

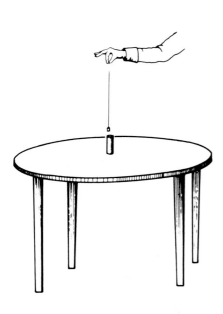

itself in matter and to confirm the existence of a basic *polarity* throughout the universe from which all organic and inorganic processes were derived.

In the pendulum's antics Ritter also detected not only *rotation* but *nutation*, a libratory motion similar to the nodding of a top. To Hans Christian Ørsted, professor of physics and chemistry at the University of Copenhagen, he wrote: "What we have, then, are the celestial movements themselves here repeated in microcosm. Could it be that the whole organism of the universe is reflected in the human body?"

At the time, Ørsted was preoccupied with laboratory experiments that sought an answer to a nagging question: What is the real nature of electricity? Ten years after Ritter's death in 1810, his efforts bore fruit when the Danish scientist laid the basis for electromagnetic theory with the discovery that electrical current flowing through a wire could deflect a magnetized compass needle. To him, as to many of his scientific colleagues, it seemed that, in his preoccupation with the pendulum, Ritter was straying from science's "highway," built with paving stones of observable fact, into byways of philosophical speculation or even mysticism. He therefore did not deign to reply.

Other scientists protested that hand-held pendulums did not move in response to physical emanations from matter but simply to an action, voluntary or involuntary, on the part of their operators. Wrote one: "It is hardly strange that bodies suspended on a string orient themselves in a manner that accords with the fantasy of the experimenter." Unimpressed with the criticism, Ritter replied: "Any supposition of error in these tests is easy to put to rest due to the fact that, even if the pendulum is given a mechanical movement contrary to the one it would naturally take, it will change back to the latter as soon as the mechanical force is no longer applied."

This exchange, with regard to a device no more complicated than a mechanic's nut hanging at the end of a bit of twine, represented yet another skirmish in the ongoing battle that has lasted to this day over the question: What actually moves the pendulum, or a rod for that matter, in the dowsing process?

To Ritter the answer was a combination of influences. Occult forces of an "animate" nature, similar but not necessarily equivalent to electricity, that were present in living organisms, dowsers included, were also imprisoned in inorganic substances. All of them could interact to cause motions in a dowsing device not only when it was in close proximity to an object under inspection but *at a considerable distance from it.*

This view borrowed, wittingly or unwittingly, from an idea of Mesmer's expounded in his doctoral dissertation that anticipated contemporary medical findings relating planetary influence to such phenomena as the outbreaks of epidemics, the conduct of the inmates in lunatic asylums, the state of health of patients (especially hypochondriacs), and the propensity of blood to clot quickly or slowly during surgical operations. Realizing that "modifications of the air," such as sound waves, could influence not only the organs of hearing but the whole of the body,

Mesmer asked: "If we assume that there exists a certain celestial power that insinuates itself in every particle of the body to its whole ensemble of nerves and the very nervous fluid itself, who would be surprised that its alterations affect the whole fabric? A force diffused in the vast spaces of the heavens influences the intimate recesses of all matter and moves and troubles the smallest particles of our bodily machines."

Believing the same force to act on pendulums both directly and through the bodies of persons manipulating them, Ritter called it *siderism,* from *sidus* and *sider* (Latin for "star"), characterized the pendulum itself as *sidereal,* and founded a journal, *Der Siderismus,* to publish articles on the new subject which he hoped would become a forum for the integration of knowledge from many branches of science.

In one of his letters to Hardenberg, Ritter warned that he could not be sure whether his friend would have success in repeating the dowsing experiments because while some eighty percent of neophytes who tried it seemed to be able to successfully operate a pendulum, only a quarter of those who manipulated the rod were successful. As for picking up emanations without the assistance of any instrument, simply by feeling them in the body, he believed this ability limited to only two or three individuals in a thousand.

All this was mere technical detail or, as Ritter worded it, "only ordinary physics," in comparison to what he next reported to his friend. "We now actually stand," he wrote, "on the threshold of a really new discovery. In the foregoing experiments, one can observe what nature, of itself, can produce under various circumstances but this is as nothing compared with what it can do if commanded."

What Ritter had stumbled upon at the start of the nineteenth century was the fact that a pendulum or dowsing rod could be used to extract pure information from the universe about any subject no matter how abstract or nebulous. This was because the instruments seemed able to produce a positive or negative movement *even when there were no physical objects present to affect them.* They appeared to respond to the desire or intent of their operators who, if they wanted, could receive a prophetically correct answer to any question requiring a *yes* or *no* answer. Thus, while holding a dowsing instrument, dowsers had to internalize a specific question, allowing it to settle into the very fibre of their beings. Should the pendulum move clockwise, a *yes* answer was indicated, should it move counterclockwise, the answer was *no.* For the hoopshaped dowsing rod, considered to behave like two pendulums working in concert, the equivalents were upward or downward motions.

The questioning process was not as easy as it appeared at first sight. Nor was it to be taken lightly. Just as in alchemy, Ritter warned, one should desire an answer with whole-hearted belief and dedication or otherwise one would obtain an unreliable one. Beside himself with excitement, Ritter also cautioned Hardenberg not to reveal his secret to anyone except Lüdwig Tieck and Friedrich Schegel who were at the time turning out German translations of William Shakespeare's plays so masterful that they

Pendulum experiment illustrated by Antoine Gerboin. "A man stands on the parquet of an apartment or in a given locale free of humidity and in which the air is not greatly agitated. He takes with his thumb and forefinger of his right hand the thread of a pendulum which he will hold about twenty centimeters above the ground on the parquet. If this operation will last for a long time, he should loop the thread several times around the last joint of his forefinger, pressing it with his thumb. In that way his hand, being more stable, will offer the apparatus a necessary degree of fixity."

129

have never been improved upon. He further warned Hardenberg to swear the translators to secrecy. "In fact," he admitted, "I used this very questioning method to ascertain whether you, as well as Tieck and Schegel, were worthy of being privy to my new discovery."

Ritter was as concerned about the moral implications of his find as were others before him. "Magic has been recreated," he added, "and, along with it, that dangerous frontier at which one is capable of deciding questions of good or evil. We are only at the beginning but I envision great things ahead along an adventurous road already welcomed last year in my address to the Bavarian Academy."*

Moral or Material?

In France, Ritter's ideas attracted the notice of a physician and professor at the medical school in Strasbourg, Antoine Gerboin, who for nearly a decade had been secretly experimenting with pendular movements ever since he had been informally introduced to them by an infantry captain in Paris—who had, in turn, learned about them on a trip to India. Impressed that a scientist of Ritter's caliber had dared to issue a public opinion on so complex and novel a problem, Gerboin decided to bring out a treatise on which he had been working for years, *Experimental Research on a New Mode of Electrical Action*, that presented 253 experiments with what he called an "exploratory pendulum."

The professor's most revolutionary conclusions were that certain persons, endowed with an "expansive" quality, were more adept at eliciting pendulum movements than others handicapped with a "deterrent" quality, and that the movements themselves could be affected by the shape or form of objects.

Gerboin's work aroused the curiosity of a brilliant young chemist, Michel-Eugene Chevreul who, like his predecessors, found that a pendulum seemed to produce a puzzling variety of movements when held over elements and compounds. After two decades of intermittent study of the phenomenon, he thought he had an explanation. In a letter to Andre-Marie Ampère, whose mathematical analysis, based on Ørsted's research, led him to found the science of electrodynamics, today called electromagnetism, he wrote: "The more these effects seemed extraordinary, the more I felt the need of verifying whether they were truly foreign to any muscular movement of my arm as had been affirmed to me in the most positive terms."

To carry out his verification, Chevreul supported his arm with a block of wood at various points all the way from his shoulder to his hand, only to find that the movement of the pendulum decreased as the block neared the fingers holding its thread. When the same fingers rested directly on the block in such a way that they could not intentionally be moved, all pendular motion ceased.

Something else bothered Chevreul. He observed that when he gazed fixedly at the movement of a pendulum as he held it, he seemed "to enter into a particular state or disposition which he

*"Physics as Art: An attempt to Interpret the Future of Physics from Its History."

130

felt might contribute to it." There was, he cautiously concluded, "an intimate liaison established between the execution of certain movements and a mental act relating to it, even if the thought is not yet the intent to command the muscular organs."

With this intuitive flash suggesting, as it did, that thought, or mind, might affect a pendulum independent of any muscular or motoric movement, Chevreul came within a hair's breadth of anticipating twentieth century experiments that have proved the ability of peculiarly gifted individuals to cause movement in stationary pendulums and other motionless objects at a distance from them solely by mental effort and, by altering the composition of matter at the microscopic level, to bend metal objects without touching them.

On the threshold of a momentous discovery that was to be awkwardly labeled *psychokinesis* (movement produced by mentation alone), Chevreul was not up to stepping across it. Instead he backed away with the lame excuse that, because his research demonstrated "how easy it was to take illusion for reality," it would be mainly of interest to psychologizers and historians of science. Nevertheless, Chevreul probably came closer to summing up the problem of dowsing in 1850 than any other contemporary scientist.

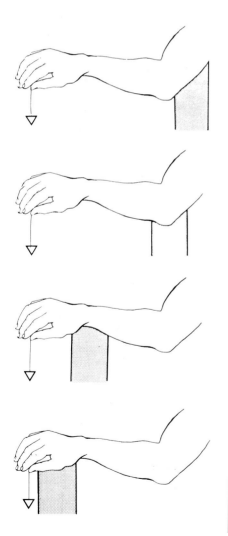

Experiment by Michel-Eugene Chevreul purporting to prove that the motion of a pendulum held on a thread is due to involuntary muscular movement. When the support lay under the thumb, all pendular motion ceased.

CHEVREUL'S SUMMARY OF THE DOWSING ENIGMA, 1850: *A dowsing device's movement can be explained either:*

1. *as being part of the* moral *world and having a* spiritual *cause derived from:*
   a. God *or the angelic hierarchy;*
   b. *the* devil *or his minions;*
   c. *the* mind *of the dowser;*
2. *as being part of the* material *world and having a* physical *cause derived from "occult" properties associated with matter which:*
   a. *the Aristotelian peripeticians called* sympathy *and* antipathy;
   b. *the Cartesians called* corpuscles, vapors, *or* subtle matter;
   c. *Chevreul's contemporaries referred to as* electricity, electro-magnetism, *or* electro-organism (Galvanism).

The movement could be augmented by the dowser's holding in his hands, together with the device:

1. *material* identical *with that of the target sought;*
2. *material* different *from that of the target sought.*

Because these two means for augmenting the device's movement were diametrically opposed, not a physical, *but a* mental, *cause would have to explain them.*

"Partisans of dowsing," wrote Chevreul, "whether practitioners or theoreticians, recognize the influence of thought *played in dowsing, whether this thought is to be equated to* will, desire, *or* intention."

"Thought," he continued, "could neutralize *or cancel out any physical cause or, otherwise, how could one explain that buried metal, which is considered to influence the rod through such a physical cause, has no influence if the dowser is seeking water, and vice versa?"*

131

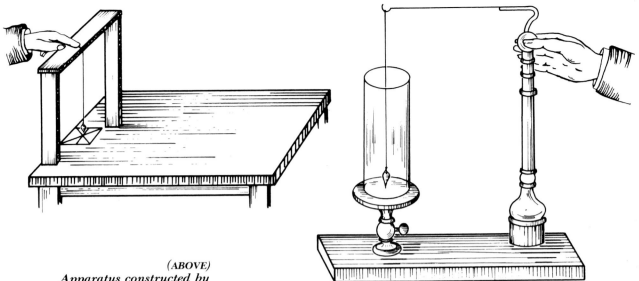

Rutter's magnetoscope

(ABOVE)
Apparatus constructed by Monsieur F. de Briche, Secretary General of the Prefecture of Loiret, France, around 1838 that ostensibly proved a pendulum's movements were not due to involuntary muscular movement. On a table a crosspiece 20 to 25 millimeters thick, 13 to 14 centimeters wide, and 36 centimeters long was mounted on two uprights 30 centimeters high. To a silk, cotton, hemp, or linen thread 21 to 22 centimeters long, a pendulum made either of a ring, a tiny ball, or a metal cylinder (silver, copper, or lead) was attached, the upper end of the thread being fixed to the crosspiece by a ball of wax which stuck to the wood. It was said that the pendulum exposed to a substance placed beneath it would rotate or oscillate whenever a hand was placed on that part of the thread lying on the upper side of the crosspiece. Monsieur Albert de Rochas in his book, Notice Historique sur les Effets de l'Od, stated that the pendulum would move as desired by a sensitive operator holding his finger on the motionless portion of the thread.

Other experimenters, however, were to come to conclusions that had narrowly escaped Chevreul. One of them, a French civil servant, de Briche, tied the thread of a pendulum around a wooden support. He touched only that part of the thread that lay against the top of the support. Though he could not have imparted any movement to the hanging bob with his hand, it nevertheless produced oscillations that varied depending upon what substance lay directly below it.

Independently of de Briche, one Rutter, a resident of Brighton, England, constructed a more complex apparatus which, because it was assumed to detect "magnetic" currents emanating from all substances, was called a *magnetoscope*. It consisted of a piece of cone-shaped sealing wax hung inside a foot-long cylinder of glass by a silken thread attached to a metal arm. The other end of the arm ran through a copper tube, widened at one point to form a spherical protuberance, to be fastened to the top of a wooden column. It was sufficient that Rutter only lightly touch the sphere for the pendulum to leap into animated motion.

The Englishman's experiments came to the attention of a famous Austrian chemist, Baron Karl von Reichenbach, discoverer of parafin and creosote, who maintained that persons endowed with something akin to Gerboin's "expansive quality" were able to sense emanations coming off substances and even identify them in the pitch dark. These "sensitives," as he called them, could also feel cold at one end of a gypsum spar crystal and warmth at the other end from which the crystal grew and visually detect flames streaming out of the two ends of a bar magnet, orange-red from its north pole and bluish-white from its south, which suggested that there was something inherently different about the two polar energies. The same flamelike emissions were seen to radiate from the left and right hands of the human body, tending to confirm Ritter's notion that it was somehow polarized. Plants, animals, and human beings, said the sensitives, were surrounded by multihued "auras" of energy depending on the state of their well-being and their age.

As had others before him, Reichenbach felt compelled to find a new name for the strange force emitted from inert and animate objects. In homage to the all-powerful Norse god, Odin, he called it *od* or *odic force* and claimed that, like Ritter's *siderism,* it was able to exert an effect at a distance as well as to travel over a silk thread and other nonconductive materials at a speed slower than electricity and even to penetrate glass. Nonsensitives could detect it only with a pendulum.

Reichenbach hurried to Brighton where he tested Rutter, and his daughter as well, and found them both to have the same high degree of sensitivity that his carpenter, Joseph Czapek, one of his most gifted subjects, possessed. When he returned to his castle outside Vienna, he constructed a device similar to Rutter's. Czapek had no trouble getting the pendulum to move simply by touching the spherical protuberance. "Sensitives" he concluded, "not only could passively *apprehend* odic energy but could actively *emit* it."

"Electrometry," "organo-electricity," "siderism," "odic force," and other new terms for an energy considered animate were as distasteful to orthodox scientists as they were appealing to antimaterialists who complained that contemporary philosophies of physics were dissatisfying because they lacked any doctrine concerning a spiritual world. "Once the nature of a spirit in man, conditioned by the stars themselves, is unshackled and can begin to shine forth," wrote Ritter's friend, Baader, "only then will it be understood that it may also be found in the lower forms of nature."

No one would have been more sympathetic to this idea than a Dresden professor of chemistry, Johann Karl Bähr, whose own pendular experimentation led him to conclude that many people able to detect forces within matter were also capable of knowing, like animals, exactly what comestibles were beneficial or inimical to their health. Labeling the forces "dynamic activity," Bähr noted that elements and substances produced pendular swings toward various azimuths and accordingly arranged them on a compass rose in a circular pattern which he felt correctly expressed the relationships among them.

In his massive tome, *The Dynamic Circle,* he wrote: "I have to assume that any educated person not influenced by the prejudices of certain learned professors will have some knowledge of these phenomena." The pendulum's uniqueness, he added, lay in its allowing anyone, however insensitive, to recognize properties of materials directly without having to take them apart or dissolve them—an affirmation seeming to imply that the budding field of analytical chemistry could be bypassed.

Bähr held that the source of hidden influence within matter was, as the philosopher Immanuel Kant proposed, not fixed but "movable in space." Specific qualities of bodies depended not on their material substance but on "inner values" recognizable only

133

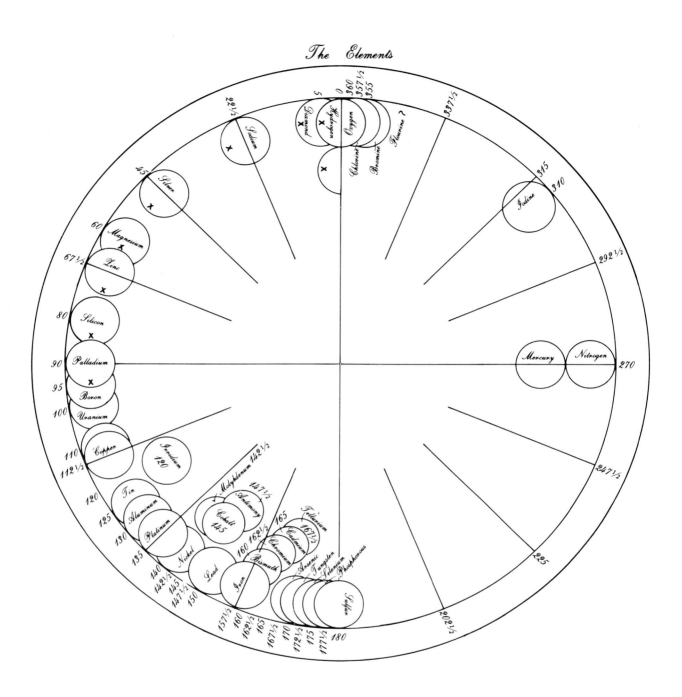

by such "outer manifestations" as the movements of a pendulum.

Bähr's system of classifying the properties of matter, elaborated on the basis of *subjective* analysis rather than *objective* proof and based on the essential claim of dowsing that, being directly accessible, knowledge needs no confirmation either by the five normal senses or repetitive experimentation, became the foundation upon which the edifice of dowsing inquiry has since been built. His arbitrary cataloguing of qualities according to a unit of angular measure on a circle, emphasizing the idea that dowsing was particularly suitable to determine *degree*, has been

134

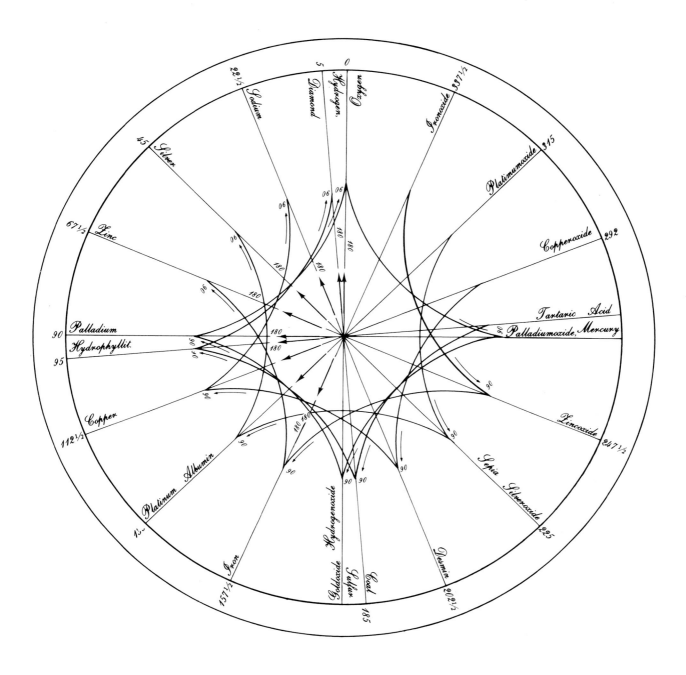

Oxygen 0 · Hydrogen 5 · Diamond · Sodium 22½ · Silver 45 · Zinc 67½ · Palladium 90 · Hydrophyllit. 95 · Copper 112½ · Platinum Albumin · Iron 157½ · Goldoxide Hydrosmoxide · Sulfur Coal 185 · Desmin 202½ · Sepia Silveroxide 225 · Zincoxide 247½ · Tartaric Acid · Palladiumoxide, Mercury · Copperoxide 292 · Platinumoxide 315 · Ironoxide 337½

Two circular diagrams worked out by Johann Karl Bähr to show attractive and antagonistic relationships between elements and compounds.

adapted under various guises to value or rate all sorts of phenomena to which, because it lacks instrumentation for their measurement, physical science can have no access. The catch in the process is, as German mining men realized in the eighteenth century, that the usefulness of data obtained in such a way depends upon the skill and probity of dowsers.

Bähr's other idea of ranking substances according to the effects produced by their "inner values" on dowsing instruments was able to endure. Between the two world wars it was taken up by Joseph Wüst, a physical chemist with a medical degree who

135

The Human Body

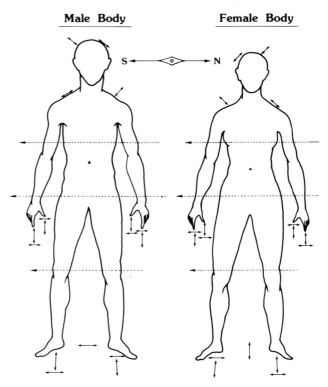

Male Body   **Female Body**

S ← ◇ → N

Two charts drawn by Johann Karl Bähr to represent polarized parts of the body.

The Hands
north-south orientation

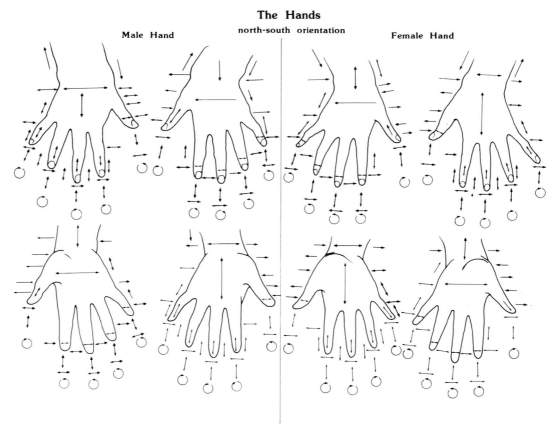

Male Hand   Female Hand

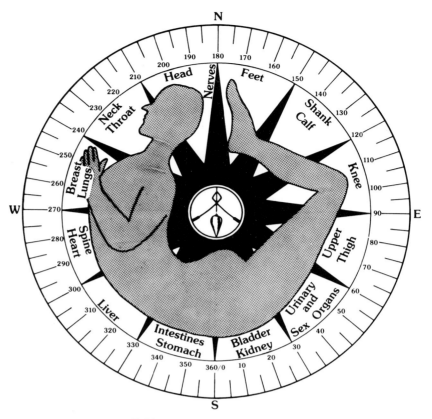

Table for Anatomical Studies

Circular table for anatomical studies published as part of a dowsing course by RGS (Radiesthesie, Geologie, Strahlen-Biologie) in Sankt Gallen, Switzerland

attracted the support of Hitler's confidant, Rudolph Hess, before Hess's ill-fated and still largely unexplained flight to England, and Joseph Wimmer, a gymnasium professor and mathematical physicist who ran a school for dowsers during World War II at the behest of Heinrich Himmler, chief of Hitler's dreaded SS.

Working at the Anatomical Institute of the University of Munich between 3 and 6 in the afternoon three times a week, they tested substances for several years, not with a pendulum, but with a fork-shaped steel wire rod, 60 centimeters long and 2 millimeters thick. Over given elements they found the rod to rotate through a specific number of degrees of arc. Inexplicably, carbon produced a revolution of 40–50 degrees, nitrogen 120–140, copper 230–250, arsenic 320–340, manganese 400–420, phosphorus 440–460, and cesium 600–620. They went on to obtain corresponding values for fifty-four elements on Mendeleyev's periodic chart. Because the figures obtained reveal no apparently logical connections, their work might seem silly on the face of it were it not for the fact that research by Soviet geologists, presently to be considered, also indicated a direct relationship between the number of rotations of a dowsing rod and underground anomalies.

Like their predecessors, Wüst and Wimmer eschewed all previous names for the active force, which they measured as traveling at a rate of 42–45 meters per second, or a little faster than the speed of sound. Instead they opted for two more:

137

Reichsführer—SS

*Field Command Post
12 January, 1943*

To: Munich-Pasing, Kirchstrasse 11

1) Dear Professor Wimmer,

My best thanks for your letter of 31 December 1942. I am as glad as you are that last year we made good progress in dowsing research and training following our get together in Zhitomir.

I wish you good health for the New Year and complete success, especially in your field of research.

*Heil Hitler
Ever yours,
/s/ H. Himmler*

*copies:
2) The Ahnenerbe
3) SS Headquarters.*

Der Reichsführer-SS   Feld-Kommandostelle, 12.Jan.43

München-Pasing,Kirchstr.11.

000518 * 13 JAN.
Akt.Z.: 9/8/1

1.) Lieber Professor W i m m e r !

Meinen besten Dank für Ihre Zeilen vom 31.12.42. Ich freue mich ebensosehr wie Sie, daß das vergangene Jahr durch unser Beisammensein in Shitomir uns auf dem Gebiet der Wünschelruten-forschung und - ausbildung doch ein recht gutes Stück vorangebracht hat.

Für das Neue Jahr wünsche ich Ihnen persönlich Gesundheit und gerade auf dem Gebiet Ihrer Forschungsarbeit vollen Erfolg.

Heil Hitler!
stets Ihr
gez.H.Himmler.

2.) An das Ahnenerbe
3.) SS-Führungshauptamt

durchschriftlich mit der Bitte um Kenntnisnahme übersandt.

i.A.

SS-Obersturmführer.

W-Radiation, after the German word for dowsing rod, and *magnetoism,* to signify an "unidentified vibration" associated with a magnetic field.

Reference to a vital energy as one physical explanation for dowsing ran into opposition from other researchers who were sure it could be fitted onto the Procrustean bed of electromagnetism. As the nineteenth century gave way to the twentieth, with Röntgen's discovery of X-rays in 1895 and the Curies' discovery of radioactivity in 1903, emanations from substances objectively measurable in the laboratory would begin to be called "particles" and "waves," the analogs of the older "corpuscles" and "sympathetic attractions." These, said promoters of a physical explanation for dowsing, were what the pendulum and the rod were capturing. Thousands of experiments were performed and shelves of books written to support this contention. For many electromagnetic researchers, as for proponents of "unknown forces," observation was data and conviction was proof.

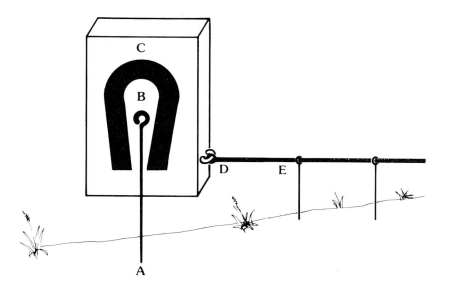

Louis Probst's invention.

To cite but one example of an instrument purportedly based on the new wave theory, French dowser Louis Probst's invention of what he called a *radio-capteur* began with a simple metal spike stuck into the earth. Its curved tip, protruding above the ground, was centered between the poles of a horseshoe magnet mounted inside a flattened box. Into the side of the box a metal ring was fitted in such a way as to intercept the magnetic field.

A wire was then attached to the ring and, isolated from the earth by a series of stakes topped with porcelain fixtures, extended in a straight line. Probst's optimistic theory stated that "waves" emitted from an underground water source or metal ore deposit were in some way "captured" by the spike and, assisted by the magnetic field, propelled along the wire. A dowser would then straddle the wire and frog-walk along it until he got a reaction. The length of that portion of the wire from the ring to the spot between his feet was supposedly equivalent to the depth of the water vein or any other object being sought. Deeper water veins would be ascertainable further along the wire.

Suitable for shallow targets, the method obviously was impractical for those at depths of one hundred feet or more underground. To get around the difficulty, Probst wound wire into coils of varying length which, arranged in series, were held to provoke a dowsing reaction if the total length of the wire contained in them was equal to the depth of a sought-for target.

The same contraption was also supposed to be adaptable for the determination of an underground target at great distance. For this particular method to work, dowsers were to station themselves with the instrument at their backs, then sidestep around in a circle until they got a reaction. By moving the instrument to a new location they could then ascertain a new line of sight which, intersecting with the first, would pinpoint a general area for more detailed on-the-ground survey.

Using this method to search for galena, near Lacapelle-Marival in the Lot, Armand Viré, working with Probst,

139

claimed to have accurately pinpointed a source of the mineral near a village 11 kilometers distant.

The whole method depended on the idea that waves from various targets were somehow received by the instrument stuck in the earth and transmitted to the dowser in its vicinity. But, as Viré noted in his book, "our sensitivity, having become more refined through practice, we noted, after a while, that the magnet was not indispensable and that the spike alone could produce the same results. Pondering this fact, we at first thought that our nervous systems themselves were receiving waves emitted by sought-for bodies like a radio receiver picks up waves from a transmitter. We therefore got rid of the metal spike . . . and after considerable practice achieved remarkable results." The whole physical part of the phenomenon seemed to have disappeared along with the unnecessary hardware.

Psychical Physics

So the same old question remained: Was dowsing basically a problem for physics or psychology? Opposing answers were proposed in the very titles of two capital works, one German, the other English, that appeared in the 1920s. The first was called *The Divining Rod as a Scientific Problem with Appendix: Conclusive Geophysical Methods* by the German Count Carl von Klinckowström, the second, *The Divining Rod: an Experimental and Psychological Investigation* by Sir William Barrett, professor of physics at the Royal College of Science in Ireland, and the cultural anthropologist Theodore Besterman.

A reading of the two books in conjunction reveals instantly that their opposing conclusions are based on fundamentally different conceptions. While the German mainly limited his subject to *field dowsing,* the Englishmen swept wider to include considerations of *remote* dowsing and to formulate a "cryptesthetic" theory—based on a word coined by Nobel

140

laureate Charles Richet that combines the Greek roots, *kriptos*, "hidden," and *esthesia*, "perception." "We claim," they concluded, "that dowsing is a purely psychological problem, that all its phenomena find their origin in the dowser's mind, that no physical theory can bear close consideration, and that the movements of the rod and of the dowser have no more direct relation to the discovery of, say, water, than as giving physical and visible expression to a mental and abstract cognition."

The either-or nature of the controversy bothered one of the most successful French dowsers of all time, Abbé Alexis Mermet, who in the mid-1930s realized that if no physical theory for dowsing was logically watertight, depth psychology could not account for it at all. Like a boatman plying between Scylla and Charibdis, Mermet tried to steer a middle course. He first evolved a complicated system comprising eleven separate physical factors that could influence dowsing, then, at a stroke, cancelled them out with the observation, passed over in silence by Probst and other proponents of physical aids, that dowsers must faultlessly *tune in* on objects being sought.

Reliance upon any physical theory was completely abandoned in 1934 by the French engineer, Emile Christophe, who was perhaps the first to clearly state that if *all* subterranean objects emitted a physical radiation, then a dowser who did not single-mindedly focus on one could react to all of them. The act of focusing Christophe called "mental orientation." He coupled it with "mental convention" in which dowsers would agree with their *selves* about what the movements in their rods or pendulums denoted. If a dowser stipulated a clockwise motion to signify a "yes" answer to a question, then, when it rotated clockwise, yes was the answer. All answers to questions, said Christophe, depended on the dowser's attention or concentration and on a wholly subjective attitude.

Christophe's "mental orientation" can be compared to the tuning of a radio or television set to capture the desired broadcast or to a radar beam sweeping the horizon. The "mental convention" is analogous to the numbers indicating radio frequencies and TV channels, or the azimuth at which the radar beam picks up a ship or a reef of rocks, thus allowing a navigator to "see" them even in foggy weather.

Christophe, and others like him, thus tried to blaze a trail away from the marshy swamps of physical interpretation toward higher ground where, scientifically unfettered, the spirit could look for answers with freedom. Von Baader's observation seemed vindicated. Dowsing was revealing the divine in man. During World War II Christophe's disciple, the Benedictine scholar, Cunibert Mohlberg, whose dowsing was used by Swiss art experts to detect whether paintings were originals or forgeries, declared: "If in heaven, God said: 'Let there be light' and there was light; on earth, man, made in God's image, could say: 'Let this or that be found,' and found it would be."

It was only after World War II that a young Dutch professor of geology at Egypt's Fuad I University, Solco Tromp, made the first serious attempt to reconcile the two basically contrary explanations of dowsing. During his work as a field geologist,

Circular dowsing "measurement circle" developed by the Swiss Benedictine, Cunibert Mohlberg, whose pseudonym was "Candi."

Tromp had met many dowsers whose erratic results had evoked in him only a feeling of extreme skepticism. About 1940, however, he began systematically to collect data which indicated to him that divining was "as real as electricity and other physical phenomena." After the war he ran a long series of scientific tests in the Netherlands at Leiden University and the Laboratory for Technical Physics at Delft. At the same time he made an exhaustive study of scattered and disparate research performed in a dozen countries from 1800 onward that today would be an excellent starting place for anyone wishing to update the material.

In 1949 Tromp's 534-page "Scientific Analysis of Dowsing, Radiesthesia and Kindred Divining Phenomena," came out under the futuristic title *Psychical Physics*. It presented an encyclopedic survey of electromagnetic activity within living organisms which, generically termed by the author the "organic field," was reminiscent of the earlier "organo-electricity," and of the "geophysical field" external to living things that included most of what was electromagnetically known about the earth and its atmosphere.

In his compilation Tromp cited a host of ignored or maligned findings that gave credence to the intuitive conclusions of earlier dowsing researchers. One of them was a mysterious vital radiation, produced by cell division and therefore termed "mitogenetic," discovered in the 1920s by the Russian cytologist, Alexander Gurwich, and confirmed by other researchers but rejected by official science. Its further study, claimed the Dutch professor, might be highly instructive for our understanding of the divining phenomenon.

The older ideas of Mesmer, Ritter, and Bähr that cosmic or sidereal activity could influence living things may be confirmable through other innovative research done by contemporaries of Gurwich that also awaits the recognition it deserves. In Europe, followers of Rudolph Steiner, the founder of a spiritual science called *anthroposophy*, used completely new laboratory techniques to prove that wheat, oat, and barley shoots increased or decreased their rates of growth in consonance with the phases of the moon or even with the positions of the more distant planets—just as had been suggested by Robert Fludd in the seventeenth century.

At Yale University's medical school, an anatomist, Dr. Harold Saxton Burr, and a philosopher, Dr. F. S. C. Northrop, teamed up to elucidate how the celestial bodies could influence life. They put forward a new "electrodynamic theory of life," since

142

confirmed by thousands of experiments, which indicated that every human being, animal, tree, plant, and microscopic organism possessed, and was controlled by, an electrical field. The "life field," as it came to be called, acted to repair, maintain, and renew cells that are the building blocks of all life forms and thus hold them in recognizable shape just as a magnet arranged iron filings sprinkled on a piece of paper into a consistent pattern. Measurable with great precision, life fields, reminiscent of "organo-electricity," were seen to vary around trees, in response to lunar phases, sunspots, and other astronomical events. As Tromp suggested, this may be potentially important in determining what is taking place in the life fields of dowsers as they perform their work.

Results obtained through efforts to unravel the web of electromagnetic forces regulating all living processes on earth were to Tromp no more or less relevant to elucidating the mystery of dowsing than the even more arcane revelations of parapsychology, earlier called psychical research. It was because workers in this fascinating new field lacked any physical data to explain such phenomena as telepathy, clairvoyance, psychokinesis, and the almost supernatural, medically inexplicable, ability of yogis and fakirs to regulate bodily processes, that Tromp conceived of a new science, *psychical physics*.

Only the combined efforts of physicists, medical men, and parapsychologists, Tromp affirmed, could come to grips with the implications of such experiments as those performed in the 1930s by the Cleveland surgeon, George Washington Crile, who showed that when lipoids, proteins, and inorganic salts were extracted from the brains of healthy, but not diseased, animals and mixed according to certain formulas, cellular bodies resembling protozoa appeared spontaneously in the mixtures. Called by Crile "autosynthetic cells," they could reproduce if fed with sterile protein solutions.

Crile's cells seemed easily akin to the vesicles produced a decade later by the psychiatrist and biophysicist Wilhelm Reich who filtered water through ordinary garden soil. After freezing the yellowish fluid for a time and thawing it again, Reich observed the formation of dense flakes which, magnified 3,000 times in his specially built microscope, revealed pulsating bodies he called "bions." They fluoresced weakly or strongly according to how completely they were imbued with a cosmic life energy that Reich called *orgone,* still another relative of Ritter's *siderism,* Reichenbach's *od,* and Bähr's *dynamic activity.*

It was only a sign of narrow-mindedness, wrote Tromp, that such experiments as those of Crile and Reich were rejected by scientists because their explanations sounded unscientific and might be completely wrong. Aware of the attempts to explain dowsing over five centuries he added: "It is not the interpretation which is important but the facts. Interpretations given even by the most prominent scientists often had to be changed during the history of mankind, but the facts remain. Most scientists of the twentieth century seem to lack the courage and the romantic feeling to tackle problems which at first sight seem incredible and without any practical prospects."

143

Three Italian dowsers holding respectively a wand, a forked stick and a rod bent into a semi-circular hoop as illustrated in Pratica Minerale *authored by Marco Antonio della Fratta et Montalbano (Bologna, 1678)*

Part Three

NEW WATER FROM ROCK?

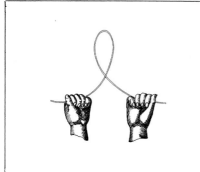

CHAPTER 8

Icebergs or "Waters of the Earth"?

". . . a thin branch from a tree or a piece of straight wire bent into a loop . . ."

Hydrologic Doctrine vs. Primary Water

In October 1977, 110 scientists and engineers gathered in landlocked Iowa to discuss a bizarre notion: Could an iceberg one mile long, 1,000 feet wide and 900 feet thick, weighing 100 million tons and containing 20 billion gallons of water, be transported from Antarctica to the Northern Hemisphere and parked next to the coast of a desert country to serve as a mammoth water reservoir?

The proposal to solve a shortage of water by moving icebergs halfway around the world was only the most recent in a long history of similar water-transport schemes that date back to the beginning of recorded history, among which canals dug into the earth, or aqueducts set above it, and the construction of ever more costly dams have been favorite choices.

By the time the conference began, a feasibility study for displacing a mountain of ice was already in the works. Commissioned by Prince Muhammad al Faisal, nephew of Saudi Arabia's King Khalid and sponsor of the Iowa meeting, it enjoined Cicero, a French engineering firm, to solve the problem of towing a gargantuan ice cube 7,500 miles to the Saudis' Red Sea port of Jidda. Some observers at the First International Conference on Iceberg Utilization estimated that tugs towing the berg, able to move no faster than a nautical snail's pace of half a mile per hour, would take nearly eight months to reach the Bab el Mandeb Strait at the entrance to the Red Sea.

Then there was the melting problem. Wilford Weeks of the U.S. Army's Cold Regions Research Laboratory protested that anyone who tried to drag an unprotected iceberg from the coldest to the hottest place on earth would end up with "nothing but a tow-line." Not disagreeing, Egyptian nuclear engineer Abdo Husseiny nevertheless waxed optimistic that, if a strong enough version of a plastic bag could be devised to retain their melt, icebergs up to five by ten miles in size could make the voyage. UNESCO hydrologists suggested that plants for the desalinization of sea water made better economic sense.

No one at the conference was aware of the fact that over eighty years ago a Stockholm professor of mineralogy and arctic explorer, Adolf Erik Nordenskiöld, had written a paper, "About Drilling for Water in Primary Rocks" which concluded that one could sink wells capable of producing water the year round along

147

the northern and southern coasts of the Mediterranean, and in the whole of Asia Minor, or exactly in those areas of the world from which conference delegates most concerned about water supply problems hailed.

Nordenskiöld, whose essay won him a nomination for the Nobel Prize in physics (he died before full consideration was given to the candidates), spent years drilling in rocky promontories and islands off the Swedish coast to bring up water for pilotage stations forced to capture rain or import water. His impetus came from his father, Nils, Chief of Mining in Finland, who told him with some wonderment that while salt water never penetrated iron mines on the Finnish coast even when they were below sea level, fresh water was always present on the rocky floors of the same mines. The Swedish scientist's extensive subsequent bores convinced him that water, produced by some process deep within the earth for which he could not account, could be contacted in hard rock.

Nordenskiöld's theory completely contradicted hydrological doctrine of his, and our own, time which insists that most of the fresh water available to living things on earth first rises as vapor from lakes and oceans to form clouds. These in turn deliver the same water, condensed by cool air currents into rain, hail, or snow, back to the earth's surface. The bulk of this precipitation trickles into rivulets, brooks, streams, and rivers to run back to the sea. Part of it is absorbed by the earth's crust, where it is

The Hydrologic cycle

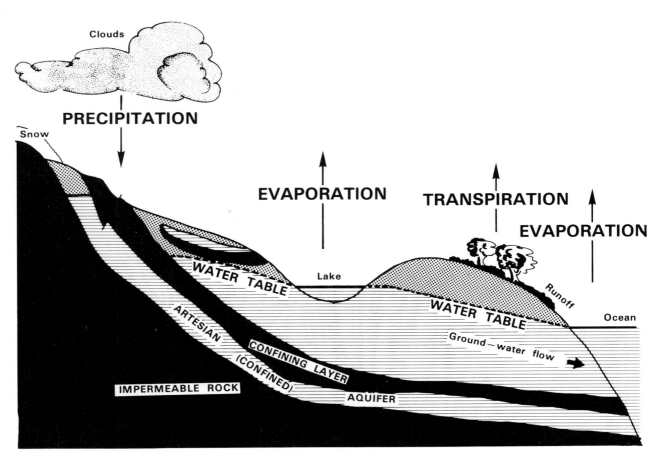

"For a century it has been known that, under certain conditions, some rocks yield hydrogen and oxygen gases which subsequently combine to form new water. In connection with the mining and recovery of gold, a natural coincidence led me to suspect, many years ago, that such a laboratory reaction might proceed within the earth. My discovery was then put to a field test by locating and drilling many water wells. The record to date is 70 producing wells out of 72 attempts, all drilled in hard rock, all located in distress areas generally considered unproductive." Stephan Riess, 1954

tapped by countless trillions of plants to be reliberated by transpiration, or seeps downward as "ground water" to collect in subterranean channels called "aquifers"—Latin for "water-carriers"—from which it can be recovered from natural springs or man-made wells. The whole circulatory process is called the "hydrologic cycle."

The Swede's new concept was to lie dormant until it was revived by a Bavarian-born mining engineer, Stephan Riess, who emigrated to the United States in 1923. Though he has never held a dowsing rod in his hands, Riess has developed a geologic theory about the origin of water which, proved by fifty years of practice, meshes well with dowsers' own deductions.

Eager to discover what California mining had to offer, he traveled to Lassen County near the Oregon border and began working his way down the Sierra Nevada range. For one mining operation with over 100,000 tons of unprocessed ore lying aboveground, Riess solved the processing problem chemically with a special catalyst known, then as now, only to himself. "News of the money those fellows made raced like a grass fire through the hills," Riess recalls, "and I had me plenty of consulting work right away."

Riess's ability to recover metal from ores attracted the attention of then ex-President Herbert Hoover, who owned large mining holdings. Hoover invited the German immigrant to join a metallurgical processing firm, in which he worked together with the former President's two sons, Allan and Herbert, Jr.

One day a load of dynamite was set off in the bottom of a deep mine at high elevation to break up ore-rich rock. After the explosion Riess was amazed to see water come gushing out of nowhere in such quantities that pumps installed to remove it at a rate of 25,000 gallons a minute could not make a dent in it.

149

Looking down into the valley below, Riess asked himself how water that had trickled into the earth as rain could rise through hard rock into the shafts and tunnels of a mine nearly at the top of a mountain range.

The temperature and the purity of the water's chemical analysis suggested to Riess that the water must be of a completely different origin than ordinary ground water. Since none of the textbooks he had studied referred to what seemed to be a completely anomalous phenomenon, he decided to look into it.

On trips back to Europe, Riess became aware that many historic castles were built on high rocky promontories such as those in the Rhineland, some of them constructed by Charlemagne's descendants. At the center of their courtyards were huge wells, often as much as eight feet in diameter with steps going into the ground two hundred meters or more, that had supplied water for centuries.

Similar wells can be found in all parts of the world. Typical is the fortress built on rocky Inner Farne islet in the mouth of Scotland's Tweed River where St. Cuthbert isolated himself from 676–687 A.D. When he visited the site in 1952, the *National Geographic*'s John E. M. Nolan nearly plunged into "a huge stone cistern filled with ice-cold water" that had supplied the saint and his fellow monks. Even more awesome is a well at La Ferriere, the stone fortress built by Emperor Christophe two thousand feet above the north Haitian plain in the early 1800s and described as "deep and clear and freezing cold, and fed by an inexhaustible spring."

In the North American West an important clue to the mystery disclosed by Riess came when, working late at night in a mine shaft, he heard a peculiar hissing sound, similar to that produced by a leaky air tank, accompanied by trickling water. He tracked the unfamiliar noise down to the ball mill, an enormous cylinder that rotates and pulverizes ore to mud by the tumbling action of steel balls and water contained within it. The water trickling out of the ball mill should normally have been found above the mud in the motionless cylinder but, to his amazement, Riess saw that it lay under a newly formed arch of mud through which hissing bubbles of gas kept rising. Holding a match over one of the bubbles, he caused a mini-explosion. What he was observing, he believed, was virgin water being liberated from ore-bearing rock by crystallization processes within the rocks themselves. He surmised that these processes had been triggered by the presence of some catalyzing agent among the chemicals introduced into the ball mill for recovering refractory gold and silver.

Riess duplicated the water-producing process in a laboratory, then turned to perfecting methods of rock analysis. He finally came to the conclusion that, in various rock strata, deep in the earth, water was continually manufactured under proper conditions of temperature and pressure and forced up in rock fissures where it could be tapped if drilled.

Classical authors, Riess discovered, tended to support his view. As far back as 500 B.C. Anaxagoras maintained that oceans were created both from rivers flowing into them and from what

150

Vitruvius's method for finding water: "To locate ground water, lie flat on the ground before sunrise with the chin on the ground in order to confine the search to what can be seen from that position. Water can be expected to lie under those places where vapors arise from the earth." Reproduced from 1543 edition of Vitruvius' *De Architecture*

Details of Water Available in Various Types of Soils, According to Vitruvius

Type of soil	*Depth at which water may be available*	*Amount*	*Taste*	*Remarks*
Clay	Near the surface	Scanty	Not good	—
Loose gravel	Lower down the surface	Scanty	Unpleasant	Muddy
Black earth	—	—	Excellent	Available after winter rains
Gravel	—	Small & uncertain	Unusually sweet	—
Coarse gravel, common sand & red rock	—	More certain	Good	—
Red rock	—	Copious	Good	Difficult to obtain due to percolation
Flinty rock & foot of mountains	—	Copious	Cold & wholesome	—

credit: Asit K. Biswas, *History of Hydrology*

he called "waters of the earth," upon which the self-same rivers depended for their own existence. Both Plato and Aristotle also supported the idea that water was formed within the earth as well as in its atmosphere.

In pre-Christian Roman times, Vitruvius, whose *Ten Books on Architecture* appeared between 27 and 17 B.C., was the first to state that water was best found, not in sands, gravels, and soil but in rocks.

In the first century of the Christian era Seneca referred to great underground rivers flowing in the planet, while his contemporary, Pliny the Elder, championing the idea that water flowed in veins, wrote that they "pervaded the whole earth within and ran in all directions bursting out even on the highest ridges."

Like the Chinese before him, Leonardo da Vinci, in his long unpublished essay, "Treatise on Water," compared the earth to a living human body. Wrote the Renaissance genius:

The same cause which moves the humours in every species of animate bodies against the natural law of gravity also propels the water through the veins of the earth wherein it is enclosed and distributes it through small passages. And as the blood rises from below and pours out through the broken veins of the forehead, as the water rises from the lowest part of the vine to the branches that are cut, so from the lowest depth of the sea the water rises to the summits of mountains, where, finding the veins broken, it pours out and returns to the bottom of the sea.

This idea did not prevent Leonardo from also opting for an early version of the modern hydrologic cycle and stating that a lot of the earth's water was the result of rainfall from clouds. As Asit K. Biswas notes in his recent *History of Hydrology:* "Characteristically, Leonardo reported an occasional doubt about certain aspects of both theories, but nothing has been found so far which would indicate that he had at any time discarded the basic concepts of either of them. In fact, the chances seem good that he believed both systems operated concurrently."

No less impressive to Riess were accounts of travelers in various parts of the Mediterranean littoral and the Near East about sources of water that laid the basis for ancient civilizations. At Cyrene in northeastern Libya the famous Fountain of Apollo still gushes from a tunnel hewn into rock just as it has done since long before the birth of Christ. In his book, *Digging for Lost African Gods,* archaeologist and explorer Byron Kuhn de Prorok described the enormous spring at Zaghuan, forty-eight miles from the site of the ancient city of Carthage near modern-day Tunis, which flows through a still-standing Roman temple on the slopes of the Atlas Mountains. Denying the usual claim that North Africa became a desert because of severe climatic change, de Prorok believed that if sources such as Zaghuan were tapped anew and ancient Roman waterways to channel their abundance restored, "Algeria and Tunisia could become the granary of Europe, as they were for 300 years under Roman rule."

In the Fertile Crescent Nelson Glueck describes the easternmost source of the River Jordan as a full-formed stream bursting forth from the base of an earthquake-battered cave in a

Over one million residents of Damascus—Syria's capital and one of the oldest continuously inhabited cities in the world—will have an improved water supply system as a result of a project being financed by a World Bank loan of $35 million. The project is the first major expansion of the city's water supply and distribution system in more than forty years. It will help increase supply of water from the Figeh Spring, an abundant supply of cheap and high-quality water from the heights above the city. Workmen at the Figeh Spring are building new separation walls in order to regulate the flow and increase the utilization of the water.

World Bank photograph by Thomas Sennett, 1977.

great iron-reddened limestone cliff, while its westernmost sources originate in one spring at the foot of a buttress of Mount Hermon and in another which "pours from the cliffs in waterfalls."

In the *National Geographic* magazine for December 1951, an article entitled "The Ghosts of Jericho" recounts that even in the recent past thousands of Arab refugees were getting their water from the *same spring* that supplied the site in *neolithic times.* Called Ain-es-Sultan or "The Sultan's Spring" in Arabic, it is identical to that "healed" by Elisha as reported in II Kings 2, 19–25.

The Ain Figeh Spring, a remarkable source of water, today supplies the entire population (1.3 million people) of Damascus, Syria, and is also the principal source of the Barada River. A report on it by the International Bank for Reconstruction and Development reads: "The principal emergence of the spring, which has been enclosed in a structure since Roman times, resembles an underground river several meters across which flows up and out of the limestone formation of the mountain. The total flow has averaged 8.63 cubic meters per second (about 132,000 gpm). The water quality is very good, its temperature and pH are relatively constant (near 14 degrees Centigrade and 7.9 respectively), its taste and color are excellent, and bacteriological contamination at the source is practically nonexistent."

153

Straight Answers

Riess's first opportunity to prove that water could be located in crystalline rock came in 1934, at Nelson, in the southeast tip of Nevada, where a mine could be made profitable only if a source of water could be found to mill millions of dollars of gold and silver-bearing ore heaped up near its shafts. The idea of drilling into a mountainside for water appeared so outlandish to his associates that Riess, fearing to make them the laughingstock of the mining industry by bringing in a conspicuous drill rig, ordered a 4 × 8 foot shaft drilled with air-compressed jack hammers.

"No geologist would dare recommend drilling for water in places like that today," says Riess. "That's why the Hoovers were so skeptical. But as we drove down and went through the upper, softer alluvium into the hard rock below, I began to get encouraged. We worked for several weeks and then, when we got down to 182 feet, boy, we hit it! The water rose so fast in that big shaft that the workers barely had time to get out of there with their jack hammer before they drowned. It came in under a lot of pressure and surged to within six feet from the surface."

Riess installed a pump in the shaft and, in his words, "pumped the smithereens out of her, on and off for three weeks, half a day, or a whole day at a time. The water ran down the canyon in a brook. There was no drawdown. She maintained her level at six feet from the surface." The new water renewed the mine's profitability and 4 million dollars' worth of bullion was shipped to the San Francisco Mint before World War II exigencies closed down operations. When mining was resumed in 1977, the local press reported that Nelson Joint Ventures was pumping water from a good well drilled on leased land. The good well was none other than that drilled forty-five years previously by Stephan Riess.

Morad Eghbal, an American-trained Iranian graduate student in geology asked Riess to elaborate on his methodology. Eghbal was keenly aware that the mining engineer's ideas did not fit into any of a series of models which geology, perhaps the most speculative of the natural sciences, has developed over decades to explain what may be happening in the unseen world below ground.

"When you consider," said Riess, "that so many of the productive mines in the world have been washed out before they could be worked out and a lot of working mines are pumping out thousands of gallons of water, you've got to ask yourself where the water comes from. I'm speaking of really big operations like the Comstock and the Tombstone."

Historians bear Riess out. Of the famous Comstock silver lode at Virginia City, Nevada, Grant M. Smith writes:

The Combination shaft intersected the Comstock Lode at the depth of 3,000 feet and entered a body of low-grade quartz on the 3,200 foot level, which proved of no value. The shaft was then sunk to the 3,250-foot point. The double line of Cornish pumps was unable to handle the water when the shaft began to make connections with adjoining mines, and Superintendent Regan installed a hydraulic pump to assist, using water furnished by the Water Company as a plunger. Later, two additional hydraulic pumps were installed. The pumps were then lifting

154

5,200,000 gallons every twenty-four hours to the Sutro Tunnel level, or 3,600 gallons a minute. This quantity lifted 3,200 feet would require about 3,000 horsepower theoretically, or with pipe friction and modern pumps and motors about a 4,000 horsepower continuous load.

On October 16, 1886, the Combination pumps ceased to operate. Within 36 hours after the hydraulic pumps were stopped the water had risen to the 2,400-foot level, filling the entire lower workings of the Chollar, Potosi, Hale & Nureruss, and Savage mines, including several miles of crosscuts.

No less impressive is Otis E. Young's description of the demise of the huge silver mine at Tombstone, Arizona:

While dewatering was going on, the related Tombstone Consolidated Mining Company attended to reopening the mines as fast as they were dried out. By 1905 the project had proved a qualified success. At the eight-hundred-foot level the pumps were raising 2.3 million gallons of water daily, while the output of the reopened mines went to the refineries at El Paso in the form of two or three carloads of bulk concentrates a day. Profits were helped along by scavenging both low-grade ore and the waste dumps of the earlier period. With a rise in world silver prices that occurred at the same time, the operation showed a profit for four years. In 1909 it was given out that boiler breakdown had shut down the drainage system and that before repairs could be effected the entire complex had been drowned beyond redemption.

Riess told Eghbal that he mainly looked for "restricted faults" or breaks in the earth's crust which rarely reach to the earth's surface. Where these vertical pipes or fissures or fumaroles did reach the surface, great natural springs of primary water occurred. "You take the creek up in Kings Canyon National Park," he elaborated, "why, it flows at several thousand gallons a minute and it is above all drainage in any direction. Moose Lake, in the same area, also has no visible watershed and that, too, flows at several thousand gallons a minute. Even in dry summer months on Mount Whitney at about 13,000 feet there is a sheer granite wall with a protrusion on its face that cups a small lake. If that lake water is rain or snow, then all we have to do is hang tanks on the Empire State Building or the Eiffel Tower and expect a constant flow of water."

"At no time is water static," Riess went on. "It is constantly changing form. It is either a liquid or gas, or it is bound up in crystalline form in rocks and minerals. The cycle of gas to liquid to crystal is repeated over and over. Oxygen and hydrogen combine under the electrochemical forces of the earth to form liquid water. Not only is water being constantly formed within the earth, but also rocks, minerals, and oil. What I seek is water in its liquid state."

During a ten-day field trip to look at various water wells developed by Riess over the last thirty years, all of which are producing as copiously as when they were first bored, Eghbal learned that the mining engineer uses a twofold approach in locating sources of water. First comes a detailed study of surface structure, the main targets of which are the identification of contacts, or places where two kinds of rock strata adjoin to create natural fissures. Such a contact zone can be found between overlying layers of sedimentary rock laid down over millennia by

155

erosion and deposition, and underlying basalt, a hard, dense igneous rock formed, like granite and other varieties, by crystallization of molten material that comes upward from deep within the earth.

"Just like igneous rock," Riess further explained, "the water I get has to be coming from great depth because it is free of leach minerals found in water flowing through sediments. It comes up through the basalt in fissures, some from 5 to 10 and up to 20 to 30 feet wide, that go down into the earth to provide vertical aqueducts."

To demonstrate to Eghbal the kind of thing he looks for in surface structure, Riess indicated a dyke, a miles-long thin protrusion of igneous rock slicing through adjacent sedimentary structures. To visualize this, one need only posit an extended strip of metal sheeting forced vertically into beach sand to create a barrier within it.

"This dyke," Riess told Eghbal, "is made up of gabbro. It has risen up through sandstone and cuts very plainly through this geology. You can see where it actually surfaces in some places from which its direction, or 'strike' as geologists have it, can be traced across country. On this gabbro contact, a seam of water is flowing down below in a big fissure maybe five or six feet wide. The dykes, penetrating as they do into the lithosphere, the rocky crust of the earth, go down to where the rock becomes fluid. The contacts on gabbro can run thousands of feet. The dykes are mostly vertical or with a very slight dip, never much less than 70 degrees."

"Do you always drill next to a dyke?" asked Eghbal.

"No," replied Riess, "if it's a displacement, I don't. You have to figure that out. You can get misled a hundred times over if you don't know your business."

"So in essence you want *to know if there are any displacement faults* that might have moved the area you're going to be drilling on?" Eghbal asked, hitting on the essence of the problem.

"Yes, it might have moved as much as 500 yards, and then you'll be off it," Riess both agreed and warned.

Riess further explained to the Iranian that if the water came up to, say, 150 feet from the surface and struck a lateral channel, it could travel horizontally for one hundred miles or more. "I couldn't give you an accurate prediction on that without first-class instrumentation and a time-consuming study of the region's geology and possibly by sinking some core holes miles apart which would give me a picture of the strata below ground," he made clear. "This would give me an idea of whether the bedrock lay high or low. The dip and strike of the bedding plane would be revealed very clearly in the cores."

Eghbal broke in: "What would happen if the water ran twenty miles in a lateral displacement and then hit another vertical fissure. Would it come up?"

"Yes," replied Riess, "if it's blocked. If it hits any kind of restriction it has to rise just as if it were coming up behind a dam and spilling over it. You could find water at one spot only 500 feet down and, maybe three miles away, it might be down at

156

At Thermal, California, near the Salton Sea, Stephan Riess drilled a well in rocky heights overlooking flatland so dry and barren as to resemble a moonscape. For over a quarter of a century it has sent a gurgling brook cascading down a slope . . .

. . . to fill a small lake surrounded, as is the nearby residence, with luxuriant vegetation. Beyond the body of water can be seen part of a 450-acre citrus orchard growing in the midst of desert terrain as arid as exists in the state. During part of the year water from the well is impounded behind an earth dam built by the citrus ranch's owner.

Photographed in 1977.

5,000 feet. It depends where the basement, the bedrock, is."

Side by side with his evaluation of structure, Riess focuses a lot of attention on the composition of rocks. Says Eghbal: "What he's looking for is which association of minerals, including water, they might contain. Think of a cocktail or a dinner party. If you know some people will be present, then you might deduce that others will also be in attendance. This is where his petrography and crystallography come in. He doesn't care about the size of the crystals in the rocks as much as their relative quantity, which gives him an idea of how the rocks have altered, or metamorphosed, over long periods of time and allows him to trace the deposition to the time of its origin.

"I also asked him if the age of a given rocky formation made any difference and he replied that, if the structure of the formation permitted an upflow of water, he didn't give a damn if it were Precambrian, or only half a million years old. It's mainly a vertical, rather than a lateral, opening between two distinctly differentiated formations that he's looking for. It's always on a contact between two walls with a space, he says. The space can be filled with impervious material, sort of like a long cork which you have to drill through to get down underneath it. He's drilled as much as 1,000 feet but when he finally broke through, he got a good well."

Eghbal inquired of Riess whether he could predict water veins through seismology, the study of subterranean structures by use of sound waves. "Very likely," was the reply, "because then I'd have a lot of stratographic information. But still I have to depend on past experience which has taken years to collect. I have to know what to look for. You can't learn these techniques in a few weeks or even a few months."

After listening to Riess's exposition and looking at his well sites, Eghbal began to wonder why in his geology classes he had never been taught some of the ideas the mining engineer was expounding. "Riess's work brought into focus some of the very problems that I tried to address to my professors," explained Eghbal, "but they always shied away from them and I could never get any straight answers."

"L'Eau des Roches"

Is primary water produced in rock and available for tapping there? Nordenskiöld and Riess are not the only ones to provide an affirmative answer to this question. Professor C. Louis Kervran, a biologist and engineer who before his retirement was a French government expert on nuclear radiation hazards, asserts that most of the wells in his native Brittany are dug into solid granite.

"Certain 'purists' declare this impossible," wrote Kervran in a 1977 essay on the origin of water found in crystalline rock. "They hold that water can only come from a permeable layer impregnated with it. A sponge, as it were, is needed, they say. This is entirely false and everybody knows it except overspecialized theorists who, even when confronted with facts, will not admit to anything that falls outside the subject matter they absorbed in school."

During his professional career, Kervran knew of so many

cases in which tunneling operations in mountain rock were suddenly flooded with water that he did not even bother to collect data on them. "The incidents were," he noted, "so banally commonplace as to be known to thousands." The floods, which in many cases literally "drowned the construction sites," says Kervran, were generally attributed by geologists to what they called "contained" or "perched" water.

Brittany's granite—termed by Kervran "primary, impermeable terrain"—has supplied water for all farm animals and humans as long as anyone can remember. Like Livingston's wells in the granite under the high Sierras, the wells in Brittany rarely run dry, even during extended droughts such as the one which struck the peninsula in 1976. So widespread is the knowledge of wells in granite among the Breton peasantry that the expression *"L'eau des roches"* or "rock water" has long existed in their vernacular.

Labeling it "constituent water," or that forming part of a whole, Kervran notes that anyone can find out how much of it any rock contains by weighing the rock before and after heating. In his view constituent water was formed at the same time as the rock itself, a lot of it hundreds of millions of years ago, by penetrating the metamorphosing rock as steam and becoming imprisoned when the rock was a precrystalline viscous paste heated to temperatures of an order of 800 degrees Centigrade at enormous pressures of 2–3 kilobars. Cooling, the rock shrank and cracked, opening up fractures leading in all directions.

On this account Kervran holds that it is difficult to find a rock even ten meters thick without such a crack or fissure, many of which intercommunicate, meeting at various angles and forming huge crevices or voids. The voids fill with water for which the myriad fissures are pathways or what Kervran terms "drainage pipes." He has even seen water protruding from such channels

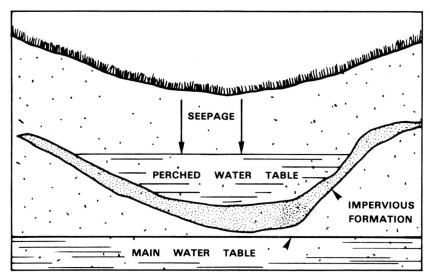

SEEPAGE

PERCHED WATER TABLE

IMPERVIOUS FORMATION

MAIN WATER TABLE

Ground water movements and perched water

where they are laid bare on the faces of cliffs.

During his years as a construction foreman building Interstate Highway 88 through the Sierra Nevada, Livingston, too, noticed similar openings oozing water, especially after heavy equipment had made cuts through rocks. Echoing Livingston's idea that the water in rock is "living water," Kervran avers that this water is generally in motion and that where the flow is more than minimal, it can be easily detected by dowsers. This explains why dowsers are, in his words, *"habitually* used in rocky regions in Brittany to pinpoint the *exact location* where one must dig to contact flowing water. The locations are detected by the dowsers with *great precision."*

During the 1976 drought in Brittany, the French Geological and Mining Bureau lent its drilling equipment, used to prospect for minerals in the Amoricain Mountains, to a crash program to find new water wells. In 1977, *Ouest France,* the newspaper with the highest circulation in the French Republic, reporting on the Bureau's work, emphasized in italic print that its wells in Brittany were *"drilled into crystalline and metamorphic terrain which has too long been erroneously reputed not to be water-bearing."*

"Why can't geologists submit to the evidence?" asks Kervran. "It is easily possible to find water in so-called impermeable rock.

Enormous boulder with fissure, photographed, 1977, in southern California. Cubic miles of so-called impermeable underground rock are laced with such fissures through which water can move at various rates of speed.

Photographs courtesy of Alain Bernard, Katell-Roc S.A., Lizio, France.

Huge circular storage well owned by Katell Roc S.A. near the Brittany village of Lizio in France. The upper photo shows the well surrounded by a fence and covered by a dome of cement through which protrude ventilation shafts. The bottom left photo illustrates the catwalk cutting across the middle of the well from which observers may peer into the crystal clear water below. The bottom right photo reveals part of the granite underwater side wall of the well.

If books on geology do not mention this, it is because all the widely known observations of this phenomenon have never yet been assembled. No synthesis has ever been made of the data, and what a shame."

To gather data on water from rock in Brittany, Kervran traveled in 1977 to the village of Lizio near Ploërmel where a local industry, Katell Roc, was bottling 300 million liters of particularly pure, almost mineral-free, water that is distributed all over Brittany and has recently become popular with "health-food" stores burgeoning in the region of Paris.

Greeting Kervran at the Katell Roc site in a sparsely inhabited countryside were three installations that might have been taken for secret underground laboratories. Surrounded by high barbed-wire fencing, each appeared to be a dome of cement some thirty-five meters in diameter, rising above the ground to a height of about four meters. Out of the domes protruded huge ventilation shafts suggesting underground activity. When the door of one of these installations was unlocked, the Katell Roc president led Kervran down underground beneath the dome. To his surprise, Kervran found himself standing on a kind of catwalk and looking into an enormous round well thirty meters across and nine meters deep. That the well itself had been dug into solid granite was clearly revealed by the side walls all the way around its circumference.

The Katell Roc president told Kervran that the well was fed by a threadlike fissure only 5–6 millimeters wide, which had been detected by a dowser. The huge cisternlike tank had been dug into the rock to serve as reservoir which is pumped off during the day and recovers each night, even overflowing to fill an additional tank of 700 cubic meter capacity.

"Where does water of such purity come from?" asked Kervran.

"I don't know," replied the Katell Roc executive. "Geologists claim it comes from rain falling on Brittany's central mountain range more than fifty miles from here."

"Then water in the wells all around Lizio should be of the same composition as yours," reasoned Kervran.

"Yes, it should," the other man agreed, "but it isn't. It's of a totally different composition. The geologists have always told me that our water is rain water. Now I wonder if they are right."

CHAPTER 9

The Politics of Water

". . . an ordinary kitchen broom . . ."

Three Wells Worth a Million

Riess decided that what he had accomplished at Nelson, Nevada, could be duplicated almost anywhere. To test his theory at his own expense, he purchased a barren plot half the size of a football field in Black Canyon, an arid rocky cleft in the Susana Knolls above Simi Valley between Ventura and Los Angeles, where all signs indicated to him an excellent chance of tapping "primary water," as he called it.

When pumped, the very first well he put down caused a brook to cascade down the hill and inundate the railroad track in the valley below. Two more wells combined with the first to produce 3,000 gpm of water, enough to supply the daily needs of 10,000 people. Visiting neighbors stared open-mouthed at his lush garden, complete with pool and an aviary filled with macaws, cockatoos, and other tropical parrots, one of which, whenever Riess started up his pump, would shriek: "Oh, boy, water, water, water!" Riess was glad to allow some of his neighbors, in dire straights for water, to pipe it free of charge from his copious supply.

News of the mining engineer's success spread throughout Ventura County and elicited increasing demands for his knowledge. The owner of the new Sinaloa Ranch was able to subdivide his property after Riess found him a source of water big enough for a housing development. When Hans Wilhelm Rohl, a multimillionaire contractor who had helped to build the strategic Alaska Highway, acquired the 5,000-acre *Rancho Dos Vientos* at the western end of Portrero Valley, Riess multiplied its worth from $100,000 to $500,000 by bringing in two wells abundant enough to create a small lake.

Two wells drilled during an extended drought on a wilting lemon orchard owned by San Francisco dentist, Dr. John C. Campbell, produced what their owner called the "best, sweetest water in the whole valley." Another citrus operation owned by the chief pathologist at the Santa Monica Hospital was saved when Riess bored him two wells each producing more than 400 gallons per minute.

None of Riess's wells was as appreciated as the one sunk for Candido Ivaro near Camarillo. A worker on the ranch of a descendant of one of the original holders of a California land grant issued by the Spanish king—for whom the town of

Picture of well in the lemon orchard planted by Dr. John C. Campbell. Discovered by Stephan Riess, it has been pumping steadily for over thirty years. Lemon groves climb hills which, without the benefit of the well's water, would be semidesert.

Camarillo is named today—Ivaro had been given twenty-six acres of land by his boss for years of faithful service. On his new holding, Ivaro spent his savings—and five years of his life—to establish a nursery of 30,000 lemon seedlings. Just as they were about ready for grafting and sale, they began dying from lack of water. The two wells on his property, drilled to 224 and 473 feet, had gone dry.

When, in 1955, Riess's wife Thelma heard of Ivaro's plight at a garden club meeting, she asked her husband to see if he could help the nurseryman, who was rumored to be so depressed at his potential ruin that he was on the verge of suicide. In the middle of Ivaro's small holding, less than fifty yards from one of the dry wells, Riess drilled to 234 feet to produce 550 gpm, an amount limited only by the capacity of the pump. By coincidence, the day following the first pumping of the well fell on *Cinco de Mayo*, the popular festival commemorating the Mexican victory over superior French forces at Puebla in 1862.

"I never knew there were so many Mexicans in the county until then," remembers Riess. "They all heard over the grapevine about Ivaro's new well and swarmed to his property for a celebration. By that time, water was filling up huge depressions on his land with kids frolicking and swimming in it. There were cases of Mexican beer, baskets of tacos, and bowls of guacamole, laughter and guitar-playing and singing."

Ivaro was ecstatic. "The pump goes night and day," he later told friends and neighbors, "and the water always stays at about

"The great two-year Western drought is over . . . For the moment, the decade perhaps, the Colorado watershed can fulfill the multiple demands made on it—but the great river is running a deadly race with human greed and government profligacy. Legal allocations of water to the mountain states of the Upper Basin, to California and the fast-growing desert states of the Lower Basin, to the Indians, and to Mexico already add up to more water than flows.

"'The West wouldn't be here,' says California Director of Water Resources Ron Robie, 'if it wasn't for water development'—but 'development' is a word that covers a multitude of sins as well. Water from Federal projects is so cheap that there is little incentive to conserve the West's scarcest and most precious resource . . . Water users, for example, are required to pay only for the capital cost of a water project, not the interest—even though the interest charges wind up being triple the capital cost.

"A portion of California's Central Valley Project called the San Luis Drain was estimated by the Bureau of Reclamation to cost $7 million in its feasibility report 23 years ago; the current estimate is $185 million, and a special task force projects it as high as $275 million. The bureau had also forecast a $300 million surplus in power sales to CVP farmers, while an Interior Department audit predicts an $8.8 billion deficit over fifty years."
— "Western Water Fight," *Newsweek* July 12, 1978

eighty-five feet in the pipe. Around here, in July and August, when everyone is pumping, the wells always drop. But not mine. It's always the same."

Riess's activities in the dry region west of Los Angeles began to irritate hydrogeologic experts at the California Water Resources Division (WRD) who were receiving reports and queries about Riess's method for water location that were as welcome to them as Willey's queries on dowsing had been to the U.S. Geological Survey. To this was added public confusion stemming from a basic question: If water was available locally in the amounts suggested by Riess's work, why were southern California politicians insisting that future supplies were *only* developable through more systems such as those that had already been engineered to transport water from faraway Lake Crowley high above Bishop on the east side of the Sierra Nevada, and from the equally distant reservoir impounded behind Parker Dam on the Colorado River?

Fanning the flames of the controversy was a two-part article in the 1953 issue of *Fortnight,* a southern California magazine: "Revolution in Water Seeking: Steve Riess Has a New Idea of How to Look for Water and 69 Wells to Support His Theory." If results mean anything to scientists, challenged the magazine, Riess's theories of water's origin ought to be investigated. It added that though they had been borne out in practice, they had all the deadweight of hydrologic dogma against them.

Fortnight diagnosed what really was at issue: the money being made in the vast water transport schemes so irresistible to California's financial and political leadership. Greed was blocking methods for locating wells which, if generally adopted and used on a large scale, would amount to the discovery of a new continent.

The article so aroused the ire of WRD officials that they at once initiated an investigation of the wells brought in by Riess. That it relied more on hearsay than on solid fact-finding was evidenced by its admission that WRD agents addressed questions to persons "living in or having knowledge of" the water situation in areas where Riess had developed wells—rather than to those property owners who were amply profiting from the wells' output. Thus, the report characterized the wells sunk for Dr. Campbell as only "apparently satisfactory according to a neighbor," though "no production data were available." The same wells continue to irrigate lemon groves today.

The WRD report characterized Riess's own wells at Simi as being placed "to pump rain and runoff water underlying the hillside." He was only mining water which had been collecting for past centuries, they added, and ultimately his wells would run dry. When he read the report to his friends, Riess laughed wryly and told them: "I have pumped 100 million cubic feet of water from those wells, a volume equal to the hill itself. If this is *contained* water, there is now 100 million cubic feet of *void* under that hill, and I don't know what's holding it up."

If the WRD experts had taken the trouble to ask, Riess could have furnished them with a tape-recording of the water flowing

VENTURA COUNTY Star-Free Press

VENTURA, CALIF., FRIDAY, SEPTEMBER 30, 1955

Headline in Ventury County Star-Free Press.

Riess Sells Water Wells for $1,000,000

By JOE PAUL, JR.

STEPHAN RIESS, Santa Susana water developer, has entered into a contract with Clint Murchison, Texas oil millionaire, to sell his water wells for an agreed price of one million dollars, it was learned today.

Attorney Guy Mann of Dallas, Tex., representing Murchison, stated that the papers have been drawn up for the transaction and that a contract has been signed by each party.

It was claimed that the purchase price of $1 million made the 200 by 80-foot plot of land containing the three Riess wells one of the most expensive pieces of real estate in California.

Mann said that the contract calls for a down payment of $50,000 with the remainder to be paid annually on a basis of water produced.

At the time time, Riess was revealed to be interested to the extent of one-sixth in the recent purchase of acreage in the Simi valley by Murchison. Attorney Mann said that Riess would participate in the ultimate development of the property industrially and residentially, the exact detailed plans for which have not been finalized.

Riess, who left today for Arizona where a company with which he is affiliated has just brought in a second helium gas well, said he was glad to have the situation clarified as to his position in the Murchison transactions. He said that his participation in the land development plan as a one-sixth interest was in payment for dropping his damage suit against Dr. M. Laurence Montgomery, former owner of the 1,600 acres of land purchased by Murchison.

"I had suffered financial damages as a result of the delay in the proposed development of the land," Riess revealed, "and in return for dropping the damage action I was given a part in the overall development plan."

LARGER PUMPS

Mann said that the first step in the program is now beginning with the installation of larger pumps on the Riess wells to determine the rate at which they will produce. As soon as this is determined, a water storage and distribution system is to be installed and by that time plans for development of the land are expected to be completed.

Riess said that he will retain his residence and the wooded garden area immediately surrounding it. Other land he owned in the valley has been included in the area to be developed.

Riess remarked that he had lived in the valley 20 years "and still I'm a stranger."

"But that's all right," he added. "What we need is 10,000 new people with 10,000 new votes in this area.

"It should be fairly obvious even to the many persons who dislike me," he added, "that with the scope of this development I'm not just a nuisance."

Riess and his theories of primary water have been the center of numerous controversies. He has opposed huge bond issues for dam building and importation of water on the grounds that deep well water is available.

At the present time, water from one of the Riess wells is serving the Susana Knolls area and has been for about two years. Riess is not charging the district for the water, the latter using the revenue from the sales to pay its debts and improve the system. Nearly 2,000 persons are getting their water from the Riess well.

166

underground made by lowering a microphone down one of the well shafts to a point some 200 feet below the earth's surface. The water rushing through rock sounded to most ears like a bubbling cauldron accompanied by distant kettledrums and reminded one minister of the church of the passage in Genesis that referred to "subterranean waters bursting forth upon the earth."

The question of productivity was finally settled, not by the biased report of the government investigators, but by Clint Murchison, Texas oil and gas tycoon who, attracted by press accounts of the Riess wells, offered to buy them. Before the sale was completed, Murchison sent his own engineers from Texas to the Black Canyon site where over a period of *eighteen months* they tested the wells to prove their worth as an endurable water supply for large housing tracts Murchison wished to develop in Simi Valley. Murchison was obviously satisfied with the tests. In September 1955, the Ventura County *Star-Free Press* reported that he had agreed to purchase the three wells for one million dollars in a deal that made the small plot of land into which they had been drilled one of the most expensive pieces of real estate in California.

From Lakeside to Eilat

When he learned of the transaction, Burton Arnds, president of Sparklett's Drinking Water, a firm supplying fresh water in five-gallon bottles all over southern California, decided to take action. Arnds had put a lot of money into a new plant at Lakeside in San Diego County where at the advice of WRD specialists he had drilled three wells, each of which initially supplied 100 gpm. Within six months, the bottler was dismayed to observe that his water supply was not only becoming progressively more mineralized—or, in folk parlance, "harder"—but was in fact beginning to run out. The water officials told him the water table below the valley was getting lower and that continued pumping might exhaust his wells. After driving all the way to Simi to have a look at what Murchison had purchased, Arnds offered Riess a contract to find him a well that could save his Lakeside bottling plant from disaster. Riess's careful study of the surface geology of the surrounding region and petrographic analysis of various rock types, led him to begin drilling, not in a brand new spot, but at the bottom of a 400-foot well that had gone dry.

When the diamond-core drill bit twisted down some 500 feet lower, it encountered a large crevice in the rock and water burst up out of the hole to spray the drillers before settling back to twenty feet below the surface of the ground. Finished in 1955, the same well continues, in 1979, to furnish 300 gpm of high-grade water. In case of emergency Riess located another equally productive well not fifty yards from the first. The second well has never been used.

"With two babies like these," Riess told visitors to the Sparklett's Lakeside plant in 1977, "we could supply all water needs for a large community. The one you see pumping is a sample of thousands we could drill in the United States and other

167

countries, to provide water at much lower cost than normal."

Arnds's good fortune, far from serving to inspire WRD officials to investigate Riess's methods, goaded them into enlisting the aid of academic geologists in their effort to discredit him. First to attack was Dr. Ulysses S. Grant, IV, professor at the University of California at Los Angeles who asked publicly why, if Riess's methods were so good, he had not published something about them in a scientific journal. Next came University of California ground water geologist, Dr. John F. Mann, Jr., who warned his television audience that Riess's ideas about a source of what he now called "primary water" were delusional.

The altercation came to the attention of Kimmis Hendrick, Chief of the Pacific News Bureau of the *Christian Science Monitor,* who investigated its background. He found that Mann had recommended a well site on a large farm newly purchased in the Anza Valley by specialty crop farmer Harry Pursche, who had already fruitlessly expended $40,000 to drill for irrigation water. Called in as a consultant, Mann told Pursche that his only chance was to probe a sand fill where "water might have collected." Five hundred and ninety-three feet and another $12,000 later, Pursche had only 4 gallons per minute, wholly insufficient for his needs.

Told of the farmer's plight by Hendrick, Riess had Pursche bulldoze a road up a 350-foot-high granite hillock and clear a flat space for a water-drilling rig. News of this undertaking spread through the valley and attracted the attention of state geologists working in the area who informed their home office in Sacramento about the development. The next day six members of the WRD arrived at the Pursche spread to warn its owner that his new attempt to locate irrigation water would only add a preposterous sequel to his lengthy saga of hard luck. One of them personally guaranteed to drink every drop of water that came out of the hard rock underlying Riess's site.

Riess's answer was to *predict before any drilling commenced* that he would strike water at 300–310 feet in a volume ranging from 300–1,000 gpm. The first water came in at 302 feet. The following morning the drill stem would not turn. Something in the hole was blocking its normal rotation. A bailer put down the

Entrance to Sparklett's Drinking Water, Lakeside, California.

168

well to retrieve whatever might be causing the blockage dredged up fistfuls of steel ball bearings. Within two days, three large bucketfuls of bearings had been removed. In an effort to prove the well worthless, someone had thrown them down the hole under cover of night to prevent further drilling.

When the well was finally finished and cased, a 500-gallon capacity pump was lowered into the hole. Powered by one of Pursche's tractors, it pumped steadily for sixty hours. Neighbors for miles around who had gathered at the well were no less dumbfounded by the find than Professor Mann who nevertheless continued to insist that Riess had "just been lucky." In spite of this belittlement, the WRD had no choice but to report that "initial production of the well compares very favorably with the best previous wells in the area. For limited periods it has pumped as much as 1,030 gallons per minute, and it has pumped an estimated 400 gpm 'nearly continuously' for over thirty days."

By 1958 Riess's exploits came to the attention of the Israeli government, which invited the mining engineer to find water for the new city of Eilat on the Red Sea's Gulf of Aquaba. After a flight to Tel Aviv, he met with then Prime Minister David Ben-Gurion and his advisors who urged him to go ahead with his search as soon as possible. Less enthusiastic were a group of leading Israeli geologists who, like their American counterparts, vigorously opposed Riess's theory of water development. "Only after a protracted session during which I explained it," Riess later said, "did they agree that my proposal had merit." This was confirmed by Israel's chief water geologist, Arie Isseroff who, in a letter, wrote: "As a geologist who is occupied with water research in arid zones, I am fully aware of the limitations of our orthodox methods in geohydrological prospecting and am much impressed by the glimpse I got of the new methods offered by Mr. Riess, recognizing the unfathomed possibilities which may be opening up before us while applying these methods. I decided, encouraged by my superiors, to cooperate with Mr. Riess's research for primary waters in our arid zones."

High in the mountainous country along the Israel-Jordan border, Riess located a well about a mile and a half from Eilat itself. "The site chosen," wrote Meir Ben-Dov in the *Jerusalem Post,* "is where a five-meter-wide cleft, running vertically through the mountain, is crossed at right angles by a similar cleft, hardly twenty centimeters across. The bowels of the earth in erupting have filled these clefts with an igneous intrusion of a soft, soapy-feeling, mottled brown rock called gabbro. The drill slowly worked its way downward, alternately in igneous intrusion and again in granite as the cleft in the rock snaked its way downward."

During the work, problems linked to cave-ins and the jamming of drill pieces beyond the Israeli drilling team's experience were finally solved when Riess's associate, James Scott, who had worked with him on many wells over the years, was sent to Israel to supervise operations.

On May 29, 1959, the *Jerusalem Post* estimated that the amount of water struck in the Riess-located well was enough to supply a city of more than 100,000 persons including industry,

Photos of California City, California and environs: a) Galileo Hill, an anomalous protruberance rising from the flat Mojave desert at the base of which Stephan Riess drilled a water well b) A huge water tank supplied by Riess' well. c) Well on outskirts of California City brought in by Riess. d) Aerial view of California City showing lake and waterfall (see also e enlargement) all created by water

air-conditioning, parks, gardens, and a dozen outlying villages. Analysis of the water, stated the newspaper, revealed that the Eilatis, used to drinking water with 3,000 parts per million of dissolved mineral salts, now had a supply with only 1/6 that amount. For his work in Israel, Ben-Gurion presented Riess with a medal and his wife with a silver-bound copy of the Talmud in English.

The astounding find was not lost on Arab leaders. Invited to Cairo by Egypt's Gamal Abdel Nasser, Riess became the only exception to a rigid years-long stricture prohibiting Americans who had visited Israel from setting foot in Arab lands. Along the Nile he located several water wells in rock for prominent

170

from Riess-discovered wells. e)
Waterfall (Courtesy of the
California City Chamber of
Commerce). f) Hundreds of
poplar trees that line many of the
city's streets, fed by Riess' well.

Egyptians before flying on to the Sudan where a revolution disrupted his planned exploration.

On a homeward-bound visit to Cyprus, Riess was interviewed in Nicosia by an English-language newspaper reporter investigating new approaches to finding water. The reporter had read a long letter written by Henry Gross, a dowser living in Maine who achieved fame when, working over a map of Bermuda on his kitchen table in Portland, he accurately dowsed fresh water in the British Island colony which ever since its settlement had depended on captured rain or imports for its needs. Gross's confirmed predictions had so impressed the celebrated American historical novelist, Kenneth Roberts, that he

171

wrote not one, but three books on Gross's dowsing finds that are now dowsing classics.*

In his letter Gross maintained that his dowsing rod indicated no less than fourteen "primary domes" of fresh water in the hills and mountains of Cyprus. Without telling Riess about the dowser's report, the investigative journalist asked the mining engineer what he thought of the possibility of finding badly needed supplies of water on the island. Riess replied: "I am convinced that abundant supplies of water are available to the people of Cyprus, right below their feet and flowing in deep-seated solid rock fissures that could be scientifically located. Man has overlooked 'primary water' that has never been seen on the face of the earth. Even more importantly, it cannot be contaminated by nuclear fallout or surface pollution as can reservoirs aboveground."

450 Miles or 450 Feet?

Back home in California Riess was approached by a group of developers contemplating the establishment of a brand new city in the Mojave Desert to provide the public with an option of living in a noncongested area. What they badly needed was a supply of water. This was all Riess needed to prove another theory he had developed—that a supply of water ran under the Mojave large enough to supply the needs of all of southern California. He knew that the agricultural empire in California's Central Valley had been brought into being by water flowing in a dozen or more rivers down the west slopes of the Sierra Nevada. On the eastern side of the divide, however, hardly any surface water flow could be observed, in spite of the fact that a massive 50 million acre-feet of water had been estimated by the U.S. Forest Service, the Bureau of Land Management, and other government agencies to collect there in winter as in the snow pack.

In the Owens River Valley along the road to Lone Pine and Big Pine east of Sequoia National Park, Riess discovered that if he walked three or four miles up into dozens of bone-dry deep gash canyons, he would encounter streams full of fish, which disappeared into the earth. He came to the conclusion that a large part of the snow-melt flowed only part way down the eastern side of the Sierra before disappearing into the crushed and fractured rocky system. If this were so, an enormous river network should be flowing underground to exit into the ocean.

To test his theory, Riess sank a series of deep wells in the desert country stretching from far up the Owens River Valley all the way to the Salton Sea out of which water exploded in geysers that shot into the air sometimes higher than the towers of the drill rigs. One of them was drilled on a plot of land he himself had purchased for a song. When it produced plentiful water, he resold at a $139,000 profit. Near an anomalous hemisphere-shaped hillock on the otherwise flat desert southeast of the hamlet of Randsburg he sunk two wells which, together

---

*Henry Gross and His Dowsing Rod, 1951; The Seventh Sense, 1953; Water Unlimited, 1957. All published by Doubleday & Company, Garden City, New York.

172

with a third drilled a few miles distant, today supply all the water for California City, as the settlement pioneered by the developers was christened.

Riess's findings were supplemented by a quarter-of-a-million-dollar study which concluded that water travelling in the fault system under the desert had nothing in common with any water in "alluvium sedimentary aquifers," *i.e.,* the water table. The chief coordinator of the study, Olindo Romulus Angelillo, a registered civil engineer, told the *Christian Science Monitor* that more than a million acre-feet flowed under the desert. "A million acre-feet," the *Monitor* commented, "is a staggering amount of water. It is enough to meet the annual needs of five million people. It is three times as much as the Los Angeles Metropolitan Water District gets from the Owens River, which for nearly half a century has been the city's main source of water supply. It is twice as much as the eighty-three cities in the Los Angeles Metropolitan area draw annually from the Colorado River. It is more than half as much as southern California hopes to get someday from the Feather River."

The Feather River Project to which the newspaper referred was at the time provoking one of the most acerbic debates in California history. It proposed to dam the river at a junction with one of its forks near Oroville, some sixty miles north of Sacramento and channel part of the impounded water hundreds of miles to the arid southland. The projected transportation system was to be the biggest water supply scheme ever undertaken in human history. Estimated in 1959 to cost at least $14 billion, it has since proved to be many billions more expensive.

Every man, woman, and child in California, and unborn generations as well, were to be saddled with water taxes to pay off bonds financing the scheme. The announcement that a huge supply of water might be tappable under the Mojave seemed to pose a threat to California's Governor Edmund G. "Pat" Brown, who had politically committed himself to the project and to the groups supporting it—bonding companies, banks, construction firms, materials suppliers, and others—who stood to make sizable profits.

As the *Monitor* summed up the enormous implications: "The find could change the whole character of the western quest for water. It conceivably could make pointless the longstanding fight between the western states over the water of the Colorado River. It could make equally pointless the divisive bickering between northern and southern California over the destiny of the Feather River."

In the midst of a heated campaign to put across to the California public the urgent need to vote for the Feather River Project, Riess contracted with the San Bernadino Municipal Water District (SBMWD) to drill wells sufficient to supply the needs of huge San Bernardino County *in perpetuo* for a sum infinitesimally smaller than that to be levied against the district as its share of the Feather River Project. Riess's first well for the SBMWD, brought in a Yucaipa, delivered 900 gpm in 600 feet of

173

solid granite. A movie of the well pumping water was screened by excited county officials to prove that county residents did not necessarily have to bear the yoke of an expensive bond issue. When the well was on the point of being accepted by the SBMWD, Riess was summoned to a private meeting with its manager who shamefacedly told him that he had been asked by Governor Brown to shut down the well. Flabbergasted, Riess asked why. "Because," admitted the SBMWD manager, "he felt that if you couldn't be stopped from running around the country bringing in maverick water wells, the whole bonding issue was in jeopardy."

Having no choice but to defend himself against political skulduggery, Riess went to court to collect some $200,000 in costs that he had personally incurred in the SBMWD drilling. The court accepted evidence from State Water Division engineers who, as Riess puts it, "had just left school," that the well he had put down would not produce the water claimed for it. Riess lost his case both in the lower and the appeals courts but finally won when the decision was reversed in the Supreme Court of California. Not wishing to add to the tax burden of ordinary citizens, he declined to sue for the full $7 million amount of his contract.

Angry and hurt, Riess carried his case to the public by testifying before a Select Committee on National Water Resources of the United States Senate in Los Angeles in October 1959. He began by pointing out that conventional solutions to an ever-increasing need for pure water differed but little from ancient methods of transporting water on mule back or through such aqueduct systems as those built in classical Roman times. Prophetically, Riess told the committeemen that not only were safe areas for dam building fast running out in the United States, but that dams represented no long-term solution because, in the end, silt collecting behind them would eventually create mudflats for beavers and waterfalls, if the dams themselves did not burst beforehand.

As an alternative, Riess proposed serious study of water flowing in rock fissures. "Why should huge sums be spent to build pipe lines over great distances when Mother Nature has created her own pipe lines?" he asked the committee. "It is certainly far more economical to pump water vertically up 450 feet than to pump it and transport it laterally for 450 miles!"

To counter the force of Riess's arguments, the California Director of Water Resources rushed into print with an *Information Bulletin* labeling the whole Mojave Desert study worthless and attacking Riess's ideas about primary water as unfounded. The newest reprise on the earlier 1954 report on the Riess wells sarcastically referred to the "purported documentary evidence" in the quarter-of-a-million-dollar study and its "specious and utterly speculative" arguments. Riess himself was termed a "purported scientist, geologist, geochemist, and philosopher," an epithet that could just as easily have characterized many of the WRD's own staffers.

The WRD's stultified approach toward an idea that merited at least a portion of its investigatory time was exemplified in the

*Golden Eagle Ranch, a
thoroughbred stud farm at
Ramona, California. Formerly
arid and barren, the valley was
converted in the 1970s to lush
pasturage with water from
three deep wells located by
Stephen Riess, thus creating a
multimillion-dollar oasis for
blooded race horses, 1977.*

Photographed in 1977

bulletin by its statement that the concept of "primary water" was not even listed in "any standard glossary of geological or hydrological nomenclature." The same could have been said for the word "blitzkrieg," which became acceptable to French generals, who could not find it in any of their standard military glossaries, only when they were overwhelmed by the reality the word represented.

The bulletin was sent to thirty-three California State Offices including those dealing with agriculture, water pollution, architecture, public works, mining, soil conservation, beaches and parks, veterans affairs, public utilities, farm and home purchases, public health, natural resources, small craft harbors, and fish and game. More ominously, copies were received by the State Director of Finance, the State Board of Registration for Civil and Professional Engineers, the State Attorney General, and the Assistant Chief of the State Bureau of Criminal Identification and

175

Investigation—the clear implication being that Riess was not only a maverick and a possible crackpot but a potential criminal meriting prosecution. The dissemination did not stop with state officialdom. Copies were sent to eleven federal officials in California, to water authorities in sixteen western states, and to twenty-eight "requesters" of information ranging from professors, engineers, consulting geologists, and newspaper editors to bankers, investment companies, and lawyers.

New Water for a Thirsty World

The vitriolic bulletin also attacked a remarkable book, *New Water for a Thirsty World*, dedicated to Stephan Riess by its author, Michael Salzman, then a professor at the University of California's School of Commerce who had served as engineer with the U.S. Navy's Hydrographic Office and became Director of the Los Angeles City Housing Authority.

During five years of research into Riess's theory of primary water, Salzman, first to translate Nordenskiöld's essay into English, came across evidence for rock-produced water in connection with one of the strangest episodes ever to appear in the annals of construction engineering. It took place in the middle of Manhattan when, in 1955, the engineering firm of Psaty and Furman, under contract to New York City's Department of Public Works, began the excavation for the foundation of an addition to the Harlem Hospital at the intersection of Fifth Avenue and 136th Street.

While removing a layer of hard rock only twelve feet below ground on Saint Valentine's day, workers were suddenly confronted with an enormous outrush of water, seemingly from nowhere, which rapidly began to fill the vast hole being opened

Michael Salzman. Photographed in 1977.

in Gotham's body. Pumps hurried to the site labored at the rate of 2,200 gpm for an entire year to keep the working area free of water. Particularly puzzling to engineers was the fact that during cold winter months the water maintained a constant temperature of 68 degrees Fahrenheit and was so pure that hospital chemists certified it could be drunk without chlorination or any other chemical treatment. A billion and a quarter gallons were pumped out of the hole day and night until twelve stories of structural steel had been erected and several lower floors decked with concrete slabs to provide enough weight to hold down the foundation of the new building against hydrostatic pressure.

In June, the *Engineering News-Record* ran a story that ended with the baffling note that neither the origin nor the constant elevated temperature of water could be explained. Of the article's readers, only Salzman responded to the challenging enigma by offering an explanation based on Riess's theory of water made in rocks. When it printed Salzman's conclusions, the journal editorialized that, despite the efforts of many agencies, the source of water flowing under the Harlem Hospital had never been determined. No hydrologist, it added, had come up with any thoughts as to its origin.

Nor has there been any comment about the anomaly in geologic or hydrologic literature in the succeeding twenty-three years.

In a foreword to the Salzman book, Aldous Huxley, the English philosopher and writer who had only recently finished his ground-breaking study of psychedelic drugs, *The Doors to Perception,* about which he was lecturing at the Menninger Clinic in Kansas, pointedly commented: "It remains to be seen whether those who are now regarded as experts in the field of hydrology and the politicians whom they advise will also agree that a good case has been made and that *large-scale experimentation is in order.*" Since then, eighteen years have witnessed no such experimentation, large-scale or small, on the part of hydrologic officials, state or federal.

Huxley's unequivocal recommendation seemed, at least, indirectly, to have won the partial sympathy of a professional hydrologist, William C. Ackerman, vice-president of the American Geophysical Union (AGU) and chief of the Illinois Water Survey Division. In an address to his colleagues at a regional meeting of the AGU in Moscow, Idaho, in October 1960, Ackerman expressed his disappointment that, for years, papers on hydrology submitted to the AGU's *Transactions* had been so recondite that most of them had been refused for publication. AGU officials had told Ackerman that, in a world expanding into space, hydrologic contributions evidenced an outworn parochialism in outlook and urged him to persuade his associates to look beyond the hydrologic cycle of the earth—which seemed to be their sole concern.

The heart of the problem, concluded Ackerman, was that hydrology had been riding for too long on the coattails of a few of its greatest exponents, whose work had been performed a quarter of a century previous, with nothing of consequence having been added in the interim.

Part Four

INDAGO FELIX:
THE FRUITFUL
SEARCH

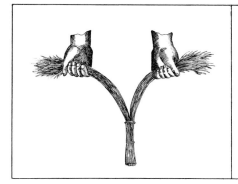

CHAPTER 10

Gusher!

". . . or a good German knockwurst *which, turning in the hands, bursts open . . ."*

The Doodlebugger and the Wildcatter

The man was hunched over an empty cylindrical ice cream carton holding in one hand what he called a "transmitter," on the end of a string, and a stopwatch in the other. The carton stood over the spot where an oil-drilling rig was spudded in to seek a new well in the hills near Aliso, California. The man kept counting to himself and, every so often, writing something in a small notebook.

After nearly an hour, the man rose and ambled over to J. K. Wadley, one of the most successful wildcatters in the oil business. "If your men drill down die-straight at the point contemplated for drilling," he said dryly, "they're going to hit an excellent commercial deposit. You're on a productive oil trend."

"How deep does the oil lie?" asked Wadley skeptically.

"At 2,700 feet, a little bit less than half a mile, and your oil zone is going to be around eighty feet thick. The well should make around 150 barrels per day." The tone was matter-of-fact, confident, and unequivocal.

Wadley looked hard at the man for a moment, trying to size him up for the tenth time. He had come highly recommended by Lee Davis, one of Wadley's close friends and a fellow millionaire who had made history when he drilled a 5,000 B/D (barrels a day) discovery well, a bore that opened up a brand new field for the University of Texas, and made it one of the wealthiest institutions of higher learning in the world.

Davis told Wadley that he had found and successfully tested a "doodlebugger," as dowsers had long been known in the petroleum industry, who was uncannily able to foretell the amount and depth of oil lying below a given spot of ground. Paul Clement Brown, the dowser, was no unlettered rustic but a graduate of the Massachusetts Institute of Technology who had worked for many years in electronic engineering and later dowsed successful wells for Robert Minkler, president of the Mobil Oil Company.

Wadley cleared his throat. "Look here, Brown," he shot out sternly, "I've worked with a few dowsers in my time. A lot of 'em will come to a wildcat location like this and tell me I'm going to get a dry hole. And nine times out of ten they'll be right. But I've never seen a one of 'em call a producer with as much confidence or precision as you just have."

181

"I have the definite impression that in dowsing I use my transmitter to send down a mental wave which is reflected by deposits of whatever I am searching for. The answering reflection is not instantaneous but has a few moments' time lag. The signal seems to proceed at exactly 90 feet a minute. I haven't any idea why. That's the reason I made a new dial on what used to be a stopwatch and graduated it in feet of depth.

"Over many years I learned accurately to delineate borderlines of underground oil and gas reservoirs, their width and length, their depth from the top of the ground and the thickness of the zones. Productivity depends upon the size of the reservoir pressures, oil viscosity, and the porosity of the oil-bearing formation. During the years I worked with J. K. Wadley, he never would drill in those areas where I said there was no oil. And people who later did drill in those areas never struck oil."

Paul Clement Brown.

He paused, waiting for Brown's comment or qualification. The dowser met his level gaze but remained silent.

"You know this well you've spotted lies right between two dust-dry holes. One was a Richfield Oil Corporation test hole, the other a well drilled by the Seaboard Oil Company. But something tells me you're right," concluded Wadley. "I'm going ahead with this project. And you'll be working regularly for me from now on." To back up his statement Wadley led Brown over to a bank of dirt in the shade of a tall eucalyptus grove, sat down next to his new oil consultant, and drew up a contract retaining the dowser at a fee of $30,000 a year.

Less than two weeks later, in his home office at Texarkana, Arkansas, Wadley looked pleased. "Well," he growled to Brown who had just arrived from California, "your prediction was pretty good. That Cascade well struck oil at 2,700 feet and it's making 150 barrels a day. We drilled three more wells into the trend and they're each producing 150 barrels as well."

Wadley then launched into the reason for Brown's trip east by informing the dowser that he had recently acquired a 9,500-acre lease at Searcy, northeast of Little Rock, Arkansas, and was planning to begin an expensive drilling program. "You go up there and estimate my chances for success," he ordered.

Brown spent several days surveying the property and, as he stated, "I found some oil and gas, but none in paying quantities. I finally decided that I might be on the wrong land, so I called on a few of the local owners who assured me that, yes, they'd leased their ground to Mr. Wadley. So there was nothing to do but call him and let him know the bad news."

Wadley's curt reply revealed his shock. "Come back to Texarkana right away and meet me in my office at ten o'clock tomorrow morning." Before Brown could reply, Wadley hung up.

Back in the office, Brown was greeted by maps of the Searcy leasehold spread out on a large table. With more than a little irritation Wadley declared: "Now, these maps you're looking at were made by two of the most accomplished geologists the oil industry has to offer. They have assured me that this is the finest

182

oil structure in the state of Arkansas and have all but guaranteed that I'll get a lot of oil if I drill up there. Not being satisfied with that, I had seismographers work over the leasehold and they agreed that I'll get oil if I drill. To triple check, I had a crew with magnetometers go over the land and they, too, have come back with a report that my chances for finding oil are excellent.

"Now those three reports and the maps that go with 'em are so much alike, you'd think they were made by the same person instead of being independently drawn. The people who worked them up are all top-notch experts in their fields. They've all promised that this structure is the best in the state."

Brown looked at the maps in silence for a few moments, then cleared his throat.

"If you drill up there, Mr. Wadley," he stated, in a word-for-word reiteration of his telephone message, "all you'll get is a showing. No matter where you put a well down in that leasehold up there, the best you're going to get is a showing of oil and probably a showing of gas, but that's the best you're going to do."

Wadley looked crestfallen. "Well," he answered, "I'm under obligation to drill up there and you are standing alone against these highly-paid professionals."

Brown stood his ground. "Mr. Wadley," he commented wryly, "to me those experts are like a band of savages dancing around a campfire, yelling and screaming to pluck up their courage and trying to make certain that the battle they have to fight tomorrow morning will bring them victory."

Wadley drilled 7,200 feet into the lease at the spot his experts believed most likely to produce instant success. The drilling was the hardest the wildcatter had ever encountered in a nearly fifty-year-long career. One hundred eighty-two drilling bits were used, costing from 125 to 345 dollars each. The total bill for the well was a quarter of a million dollars.

"He got a showing of oil, and a showing of gas," recalled Brown, "and that's all he got. He didn't do any further drilling on that structure."

A third assignment involved one of Wadley's associates who had drilled three 75 B/D wells in fractured limestone near the Red River, north of Vernon, Texas. A fourth well was planned for the same area but, doubtful about its potential success, Wadley asked Brown to check it. This time the dowser reported to his boss: "They're sitting right on top of oil at that well. All they have to do is drill straight down to get it. But its potential production is only small potatoes compared to what the land across the road will produce. Do you have it under lease?"

Wadley shook his head. "For years everybody's said there's no oil on that side of the road," he commented. "It's been studied by a whole bunch of experts and they're all unanimous. So no one has leased it."

Brown took Wadley to the prospective site and, within a day, convinced him that the main oil-bearing structure in the area lay across the road in a northwesterly direction. After obtaining a lease on the land, Wadley brought in twelve excellent oil wells, then admitted to Brown that another dowser by the name of

183

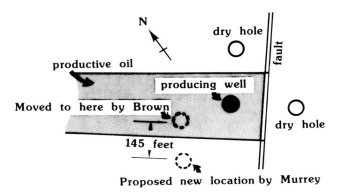

Map of Murrey's projected oil well and Brown's correction.

N

dry hole

fault

productive oil

producing well

Moved to here by Brown

dry hole

145 feet

Proposed new location by Murrey

Murrey, whom he had assigned to check the terrain, had completely missed the new field. "He predicted a lot of paying wells for me but they turned out to be nothing but dry holes," Wadley went on. "And the funny thing is that, after we parted company, he went down to Abilene, Texas, where, working for himself on his own lease, he drilled five wells all at the same time. Every one of them was a big producer. Since then, I've heard his luck's run out."

Spurred by curiosity, Brown made a trip to Abilene and looked up Murrey. He discovered that, before his run of "bad luck," Murrey had expanded his original lease and actually brought in over 200 producing wells, discovering three new oil fields in the process, all by dowsing. Then, as Brown found out at the new site Murrey was working, he had made a common oil dowsing error.

"He'd moved over onto 'feeder beds,'" explained Brown, "where the oil lay in numerous little stringers. It was evident to me he'd never learned to dowse for oil properly and was not able to distinguish scattered deposits from the wide, solidly productive reservoirs he'd found earlier. After putting down sixty-eight dry holes, he stopped drilling. When I caught up with him he was scratching his head."

Murrey asked for Brown's help: "I seem to have a field with only one producing well," he explained, "I've drilled two holes northeast and southeast from it and no more than 200 feet away, but no success. I'm planning to punch a third one in to the southwest. Will you see if I'll get oil?"

What Brown found was that if Murrey drilled in the spot projected he would come up with a third loser, but if he moved only 145 feet northward and about the same distance west of the producing well, he'd have a winner. "Your stake is located only one hundred feet from the edge of your productive reservoir," he chided Murrey, "over little stringers of oil leading away from it."

Although his own dowsing had indicated to him that no oil was to be found at the spot proposed by Brown, Murrey nevertheless followed the proffered advice. That the well produced a handsome 300 B/D can be confirmed by anyone who consults the Texas Railroad Commission's oil records.

Paul Brown had been working on electronic methods to search for oil and gas when one day he saw several men prospecting for a new well site with "doodlebugs," as a host of dowsing devices worthy of Rube Goldberg are generically termed in wildcatting circles. After experimenting with most of them, Brown opted for one of the simplest, a cylinder filled with petroleum hanging on the end of a string.

Taking out a stopwatch with its face graduated, not in minutes of time, but feet of depth, Brown explained his procedure: "I press the button on the top of the watch, starting it from zero, and hold my pendulum steady and motionless. The watch reads off ninety feet of depth every minute. At one point, when the watch has recorded a given depth, say 5,000 feet, the pendulum will start swinging in a circle counterclockwise, at which point I will say, 'In.' That depth indicates the top surface of a bed of oil-producing sand. The pendulum will continue to rotate counterclockwise until the watch hand reads 5,120 feet, whereupon it will stop. At that point I say, 'Out.' I have reached the bottom of the oil production zone and know it is 120 feet thick."

Using the same method, Brown proceeds down into the ground locating any oil zones deeper than the first one encountered. By noting the intensity of the twirling motions he can, he says, predict the amount of oil a well will produce from a given zone. These he classifies in one of four categories: "not commercially productive," "good," "very good," and "excellent."

An Expert Impressed

Asked who might substantiate his fascinating account of his oil-dowsing ability and corroborate his accuracy, Brown replied laconically: "Well, there's Chet Davis. He's a registered petroleum engineer with nearly forty years experience in the field. He'll support my claims."

A graduate of the California Institute of Technology, Chet Davis, supervising engineer for California field operations for one of America's largest oil companies, related how one morning a promoter walked into his office to announce he was in touch with a man whose mysterious method of finding oil was fantastically accurate.

Davis at once grew uncomfortable. "Listen," he told his interlocuter, "I'm a professional oil man. I'm not going to stake my reputation on some magician. Even if he really does have something to offer, I wouldn't get a good reception with our geophysicists or geologists who'd be against him if only because he'd be putting them out of a job."

For years, Davis had run across "doodlebuggers" who had sworn they could find oil without error, but every time the engineer took one of them out into the field he could never pass even a simple test. "All of them always wound up with some alibi," says Davis, " 'Today the chemistry of my body has changed' or something like that. It was really pathetic, sometimes tragic."

Refusing to be put off, the promoter continued over a period of weeks to paint so rosy a picture of his oil finder's prowess that finally Davis's curiosity was fully aroused. Partly because the man represented to him was a fellow engineer reputed to use an electronic instrument in his oil location work, Davis decided to see if someone could find producing oil and gas wells at a rate better than the average one in twenty-five that the oil companies were achieving. Over an eighteen-month period the anonymous oil locater was provided by Davis with the exact physical locations of thirty-five wells to be drilled in various parts of the state and requested through the promoter to make written predictions about their potential productivity or lack of it. These could later be checked either against oil company scouting reports or against the *Munger Oilogram,* a daily scouting service providing data on the progress of any wildcat or development well drilled in California.

Concerned with more urgent business for several months, Davis did not bother to glance at the predictions that had begun to trickle in. So insistent was the promoter in pressuring him for a report, however, that the oil engineer devoted the better part of one Christmas vacation to a careful comparison of the forecasts with published drilling results.

When he was through with this task, Davis was thunderstruck.

"After double-checking the data," he says, "I found to my utter surprise that, of thirty-five wells I'd assigned him to check, only seven had predictions which did not match results. He seemed to have scored an 80 percent accuracy rate, which to me was just fantastic. I was puzzled by the seven misses mainly because they were all in the same locality. So I had one of my scouts check them.

"Well, so help me God, I found that every one of those wells had been bored *vertically.* The oil finder predicted they would be dry holes, and he was right. After drilling the seven dry holes, the company came back and drilled directional holes and then every well became a producer. The oil finder had all thirty-five wells 100 percent correct! I didn't think anyone in the oil business would ever believe it."

Typical among the predictions was one made for the Zel Rol No. 1 well owned by the Supreme Oil and Gas Corporation in the Shafter Gas Field: "Commercial production would not be developed if the hole was drilled straight down at the surface location selected by Supreme. Only *five feet* of gas sand would be developed, insufficient for a commercial well. However, if a location *150 feet southeast* from the selected site were to be drilled, two productive gas sands would be hit, one just below *4,050 feet,* the other at a depth of about *4,320 feet.*"

The result for the same well read: "Supreme drilled the well at their selected location. There is only *five feet* of sand present. The hole was then redrilled to a subsurface location about *150 feet southeast* of the selected site. The electric log of the redrilled hole shows a 15-foot sand development between *4,060 and 4,075 feet* and a 35-foot sand development between *4,315 and 4,350 feet.* The well was completed, producing from both zones."

Eventually introduced to Davis, the man who had made the almost unbelievably accurate predictions was none other than Paul Clement Brown with whom Davis next began a series of weekend field tests to further check his ability. As he reported: "The first place I took him to was the Castaic Hills Field on which I had electric logs for three wells. This is a field where the

186

SHORT SUMMARIES OF TYPICAL PREDICTIONS BY PAUL C. BROWN AND ACTUAL RESULTS.

	Predictions	*Results*
Signal Oil & Gas Co.	Some shows only below 11,000 feet but not commercially productive.	Oil shows at about 11,000 feet. Well abandoned as nonproductive.
Standard Oil Co. KCL 27-3	Well will discover a new field. Oil sand about 40 feet thick at about 7900 foot depth.	Well completed as a new discovery. Oil produced from 7904 to 7943 feet depth.
Standard Oil Co. "67" 21-10	Well will be a dry hole.	Well drilled to 12,705 feet. No oil encountered.
Standard Oil Co. KCL 34-3	Well will be a dry hole. All zones wet.	Well drilled to 8400 feet. Objective sands wet.
Standard Oil Co. 9Z-523	If drilled straight, well will find all objective sands wet. If redrilled to SW commercial production will be possible from two upper sand series.	Straight hole drilled to 9991 feet. All sands wet. Well redrilled to SW. Two upper sand series produced 1268 B/D and 220 B/D
Standard Oil Co. 9Z-534	Well will find all sands wet. Possibly a marginal well can be obtained in Phacoides sand. Fracing will be necessary to establish commercial production	Well drilled to 9290 feet and all sands wet. Redrilled. Phacoides sands yeilded 50 B/D. After fracing well produced 265 barrels a day.
Getty Oil Company Morris USL-581	Upper and lower Carneros sand series will be productive if hole drilled straight down.	Well completed as a dual upper and lower Carneros Zone producer.
Standard Oil Co. 4Z-518	Only upper Carneros sands will be productive.	Well completed as an upper Carneros zone producer.
Rothschild Oil Co. Kliewer No. 1	Well hole will result in finding the objective sand wet.	The objective Stevens sand was wet.

formations dip steeply at about a 45 degree angle. If Brown really had the ability to pick the top of a formation and determine the thickness of the oil sands, I figured this would be a good place to test him, because I could take him first to a well high on the structure, then to another well low on the structure."

At the first well Brown took out his pendulum and inserted it in an empty gallon-size ice cream carton to protect it from side winds where it could twirl beyond the gaze of his companion.

"It was the strangest procedure I ever saw in my life," Davis recalled. "I was told the thing inside the can was a type of

187

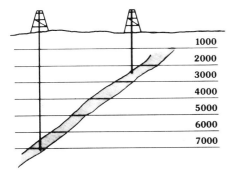

Oil formation dipping at an angle

1000
2000
3000
4000
5000
6000
7000

electronic transmitter which pumped energy into the earth at the rate of 90 feet a minute. When it encountered oil, the signal was supposed to echo back. Whatever he was doing, Brown gave me a depth for the top of the oil sand, down about 3,000 feet, which came to *within five feet of the mark.* It was barely 15 feet thick and he called it at *12½ feet* thick. I was impressed to say the least."

Davis knew that the second well, drilled into the lower part of the structure, once an oil producer, had been converted into a water-injector, meaning that water was being pumped into it from above the ground to move subterranean oil after gas pressure had dissipated. After the conversion the oil pump had been left in place so that anyone seeing it for the first time could infer that it was, or had been, a producing well.

Within minutes, Brown told Davis: "You know, this well is sort of strange. I get a very weak indication of oil here. There's a trace of oil at 7,000 feet but it's not commercial."

"You've hit the nail on the head again, Paul," Davis said elatedly. "You're just incredible."

At another oil field that same day Brown was no less successful. Said Davis: "To make a long story short, I took Brown to three wells there and he told me which were productive and which were not and, again, he was staggeringly accurate about the depths and thicknesses of the zones."

During years of oil dowsing for Wadley, for which he still receives royalty checks, Brown was able to travel extensively throughout the United States, from the Pacific to the Midwest. He estimates that he may well have walked over 10,000 miles in his prospecting work. His overall findings recorded on maps are so extraordinary that, if one day proved correct, they could revolutionize geological theory. According to Brown, oil deposits, far from being randomly distributed under the face of the planet, are laid out in reservoirs arranged in almost arrow-straight lines, each nearly equidistant from its neighbors.

"It's as if they were obeying some natural law," Brown surmises. "They are all linearly arranged but located at different depths. For instance, if you go to the big oil field at Lompoc, California, you'll find that most of the producing wells up there are all arranged in straight lines. If you search out the dry holes, you'll find out they're not in line. It's the same thing in the Los Angeles Basin, and a lot of other places. In various regions quite a number of the rectangularly outlined oil fields are actually under production and more are being wildcatted! The straight alignments of deposits are not suspected because so many dry holes have been drilled outside them and because only some portions of the deposits have been brought into production, but their extensions have remained undiscovered. The deposits are also at varying depths."

Brown holds the heretical belief that as much or more oil remains to be discovered in the United States as has already been pumped from below ground. Many oil companies, he says, look laterally for extensions of fields when they actually should look deeper. While dowsing the Santa Fe Springs Field for Wadley near Whittier, California, Brown could find no extension beyond

Map of the "Big Bend" region of Texas showing principal reservoirs of oil and gas according to Paul Clement Brown (adapted from a Malco road map). Parts of some of these reservoirs have been exploited. Others have been overlooked.

its edges. Then he went into the field itself and determined that the richest pay zones were deeper than any of the wells that had been drilled. Because of the cost involved to go to the 8,000 plus feet of depth that Brown recommended, Wadley elected not to drill. At 8,100 feet, another oil outfit struck an oil deposit so productive that several more companies moved seventeen rigs into the Santa Fe Springs Field and redrilled most of the wells in it. Today nearly the whole production in this field comes from these deep wells.

"The extension Wadley was looking for was not beyond but

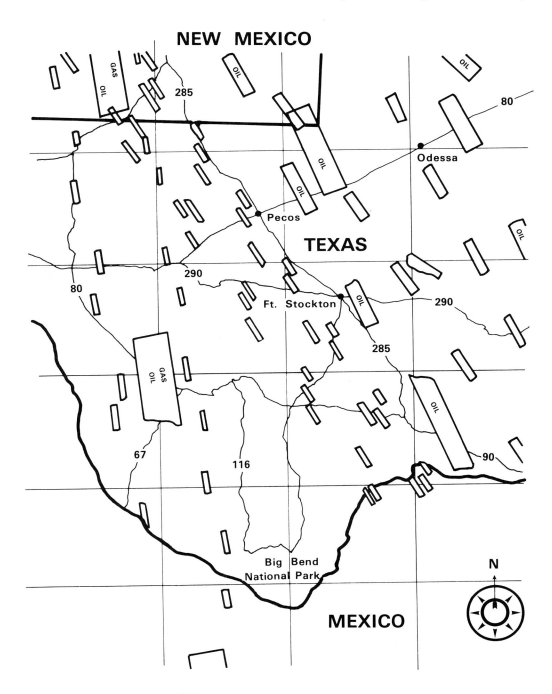

below the field," affirmed Brown. "That's the case for a lot of fields. We have a tremendous supply of oil in this country. The oil companies just don't know where to look for it."

Recent headlines more than substantiate Brown's allegation. Abandoning dry land, major U.S. oil companies have spent billions to acquire offshore leases that have proved bitterly disappointing. In August 1977, the *Los Angeles Times,* in a story headlined "Oil Hopes Ooze—Hundreds of Millions Paid For Only Dry Holes So Far," noted that three of the majors had shelled out $560 million for the right to drill for oil and gas in the Gulf of Alaska. During the first year of operations only dry holes were drilled in what the oil men held to be the most promising tracts.

Off the East Coast of the United States attempts to find oil or gas have been no less discouraging. In June 1977, the Continental Oil Company, first to complete a well in the Baltimore Canyon opposite New Jersey, came up with a dry hole at what it considered its potentially best site. Continental's expensive miss was matched the following month by the Shell Oil Company, whose first exploratory well drilled to 14,000 feet under the ocean floor seventy-three miles east of Atlantic City—and a bare two miles from the unsuccessful Continental bore—failed to find any commercially valuable hydrocarbons.

About the failure, the *New York Times* reported: "Industry analysts disagreed on how serious today's Shell development was. Some said that it increased the odds against any significant discovery in what had been considered, potentially, the area's most fruitful geological structure, the Baltimore Dome . . . If the area does not prove successful, it would be reminiscent of results elsewhere in offshore drilling. The so-called Destin Dome in the Gulf of Mexico produced nothing of value, although the oil companies paid $1.49 billion for leases there. The Gulf of Alaska brought nothing on lease costs of $572 million. The Tanner Banks off San Diego brought no commercial find on leases costing $438 million. There was little oil in San Pedro Bay near Long Beach, California."

In view of their track records, one may well ask why the major oil companies do not use the services of a competent oil dowser like Paul Brown. Asked what the biggest obstacles to finding oil by dowsing might be, Brown answered: "That's very simple. *The* one biggest obstacle is the skepticism of leaseholders, operators, and financiers. The hardest task is to convince an investor that my methods work. Geologists and the geophysicists in the major oil companies are my worst enemies. All their professionalism and book-learning is threatened by my approach. I can beat them every time by a large margin when it comes to finding oil and gas."

The Truly Scientific Approach

From his contacts with leading oil and gas operators over a quarter of a century, Brown learned that many important oil fields were discovered, not by geologically trained technicians, but by gifted dowsers like himself. One of his earliest clients was C. B. Eddington, a well-known Los Angeles oil producer who had

190

been in partnership with the equally well-known Sam Mosher.

"Eddington had faith in me," he recounted, "because he knew that dowsing had discovered big fields. He told me that the founder of the Union Oil Company, Lyman Stewart, located the big field at Lompoc, California, just to name one, by dowsing. A history of Union Oil entitled *The Black Bonanza* only alludes to Stewart's dowsing ability but doesn't tell the story truthfully."

While working with Wadley, Brown was sent to what he calls the most productive oil field in the United States between Marshall and Longview, Texas, where he learned from local landowners that the initial discovery well had been brought in by a famous dowser, Ol' Dad Joiner. Before Joiner's appearance on the scene, leading oil men who had drilled a number of dry holes on the top of an anticline doubted the area would ever be fruitful. Against the best geologic advice Joiner, then seventy-four years old, located his well on the western flank of the anticline where his dowsing predicted a lot of oil to lie.

"When they drilled Ol' Dad Joiner's location," said Brown, "the well came in at a tremendous 5,000 barrels per day on a 160-acre lease. The old lady who owned the land had a flock of Leghorn chickens, pure white, just as if they'd been laundered. When the well came out of the ground it gushed up into the air and rained down on those chickens and turned 'em into speckled black-and-white Wyandottes. The old lady was madder'n hell."

Another dowser was responsible for one of the most spectacular oil strikes in America, the Lakeview No. 1 well in California. "It blew in at 11,000 barrels a day," says Brown, "a real gusher way up in the sky. It soon increased to 100,000 B/D and ran like a stream. They damned the flow with sandbags and recovered more than three million barrels from the reservoir behind it. Union Oil had more oil than they knew what to do with. The price fell from about $1.39 a barrel to about 39 cents per barrel. You can still see some of those sandbags lying there today, a little way south of Taft, California. I've been on the spot. Gushing only stopped when the drill hole suddenly collapsed and the rig went down into the depression."

Since that fabulous time, no well of comparable size has been found anywhere in the United States, but Brown has determined that if a new well were sunk at the same location and properly controlled, so that it did not blow itself out, it could be extremely productive. Informed of the prospects, Wadley tried to obtain a lease but failed because the land was owned in fee by Standard Oil Co. "The oil still is there," says Brown. "On my dowsing scale it reads 'maximum.' I could guarantee 5,000 barrels a day if the well were drilled by conventional methods since the most friable sands in the United States are in that reservoir."

Stressing that it took him years to learn his dowsing techniques, Brown complains that a great deal of suspicion about dowsing in general, and oil dowsing in particular, stems directly from the practices of neophytes or boasters who promise what they cannot deliver.

"Most beginners," he says, "think that because so-and-so can read oil, so can they. It looks so easy. They are always so positive. They'll go out and set up a rig on a bunch of stringer beds like

191

Murrey did. The oil they read may collectively add up to a sizable amount. But if they'd read each bed individually, they'd have found that the beds just added up to a bunch of stringers. When the well is drilled, it comes up with just a showing and not enough for production. I've seen that happen over and over again with dowsers who don't have sufficient experience, and that's why dowsing has too often been extremely risky for wildcatters who tried it. Time and again they select undependable dowsers who don't know how to read underground deposits of oil like they should be read. Amateur dowsers overread small deposits of oil and fail to estimate the size of good reservoirs. They are too sure of themselves. I made my own mistakes in the early days but fortunately not in any place where Wadley drilled. I learned from those mistakes and corrected myself."

Brown has recently been successful in dowsing not only for oil and gas but for minerals as well. He has found the first deposit of a rare platinum-bearing ore ever located in the United States. Opening a U.S. Geological Survey Map, the "Devore Quadrangle," he pointed to an area in the San Bernadino Mountains and stated: "Up here I found a vein of ore over 600 feet wide and about four miles long interlaced with veins of platinum ore twenty to twenty-two feet wide. I didn't know what the ore was when I first came across it, but when I dowsed it, I came up with a lot of platinum. So I sent a sample of the ore to the top platinum expert in America."

So intrigued was the expert with what he saw that, the day after receiving the package, he took a plane from Chicago to Los Angeles to meet Brown. The dowser took him up to a 3,000-foot elevation where there were outcrops of the same ore. The expert reached down and picked up a sample from alongside the trail and, without saying anything, stuffed it into his coat pocket.

The following morning as he handed the sample back to Brown, he asked the dowser: "Do you know what you're looking at?" As Brown shook his head, the reply came: "Well, that's laurelite. It's a complex platinum-bearing ore widely exploited in the Soviet Union, which produces about a third of the world's platinum and exports a lot of the metal. I've never before seen a trace of it anywhere in this country."

Brown also told the story of his first large uranium find while on assignment for Wadley: "I'd not so much more than got acquainted with him than he sent me up to the Ambrosia Lake area near Grants, New Mexico, where he had drilled an expensive dry hole. He wanted me to determine if the rest of the area was devoid of oil. So I went up there and I found the reason why they weren't finding any oil was because there wasn't any oil up there. I came back and told Wadley: 'Chief, there's no place to drill for oil up there but your lease covers the finest deposit of uranium I've ever seen. You should go for that since the same lease allows for the development of both oil and minerals.'"

Wadley considered the matter for a few days, then told Brown: "I leased that land to drill for oil. I don't want to fool with uranium. I'm going to quit-claim it back to the owners."

"And that's what he did," admitted Brown ruefully, "but a

192

short while later it produced six million dollars' worth of uranium for its owners. He'd walked away from six million just like that!"

Brown holds that uranium deposits, like oil, not only follow straight lines on the earth's surface and have nearly equal spaces between them but also lie much deeper than suspected by professional geologists. One major oil company, said Brown in 1977, was planning to core-drill for uranium in New Mexico down to a total depth of 3,800 feet. Brown's own tests in the same area have indicated that no commercial deposits of uranium would be found. "The real McCoy," he asserts, "starts at 4,905 feet and

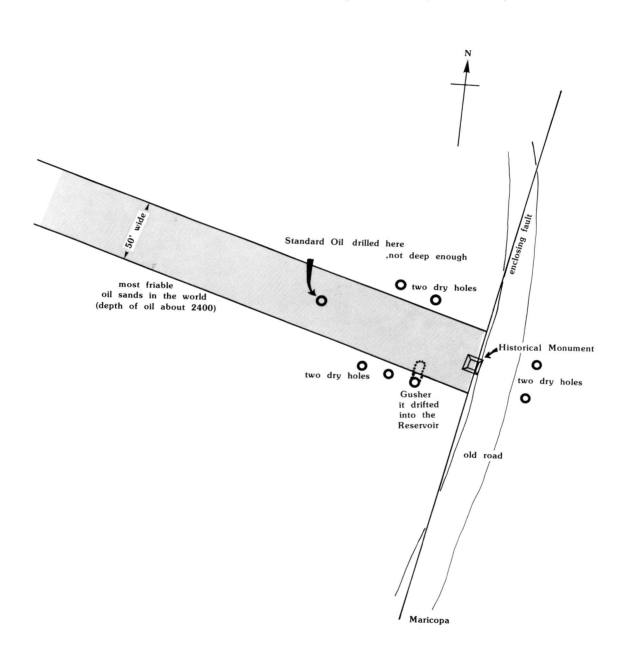

Photographs taken in the San Fernando Valley, California, 1977.

"*I wouldn't know how to explain the whole thing anymore than one can explain how a baby learns to walk or a young bird to fly. But I am able to dowse for natural resources not only while on the physical sites themselves but with the help of a map.*" *To demonstrate how this seemingly unthinkable process works, Brown put the tip of his pencil down on a map where a spot indicated the top of a mountain peak.*

"*I like to start on a peak,*" *he said,* "*I don't know why. I then project myself, not physically, but mentally, down into the section of country surrounding the mountain. I put my pendulum, containing whatever it is I'm searching for, into motion so that it will swing. It settles into a backwards and forwards motion along one azimuth and I get behind it to see exactly what direction it is tracing.* "*When I see the line clearly, I mark it with a ruler.*"

"Then I begin over again at approximately right angles to the line I've marked and when the pendulum settles into an even back-and-forth swing again, I draw another line. Where the two lines cross, that's my starting point.

"From the starting point, I use the self-same pencil and begin moving it away in any direction. At the same time I set my pendulum to rotating. When the spinning stops, I know I've reached the approximate boundary of the deposit. Of course, this can only be precisely determined by going to the location itself and shooting straight down. I've done this from the ground, from automobiles, from helicopters, and from airplanes."

Paul Clement Brown.

Well dowsed in the 1950s by Paul C. Brown for J.K. Wadley, was purchased together with storage tanks as the first step in its entry into the oil business by the Occidental Petroleum Company, today a giant oil and gas producer that has recently signed a multi-billion dollar deal to develop hydrocarbon resources in Siberia.

runs down to 5,000. It has to be deep-mined. But the company won't find it because they're going to stop short of it."

On one map of New Mexico Brown has drawn a line running almost due north from Culbertson County, Texas, to Trinidad, Colorado, which he maintains is a gold streak, or vein of gold. "Years back, a man mined on this vein," he recounted, "and took out real rich ore. He found it by dowsing. He located a cavity, a kind of underground cave, where he didn't have to do much digging. The ore he brought out he took to town and the gold he pounded out of it made him enough money to last him six months or so. Then he'd go in and get another load. When he died, hundreds of people looked for his mine but no one could

find it. The vein is about twenty to twenty-two feet wide. Much of it is about forty feet below the surface. It contains more gold than you can shake a stick at, real rich ore."

Self-effacing, almost shy, Paul Clement Brown is not the type of man to boast of his exploits, but it's a fact the Occidental Petroleum Company got its start in the petroleum industry when it bought ten producing wells that had been successfully dowsed by Brown for Wadley. "It was on a seven-acre lease, later increased to nearly 300 acres, in the Dominguez Hills area north of Long Beach, California," recounts Brown. "A couple of fellows had it and wanted Wadley to lease it. He told me to look it over and if I found oil in paying quantities, he'd drill. I showed him a place where the oil deposits lay against a fault. We traveled that fault quite a way, anywhere the station wagon could get up to it.

"The funny thing was that the Union Oil Company had a lease across the street adjoining the seven acres, but when their geologists said there was no oil under it, they quit-claimed it back to its owners. So Wadley leased this and some more land to total about 300 acres and I made an initial location and we came up with 886 barrels a day. A number of Union Oil Company wells in the vicinity were doing only five to seven barrels.

"My well was a discovery well. We drilled eleven more wells and we hit oil every time in quantities from 900 to 1,100 barrels a day. We put chain link fences around them and put in two 1,000-barrel tanks for each well and painted them aluminum. It looked all very neat and clean. Occidental Petroleum bought ten of the wells. That's how the company got its start in 1955."

"What I'd discovered was a fault block arrangement the Union Oil men hadn't been able to locate. The chief engineer at Union got fired on account of my find. They told the whole geology department they'd fire all of them if they couldn't do better than that. So they came in and made a location adjacent to ours, about 330 feet away.

"Wadley told me to wait until after all their people had left the site, then take a reading on their proposed well. I told him that if they drilled straight down, they'd get a dry hole but that, if they slanted over toward our new producer, they'd get a good well because they'd come into the same fault block deposit.

"So that's what they did. And they drilled eight more wells offsetting our lease and all of them were slanted over to end up adjacent to our lease boundary. They put one well down right under one of our tanks and it produced 2,800 barrels a day. We requested them to run a survey and, sure enough, it showed they were under our lease, so they plugged up their well back to their line and it didn't produce much anymore."

Asked whether his cylinders, each filled with a specific material in its pure state, were really essential to his work, or whether the whole of it was basically a mental act, he replied enigmatically and poetically:

"You know, that's a good question. As a man says, 'The spirit moves me.' What I have done is what any man can do with the right spiritual approach. And that approach is the truly scientific one. They'll tell you dowsing isn't scientific but I'll tell you it is scientific if you do it the way it should be done."

197

SECRET FINDER DEVICE USED

Sunken Ship With Millions in Aztec Gold Believed Located

On 27 August 1969 the **Los Angeles Times** *ran the above headline on its front page. The accompanying story referred to a sunken 85-foot 16th century caravel,* **Trinidad,** *the long-lost ship of Francisco de Ulloa, one of the lieutenants of famed conquistador, Hernán Cortés, which historians believed to have foundered in 1540 at the mouth of the San Luis Rey River near the present-day town of Oceanside.*

Wilfred Takasata, a 41-year-old diver from San Pedro became obsessed with finding **Trinidad** *when he read an article about the ship written by Dr. Joseph Markey, an amateur archaeologist who claimed de Ulloa landed in California two years before its "historical" discovery by Juan Rodriguez Cabrillo. Markey based his opinion on* **Trinidad's** *log discovered in the archives of the Spanish city of Seville.*

In 1968 the California Lands Commission granted Takasato exclusive rights to search the waters off Oceanside for the wreck, purportedly carrying over $50 million dollars worth of gold. When friends introduced Takasato to Paul Brown, the oil dowser was invited to assist in locating the long-lost vessel.

Armed with a pendulum, referred to by the newspaper as a mystery device called an "attractometer," Brown triangulated a location some ¾ of a mile off the California coast by taking directional readings from Oceanside and San Pedro. He then went aboard **Gleaner,** *the treasure-hunting expedition's ship which he piloted with his pendulum over the area he had pinpointed from shore.*

"We made several runs to get a precise fix," says Brown. "The ship proceeded very slowly. I'd tell 'em: 'Now the target is right under the wheelhouse, now its exactly under the stern.' Finally they dropped their marking buoy."

Divers went down in 5 fathoms of water at the site to clear away a large patch of sand 6-8 feet deep whereupon portions of a 50-foot segment of rotten timber and caulking were brought up. Laboratory analysis and dating of the debris indicated that the remains were probably those of **Trinidad.**

The find was made in 1969. Since then no one has been able to solve the problem of raising the treasure ship made particularly complex by ocecan currents which replace sand over the hulk almost as fast as it is removed. **Trinidad** *thus will be raised when someone comes up with a solution . . . and the money to pay for it.*

CHAPTER 11

The U.S. Marines Learn to Dowse

". . . two candle snuffers . . ."

A Village's Unseen World

Concurring with Paul Brown about the need for a spiritual approach in dowsing is Louis Matacia, a professional land surveyor who, as a consultant to the United States Marines, was asked to take time out to view a film in November 1966. In the projection room of the Marines' Development and Educational Center at Quantico, Virginia, Matacia saw Robert McNamara, then U.S. Secretary of Defense, appeal for new ideas that might help to answer insoluble military problems.

One problem that particularly attracted the surveyor's attention was the sight of U.S. Marines helplessly looking over an expanse of Vietnamese jungle terrain for openings of enemy underground tunnels. Matacia grew excited. As a professional dowser with an impressive record, he himself had always been able to find underground utilities, with nothing more than a pair of rods cut from coat hangers. Why wouldn't the same technique work for tunnels?

When Matacia volunteered to demonstrate his dowsing skill, a large group of Marine officers gathered in the basement of Quantico's Landing Force Development Center. As they stared incredulously, Matacia got out two L-shaped metal rods, of so narrow a diameter—3/16 of an inch—that they might also properly be termed wires. Holding them in his hands so that they pointed straight ahead of him, he walked across the basement under several water pipes exposed in the ceiling. Each time he crossed under a pipe, all present could see the rods in his hands swing outward and align with it.

The reaction of the audience was not one of universal awe. Some of its members glared at Matacia in hostile disbelief. But since the majority of the onlookers, as well as the rods, seemed to be responding well, Matacia decided to release more "top secrets." In his soft Virginia countryside drawl he told the Marines that, with the help of his rods, he could tell through which of the pipes overhead water was running, indicate how many degrees off the horizontal they were sloping, or find pipes below ground. He could determine whether an underground pipe were made of iron or copper or whether it served as a sewer or a water pipe and he could pinpoint its thickness and its depth. Hearing these assertions, some of the officers began to snicker

199

Louis Matacia marking the course of a lost underground pipe for contractors. The pipe's exact location was determined with a pair of L-shaped rods. (Photograph courtesy of Louis Matacia.)

derisively and walk away. Others shook their heads pityingly as if confronted by a man suddenly gone mad. A few of the more courageous, eager to learn more about Matacia's seemingly miraculous art, pressed for more information.

Major T. F. Manley was an officer receptive and broad-minded enough to look further. At his initiative a full-scale test of what now were called "Matacia's wire rudders" was scheduled for November 14, at 14:45. The site selected was a mockup of a typical southeast Asian village, complete with thatched huts, pig pens, rice paddies, wells, sampans floating on a river, bridges, trails, and even graves. Located on the Quantico base, the village was used for tactical training of Marines on their way to Vietnam.

Scattered throughout the village were devilish booby traps similar to those devised by Viet Cong guerrillas: "pungi pits" into which a man could step to have both sides of his leg from ankle to knee impaled by sharp steel spikes covered with excrement to guarantee almost instant infection; trip-wired grenades festooned in series along a trail to be detonated simultaneously by a single VC hiding in a tree; and other representatives of a homemade arsenal. Below the ground ran the unseen world of the village: a network of tunnels, secret rooms, weapons caches, stores for supplies, and hiding places for the enemy. What the Marines wanted to know was whether Matacia could locate the subterranean passageways while walking with his "wire rudders" on the firm ground above them.

Hardly had Matacia arrived on the scene than he set to work, the Marine observers trailing after him. As he passed between two houses at the edge of the village, his parallel rods, protruding in front of him like the antennae of some insect, eerily swung outward to point directly at the houses now on either side of him.

"Well, now, that's got to be a tunnel of some kind," he said unhesitatingly. The Marine observers only silently nodded their assent. A white ribbon was laid between the two houses to formally record Matacia's finding. After careful work with a single "rudder," Matacia then stated that the tunnel sloped downward from one of the houses to the other. When none of the military seemed to know whether this was true, a Marine captain entered the tunnel system from an opening in yet another house. He returned to report that there was over a foot of water at the end of the tunnel Matacia had said would be deeper than the other.

On and on Matacia coursed through the village, discovering not only more tunnels but underground communication wires and pipes. He next entered a larger house to declare there was a large cave beneath its floor. This turned out to be what Marine tactical instructors called the "Hidden Room."

Outside another house, a captain asked if his method would allow a man to find a false wall. Matacia walked around the house and unerringly found the asked-for target behind which several guerrillas could easily be concealed. When he had surveyed the entire village, his successful finds were transcribed onto a map. The officers crowded around to look. Not one of his calls was in error. Most of the underground "system" had been revealed, and Matacia had performed this feat in less than half an hour.

By now the Marines were themselves trying to locate tunnels with extra sets of rods, cut with pliers from ordinary metal coat hangers that Matacia had brought along with him. Some of them had instant success. When a Major Townsend appeared on the scene, Matacia invited him to try a set of "rudders." Townsend, who had never in his life seen, let alone held, such a set of dowsing rods, took them in his hands and stepped out resolutely across the village terrain. When he had moved a certain distance in a straight line the rods, to his utter surprise, spread outward, stopping at right angles to his line of march. He told Matacia that he was standing over a tunnel he knew to be two feet underground at that point.

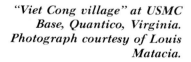

"Viet Cong village" at USMC Base, Quantico, Virginia. Photograph courtesy of Louis Matacia.

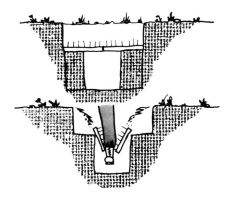

(ABOVE) Booby trap. A man stepping into the punji pit hits two boards or steel plates with steel spikes affixed, the boards or plates then pivot, wounding the leg above the area protected by the boot. (Courtesy of the United States Marine Corps.)

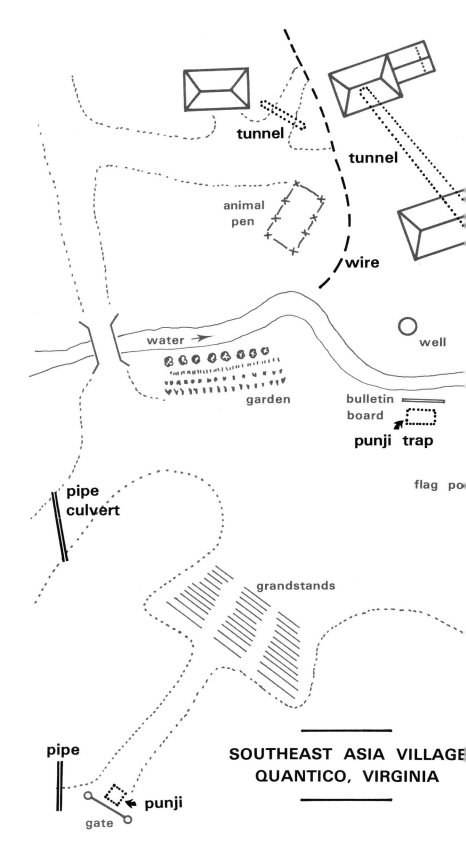

tunnel

tunnel

animal pen

wire

water

garden

well

bulletin board

punji trap

flag po

pipe culvert

grandstands

pipe

SOUTHEAST ASIA VILLAGE
QUANTICO, VIRGINIA

punji

gate

(RIGHT) Map of mock Viet Cong village at USMC base, Quantico, Virginia, showing Matacia's dowsing successes. (Courtesy of Louis Matacia.)

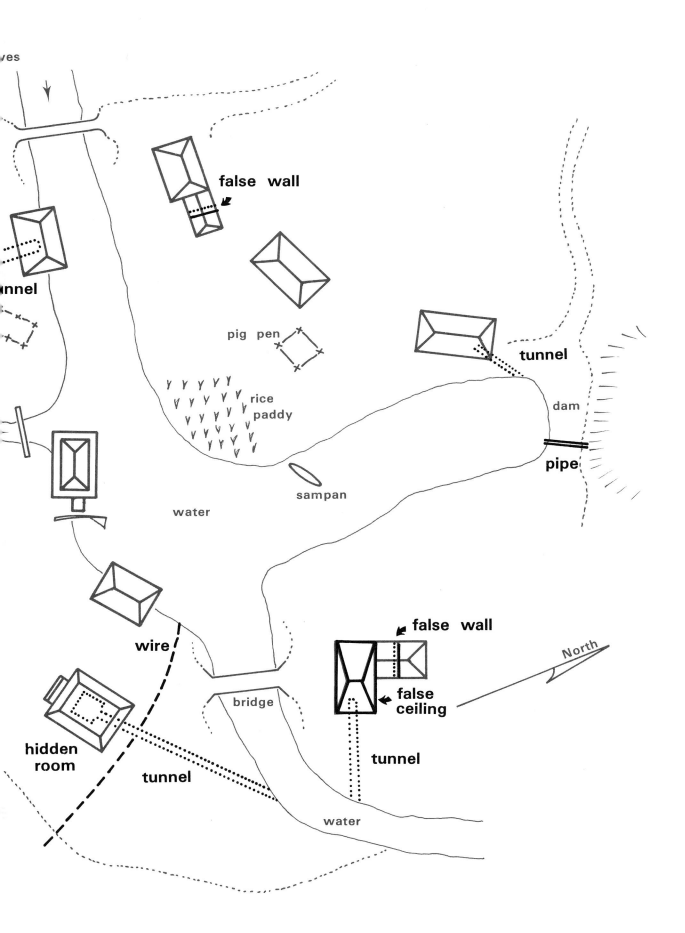

ves

false wall

tunnel

pig pen

rice
paddy

tunnel

dam

pipe

water

sampan

false wall

North

wire

false
ceiling

hidden
room

tunnel

bridge

tunnel

water

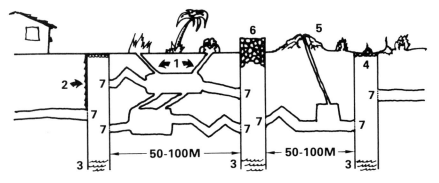

Well-Tunnel Complex above was discovered near Ben Cat in September 1965. It is a series of multi-bunker tunnels with angled connecting tunnels. Each bunker has space available for fifteen to twenty men. The entrances to and exits from the VC bunkers are built into the walls of actual or simulated wells which are twenty to thirty meters deep. Access to these skillfully camouflaged entrances and exits is by way of notched dirt steps or by the use of long notched bamboo pole ladders. These wells also serve as deep pit man traps. (Courtesy of the United States Marine Corps.)

1. **AIR VENTS**
2. **NOTCHED DIRT STEPS**
3. **WATER**
4. **CAMOUFLAGED COVER**
5. **CAMOUFLAGED VENT HOLE**
6. **NORMAL WELL TOP**
7. **CAMOUFLAGED ENTRANCE COVERS**

As Matacia was talking, Townsend noticed a captain passing by. He hailed him abruptly: "Look, just for the hell of it, do you have a minute? We are from the Development Center. Take these rods and hold them loosely in your hands, like this. Now just walk forward and see what happens."

The young captain, who had not the slightest idea why he was being asked to do what seemed to him an imbecilic task, took the rods in his hands and moved out as he was told. When he was over the tunnel, the rods spread apart. Major Manley, who had been holding his breath in anticipation, almost whooped his next question: "Did you feel those rods turn in your hands, Captain?"

The officer stammered: "Yes, but what made them turn? I didn't change my grip on them."

"That's a first time for him, isn't it, Major?" said Matacia. "It goes to show how basically easy it is. A little experience and anyone can proceed through a village, walking between buildings and around buildings to determine any subsurface structures. I believe I can tell how big underground caves are by outlining their edges."

Flushed with success, that same evening, in his home in Falls Church, Virginia, Matacia wrote a solicited letter to Major Manley which, together with its accompanying documentation, outlined a series of potential applications of dowsing which Matacia thought would "enhance current Marine Corps operations in Vietnam and save many lives." After reviewing what had been accomplished during one afternoon at Quantico, Matacia confidently stated: "I know it will work in other areas. Its applicability is limited only by the imagination of the users. It is inherently simple, easy to teach, and the equipment costs almost nothing." Matacia suggested to the USMC that it undertake a testing program to realize the full potential of his technique and informed Manley that he would be available for further demonstrations and discussions, should the Corps be interested. Together with the letter, Matacia sent along a notarized specification explaining how to operate his "rudders."

204

Marines being taught dowsing at Quantico. Photograph courtesy of Louis Matacia.

Matacia, who up to this point had donated all his advice to the Marines for nothing, waited expectantly for an answer, but searched his mailbox in vain as the days went by. Several weeks and many casualties later, he began to think the entire potential of what he had demonstrated was being shelved. So he took it upon himself as a private citizen to write an appeal to the U.S. Defense Department moguls on his own land surveyor's letterhead.

Estimating that only one out of ten recipients would pay any attention to his letter, Matacia upped the odds and wrote to twelve different Defense Department research agencies and military commanders, including the Special Warfare Agency; the Commanding General of the Experimentation Center at Ft.

Reproduction of Observer *article.*

First In Vietnam

THE OBSERVER

Published Weekly For U.S. Forces In Vietnam
(Circulation: 73,000)

Vol. V, No. 45   SAIGON, VIETNAM   March. 13, 1967

Shades of Black Magic

Marines On Operation Divine For VC Tunnels

Da Nang (USMC) — An old-fashioned method of locating water in arid areas, the divining rod, has been updated and put to military use in Vietnam.

A method for locating underground structures and other objects by use of wires, "Matacia's Wire Rudder," was used by Marines during the final three days of Operation Independence, three miles west of An Hoa.

Matacia's Wire-Rudder is two identical wires, 3/16 inch in diameter, bent in the shape of an "L" with an overall length of 34 inches. The longer side of the "L" is 26 inches in length.

Marines operate the divining rod by holding one in each hand, level with the ground, pointing in the direction of their movement. As the carrier moves over, under or along a hidden structure,

the wires will swing into alignment with the structure.

Introduced to Marines of the 2nd Battalion, 5th Marine Regiment, the divining rods were greeted with skepticism, but did locate a few Viet Cong tunnels.

Private First Class Don R. Steiner, Shadyside, Ohio, a battalion scout with the 2nd Battalion, 1st Marine Regiment, tried the rods for the first time on a recent patrol. The rods spread apart as Steiner passed a Vietnamese hut.

Upon checking inside the building, Marines discovered a tunnel that led to a family bunker underneath the trail, right where the rods had reacted.

In this day of nuclear powered devices, it may seem that there is still room for the old, if you happen to be a believer.

Belvoir, Virginia; the Advanced Research Projects Agency; the Department of the Army's Chief of Research and Development; the Defense Intelligence Agency in Washington, D.C.; and the Commander-in-Chief of the U.S. Armed Forces, Vietnam.

Matacia received discouraging replies. Typical was one from the Office of the Chief of Research and Development of the Department of the Army. It said it had run its own investigation of his proposed technique and found it unacceptable because "there is a low probability of making usable interpretations of the rods in an unfamiliar situation," and because "confirming criteria cannot be established to inform the operator that the method or the rods themselves are functioning properly or accurately."

Even as the Pentagon was turning Matacia down, Marines in Vietnam were scoring successes with his "wire rudders" in the field. *The Observer*, a weekly published in Saigon for U.S. forces in Vietnam, made first public reference to dowsing by American troops in combat.

Evidence began piling up that the top brass in Saigon was seriously interested in the tunnel-finding technique. The Development Center at Quantico received several positive reports about dowsing from the American Commander-in-Chief in Vietnam, stating that Marines were unearthing not only tunnels but caves, buried objects, caches of food and ammunition, and even secret messages buried in bamboo tubes. Though the Commander-in-Chief himself requested more information about the strange searching technique, Pentagon scientists had nothing to supply.

The biggest public boost for Matacia came on October 11, when Hanson Baldwin, the prestigious military expert for the *New York Times*, sent his paper a dispatch from Camp Pendleton, the USMC base in southern California. Wrote Baldwin: "Coat-hanger dowsers, as they are called here, are not included in Marine Corps equipment manuals. But, according to Marine officers, they have been used in Vietnam with marked success in the last year, particularly by engineer units of the 1st and 3rd Marine Divisions, which are engaged in mine detection and tunnel destruction. The dowsers supplement the familiar battery-powered mine detector, a complex device that emits a warning signal when it is passed over a buried metallic object, and the hunt-and-probe method—detection with bayonets."

In Baldwin's presence, Major Nelson Hardacker, commanding officer of the 13th Engineer Battalion, 5th Marine Division, demonstrated the dowsing technique to a group of Marine officers. He pinpointed a tunnel and determined the angle of its slope. A lieutenant colonel who did not know where the tunnel was also found it, with the help of coat-hanger rods. Finally, Baldwin himself tried the rods and located a tunnel unknown to him.

The *New York Times* correspondent put into the record the fact that the history of coat-hanger dowsing by the Marines "seemed" to have originated with Louis Matacia, who was not getting solid recognition for his efforts. In his conclusion Baldwin noted that despite the fact that Matacia's "rudders" had been tested and demonstrated both at Pendleton and Quantico, they had yet to be officially adopted by the Marine Corps. In spite of this, the unofficial use of the device was spreading. Marine engineers at Pendleton swore by them, even though they knew no more about *how* and *why* they worked than did academics or intelligence experts.

D-Day at Camp Lejeune

Baldwin's report and the continuing dowsing successes of Marines in combat in Vietnam now laid the basis for an extraordinary day-long dowsing demonstration staged for military personnel. On May 12, 1968, at 8:00 hours, two groups of men gathered in the Office of the 2nd Marine Division at the USMC's Counter Guerrilla Warfare Command (CGWC) in Camp Lejeune, North Carolina. The first, consisting entirely of Marines, included a group of field-grade officers curious to learn about what they had heard was one of the wierdest imaginable approaches to intelligence-gathering. On hand, too, were a Captain Piatt plus six noncommissioned officers, all instructors at CGWC and all Vietnam combat veterans. Their assignment for that day: training in dowsing.

The second group comprised six professional dowsers: Leonard Brown, a water locater from Upper Black Eddy, Pennsylvania; Arthur Sowder, who had often dowsed water for the U.S. Forest Service before he retired; Lewis Gilstrap, a cybernetics expert who had carried on private research on dowsing; Hugh McCotter, a Florida engineer working for the Dixie Precision Manufacturing Company; Carl Schleicher, a systems engineer; and Louis Matacia.

During Matacia's initial briefing, a colonel rudely interrupted to remark that, as far as he was concerned dowsing was no better than witchcraft and the demonstration could only result in a waste of time for all concerned.

Eyeing the colonel cooly, Matacia softly asked: "Sir, do you

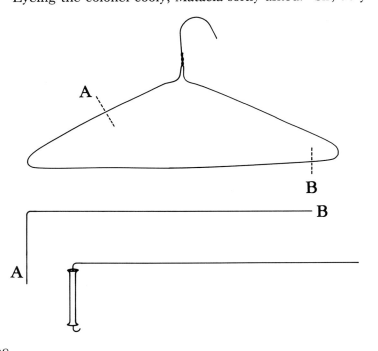

How to make an angle rod from a coat hanger, as first conceived by Louis Matacia.

have an artillery piece on this base?"

"Yeah," the reply was gruff, "there's a 105-millimeter howitzer."

"Well, from right where we're standing we're going to give you its azimuth and its distance to the nearest one hundred meters," stated Matacia flatly. He then asked Brown to hold his nylon Y-rod at the ready and pivot slowly in place. When the rod snapped down, several Marines uttered exclamations, leading both dowsers to believe they were right on target. Brown raised his rod again and Matacia began counting aloud: "One hundred meters, 200, 300, 400, 500, 600," at which point it began moving imperceptibly but slowly downward. "The howitzer is on the azimuth indicated and 600 to 700 meters from the building where we're standing," announced Matacia. The colonel strode into an adjoining room to check a map of the Lejeune base. When he returned, he reported that Matacia had fulfilled his boast to the letter. Not a whisper broke the silence that followed.

Matacia then passed out L- and Y-rods to each Marine scheduled for training. McCotter distributed "Magnetomatic Locators," telescopable antennas which could be recessed into their 6¼ inch hand grip when not in use, that he had developed in Florida for contractors dealing with excavation problems.

Setting the tone for the day's proceedings, Matacia announced: "Gentlemen, we are here at our request and our expense and through the courtesy of your commanding officer to demonstrate to you what can be accomplished with the techniques and tools of dowsing, and to teach you these techniques, step by step, from the fundamental to the most sophisticated. We are not trying to *sell* you, or the Marine Corps anything, but we are trying to *give* the Corps the benefits of our collective experience which we believe is particularly applicable to counterguerrilla warfare measures. We will demonstrate and prove to you, beyond the shadow of a doubt, things that, if you read about them in books, you would believe to have come straight out of science fiction. All that we ask of you is to maintain an open mind and bear with us."

Before the day was over, went on Matacia, the Marines would know how accurately to locate snipers, booby traps, bunkers, pillboxes, or anything else concealed in a combat zone. They would learn how to get out of the jungle safely without a compass by simply using a device cut from the undergrowth, in any weather, day or night. They would be able to find underground mines, hidden caches of arms, and tunnels and tell how many persons and what type of equipment were hidden in them without going below ground. Finally, they would gain the ability to pinpoint, from nothing but the map of any given area, installations such as gun or radar emplacements, troop concentrations, airfields, and other targets of military interest anywhere in the world.

When Matacia asked for questions, the Marines sat in stunned silence. Captain Piatt could only murmur: "Please proceed."

Matacia next admitted that he knew of no explanation for how dowsing worked. Nevertheless, he added, anyone could master the art with the possible exception of mentally disturbed

209

MacCotter's "Magnetomatic Locator" demonstrated by a U.S. Marine. Photograph courtesy of Louis Matacia.

individuals, morons, and professional skeptics.

He then asked Sowder to show how a dowsing rod could be employed in lieu of a compass for orientation in unfamiliar territory. The retired forest ranger rose, took up his forked nylon rod and slowly rotated in place, asking aloud: "Which direction is magnetic north on the earth from here?" He had turned no more than 100 degrees when his rod abruptly snapped down. Raising his arm Sowder pointed in the direction indicated and asked: "Can anyone tell me if I'm pointing to magnetic north?"

After checking with his compass, one of the Marine sergeants said: "Correct, right on target."

Captain Piatt broke in to inquire of Matacia whether he could use the same technique with which the dowsers had found the howitzer earlier that morning to locate a model Vietnamese village called Tri-Me No. 1, the siting of which was known to every Marine on Camp Lejeune but to none of the dowsers. In less than a minute Matacia fulfilled the request, adding: "Now, I'll tell you how far away it is, Captain. Do you want it in feet or meters?"

"In meters," said Piatt.

"Do you want the distance to the center of the village or its edges?" pressed Matacia.

"The center."

Taking a glass ball attached to a string from his pocket, Matacia held it between his forefinger and his thumb and, facing in the ascertained direction, asked, "Is the distance from here to Tri-Me No. 1 more than 1,000 meters?" After a 12-second pause, the ball swung slowly in a clockwise direction which to Matacia indicated an affirmative answer.

"Is it more than 2,000 meters?" inquired Matacia.

The ball continued its clockwise swing.

"More than 3,000 meters?"

The ball slowed, stopped, then reversed its swinging direction.

"Okay," Matacia told the Marines, some of whom were

210

Louis Matacia (Photograph by George Vitas.)

staring at him with mouths wide open, "it's between 2,000 and 3,000 meters away. Let's see if we can get a closer fix."

By counting from 2,000 upward by 100s, he obtained a reading of between 2,400 and 2,500 meters.

"I can get closer than that, Captain, if you want," he challenged.

"No," replied Piatt, "that won't be necessary. The village is approximately 2,400 meters distant."

Buzzing with excitement, the group walked to Tri-Me No. 1, where they found a cleared area with a hut, a watchtower, and an earth bunker. One of the sergeants was asked by Matacia to shut his eyes, then rotate three times on the same spot. "Now keep turning," he further instructed, "and while holding the magnetomatic locater, with its antenna pulled all the way out, in your hand, ask for the direction for the entrance to the bunker."

The sergeant turned until at one point he felt the rod twisting to the right in his hand. He stopped his motion and opened his eyes. To his utter surprise he was facing the bunker's entrance about seventy-five feet distant.

Told that a tunnel existed somewhere in the cleared area, Matacia used a single "rudder" to find it between the hut and the watchtower and correctly ascertained its depth at six feet below ground. Captain Piatt asked slyly: "Can you tell me if there are people in the tunnel?" Standing directly over the tunnel, Matacia asked: "Are there any human beings inside the tunnel I'm standing over?" The ball twirled in the direction denoting an affirmative answer. Matacia's dialogue with himself continued.

"Are there more than five people?"

Negative swing.

"More than one?"

Another negative.

"Is there one person down there?"

"Yes," rotated the ball.

Looking fixedly at the sphere, the captain solemnly nodded his head and admitted that the Marine he had ostensibly sent for cool drinks half an hour previously had actually been ordered to go into the tunnel and stay there until summoned out.

The increasingly impressed Marines were subjected to an hour of instruction in the use of every kind of dowsing instrument, after which Matacia instructed one of the CGWC cadre to conceal a trip wire along a trail leading southeast out of the clearing. Followed by the others he advanced down the trail with his Y-rod and said in a loud voice: "When I am five feet from the trip wire, wherever it is, my rod will snap downward to warn me of its presence." Five feet from the concealed wire, down went his rod.

After a break, Matacia next demonstrated the same technique employed by Paul Brown for oil or ore deposits to locate a mock POW camp on a topographic map. Not completely satisfied with his initial location, he kept holding the pendulum in his right hand while moving his left hand, palm down, above the map. When it was directly over the lower right corner of the map, the pendulum began twirling actively. Seeking more precision, he put the point of his index finger on the area and moved it slowly until

The most common type of booby trap consists of a trip wire stretched across a trail, anchored to a small bush or tree and to a friction type fuse in the grenade. Most other booby traps are a variation on this basic idea. Courtesy of United States Marine Corps.

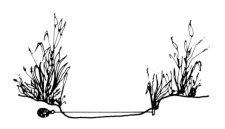

211

Matacia demonstrating how his "rudders" would respond to a concealed manhole . . . or buried corner of a building foundation. (Photographs courtesy of Louis Matacia.)

it was above the crest of a hill overlooking a river, whereupon the pendulum renewed its spinning motion.

"The POW camp must be right near here," he affirmed.

"You couldn't be much closer," explained Captain Piatt who put his fingertip alongside Matacia's. "You're right next to it. The camp's exact location is under my finger."

The group moved two miles east of Tri-Me No. 1 to a forested area interspersed with pathways along one of which a cache of military supplies had been buried: The captain asked Matacia if he could locate the cache. "Well, I'll try," said Matacia, "but I'm not sure I can guarantee success. It's late in the day and I've been dowsing for several hours now. This has sapped a lot of my energy." Within a few moments his dowsing led him to a large circle of ashes, the remains of a burned out campfire.

"This seems like a crazy place to bury supplies," he commented, "but this is where I find the cache."

"You've hit another bull's-eye," said the captain, "and though it appears crazy, that's exactly where a lot of caches have been found in the Vietnamese jungles. The guerrillas dig holes in the ground, bury a quantity of material for future use, then build their fires over the filled-in holes to make it easy to find them later on."

Matacia grinned. "Do you want me to tell you what's in this cache?" he asked. "Give me a list of the possible items it might contain." The captain listed six: ammunition boxes, unboxed ammunition, food, clothing, medical supplies, and weapons. Matacia stated that all items were present except unboxed ammunition and weapons. Sowder and Brown came independently to the same conclusion. The threesome proved 100 percent correct.

As the whole group trooped back to the headquarters building, the Marines told the dowsers that, from what they had seen and done, they were convinced that dowsing could help them enormously in antiguerrilla warfare and self-preservation.

Their attitude was later summed up by McCotter: "I wouldn't have believed it, unless I had *seen* it. Personally, I learned more in eight hours than I had in some thirty years' contact with the subject, and all my preconceived notions about dowsing phenomena are hereby jettisoned. Despite some statistics which maintain that only one-third of all people can dowse, we wound up at the end of the day with all participants being able to get good dowsing reactions, even though some had initial difficulty because of lack of confidence."

Conviction, Confidence, and a Sixth Sense

This opinion was evidently not shared by higher military authority. McCotter's persistent communication with the U.S. Defense Department throughout the rest of 1968 elicited no interest in either further demonstrations or research on dowsing, the principal objections being that the technique was not a "measurable science" or "100 percent reliable." "But what military device is 100 percent reliable?" McCotter countered. "Rifles jam, shells and bombs fail to explode, communications get 'fouled up.' The history of warfare is full of such failures at critical times."

The Corp's final rejection of dowsing was expressed in 1971 in a letter written at the direction of the Commanding General, Marine Corps Development and Educational Command, at Quantico, Virginia, which stated that several applications in the use of dowsing had been evaluated with "varying degrees of success" but that in no case was the Corps "able to determine a scientific basis for the success or failure of the techniques/instruments employed." Reasoned the general:

The "cause" of an effect is just as important as the results produced in order to formulate doctrine, organizations and techniques in the form of military publications addressing the subject. This essential causal determination will apparently continue to remain an unknown with regard to those techniques/instructions no matter how many times they are investigated. The Marine Corps will again become interested in dowsing only when it can be conclusively demonstrated that the average Marine can employ the technique without regard to his personal convictions, confidence level, or subconscious development.

In the days when the American West was still the frontier, Indian and white scouts were attached to units of the U.S. Cavalry to guide them in unfamiliar territory and help them to avoid ambush. The scouts were necessary exactly because they did not have "average," but highly sophisticated, talents requiring great personal conviction, an extraordinarily high level of confidence, and even a "sixth sense" to warn them of impending danger.

In wilderness areas all over the world native "trackers" have been employed to follow the trails of fugitives just as bloodhounds are used to track down escaped criminals, even though the

PROPERTY OF RONALD SMART, CULPEPPER, VIRGINIA. *Photographed while drill rig was boring a 565-foot well which produced barely a quart of water per minute. As the work was proceeding, Louis Matacia put down a peg, topped with a bit of white cloth, some eight feet from the unsuccessfully bored well. He predicted that water would be tapped at 40, 90, 198, 230, 260, and 290 feet. The well was drilled on May 4, 1977, to a total depth of 265 feet in solid rock and produced 8 gallons of water per minute or thirty-two times the amount from the first well nearby.*

trackers' skills were often beyond the ken of the intelligent urbanized individuals who put them to good use.

If *use* of a method rather than its understanding is the crucial criterion for its employment, then able dowsers, it would seem, are no more or less rare these days than the trackers and scouts of yore. The insistence by the USMC that a technique be able to be mastered by every man in a company, battalion, or regiment before it can be put into practice may therefore be misplaced.

The unstated question lurking behind military rejection of dowsing as an intelligence-gathering method necessarily must be: "If we admit that dowsing by *our* forces can locate military targets, then we must necessarily admit that it can just as successfully be brought into play by *their* forces." Since there is no known counter to the dowsing skill, the very idea of its usefulness thus becomes a sword with two edges.

Ironically, dowsing is also a threat to military establishments everywhere for if, to cite but one example, an enemy's submarine fleet could be tracked with so simple a technique, what would become of the vast technological edifice of antisubmarine warfare?

CHAPTER 12

Ships and People in Trouble

". . . a tailor's scissors pressed at its rivet . . ."

The PCE
"Nhat-Tao HQ-10"

The Paracel archipelago comprises half a dozen uninhabited rocky protuberances nearly 300 miles off the east coast of Vietnam and due south of the Chinese Island of Hainan. Long disputed by the Chinese and Vietnamese, their possession assumed new importance in 1974 when it was reported that the chances of one day striking offshore oil in their vicinity appeared to be improving. When a task force of Chinese ships landed troops to assert Peking's sovereignty, the South Vietnamese admiralty sent a flotilla to repel them.

The Vietnamese officer in charge of intership communication was Captain Vo Sum, who had been introduced at the age of seven to the possibility of hunting for anything lost or missing with the help of a pendulum by his father who read aloud to him from a large collection of French books on the subject.

What especially motivated Vo Sum to learn how to get answers to questions simply by holding a weight on a string and watching its gyrations, was the sight of his father sitting alone at his desk, pendulum in hand, searching for Vo Sum's elder brother who had disappeared somewhere in France. By watching the pendulum's movement, the father came to the horrifying conclusion that his missing son had fallen severely ill and had died in Marseille. It was not until several years after this sad finding that a Vietnamese, returning to his homeland from Marseille, visited the older man to relate that his son had in fact expired in the French Mediterranean port.

When the publisher of a new weekly, *Khoa-Hoc-Huyen Bi*, meaning "Occult Sciences," invited Vo Sum to contribute an article, he decided to reinvestigate the searching method taught him by his father which he had completely abandoned for over fifteen years. Several weeks of practice and three articles later Vo Sum came to the conclusion that he might be of great service to his compatriots if he could apply dowsing to the search for some of the thousands of persons who had been lost during the protracted hostilities in Vietnam.

With the permission of *Occult Sciences'* editor, he introduced a "Mail Box" column in the magazine suggesting that, with his help, individuals might be able to locate their kinsmen who had disappeared in the wartime confusion. Clients were invited to send him photographs of their missing relatives over which Vo

Captain Vo Sum at the time of his service in the Navy of the Republic of Vietnam.

Sum suspended an inch-wide ball of ebonite on a string. When the ball turned clockwise, this indicated to him that the subject was alive. If it turned counterclockwise, the subject was dead. Waiting until nearly midnight to enhance tranquility and heighten concentration, he next tried to locate living subjects' whereabouts by moving the pendulum slowly over a map until it twirled forcefully over one spot.

As he continued dowsing for missing persons, Vo Sum was amazed to note that many of them seemed to be concentrated in half a dozen specific and limited areas, three of them in Laos and Cambodia where he believed he might have stumbled upon the exact coordinates of enemy prisoner-of-war camps unknown to South Vietnamese and American military authorities.

Realizing that American government officials were eager to learn whether downed U.S. Navy and Air Force pilots had survived and, if so, where they were being held prisoner, Vo Sum wrote a letter to the U.S. Ambassador in Saigon, Ellsworth Bunker, offering his services in locating missing military personnel, only to receive a discouraging reply from the Second Secretary of the U.S. Embassy, William F. Eaton.

Eaton's letter oddly stated that "while we appreciate your offer to assist in locating U.S. prisoners of war, we believe that only the Government of North Vietnam is capable of supplying the U.S. Government with an accurate and complete accounting of the present whereabouts and conditions of U.S. prisoners of war and those missing in action." After recovering from his disappointment at Eaton's categorical rejection of his services, Vo Sum realized that he had made a cardinal mistake by violating what many dowsers hold to be a basic ethical law: Never offer a service to anybody unless they ask for it and really need it.

He therefore decided to concentrate on helping his countrymen find missing relatives and simultaneously began to teach dowsing through a home-study course, advertised in *Occult Sciences,* consisting of twenty-four written lessons to be mastered over a period of six months. At the beginning of 1974, 144 persons, representing every province of South Vietnam, had enrolled in the course.

During the 56-minute naval engagement with the Chinese that came to be called the Battle of the Paracel Islands, a Vietnamese patrol craft escort (PCE) received a direct hit by a Chinese surface-to-surface missile which disabled her electronic communication equipment. As officer responsible for maintaining contact with the stricken vessel, Vo Sum resolved to try to locate her with his pendulum. Using only her name, "Nhat-Tao HQ-10," written on a piece of paper as an identifying key, he marked a preliminary position for the escort vessel on a nautical chart at 16 degrees 18 minutes North and 111 degrees 16 minutes East at 10:00 hours on January 20 (point A on the chart). The ship was moving, said Vo Sum, in a south-southwesterly direction.

Having no other information to rely on, the operations chief of the Vietnamese task force, Admiral Tran-Van-Chon, decided to base rescue operations on Vo Sum's findings. Twenty-four hours later, Vo Sum's dowsing gave him a second position (B on the chart), with the stricken PCE still drifting in the same direction,

GENERAL PATTON'S WATER DOWSER

Ralph Harris, a Californian realtor, was born in South Boston, Virginia, where he learned to dowse for water from his grandfather who died at ninety-nine years of age. After enlisting as a private in the U.S. Army in 1941, Harris, promoted to the rank of captain, participated in the landing of American forces in Morroco commanded by General George Patton. His account follows:

"The Germans had blown up all the water wells in the area when we landed not far from Casablanca. The army engineers were drilling in the sandy desert country to no avail. A lot of water was being pumped ashore from ships and trucked to the troops. One of our geologists said there was no way to pinpoint water without first bulldozing the sand away so he could see the underlying formations.

"When I found out how badly our army needed water, I decided to inform General Patton that I could find it by dowsing. I had a hell of a time trying to get to see him but finally I came face to face with him. When I told the general what I could do, he only asked: 'What do you need, Captain?'

"I replied: 'All I need is a forked willow switch.'

"Patton immediately reached for his field telephone, called his aircorps commander and said: 'I want a willow tree flown in here as soon as possible.' The aircorps officer must have asked a rude question because Patton shouted: 'No, I'm not crazy! I want a willow tree! I don't give a damn where you get it but I want it in here on the double.'

"So the next day they flew in a willow tree not quite the height of this room with plenty of cuttable forked sticks on it. I cut one and went out and found what seemed to be an underground river 300 feet wide and 400 feet down to water and 300 feet deep running under the arid desert. I took a colonel of engineers out there to show him where to drill. He said there couldn't be any water there.

"I challenged him: 'Colonel, would you like to bet some money on that? How about 5,000 dollars? I've got that much in my account. Would you like to put up 5,000 that there's no water here? Would you like to do that, Colonel?'

"He said: 'No, I wouldn't.'

"'Well,' I said, 'then what you're saying is just talk. Why don't we drill and see. General Patton is backing me to find water.'

"So we drilled a well down to 700 feet and we got 2,000 gallons per minute.

"I located similar wells for the army in other desert areas. You could find an underground river every few miles. The water didn't form in domes in that country, it ran in rivers. I located a lot of water, wherever we needed it. A total of seventeen big wells.

"I never got any recognition for this work. I should have been promoted to major. If I'd asked General Patton for it, I think he'd have given it to me. He was a rough man but fair and he was a genius."

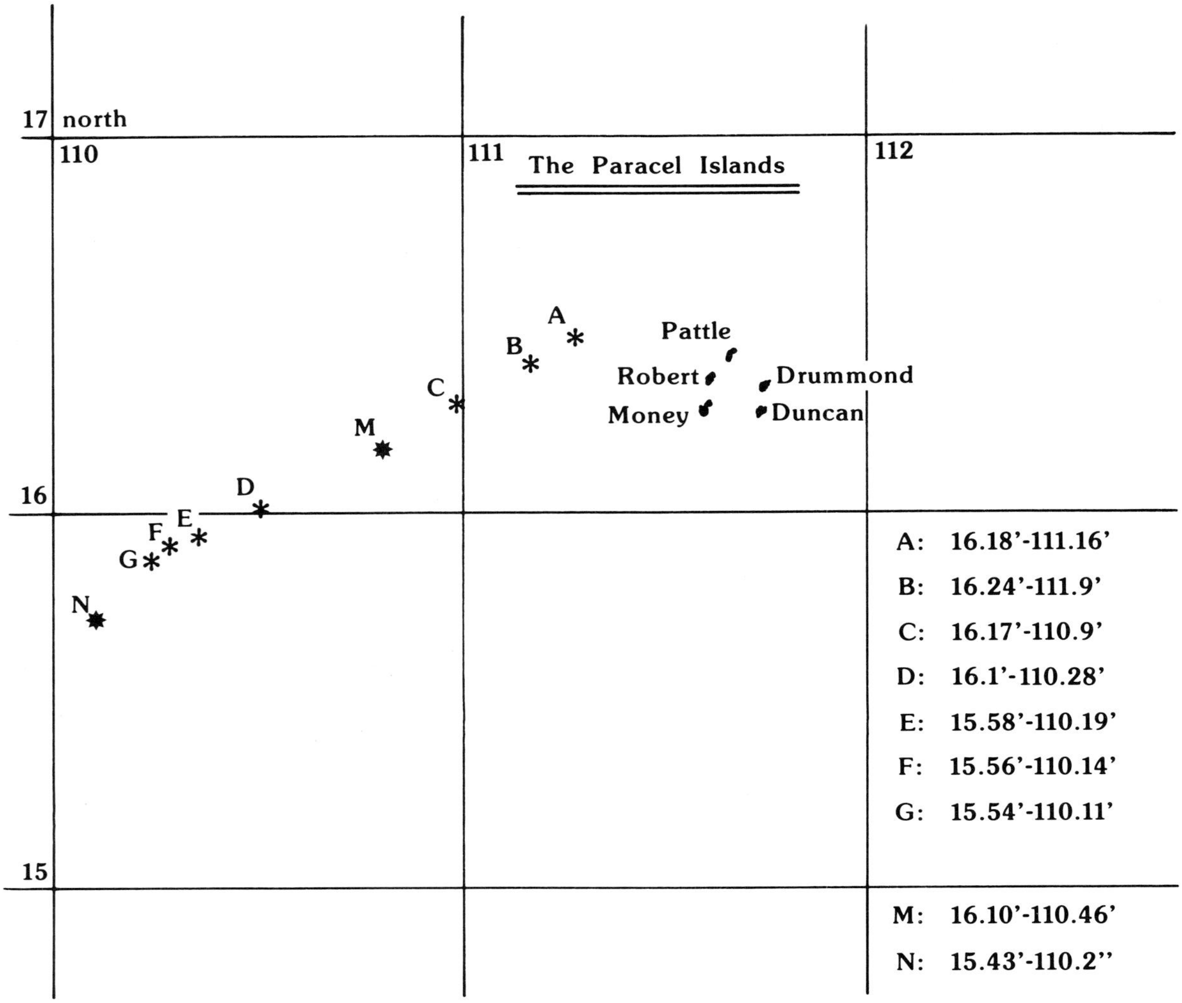

17| north
110   111   The Paracel Islands   112

                                    A
                                B   *
                                    *   Pattle
                        C   Robert   Drummond
                            *   Money   Duncan
                    M
                    *

16   D
                *
            F E
        G * * *
    N
    *

15

A: 16.18'-111.16'
B: 16.24'-111.9'
C: 16.17'-110.9'
D: 16.1'-110.28'
E: 15.58'-110.19'
F: 15.56'-110.14'
G: 15.54'-110.11'

M: 16.10'-110.46'
N: 15.43'-110.2''

*Naval chart indicating positions
of disabled ship and raft.*

240 degrees. Air search was hampered by an order to South
Vietnamese pilots to keep their planes away from the 16th
parallel in order to avoid possible entanglements with Communist
MIG aircraft.

On the third day, at 10:00 hours the Captain's pendulum
gave a third reading (point C) and, at 18:30 that evening,
twenty-three members of the Nhat-Tao HQ-10's complement,
now on rafts, were rescued by a Netherlands merchant vessel,
Skopionella, out of Hong Kong (point M). Vo Sum was warmly
congratulated by the commodore commanding the task force for
having accurately determined the exact position of the crippled
escort.

The rescued crew members reported that two of their
number had been seen floating away on a wooden raft which Vo
Sum proceeded to dowse, finding its position to be 16 degrees 1
minute North and 110 degrees 28 minutes East (point D),
heading south-southwest, at 13:25 hours on January 24. Vo Sum
gave three more positions (points E, F, G) during the same

218

afternoon. At 18:15 that evening the raft was sighted by an observation plane at 15 degrees 43 minutes North, 110 degrees 2 minutes East (point N), but the two men were no longer on board.

Opium Smugglers Apprehended

Vo Sum's exploit caused a sensation in Vietnamese naval circles. Two captains asked him to teach them his method of search. An admiral and a commodore expressed interest in it but complained that, because of their exalted ranks, they could not go on record as practicing dowsing to locate vessels at sea for fear that they would be accused of "superstitious practices."

In the summer of 1974, news of Vo Sum's feat came to the attention of Captain P. M. Khue, Assistant Chief of the Vietnamese Navy's Sea Operations Command. On June 26, he invited Vo Sum to his office, hoping that the same strange ability that had allowed the rescue of the "Nhat-Tao HQ-10" crewmen would be of assistance in solving a problem that was plaguing him.

Naval operations were at that time divided between a River Operations Command which had charge of a vast southern area of the country laced with rivers, canals, and swamps, and the Sea Operations Command which supervised all shipping from the coastline out to deepest water. The two principal tasks of the Chief of Sea Operations were the prevention of enemy infiltration

TABLE

Time	Point on Chart	Coordinates in Degrees
11:00	A	7.42 N 105.29 E
13:00	B	7.53 N 105.43 E
15:00	C	8.06 N 105.57 E
16:00	D	8.32 N 106.40 E

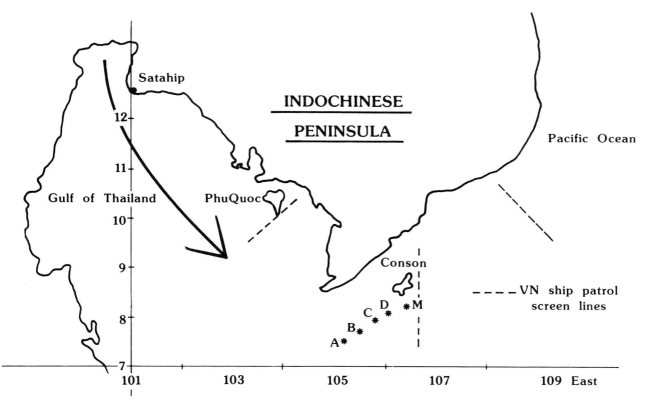

Naval chart indicating positions of opium smuggling vessel.

into South Vietnam from the high seas and the apprehension of smugglers anywhere off the coasts.

Khue told Vo Sum that the command had completely lost track of a junk, numbered 93393, out of Satahip, a Thai port on the Gulf of Thailand, which the international police organization, Interpol, had reported to be carrying a load of six tons of raw opium. The vessel was active in one of many smuggling operations in which up to ten tons of drugs, including heroin, originating in remote areas of Laos, Thailand, and Malaysia where it was grown for worldwide markets, were clandestinely shipped each year to Hong Kong and other Asian ports. The secret shippings were extremely profitable, one ton of raw opium selling for close to a million U.S. dollars and 100 kilograms of heroin for two hundred thousand.

Taking his pendulum from his pocket, Vo Sum first asked a key question: "Should I or should I not work on this problem?" When the pendulum's motion indicated a "yes," he then posed himself the following successive questions:

—Is junk number 93393 actually carrying opium? *Answer:* Yes.

—Will this opium be seized by the navy before midnight? *Answer:* No.

—Will it be seized on June 27 at 1:00, 2:00, 3:00, 4:00, or 5:00 A.M.? *Answer:* No.

—Will it be seized at 6:00 A.M. on June 27? *Answer:* Yes.

—Will all six tons be seized? *Answer:* No.

—Will two-thirds or half be seized? *Answer:* No.

—Will one-third be seized? *Answer:* Yes.

The replies having predicted that further work on the problem seemed worthwhile, Vo Sum next took a 5 × 7 inch colored photo of a junk—a vessel with a top speed of ten knots, 14 meters overall and 3 meters abeam, weighing ten tons with a crew of eight—from the Sea Operations Command files. He changed the number of the ship shown in the picture to the number which had been reported for the presumed smuggler, 93393, and laid it near the top of the chart to focus his attention upon the exact target sought.

Precisely at 11:00 hours, Vo Sum located the junk at a point A on a large chart, showing the whole of the southern tip of the Indochinese peninsula and the Gulf of Thailand, and noted that she was sailing at an azimuth of 55 degrees, or approximately northeast by east.

During the afternoon the captain made three more readings at 13:00, 15:00, and 16:00.

Operating on Vo Sum's data radioed to him from shore, the commander of a South Vietnamese destroyer-type HQ-4 reported picking up a junk on her radar screen (exactly at point D) at 16:00 hours. The naval vessel gave chase and finally caught and boarded the junk at 20:15 hours (at point M), 6.5 miles from Conson Island, site of a notorious prison established by French colonial authorities and maintained, after South Vietnamese independence, by the Saigon government.

Vo Sum was puzzled that the junk should have been captured so soon. He had predicted to Captain Khue that the opium would be taken into custody only at six o'clock in the morning, the following day, June 27. Since the junk had been overtaken ten hours earlier, it seemed that his forecast for the time of the seizure was wrong. The junk was searched for opium from the time of its capture to 1:00 A.M. on June 27, at which point the destroyer radioed the Sea Operations Command that its crew members had been able to find only a cargo of vegetables, ice, and fish, but no drugs of any kind.

Khue looked at Vo Sum askance.

"It looks like you're mistaken," he chided.

Undeterred, Vo Sum checked with his pendulum for contraband opium aboard the junk and received a strong positive indication that it was in fact present. He turned to Khue.

"Order the search to continue," he demanded. "Have them turn that junk inside out!"

The doubtful Khue complied.

Upon receiving instructions to continue hunting for the opium, the search party now decided to probe all the way to the bottom of certain tanks packed with ice and fish. At 2:30 A.M., they came upon their first batch of raw opium. Spurred by this initial success, they continued searching and, precisely at 5:00 A.M. on June 27, the destroyer commander reported to Khue that

Gordon MacLean dowsing time of an oil tanker arrival near the Portland Head Lighthouse in Maine. (Photograph by Alice Brown.)

Gordon MacLean, a chemical engineer now in his eighties, still works full time directing the analytical laboratory for Pine-State By-Products, a manufacturer of poultry feed in South Portland, Maine. On sunny days, MacLean will take visitors out to the Portland Head, a promontory dominated by a lighthouse at the entrance to Portland Harbor which commands a view of the eastward sea horizon.

Knowing that an endless procession of oil tankers advances on Portland to deliver fuel for distribution throughout Maine and other parts of New England, MacLean smilingly asks his companions whether they would like to know the exact time the next tanker will appear on the horizon on its way into the harbor. When the offer is accepted, he takes from his pocket a small, supple Y-shaped rod made of plastic and sweeps the horizon. At a given azimuth the rod dips.

"That's where the next one will appear," chortles MacLean. "Let's see how fast she's moving. Is it 18 knots, 17, 16?" The rod remains motionless. "Is it 15?" The rod dips. "Is it between 15 and 16 knots?" The rod dips again. "Is it 15.1 knots?" No dip. "Is it 15.2, 15.3, 15.4?" Still no dip. "Is it 15.5?" The rod once again dips down vigorously.

MacLean grins. "Well, now we have the speed, let's get the distance." By a similar procedure this is determined as forty-seven nautical miles away from the point where the tanker should appear. By a simple arithmetical calculation, MacLean forecasts that the tanker should show up within three hours and two minutes.

And it does. And MacLean has repeated this incredible feat many times for scores of witnesses.

they had found 2.1 tons of opium all told. Vo Sum's dowsing prediction had turned out to be almost 100 percent correct.

He was hopeful that his success in locating the junk would allow him a share of the $40,000 awarded by the Vietnamese Government's Customs Directorate to any agency or individual involved in the successful seizure of two tons of opium. Usually the persons responsible for locating a vessel carrying that amount of contraband received 40 percent of the award, the rest of the sum being divided between all participants involved in the operation, crews aboard ship, and workers ashore.

The check that came to him in the mail amounted to a paltry $10, an indication, as Vo Sum put it later, "of what nondowsing officials think of our unusual service."

"Operation Farewell"

During the last part of 1974 and the early months of 1975, when the fortunes of the South Vietnamese Army were evaporating with each passing day, requests to find missing relatives and friends mushroomed from an average of fifteen to more than one hundred a week. Faced with the mounting demand for dowsing services, Vo Sum enlisted six volunteers from the new Vietnamese Society of Dowsers he had organized to help him with the work. Provided free of charge, the dowsing activity (which Vo Sum later called "Operation Farewell" in memory of the tragic events leading up to the fall of South Vietnam to its Communist adversary) became most intense from March 12, 1975, onward and ended on May 30 with the fall of Saigon.

As Vo Sum was to report: "We practically had to work round the clock. During the day, my wife and two daughters registered new clients and provided answers to others who had come to inquire a few days before. It was also my wife who had the heavy burden of tactfully informing supplicants that our dowsing had determined that their loved ones were no longer among the living."

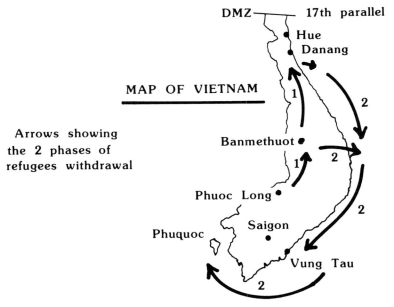

MAP OF VIETNAM

Arrows showing the 2 phases of refugees withdrawal

DMZ — 17th parallel
Hue
Danang
Banmethuot
Phuoc Long
Phuquoc
Saigon
Vung Tau

The first phase of the fifty-day period lasted until March 29, when the city of Ban Me Thuot in the mountainous highlands fell to the enemy, unleashing the start of a massive retreat by soldiers and civilians. Most of the results obtained by Vo Sum and his colleagues in their searching work during this period showed a precipitous movement of persons toward the northern provinces not yet occupied by the Communists, a migration corroborated by subsequent dispatches.

In the midst of a steady avalanche of foreboding news, Vo Sum received word from two students who had completed his dowsing course that their newfound ability had at least helped to save the lives of soldiers in the field. The commander of a military post at Chikara in mountainous Pleiku province wrote to say that one of his noncommissioned officers who had been taught to dowse by the naval captain was using his art to insure the outpost's survival in the face of unrelenting enemy pressure.

Sergeant Nguyen-Minh-Phuong spent part of each afternoon in the fort's operations room dowsing for possible surprise enemy night attacks. After concentrating on the problem and focusing his attention on a hand-drawn map of the fort, he asked: "Which part of this post or its outlying defenses will be assaulted tonight?" Following the location of the threatened area, he then put the question: "What will be the time of H-hour?"

The post commander informed Vo Sum that while, at first, he put no credence in Nguyen's intelligence, over a period of several weeks the noncom's advanced warnings proved to be so accurate that he began ordering his forces to prepare for an assault according to the information supplied by the dowser. This stratagem markedly lowered casualty rates and bolstered the flagging morale of the post's defenders.

Two weeks prior to the fall of Ban Me Thuot, the captain met another of his students, Hoang-Van-Nam, in Saigon, who rushed up to him saying: "Honored teacher, the techniques I learned from you have saved my life. Had I not learned dowsing, not only I, but many soldiers in my unit, would probably have perished three days ago."

Hoang went on to relate that his company had become scattered while retreating before a rapid enemy advance and that he found himself lost in the jungle. After hours trying to find his companions, he at last saw footprints in the soft earth of a trail. Pulling his pendulum from his pocket, he ascertained that they had been made by fellow platoon members. Over the next five hours, guided by his dowsing alone, he made his way through totally unfamiliar territory and finally came across his company bivouacked on a hill.

The company commander, who had believed Hoang dead, was so surprised by the means the soldier had used to find his way back to his unit that he asked him on the spot which direction the company should proceed in order to avoid enemy forces. After posing questions to himself over a quarter of an hour, at 11:00 hours Hoang came up with a surprising answer: "Captain, we should not move out at all," he asserted, "because, at 15:00 hours, we shall be picked up by helicopters."

223

ABOVE Bob Ater demonstrating "dropping in" and BELOW "channeling" while dowsing with a pencil. (Photograph by Bill Halas.)

Several officers and noncoms openly laughed at this prediction. It seemed wholly unlikely, during what was amounting to a holocaust, that the high command would send helicopters to rescue one stray company. The captain nevertheless decided to risk a four-hour wait to see if Hoang's hopeful prediction would materialize. Just after 15:00, when they were beginning to doubt the dowser's prognosis, the men heard the roaring of engines from a squadron of helicopters moving toward them from the south. One of the soldiers immediately fired an emergency flare. When the unit on the ground had been properly identified by radio, the helicopters landed and the men were airlifted to safety.

In April requests to find missing persons became so numerous that, in order to obviate an overwhelming number of clients from coming to his house, Vo Sum began publishing results in *Trang Den*, a well-known Saigon daily. A standardized form, used to send answers to the paper, provided information on whether a given subject was dead or alive as well as a precise location for the living body or the corpse.

During the second phase of the search operation most of the locations indicated a streaming of refugees, first toward the east coast, then southward by sea to the coastal city of Vung Tau and the island of Phu Quoc, the westernmost portion of South Vietnamese territory south of Cambodia where facilities to care for refugees had been hastily organized. Because of the general confusion during the debacle, Vo Sum and his team had to rely on clients to tell them whether their dowsing predictions had turned out to be correct or not. Many of them never bothered to report back. Nevertheless a great many successful cases were confirmed.

A typical happy ending involved Vo Sum's naval colleague and assistant, Commander Ho-Duy-Duyen, who anxiously wished to learn what had happened to his sister. Five months pregnant, the woman had fallen from a crowded naval vessel leaving the Cau Da pier in the port of Nhatrang. Witnesses saw her finally pulled from the water and stretched out on the dock where she lay motionless. Vo Sum told his colleague that his sister was not dead, as observers had suspected, but had somehow managed to get all the way to Phu Quoc Island. Two days after Vo Sum's optimistic prediction, the commander received a call from the refugee camp at Phu Quoc to say that his sister had been put on a plane for Saigon. The overjoyed brother, who had been unwilling to believe that his sister had not perished, rushed to the airport to meet her.

After learning of Duyen's sister's case, Chief Petty Officer Tran-Ngoc-Quang of the Naval Logistics Command came to Vo Sum's office bearing a photo of his son, Tran-Ngoc-Binh who, as the father related, had withdrawn with his infantry unit from Pleiku in the Vietnamese central highlands. Intercepted by a Communist patrol, the unit suddenly was decimated by an exploding land mine. Amidst the panic and confusion, one of Binh's close friends escaped to make his way to Saigon to tell Binh's disconsolate father that his son had been wounded, perhaps mortally.

224

After working quietly for several hours over Binh's picture, Vo Sum told the parents the next morning, a Tuesday, that Binh had indeed been wounded, though not seriously, and would contact his family within two or three days. Late Friday afternoon, Chief Quang ran into Vo Sum's office with tears in his eyes. "I've just received a letter from my son," he almost sobbed, "he's in the 2nd Corps Field Hospital, nearly recovered from his wound, and will be released soon." As Vo Sum wrote in a letter: "The tears of joy in the eyes of a fifty-year-old father learning that his son was alive and would soon come home was one of the most cherished recompenses I ever had for my dowsing."

From his experience in training dowsers, Vo Sum, now living and working in San Diego, California, has come to the conclusion that the greatest stumbling block to progress in dowsing is overconfidence, which leads to a lack of precise formulation of questions and thus wrong answers. When failure is encountered, he says, this often leads in turn to a depression, which causes many novice dowsers to abandon the practice as hopeless. But if a dowser is able to stick to it and practice assiduously, there is no answer he will not be able to provide to the five basic questions of the intelligence game: How? What? Where? When? and Why?

Lost in the Wilderness

Equally encouraging is Robert Ater, a Baptist minister turned doughnut maker and high school custodian in Bath, Maine. "Everything has to be somewhere," he says simply. "You may not know exactly where the person or thing you are seeking is but you know it is out there. State exactly to yourself what you wish to find. Become involved in it personally. Dowsing is a natural function in man. Ancient peoples knew this. Primitives in our own time demonstrate powers of the brain that are occluded in so-called civilized persons."

Ater dowses with a pencil. "I use two basic positions," he explains. "The first I call 'dropping in' on a location from a short distance above a map. The second I call 'channeling' because this best describes what it feels like when I follow a trace on the map. It's as if my pencil is traveling in a well-defined groove."

One cold April evening, the six o'clock television news reported that two University of Maine students were a day overdue on a hiking trek into New Hampshire's White Mountains where a fierce late-season blizzard was sweeping the Presidential range.

"What if they were my boys?" wondered Ater, who had two student-age sons of his own. Spurred by the thought, he spread a Texaco road map out on his kitchen table and located Mount Washington, whose 6,288 foot summit, highest east of the Mississippi, was the goal of the two hikers. Holding a pencil in his right hand as if he were about to write a letter, he pointed its tip downward over Crawford Notch where the students were reported to have parked their car. Staring fixedly at the pencil he asked himself: "Exactly where is the trail the hikers took as they began their ascent?"

The pencil advanced slowly, retreated, then advanced again,

225

as he "felt" along the path. Ater's excitement surged as it traveled on the cream-colored section of the map indicating the mountainous area and finally settled on Pinkham Notch, eight miles to the northeast of its starting place.

"In an instant," Ater later reported, "I knew that the two students had started out not from Crawford, but from Pinkham Notch. I accepted this without question, wholly confident I was on the right track." His pencil then moved around Mt. Clay, across the base of Mt. Washington to a point between Mt. Adams and Mt. Jefferson where it abruptly stopped.

Sure that he had located the place where the two students had taken refuge from the storm, Ater, who had neither a car nor a telephone, ran three blocks to the nearest public phone booth and called the observatory atop Mt. Washington to give weatherman Jonathan Lingol the coordinates he had pinpointed. To Ater's surprise, Lingol, not at all skeptical, carefully wrote down the information mainly because the area Ater had plotted had been considered too far away from the hikers' supposed route and consequently had not been searched.

The uses for dowsing these days are far more diverse than they were only a few decades ago. Some "specialist" practitioners of the art have become particularly adept at solving specific problems more rapidly and efficiently than any of their competitors using nondowsing means. An unusual example of specialization is the work, known to hundreds who have benefited from it, of the late Marcel Triau, a French-born dowser who, after emigrating to the United States, over many years used a pendulum to diagnose engine trouble in automobiles at the Texaco station he operated in Canaan, New York. Triau's expertise in adjusting points for timing won him a special commendation at a training course for automobile mechanics where he was able to finish assigned tasks long before his fellow students who were using sophisticated testing equipment.

Marcel Triau demonstrates his pendulum diagnosis for engine trouble at the annual convention of the American Society of Dowsers in Danville, Vermont.

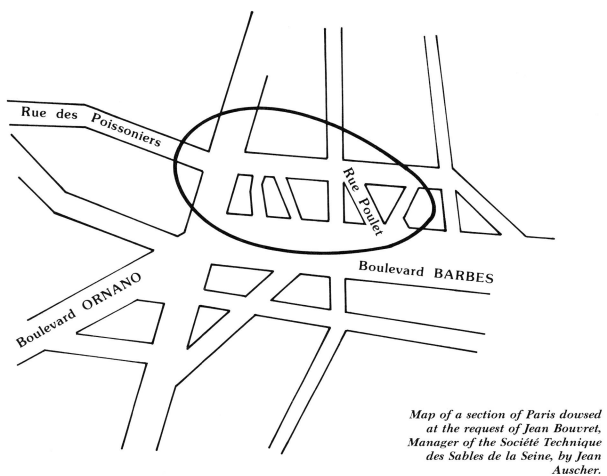

Map of a section of Paris dowsed at the request of Jean Bouvret, Manager of the Société Technique des Sables de la Seine, by Jean Auscher.

Jean Auscher at work in his study. Paris, 1978. (Photograph courtesy of Professor Zbigniew William Wolkowski.)

One week after the students had begun their journey, a weary Appalachian Mountain Club search party heading north from the observatory in deep snow found the students in a shelter on Edmund's Col midway between Mts. Adams and Jefferson. Weather conditions were so severe that it took another full day to bring them out of the wilderness to safety.

"All too often," says Ater, "dowsers never get any feedback when they make searches of this kind. I was therefore particularly happy to get an appreciative letter from Mr. Lingol thanking me for my effort and affirming that the two hikers were found exactly where I predicted and their car had indeed been parked at Pinkham, rather than Crawford, Notch."

Like Vo Sum, Ater counsels beginning dowsers to persevere. "Anyone trying my method," he says, "should never be discouraged by lack of immediate success. I have been working with it for several years and am still developing my talent. The key is practice and more practice, especially on things that can be readily proven. If you can develop a passion for the art and really enjoy it, you will undoubtedly be successful."

No dowser has enjoyed more success than the French engineer, inventor, and gifted artist, Jean Auscher, who more than once has been able to assist police officials in solving crimes.

227

When safe-crackers rifled the safe of the société Technique des Sables de la Seine in Paris, the firm's manager, Jean Bouvret, asked Auscher for help in recovering the 2 million francs that had been stolen. Using a special *scripto-pendule* of his own design that traces patterns on paper with India ink, Auscher established that two thieves involved in the theft should be living in an area delimited by the oval his pendulum traced on a map. A police investigation flushed one of them out of an apartment at the foot of the Rue des Poissoniers, the other from his lair in the short Rue Poulet, or at opposite ends of the oval. "We are especially in your debt," wrote Bouvret to Auscher, "because now that our employees are no longer under suspicion, our insurance company is going to cover our loss."

The uses for dowsing appear to be innumerable and far more diverse than even a few decades ago. Given the original application of dowsing to search for mineral ores in Europe, one may ask whether, since its fall into desuetude in the eighteenth century, any trace of mineral prospecting with divining rods still remains alive on the continent. Not only is the answer to this question affirmative, but in one European state the practical use of dowsing to find mineral resources seems to have been expanded to dimensions undreamed of by early German miners.

The prospecting work is carried out by dowsers who, for the most part, are highly trained specialists in geology and mineralogy, and who insist that dowsing can help to unearth mineral treasures in a country that covers 1/6 of the earth's land surface.

That country is the Union of Soviet Socialist Republics.

CHAPTER 13

Pay Dirt

". . . an intertwined fork and knife . . ."

The Biophysical Method

In the early spring of 1968, a group of 236 Soviet geologists, geophysicists, hydrologists, biophysicists, medical doctors, physiologists, and psychologists from ninety-eight research institutes and economic planning bodies all over the USSR assembled in Moscow at a "Seminar on the Problem of the Biophysical Effect." Sponsored by the Section for Technical Parapsychology and Biointroscopy of the Society for Science and Technology of the Instrument Building Industry, the seminar's attention was focused on the *volshebnii prut* used in the art of *lozakhodstvo,* as the "magic rod" and "dowsing" were known in old Russia.

The new appellation "biophysical effect" (BPE) and its corollary, the "biophysical method" (BPM) were probably inspired by the life work of Professor Leonid Vasiliev who specialized for thirty years in the study of telepathic communication at the Institute for the Study of the Brain and Nervous Activity in Leningrad.

During the Stalin era when psychological research was strapped into an ideological straight jacket, Vasiliev had to work all but anonymously, but after the advent of a much freer intellectual climate under Khrushchev, he finally was able to publish his classic *Mysterious Phenomena of the Human Psyche* in 1959. One year later he brought out another volume, *Biological Radio Communication,* formally introducing the thesis that biological organisms were capable of transmitting and receiving information on an unidentified carrier wave. Since a similar unidentified wave had long been postulated to account for the dowsing phenomenon, it seemed logical to find a new name for the searching art that, dispensing with magical overtones, would retain Vasiliev's idea of a link between physics and biology. The "biophysical effect" can therefore be credited, directly or indirectly, to the Leningrad professor.

Just as dowsing migrated westward out of Germany, so it diffused eastward to Russia where miners in the Ural Mountains were using it to discover ore more than three centuries ago. Before World War I, it was employed to locate water for construction crews building the Amur railroad in the Far East. At the Moscow seminar the Georgian hydrological engineer, Georgii I. Kevkhishvili recounted how, before World War II, he was

229

Georgii I. Kevkhishvili (second from left) and other dowsers on Moscow television. (Photograph courtesy of Dr. Alexander P. Dubrov, Moscow, USSR.)

employed by the Red Army to find badly needed water for temporary military encampments in the drought-stricken North Caucasus. He has recently deposited a complete archive on this and other exploits at the Academy of Sciences in Tbilisi, capital of the Soviet Republic of Georgia.

During the war, two more engineers, Evgeny Simonov and Boris Tareyev, made public their dowsing findings in *Elektrichestvo,* a leading electrical engineering journal. "We have found it possible to locate a three-phase electrical cable underground," they wrote. "The direction of the rod's deflection, up or down, makes it possible also to determine the direction in which the power in the cable is moving. A person armed with what has been called the 'magic rod' becomes an unusually sensitive electrophysical device. The forces in the rod are thousands of times stronger than those operating galvanometers. Though their cause cannot be explained simply as an effect of electrostatic or geomagnetic fields, it is no longer a question of magic as our forebears in the Middle Ages believed."

About the same time, no less an academic authority than Gerasim V. Bogomolov, a professor of hydrogeology and a member of the Byelorussian Academy of Sciences, who had taught himself to dowse, was accurately predicting the depth and dimension of many water veins he had discovered as well as the diameter of underground pipes and electrical cables.

Soviet Geologists Back Dowsing

In 1966, a doctor of geology and mineralogy, Nikolai N. Sochevanov, who today works for the USSR's Ministry of Geology as one of the leading Soviet specialists in geochemical prospecting, opened the modern era of Soviet dowsing with presentations of his findings to several scientific societies in Leningrad, including one devoted to space age technology under

230

> "We hydrogeologists know that electromagnetic phenomena can occur also during the filtration of underground water through rocks. As the water flows around the rocks, the water particles execute complex oscillatory movements. Even here electromagnetic waves can appear, their length depending on the speed of the underground stream. But man's organism, as is well known, is even more sensitive than some physical instruments. For instance, smell allows us to catch the presence of a countable number of airborne molecules of a given substance. It is easy to conceive of a man holding a wire rod—a closed oscillating circuit—tuned precisely for the oscillation range of underground water. The human organism simply becomes the signal amplifier as the impulse travels through the nervous system to the hand muscles and the operator, probably unwittingly, turns the rod which thus is most likely something akin to the indicating needle of an instrument."
>
> Professor G. V. Bogomolov
> as quoted in *Tekhnika Molodezhi*, No. 8, 1967.

the aegis of the Soviet Ministry of Defense. Sochevanov described his testing the dowsing ability of forty subjects, at least four of whom were able accurately to detect a current of water that hydrogeologists knew to be filtering through a huge earth dam regulating the flow of the Chu River near Lake Issyk Kul in Central Asia.

Sochevanov developed a series of U-shaped rods made of different metals designed with special handles so that they would not just dip downward or upward, like the old forked stick, but make one or more *complete revolutions through 360 degrees*.

"It thus became possible," he reported, "to record the number of revolutions made over a given period of time or interval of distance as a dowser moved or was moved along a given traverse. This allowed a degree of quantitative analysis to be applied to the biophysical effect."

In northern Kirghizia, Sochevanov observed that the strange revolutions over water veins and known ore deposits would often coincide with instrumentally measured electrical potentials above them. When one dowser walked over a lead-zinc deposit ten meters below the ground's surface at Arsy, his U-shaped rod made eighteen complete rotatory movements. While seated in a slowly moving automobile the number of revolutions over anomalies was reduced by a factor of 1.5–2 and by much more as the speed of the vehicle increased. Cloth and rubber gloves had no effect upon the rotation but, totally inexplicable to Sochevanov, gloves made of leather seemed to completely block it in certain operators. When an electric wire carrying a 15-volt current was wound around a dowser's wrists, the number of revolutions decreased to as much as a quarter of their original amount as it did when a horseshoe magnet was brought close to the back of their heads.

In 1967 two articles on geological prospecting appeared

231

simultaneously. The first, published in *The Prospecting for and Conservation of Mineral Resources* by a team of four nondowsing geologists, pointed to the time-consuming difficulties of accurately locating new deposits. The other, suggesting a new way to speed up the process, came out under the title "The Biophysical Effect in Geology." Its author, Valery S. Matveyev, then working at the Kazakh affiliate of the All-Union Scientific Institute for Geophysical Prospecting in Alma Ata, described experiments in which the revolutions of U-shaped dowsing rods correlated with the location of a deposit of copper-zinc ore in the Tasty-Butak field and over a gas-pipe line running from Bukhara to the Urals. Matveyev recommended that in the future it would be appropriate to devote more study to the seeming dependence of a rod's rotation on its composition and dimensions, for "if the most suitable rod were used, it might be possible to zero in on significant commercial deposits and avoid the 'little stuff'."

By the end of 1967, tens of thousands of BPM experiments had been performed all over the Soviet Union from the Trans-Baikal region and Buryat Mongolia to the Caucasas and the Kola Peninsula north of the frigid White Sea. Of 240 dowsers used, 53 of them exhibited the ability to measure, through the rotation of their rods, anomalies associated with known ore deposits and geological faults and the distribution of underground water courses. It appeared, reported Sochevanov in an interview with the popular Soviet magazine *Around the World,* that the biophysical effect was observable over sulfide ore bodies and disintegration zones covered with 50–70 meter thick layers of clay; under high-power electric lines; and over water mains, electric cables, and gas pipes. Most important, the experiments were reproducible. It seemed that over any section of a traverse the rod makes exactly the same number of revolutions, which means that graphs can be drawn of the 'intensity' of the rod's action and compared for different operators on a given day or for a single operator at different times of the year.

Particularly sanguine about the potential contribution of dowsing in geology is the Tashkent geological engineer, Boris V. Bondarev, whose doctoral dissertation, "Use of the Biophysical Method in Geological Prospecting," was approved by a high commission of his superiors specially created to review his work. The commission assigned Bondarev to locate underground objects completely unknown to him. "Within a half hour," reported the Soviet magazine, *Uzbekistan,* Bondarev correctly located fifty biophysical anomalies as proved by their mapping." A protocol drawn up to attest to the finds was certified on the spot by commission members.

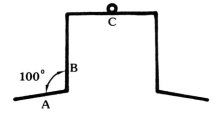

Soviet Dowsing Rod. "On the Biophysical Method in Geology" (see Bibliography) by Valery S. Matveyev, gives the following data for four variants:

	diameter	A	B	C
		(in centimeters)		
Steel rod No. 2	2 mm	18.5	16.2	15.2
Steel rod No. 3	2 mm	18.2	17.8	14.0
Aluminum rod No. 4	2 mm	18	7.5	13.3
Copper rod No. 5	2 mm	18	7.9	13.3

"Using several different rods, BPM anomalies were noted over ore bodies. In our opinion, those for steel rod No. 2 better indicate the morphology of the ore bodies as well as their content of useful minerals than the potentials recorded by electrical instrumentation. Over ore bodies between stakes 30 and 46 are three BFE maxima, the intensity of which increases in an easterly direction. Because of the absence of test bores, the nature of the first maximum (between stakes 30–33) is not certain. The second maximum (between stakes 35–40) exactly coincides with the westernmost edge of ore bodies which lie nearly horizontal at a depth of 23–35 meters. The third, most intensive, maximum (between stakes 40–46) corresponds to an overall increase in size of vein-shotted copper ores and to their relative proximity to the surface, as well as to the location of bodies of solid copper-zinc and zinc ores. In the same profile still another biophysical anomaly (between stakes 62–66) was detected which is correlated with contacts between layers of diaboses, spilites, and pophyrites. This anomaly is detectable with steel or aluminum, but not with copper rods. It would appear, therefore, that the selective capacity of rods made from different metals can be utilized to differentiate the geological nature of different biophysical anomalies, in this case between those connected to ore and those connected to contacts. Where the electrical method marks an anomaly linked to carboniferous limestone (between stakes 75–90), no biophysical anomalies were detected by the rods.
—Valery S. Matveyer*

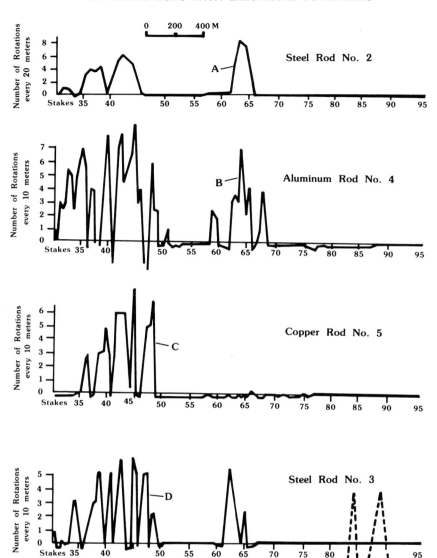

COMPARISON OF REACTIONS
OF METAL RODS WITH ELECTRICAL POTENTIALS

233

The same magazine hinted that dowsing had probably been used in Uzbekistan for as long as anyone could remember. "How did our ancestors find water in the Kyzyl Kum desert?" it asked rhetorically. "We know that, in those days, there was no drilling based on geological prospecting and the water in those wells stands at depths of 300 meters and more!"

Statements by Soviet Geologists

"The biophysical method (BPM) established that the general direction of tectonics in the western part had a strike bearing 320 degrees. The strike located was later confirmed by electromagnetic and magnetic surveys . . . The use of the BPM, in combination with complex geophysical methods, permits one to obtain a fairly clear picture of the tectonic structure of an area under study."
Mikhail F. Komin, Moscow

"The study of the structure of tin deposits in Kirghizia and Tadzhikstan used the BPM accurately to pinpoint the location of ore bodies. It included the determination of the strike of large fractured zones as a result of which a major role was seen to be played by northeast and meridinal fractures in the siting of two deposits of rare earth-tungsten-tin complex ores . . . Taking into account the results obtained, one may assert unconditionally that the BPM is expedient for the study of the geology of ore deposits, particularly tin."
Tatiana A. Burova, Moscow

"In principle, the great accuracy of the BPM in determining the location of objects causing the anomaly (plus or minus 1–1.5 meters) offers the possibility of putting the prospection of overlain deposits of ore on an entirely new footing. Instead of awaiting the results of costly multistage operations—deep geochemical analyses, the working out of anomalies, and their subsequent verification—one can move directly to prospection and evaluation of ore deposits . . . So far, the limited application of the BPM in exploratory work in northern Kazakhstan in no way reflects its enormous potential. This state of affairs will continue until the BPM has been officially recognized by the Ministry of Geology."
Anatoly M. Grigoryev, Tselinograd

"My methodology, developed with a horizontally oriented rod, allows me to solve the following problems: (1) The determination of the width, thickness, depth, and flow of underground water courses; (2) to state whether gold is present in ores and to predict its amount down to values equal to only tenths of a gram per ton; (3) to find "blind" bodies of ore at depths down to 300 meters; and (4) to locate contact points between rocks of lithogically different ages."
Boris Bondarev, Tashkent

As a country second only to South Africa in gold production, the USSR could well profit from Bondarev's and other dowsers' faculties to unearth new deposits of the yellow metal so crucial for financing Soviet imports of grain, industrial equipment, and technological know-how. The Altynopkan Field Expedition to which Bondarev was attached in 1967 recorded that the dowser

---

on the Use of the Biophysical Method

"Using the BPM we were able to differentiate between chemical compositions in subterranean water flows originating from the right and left banks of the Oka River . . . A map showing chlorine concentrations in alluvial aquifers supported a schematic drawing made on the basis of biophysical data for water movement in Permian sediments. BPM estimates of flow rates in these sediments revealed an average rate of speed of 0.87–1.35 meters over twenty-four hours for the first system and 0.59–0.96 meters for the second. The greater rate in the fissures of the first system was confirmed by the presence of larger karst voids in this direction."
Alexander A. Ogil'vy, Moscow

"Even the few examples we have presented reveal the tremendous opportunities linked to the use of the BPM in geology. The method is simple, mobile, inexpensive, and permits the discovery at significant depth (100–120 meters) of deposits undetectable by ordinary methods."
Valery S. Matveyev, Alma Ata

"In the USSR the biophysical method is used to solve various geological problems in the deposits of polymetals, gold sulfides, gold-quartz, copper-molybdenum, copper-bismuth, rare metals, tin-tungsten, tin-polymetals, monomineral tin, magnetite, siderites, bauxites, muscovites (in pegmatites), and others.

A number of problems are also being solved in geological mapping with the aid of the biophysical method. These include the tracing of disjunctives, tectonite and mineralized zones, the establishment of the strike and direction of the predominant fissured zones in this or in other areas, a more precise determination of geological contact zones, and the correlation of geophysical anomalies between profiles.

The biophysical effect is used in geological practice to locate underground water and ores, to disclose the contours of ore bodies, and to pinpoint in the region of ore deposits known "barren" sections where the presence of ore is likely not to be expected. With the help of the BPE it is possible to specify the depth of the disturbing object (ore body, subterranean streams, etc.). Other geological problems are also being solved. The qualified use of the BPM makes it possible to lessen the costs of drilling and allows more effective prospecting for minerals.
Alexander K. Bakirov, Tomsk

proved extremely accurate in determining the locations of known gold and polymetal ore deposits and was able to find previously unknown ore zones in the Burgundinsk Field.

According to another report written by the Almalyk Geological Expedition, during an experiment in the "Bichanzor" gold fields, Bondarev examined a series of trenches with his rod and consistently stated which of them contained gold ore and which did not. In a series of articles in the *Uzbekistan Geological Prospector*, Bondarev noted that it was only because of the large number of unsubstantiated hypotheses put forward to explain dowsing scientifically that the biophysical method has thus far not been widely used in geology. "But," he added, "the absence of theory applicable to this question has not entirely impeded its practical use."

Bondarev stressed that any dowsing task requires detailed study of the problem in all its technical details. In reply to an inquiry by a Communist party official in Kokpatas who had asked him how some men discovered to have the dowsing gift might be put to work, he wrote: "I sincerely greet you as supporters of the oldest prospecting method in the world. Always remember that we, like sappers, cannot afford to make errors because science cannot yet defend us against the large number of skeptics who oppose us. In addition to competence in the biophysical method, it is highly essential that operators know a lot about geology and its methodology. Despite its seeming simplicity, a dowser's work, in its intricacy, can be compared to that of a jeweler."

Bondarev's experience has allowed him not only to define precisely the dimensions and depth of underground water currents, but to quantitatively and qualitatively forecast the presence of gold in complex ores down to a tenth of a gram per

Two charts drawn by Professor Alexander G. Bakirov correlating dowsing rod rotations with ore bodies.

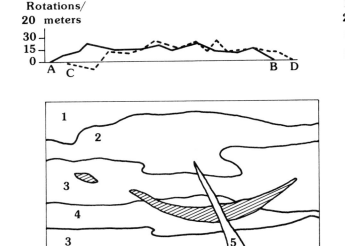

Graph of a biophysical anomaly over a copper pyrite deposit. 1—4 Pillow structure of lavas. 5 Diabase vein.

A—B, using a cast iron rod.
C—D, using a steel rod.

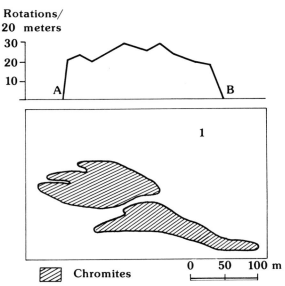

Graph of a biophysical anomaly over the northern part of ore bodies 3 & 4 in the '40 Year' chromite deposit in the Kazakh SSR.   1) Serpentized dunites.

A—B, graph.

ton and to pinpoint contacts between rocks of lithologically different ages.

In another article in *Geologorazvedchik Uzbekistana,* published on December 30, 1969, Bondarev discussed the effectiveness of the BPE in prospecting. "At the present time," he wrote, "from the moment mineral ores are located to the time of their actual exploitation, a long period intervenes during which maps are studied and small and large-scale drilling tests performed. Expensive methods are used during the prospecting of a mineable deposit to determine its contours. As a rule, a significant amount of drilling is done through hollow intrusions. Moreover, in the course of exploiting a deposit, geologists often ultimately reveal that it is not as large or extensive as it was thought to be. Using the biophysical method, I have shown at the Kanzhol silver-polymetallic ore field why, in the presence of a low surface content of silver and polymetal, old-time prospectors were able to locate silver ore at depths of fifty to seventy meters. With dowsing, each prospecting hole can be sited so as to directly contact or cross the desired mineral even in the case of 'blind' ores that are macroscopically indeterminable."

In 1971, Soviet geologists continued to report enthusiastically on the potentials of dowsing at the 2nd Seminar on the Biophysical Effect held in Moscow in March. Among two dozen reports were those at A. M. Grigor'ev, who described how, in the Caucasian Mountains, he was able systematically to compare his own dowsing results with standard search methods and show them to be more effective, and Y. K. Mel'nikov, who announced that in Karelia, east of Finland, his test bores made on the basis of dowsing came up with "pay dirt" far more frequently than those pinpointed by other methods. To coordinate future work, the conference also elected an "Interdepartmental Commission on the BPE" which, because its activities are not included in the USSR's overall economic plan, can be considered a private body rather than an official state organization.

Opposition by Conservatives

That the new commission was not universally viewed without prejudice in Soviet geological circles could be gleaned from the fact that the conference resolved to ask the Ministry of Geology to organize its own expert commission for testing BPM operators in the field and evaluating the method's overall contribution to geological prospecting. It also requested the Ministry of Higher and Middle Specialized Education to allow optional lectures on successful BPM fieldwork to be included in the curricula of Geological and Geophysical departments at Moscow State University, the Leningrad Mining Institute, and other geological faculties in order to prepare budding field geologists to use the BPM in geological mapping.

Resistance to dowsing on the part of conservative or skeptical geologists, hinted at both by Bondarev and the conference's official resolutions, finally surfaced soon after Soviet work with the BPM was positively presented to foreign scientists.

237

At the First International Conference on Psychotronic Research held in Prague, Czechoslovakia, in 1973, Dr. Alexander Bakirov, a professor of mineralogy at the Tomsk Polytechnical Institute—a sort of Siberian MIT—who represented the Interdepartmental Commission, told delegates from fifteen countries that he was using dowsing "biophysically" to locate ore bodies as deep as 3,000 feet underground and to make geological maps from aircraft traveling 200 meters above the earth's surface at 200 kilometers per hour. His data, said Bakirov, so well accorded with other geoprospecting methods that he believed it would prove, in the long run, to be as effective as standard search methods, and hundreds of times less expensive.

The conservatives' sortie came in 1975 in the form of an article published in the official *Geology of Ore Deposits* by three ranking members of the profession. They attacked dowsing not on the merits of the physical data it had produced but because, in their opinion, it was a branch of *parapsychology,* a field specializing in the study of telepathy, clairvoyance, and other modes of extrasensory perception equated by many senior Soviet scientists to charlatanry.

"It is hardly worth taking the time to evaluate dowsing," the authors sarcastically began, "or the 'problems' connected to it. We certainly do not intend to dissuade dowsers since those who believe in parapsychology are never affected by the truth. It is to the broader geological fraternity that we appeal."

What particularly irritated the antagonists of dowsing was the claim by its adherents that they could "tune" to any type of mineral resource of interest to them. Christophe's "mental orientation" was thus rejected as so much nonsense. The authors laid great stress on lack of dowsing success in the area of the Kursk Magnetic Anomaly where it was alleged that Sochevanov and a dowsing colleague were unable, while under test, to detect known strata of iron quartzite. They then dredged up accounts dating back to 1900 of unsuccessful tests of dowsers in several western European countries. In their harshly worded conclusion they stated, *"Work done with the BPM is a harmful illusion and has no connection whatsoever with scientific methods of prospecting."*

Less than a year after the appearance of the negative article, *The Geology of Ore Deposits* published a counterattack, "Yes, the Biophysical Method Does Exist!" by Bakirov, Sochevanov and two other authors.

Why, they asked, was no mention made by their adversaries that the BPE was under study by scientists at the USSR Academy of Sciences' Institute of Biophysics and Institute for the Problems of Information Transmission? Why did they not admit that their evidence on the apparent failure of dowsers in the Kursk Magnetic Anomaly failed to shake the opinion of dozens of scientists that a single experiment was wholly inadequate to justify condemnation of a method being used successfully by hundreds of operators? How could anyone not believe the irrefutable data provided by the southern Urals Hydrology Unit on water supplies discovered by dowsing geologists which permitted a sharp rise in the percentage of successful wells drilled for collective farms? Or the documented case of a successfully dowsed well drilled for the village of Glinka in the Donets Basin that brought in water at a rate of 6 cubic meters per hour? Or another 7-cubic meter well which solved the water-supply problem for the "Soviet Ukraine" collective farm? Or the fact that an engineering firm in Chelyabinsk had disclosed that dowsing had produced 1,120 wells up to November 1975, with a failure rate of only 6 to 8.5 percent for four different dowsers? Or the successful location by dowsing of industrially important mineral deposits in the Yenessei Mountains after normal geological prospecting had failed to find any ore over a period of many years? Or, during a helicopter flight, the pinpointing by dowsing of places where soil erosion was threatening to crack a 400-kilometer gas pipe running from Ukhta to Torzhok?

"Our considered opinion," they noted in conclusion, "is that with respect to the critical article under examination the law formulated by the English writer, Arthur Clark, in 1974 is highly relevant: 'When a leading elder scientist states that a given idea is realizable, he is almost always correct. When he states that a similar idea is not realizable, he is likely to be wrong.' "

Entrenched opposition to dowsing has not deterred Soviet dowsing geologists, whose results have proven the worth of their method. In 1977, a book containing ten essays on hydrogeological research published by the Production and Scientific-Technological Institute for Engineering Research in Construction included one entitled "The Biophysical Method in Hydrogeological Prospecting." Author Alexander Nikolaevich Ogil'vy concluded that the main advantages of dowsing in the search for water were the simplicity of the equipment required, the speed and ease of the method's practice, and the scope of hydrogeological problems that could be solved by it.

Even earlier, in his widely circulated textbook, *Geophysical Prospecting Methods,* Ogil'vy made bold to state: "The body is a living organism plus a conductive circuit that reacts to some distortion of electromagnetic or other unknown physical fields that arise around ore deposits, moving underground water, or breaks in rock layers. There is nothing mystical in this. It is merely the newest problem that has appeared to disturb many scientists in our country and abroad. Who knows, today we may be witnessing a rebirth of the oldest prospecting method in the world which, when put on a scientific footing, will lead to the solution of problems that defy the most modern geophysical methods."

In February 1978, the president of the Interdepartmental Commission, Nikolai Sochevanov, gave a long lecture to the physics section of the Moscow Society for Natural Scientific Investigation in which he advanced an hypothesis that an entirely new physical field, distinct from gravity or electromagnetism, might play an important role in the dowsing effect. His experiments to objectify the field, including some which purport to demonstrate how animals and plants can communicate or react to one another at distance were well received by his fellow scientists and have been included in a long scientific monograph on dowsing to be entitled "The Riddle of the Ages."

239

The Archaeological Connection

Professor Ogil'vy's nephew and namesake, Alexander Alexandrovich, a hydrological engineer and well-known dowsing professional, was confronted with the task of carrying out on the grounds of the Soviet capital's Ostankinsky Palace, a search for an underground drainage system all traces of which had become lost to memory. Witnessing the procedure was a young mechanical engineer embarking on a career in the preservation and restoration of historical monuments, Alexander I. Pluzhnikov. When digging proved Ogil'vy's dowsing accurate, Pluzhnikov was sold on the method. "That same day," he remembers, "I became a dowser."

Pluzhnikov's dowsing exploits in archaeology over the next several years attracted the attention of the well-known Moscow architect-restorers Nikolai I. Sveshnikov and Nikolai I. Ivanov who are engaged in the restoration of sixteenth to nineteenth century Russian monuments. They invited Pluzhnikov to come, one Saturday morning, to old yards in Moscow marked for rehabilitation as an architectural memorial where they were trying to find buried remains of an old building. Pluzhnikov immediately took from his bag two metal rods, colloquially termed "twin mustaches," and within a brief period of time stuck a series of tiny flags into the earth to mark the contours of the building's foundations underground.

When shoveling revealed the foundations to be where he had indicated, Pluzhnikov was asked how in the world his method worked. "My colleagues judge me to be an experienced mechanical engineer capable of analyzing any construction," he replied, "but I can't begin to explain the 'mechanics' of this method, though I've been training in it for almost four years, and have successfully found artifacts buried at depths up to twenty meters."

Impressed by Pluzhnikov's demonstration, Ivanov invited him to take part in the reconstruction of a battlefield near the village of Borodino, the site of one of the bloodiest engagements of the War of 1812 fought by defending Russians against Napoleon's invading armies. The long-standing project is formidably complex. French and Russian topographical maps drawn immediately after the battle itself were thought to depict all artifacts of interest, but many of those still visible aboveground have since been found to be inaccurately charted. Moreover, historical documents have revealed that only a fifth of the most important fortifications, mass graves, and other objects were sketched. During the past century and a half the field itself has been altered by incessant plowing and the construction of new roads across it. Groves of trees have grown, been cut, and grown again. The confusing situation hardly eased when, during World War II, still another battle took place on the field between Soviet Russians and Nazi Germans.

Pluzhnikov's contributions to the restoration have been spelled out in a long article, "The Application of the Biophysical Method to Researching and Restoring Historical and Architectural Monuments," published by the Scientific Research Institute of the Russian Republic's Ministry of Culture.

Drawings by Pluzhnikov of his "twin mustache" rods, taken from his article "Possibilities for and Results of the Use of the Biophysical Method in Researching and Restoring Architectural Monuments" (see Bibliography).

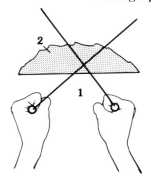

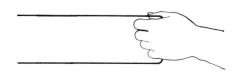

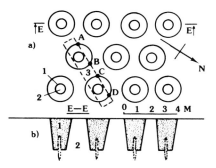

"Wolf-Holes:"
a. Bird's eye view b. Cross Section
1. Hole 2. Sharpened Picket 3.
Section of excavation through two
holes. ABCD) Points indicating
border between originally
excavated and virgin terrain.

Alexander Pluzhnikov dowsing at
the battlefield at Borodino.
(Courtesy of Dr. Alexander
Pluzhnikov.)

Of the many fortifications on the Borodino battlefield, the most historically controversial has long been the so-called "Rayevsky battery," the details of which have been contradictorily represented on maps. Only by dowsing was it possible to accurately locate a network of "wolf-holes"— chimneylike cores cut into the ground designed to break the legs of attacking cavalry horses—one hundred meters in front of the battery that had long since been filled with earth and overgrown with grass. "One can imagine," says Pluzhnikov, "how hard it would be to find such old holes under a uniformly plowed field by any means other than dowsing!"

Pluzhnikov also detected a large number of former excavations and common graves in the area of the battery, inside the redoubt, and within the *flèche*—a field fortification in the form of a blunt angle—commanded by Russian General Bagration who was killed during the battle, as well as near the command post of Napoleon himself, and in several other areas. Under the spot from which the French emperor directed the battle, bodies

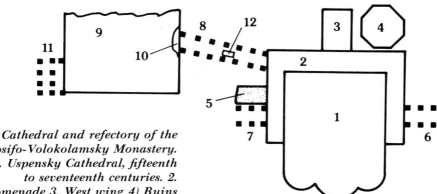

Cathedral and refectory of the Iosifo-Volokolamsky Monastery. 1. Uspensky Cathedral, fifteenth to seventeenth centuries. 2. Promenade 3. West wing 4) Ruins of the fifteenth century bell tower 5. Ruins of the most recent wing 6 and 7. Foundations corresponding to the northern and southern wings 8. Foundations of the 1504 passageway 9. Sixteenth century refectory 10. Ancient doorway at the level of the second floor. 11. Foundations of a 1530 wing. 12. Proposed gravesite of Malyuta Skuratov.

of fifteen to eighteen men appear to have been arranged with their feet pointing north in ordered rows of graves, says Pluzhnikov, the remains presumably being those of French generals and field-grade officers taken to Napoleon's headquarters to be buried with military honors.

Spreading the news of Pluzhnikov's seemingly uncanny talent, the newspaper *Leninskoye Znamya* in an article, "Those Who Can Look Into the Earth," put forward the case of the Iosifo-Volokolamsky monastery, founded in 1479 northwest of Moscow, which has undergone repeated destruction. Restoration work has been returning the monastery's buildings to their original pristine splendor. During the course of a single day Pluzhnikov was able, through dowsing, to explain many features unknown to the restorers and to offer clues on how to proceed with their work that has been making slow progress for nearly two decades.

Historical records made plain that the monastery's Uspensky cathedral and huge refectory had still been connected even as late as the eighteenth century by a passageway built in 1504, under which Malyuta Skuratov, head of Ivan the Terrible's *Oprichnina*, the Russian secret police of that day, may have been buried. Dowsing revealed seven columns on either side of the passageway and a grave between the third and fourth columns in each row counting from the north.

Pluzhnikov also used his technique to survey the former estate of Tsar Boris Godunov near the village of Bol'shye Vyazemy where, though dusty documents described the one-time existence of a magnificent palace surrounded by palisades and a moat, only a rickety old bell tower remained. Within the course of a single day he charted outlines of the palace's foundations, the bases of a series of wooden towers, and a moat long since filled with earth. When he was finished, his sketch revealed the entire ground plan of the medieval imperial residence that agreed in most particulars with its detailed description in centuries-old manuscripts.

Still another historical city studied by Pluzhnikov was Serpukhov under which, as legend had it, tunnels had been dug in medieval times to serve as escape routes and hiding places for monks and their dependents threatened by marauding bands of Mongols and other Asiatic invaders. By carefully plotting his findings on a map, Pluzhnikov made the discovery that the tunnel network interconnected three strategic areas of the town, namely the kremlin, or citadel, and the fortified Vysotsky and Vladychny monasteries founded in the fourteenth century. Several kilometers long, the 7-foot wide tunnel was found to pass under the Nara River at two places. "The whole system was mapped in slightly less than eight hours," wrote Pluzhnikov. "No other methods could have located it in so short a time."

Pluzhnikov is happy to prove the worth of dowsing in archaeological work to anyone willing to stop, look, and listen. Many of his Moscow colleagues, he says, "believe mainly in their shovels as prospecting tools, but others from Leningrad and Volgograd have adopted my dowsing methods to hunt in

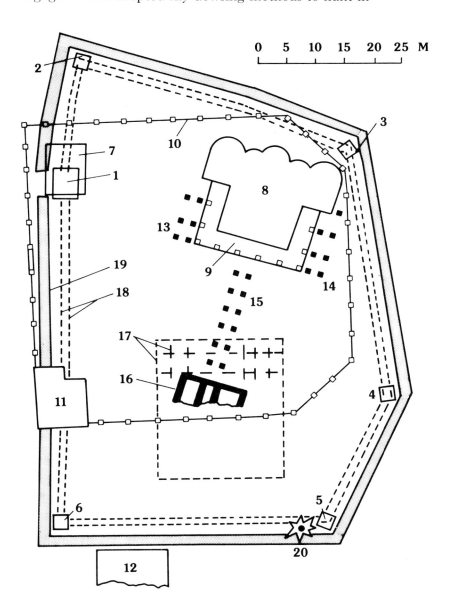

Fortified estate of Tsar Boris Godunov 1. to 6. Old sixteenth century wooden towers 7. Bell tower existing in the sixteenth and seventeenth centuries 8. Sixteenth century cathedral 9. Promenade 10. Existing stone defenses 11. & 12. Eighteenth century buildings 13. & 14. Foundations of wings 15. Foundation of a former passageway to the cathedral. 16. Sixteenth century stone palace 17. Masonry in the foundation of a sixteenth century wooden palace 18. Course of sixteenth century defenses (thin wooden structure side by side) 19. Sixteenth century moat 20. Oak tree

243

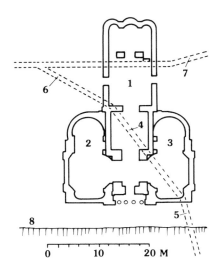

The Troitsky (Trinity) Cathedral in the Kremlin at Serpukhov. 1. Existing cathedral with walls, sixteenth to seventeenth centuries; 2.—3. Existing additions, nineteenth century; 4. Underground passageway; 5.—7. Portions of the passageway leading respectively to the Vladychny monastery (under the Nara River), to the old suburb, and to the Vysotsky monastery; 8) Crest of the river bank.

Dr. Alexander Pluzhnikov dowsing for underground stone and wooden remains of the Alexandrova Sloboda, one of many settlements in feudal Russia which, exempt from taxation, were called "free." The settlement was destroyed at the beginning of the seventeenth century and the population dispersed. 1971 digs corroborated Pluzhnikov's 1970 dowsing of various subterrenean anomalies.

southern Russia for remains of settlements such as those established by ancient Greeks on the Black Sea littoral."

They have also been used in Central Asia by geologist Bondarev who was assigned to pinpoint metallic objects thought to have become buried over the centuries at depths up to five meters around the Chacha Citadel near Tashkent's "Shark" furniture factory. The head of the dig reported: "The experiments must be continued but, so far, their results indicate that this autumn, when we begin excavation of the Afrasiaba Citadel, Bondarev will be able to let us know in advance the placement and depth of objects to be excavated, as well as voids, that exist under thick layers of earth and this will greatly facilitate our work. It appears that the use of the biophysical effect can reduce manual labor in archaeology and speed up digs."

FOUR WELL-KNOWN SOVIET GEOLOGICAL EXPERTS. *As described by Dr. Alexander P. Dubrov, author of* The Geomagnetic Field and Life *and a proponent of dowsing, they are:*

"1) The well-known Soviet dowser and geophysical engineer Alexander Bazhenov engaged in prospecting work. I can add that he is one of our best dowsing specialists and, like Pluzhnikov, has worked on projects for the restoration of old architectural monuments (in Estonia) as well as in geological work.

2) The Soviet dowser Tatiana Burova during an ore-seeking traverse in the mountains of Kirghizia. Since Burova's pronouncements on dowsing are included in the book, they need no further amplification on my part.

3) Soviet master dowser Semyon M. Yogin demonstrating his self-designed P-shaped device during a search for copper-nickel sulfide ores. Yogin devotes a great deal of time to the biophysical effect and works very productively in this area. He holds his unique instrument in either hand. Over complex copper-nickel sulfide ores it turns at an angle up to 210 degrees but over tectonic disturbances it makes a 180 degrees turn to the left. In Norilsk in the dead of winter he works holding the instrument with a heavy fur glove.

4) Engineer and biophysicist Vasily S. Stetsenko, searching for underground water within the Ukrainian crystalline shield in 1978."

One Man's Way

The Russian's pioneering application of dowsing to cultural history has elsewhere been matched only by a Scots infantry general, Jim Scott Elliot, who, after his retirement, began to develop a keen interest in archaeology. While living in his native Dumfriesshire, a Scots border county washed by Solvay Firth, he began studying the intricacies of archaeological field excavation and was simultaneously introduced to Viscount Henri de France's *The Elements of Dowsing.* At once he saw the potential connection between dowsing and archaeological search. With the assistance of a local water diviner he, too, taught himself to dowse.

After a long period of diligent practice and self-questioning, during which he endured condescending smiles from his family and odd looks from his colleagues and friends, he began to get results on self-assigned tasks around his home. His first practical attempt concerned the "Wishing Well," a half-moon-shaped concrete ornamental basin, twelve feet in diameter, which lay halfway up a hill behind his house. The center of the well's overflow system, inoperative for years, was visible slightly off center and, though no one knew for sure, it was assumed that it led down hill to the southwest. Excess water from the well flowed through an improvised cut in the basin's wall through a shallow ditch to create a sea of mud whenever the overflow was especially heavy.

With the idea of clearing the long-since blocked pipe, Scott Elliot circled around the basin's edge with a dowsing rod and got a reaction, not at its supposed southwesterly location, but at the northern side of the basin which he marked with a wooden peg.

Jim Scott Elliot, Major General (retired) map dowsing for archaeological artifacts. (Photographed by Juliet Muskett.)

"The generation that I belong to is skeptical and always asks for proof that dowsing works. On the other hand, the young are open and prepared to 'have a try' and use it. Officialdom of all kinds does not accept it. Nor does science, though we have a number of scientists and geologists in our British Society of Dowsers.

"It is essential that we, as dowsers, overcome this barrier of officialdom, and I believe we can only do this by successful results. To achieve this I suggest we must cut out inefficient dowsing as far as is possible, and so demonstrate by accurate work by qualified dowsers, that dowsing not only works but can be useful, and in a money-mad world, a saver of time, labor and money.

"So may I urge that we expect from the qualified dowser an outlook that expects nothing short of success—not boastfully but humbly—based on a quiet acceptance of an ability, gifted to us, but developed by hard work and trained in the harsh field of experience where success and failure mean much to one's professional integrity." from an address to the 1973 Convention of the American Society of Dowsers by Major General J. Scott Elliot, C.B., C.B.E.

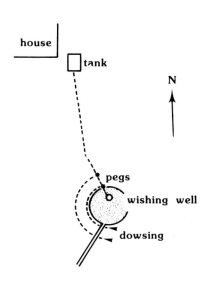

Diagram of pipe. Adapted from **Dowsing: One Man's Way** *by J. Scott Elliot.*

A second peg was put down when another location was found on a wider circle. Scott Elliot was happy to observe that both spots lined up with the overflow's rose. Digging into the ground along the hypothetical line, the general found a lead pipe eighteen inches down. Further dowsing and digging determined that the pipe followed a slightly bent course into an underground tank, a forgotten relic of the days before public mains connected the house to the municipal water supply.

Sometime later a local farmer reported to the general that a small black patch would appear on one area of his land whenever it was plowed. Scott Elliot's dowsing around the patch told him that there was something unusual under the top soil. Extensive excavation in the late autumn of 1965 and the spring of 1966 revealed, to quote the general's report, "an early Bronze Age fire pit not recognizable as a known form." Two possibilities came to mind: a deer roast or, as seemed more likely after extensive research, a place for human cremation.

Word of Scott Elliot's dowsing spread beyond his home county and he quickly found himself asked to check the possibility of archaeological remains on properties in other parts of the United Kingdom. In 1968 the owner of a cottage in Swinbrook, near Oxford, asked him whether there might not have been an old habitation in her garden as suggested to her by, as the general put it, "what we Scots would call a 'fey woman.'"

During a visit to the property in 1969, the general could find nothing on the surface of the garden grounds to indicate the presence of a site. Because he finds it easier to work out intricate details on a map, before undertaking a dowsing survey on the ground, he returned home with a 1:2,500 map showing the garden, and, after enlarging it by a multiple of four, was surprised to detect what appeared to be a 35-by-60 foot construction under the lawn at its western edge. A subsequent dig, to quote the general's unpublished account, "unearthed several floors, one beautifully laid out and firm, the remains of what is thought to have been a hearth, a line of stake holes running at a gentle curve well cut into sandstone and accurately spaced, and two sharp-end ivory tools beautifully shaped and polished. The site was found *entirely by dowsing means.*"

The next year, the general map-dowsed the garden and orchard of the Manor House at Chieveley, a village in Berkshire, and predicted the presence of a complex site including three periods: Iron Age, circa 50 B.C.; Roman circa 80 A.D.; and Saxon circa 850 A.D. The dates were also determined by dowsing. After field dowsing seemed to confirm a site, trial excavations in 1973 and 1974 at three selected spots produced a large ditch, probably Roman Punic of the first century A.D. and a smaller ditch and an entrance. An extension of the original cut exposed a considerably quantity of carbonized wood radio-carbon-dated at 808 A.D. ± 80. The third cut revealed a large ditch, possibly Roman Punic. "The main point of my work at Chieveley," said the general to visitors at his suburban London home, "is that up to the time that map dowsing pinpointed it, the site was completely unknown to archaeology. But with just three small cuts, we have proved a continuous series of existences going back to pre-Roman times."

247

Scott Elliot is disappointed that he has not yet been able to persuade professional archaeologists to take up dowsing as a time-saving adjunct to their work. At one meeting in Edinburgh, during his early days as a dowser, he spent some time trying to interest a group of eminent Scottish archaeologists in the use of dowsing but, as he puts it, "got nowhere." As he was about to leave, one of them asked if a dowser could find a piece of metal in a man's body. The speaker then slipped off his jacket and lay over a table saying that he had a piece of shrapnel in his back since World War I and could the general find it? In front of five smiling onlookers the general, who had never before used dowsing for such a purpose, and was therefore inwardly anxious, used his pendulum to search the man's torso and within three seconds put his finger on one part of the man's back. At the feel of Scott Elliott's fingertip, the man exclaimed: "You've got it!"

Still another test came from a professional geologist who, doubtful of the worth of dowsing, suggested the general outline a bed of alluvial tin under an extensive meadow. Though he had never dowsed for underground mineral deposits, he worked over the field and, within half an hour, marked out on the ground what he believed to be the edges of the tin bed. When the geologist returned from a meeting, he examined the survey, then told the general that he had earlier established the bed's boundaries by pitting across the meadow. Scott Elliot's findings had coincided with his own.

In a book written about his dowsing experiences, Scott Elliot concluded from this experience that it was of primary importance that dowsers possess a level of confidence requisite for success and be bold enough to try something they had never done before, while at the same time remaining oblivious to onlookers so that their minds could work without interference. To underscore the fact that there was no rigidly prescribed dowsing method, but rather a style suitable to a given individual, the general entitled his book: *Dowsing: One Man's Way.*

How many hours, days, months or whole digging seasons may be saved in future years if archaeologists will see fit to use the services of competent dowsers? The answer may have been provided by Dr. Froelich Rainey, former director of the University Museum of the University of Pennsylvania, whose associate, Rodney Young, was excavating a huge mound 150 to 175 feet high and 600 to 800 feet in diameter in Anatolia in search of the tomb of the Phrygian King Gordius, father (or son) of the fabled King Midas to whom Dionysius was reputed to have given the power to turn anything he touched into gold. A knot devised by Gordius so intricate that no one could untie it was cut by Alexander the Great with his sword when the Greek heard an oracle promise that whoever could untie it would be next ruler of Asia.

While on a trip to Vermont from his retirement home in Cornwall, Rainey paused to write: "Young dug at Gordion, capital of the ancient Phrygian empire, for about twenty-five years. I spent alot of time there and urged him to dig the largest of the burial mounds at the site. At the time, Kenneth Roberts got the Maine dowser, Henry Gross to try to find water for us at Tikal,

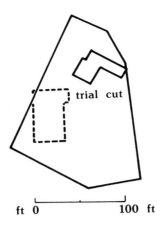

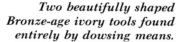

Map of Swinbrook property. Adapted from Dowsing: One Man's Way by J. Scott Elliot.

trial cut

ft 0   100 ft

(Courtesy of Major-General J. Scott Elliot.)

Two beautifully shaped Bronze-age ivory tools found entirely by dowsing means.

cm

Guatemala and Henry went there with me. No luck. But at the same time we talked about Gordion and with a large scale map of the site he dowsed over the map and then said Rodney would find the tomb in the *southwest* sector of the great mound.

"Rodney, a classicist, thought nothing of this and so we excavated for two whole seasons and finally struck the tomb in the *southwest* sector. We tunneled about four hundred feet into the tomb and found a great chamber undisturbed, very rich in bronze objects, but no gold. Gordius was in the tomb under forty layers of woolen and linen blankets in a four poster bed.

"Rodney never referred in any publication to Henry Gross and his dowsing."

*In a bucolic German landscape
the tiny figure of a dowser begins
a traverse over veins of metal
revealed in Balthasar
Rössler's* Speculum Metallurgiae
Politissimum *(Dresden, 1700).*

Part Five

CHALLENGES TO SCIENCE

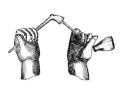

CHAPTER 14

The Sixth Sense of the Anthropomagnetometer

". . . two clay pipes . . ."

Granted by God to Many

In an April 1978 issue of the *Saturday Review,* James Trefil, a physicist at the University of Virginia, provides a kind of "restaurant guide" to ideas considered unorthodox or downright "kooky" by conventional science. To those he feels are "moving into a respectable position on the frontier of science" he awards a scientifically "palatable" four stars, but there is only one in this category: the existence, somewhere out there, of *extraterrestrial intelligences.* Further out on the frontier he situates *extrasensory perception* and *accpuncture* which, because they "still don't have wide acceptance," are awarded a scientifically "tasteless" three stars. Beyond them in a fringe area lie subjects in a scientifically "unappetizing" two-star category that, according to the physicist, "probably never will amount to anything." UFOs and abominable snowmen fall into this bracket. A lowly one star is pasted on scientifically "inedible" topics hovering at the extremity of the fringe, such as the mystery of the Bermuda Triangle, the Loch Ness monster, astrology, remote viewing, and spoon and key bending "a la Uri Geller." With respect to the latter Trefil simply comments: "Forget it."

Nowhere in his article on pseudoscience does Trefil refer to the lengthy Puthoff-Targ experimentation on remote viewing at the Stanford Research Institute or to brilliant research performed by American, French, and British physicists and metallurgists on the ability of gifted young people to bend metal objects at distance.

When it came to dowsing, Trefil at first found himself straddling a fence. "Ordinarily," he wrote, "I'd give this one star, but a student recently showed me not only that he could locate an underground water pipe but that I could too. There's probably a neurological explanation."

If Trefil had sampled his scientific literary menu a little more carefully before cloaking himself in the mantle of the "Duncan Hines" of physics research, he would have found that a scientist and fellow-Virginian had published an article in the *Virginia Journal of Science* eight years before Trefil's *Saturday Review* contribution appeared. Only the first in a long series of subsequent papers, it put forward a convincing explanation for field dowsing.

The saga behind its conclusions could begin on Hallowing

253

Dr. Zaboj V. Harvalik of Lorton, Virginia, 1977, with some of the equipment he designed to test dowsers' sensitivity to an artificial magnetic field. The "black box" on the table is a DC variable power supply that permits variations of current flowing through the ground, thus varying the intensity of the magnetic field to which the dowser is exposed. Next to it is a "randomizer," a device permitting the switching "on" and "off" of the electric current without the dowsers or Harvalik himself knowing it. This randomizer establishes a "double blind" experimental condition.

Point, a spit of land jutting into the two-mile-wide Potomac River opposite a rocky protuberance called Craney Island. One sunny spring afternoon in 1968 anyone passing a modern house of stucco and glass facing the island could not have failed to notice a crowd of people gathered in the front driveway. One after another they were walking with dowsing rods in their hands over an empty stretch of ground, one spot in the middle of which seemed to provoke an action in the rods. Anyone unfamiliar with dowsing might have concluded that the inmates of some madhouse had invented a new game.

What actually was taking place was a scientific experiment devised by Dr. Zaboj V. Harvalik, a professional physicist and scientific advisor to the U.S. Army's Advanced Material Concepts Agency, a 100-man top secret unit, which was assiduously planning America's army for the year 2000.

Harvalik's interest in the dowsing phenomenon began in the early 1930s when, in his native Czechoslovakia, he encountered a peasant walking over his acreage with a forked branch cut from a willow tree. When the peasant explained he was looking for water, Harvalik asked whether anyone could do likewise.

"By no means," the peasant replied gruffly, "this talent is granted by God only to a few."

Harvalik was skeptical. While finishing up his studies for a doctorate in physical chemistry, he had taught himself to manipulate a rod and had poured over existing literature on dowsing—but the more he read, the less sense he could make of its seemingly contradictory conclusions. When he emigrated to the United States, he continued to ponder the scientific aspects of the method while teaching physics at the University of Missouri. In one of his earliest experiments, he noticed that whenever he stepped across an electric wire on the ground with a current running through it, the dowsing rod he was holding would react just as if he, or it, were a compass.

The idea of using an electrically charged wire came from a book, *Physics of the Divining Rod*, published just before the war by two English engineers, J. Cecil Maby and T. Bedford Franklin. Trying to explain the whole process as a simple reaction on the part of dowsers to electromagnetic waves, they attracted the wartime interest of the Ministry of Defence, which was bent on discovering ways to detect targets at a distance until the perfection of radar rendered their methods obsolete. Only much later did Maby realize that the relatively low sensitivity of the instruments he was using was not up to the task he and his colleague had assigned themselves. He abandoned his strictly scientific attitude and, in his *Confessions of a Sensitive*, allowed that to explain dowsing solely on the basis of electronics was like trying to stage *Hamlet* without the Prince of Denmark.

Harvalik's attention was caught by the English researchers' belief that the magnetic component of an electrical current—or the magnetic *vector* as it is known in science—might play a specific role in dowsers' location of subterranean objects in the field. He was also aware that the Director of the Physics Laboratory at the Ecole Normale Superieur in Paris, Yves Rocard, had affirmed in his book, *Le Signal du Sourcier*, that what dowsers were detecting was a *gradient*, or slight change, in the earth's magnetic field aboveground which he believed to be caused by electric currents from water filtering through the earth below.

To test this idea Rocard wrapped a coil of electric wire around a 1 × 2 meter wooden frame to see whether dowsers walking through it could obtain a "signal" when the current ran through the wire. General results indicated a positive answer, but less than 100 percent accuracy suggested either fatigue or boredom in many subjects after a short period of testing or misplaced anticipation as demonstrated by their being more often wrong on positive than on negative calls. Rocard, whose only

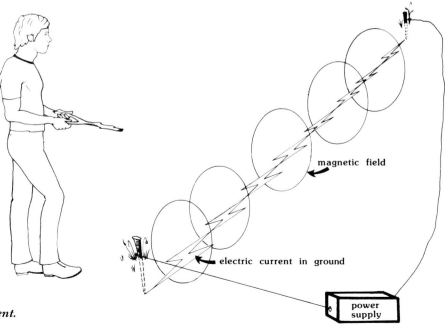

magnetic field

electric current in ground

power supply

Illustration of Harvalik's experiment.

255

reward for his pioneering research was a demotion in the French scientific and educational hierarchies, also swept an electrically activated coil over the bodies of dowsers and was led from their responses to conclude that they might be detecting a magnetic signal somewhere in the region of their elbows.

Considering the research performed up to 1950, Harvalik realized that electrical waves could easily *induce* current in a "loose" wire from a wide variety of sources, even when it was not supplied directly by a generator or a battery. After moving to Virginia to undertake research on explosives with the U.S. Army Corps of Engineers at Fort Belvoir, he decided to eliminate the wire and thus unequivocally prove not only a dowser's sensitivity to a magnetic field but also the degree of sensitivity.

During the weekends which he allotted for his dowsing research he pounded two short pieces of water pipe sixty feet apart into the earth near his driveway and connected their exposed tips with wires to a battery. Membered into the circuit was an instrument which allowed him to vary current intensities from zero all the way up to 150 milliamperes.

When the direct current reached the pipe charged negatively, it then ran through the ground to the one charged positively and back to the battery. The current in the raw earth between the pipes produced a magnetic field above it, its strength varying proportionately with the amount of current flowing in the circuit.

Using himself as his own subject, Harvalik walked along a traverse between the two pipes holding a dowsing device in his hands. When the current was off, the rods remained parallel. When it was on, the device reacted, indicating a response that became strongest when the current flow reached 50 milliamperes.

Over several years, Harvalik tested friends and Fort Belvoir colleagues, many of whom first became aware of their dowsing ability when run through his electromagnetic obstacle course. After hundreds of hours of tests, he was able to determine that 80 percent of his subjects could initially obtain a dowsing signal at a current strength above 20 milliamperes. The rest could continue successfully to record signals down to 2 milliamperes and a select few obtained reactions when only half a milliampere passed thru the ground. Sensitivity to magnetic fields, it appeared, was as variable as hearing or sight.

In late 1968, while Louis Matacia was initiating the Marines into the practical aspects of dowsing, Harvalik formally presented his research in a lecture, curiously entitled "The Anthropomagnetometer," on the scientific how and why of the technique to an audience of scientists from Fort Belvoir's Detection, Intrusion and Sensor Laboratory.

"I would like to describe a potential tunnel detection instrument," he began, "which consists of a mechanical indicator and a highly complex electronic system of networks probably reacting to magnetic anomalies." As his listeners were each imagining their own versions of a space age "black box" filled with electronic hardware, Harvalik went on to explain that the "mechanical indicator" was nothing more than two L-shaped rods and the "highly complex electronic system" was the body of a human being. He then added quietly: "I would venture that by now you recognize that this instrument is a form of divining rod."

What the collective reaction to this statement was on the part of the army specialists, many of whom had never heard of a "divining rod," Harvalik does not know. But he left no doubt in their minds that a human being was a living magnetometer of incredible sensitivity. "If one assumes that man is able to detect magnetic anomalies by utilizing dowsing techniques," he declared, "one is utterly amazed by the sensitivity of the human body to such anomalies. Magnetometric measurements indicate that a dowser reacts to magnetic gradient changes of weak as one millimicrogauss or, expressed another way, 10^{-9}, or 0.00000001, gauss.

Harvalik made clear that magnetic anomalies producing such weak changes in the earth's magnetic field can be found almost everywhere. They can be caused by local variations in magnetic properties of the soil, by discontinuities due to buried boulders, trash, or corpses, by cavities such as culverts or tunnels, by slow-flowing ground water or fast-flowing subterranean water streams, or even by the root systems of trees and shrubs.

Two years later, at his next lecture before the annual meeting of the Virginia Academy of Sciences in Richmond, Harvalik, unwittingly utilizing the Russian adjective of which he knew nothing at the time, characterized dowsers as "biophysical magnetometer-gradiometers" and stated flatly that, far from being "granted by God to a few," the dowsing ability could be inculcated and vastly improved through practice. The majority of beginners, Harvalik found, were able within hours to detect weaker and weaker magnetic fields, especially if they drank a tumbler or two of water before testing. Even apparently hopeless cases, with no initial aptitude, found their sensitivity suddenly awakened after imbibing a relaxing noggin of bourbon. "One might possibly explain the enhancement of a dowser's sensitivities after an intake of water," says Harvalik, "by reference to the water-controlling functions of the kidneys and the magnetic properties of water in a biological environment. It might be conjectured, however vaguely, that the water acts as a dilutent to concentrate the diamagnetic environment of the kidney region and thus behaves as a magnetic field concentrator."

At the end of his lecture, Harvalik was surprised that, of forty scientists in the lecture room, none asked him a question from the floor. His astonishment was only partly dispelled when later, in the men's room, a dozen younger members of the group crowded round him with queries.

"Why on earth didn't you put these questions to me during the official session so they could be included in the proceedings?" he asked, only to receive sheepish replies from his interlocuters that they were afraid overt interest in a subject considered scientifically irrational might jeopardize their careers. One older man, chairman of a well-known university's physics department, admitted to Harvalik that, as a skilled field dowser, he had been privately interested in the subject for thirty years, but had never heard a clear and physically acceptable explanation for it until Harvalik had provided one.

257

With his research safely incorporated in the scientific annals, Harvalik resolved to find out what else dowsers might or might not be capable of confirming. At this point, he was visited by Professor Duane Chadwick of Utah State University's Water Research Laboratory, who was trying to correlate signals obtained by dowsers over a given terrain with those recorded by a cesium magnetometer. His investigation of dowsing, the first and only one partly funded by a government agency, the U.S. Department of the Interior, incorporated observations on twenty-three of Harvalik's experimental subjects, but its less than convincing results led only to the conclusion that the whole issue "warranted further study."

Since it was known from research at MIT's National Magnetic Laboratory that the most sensitive magnetometer yet invented could detect weak magnetic fields issuing from the brain, he erected a wall-like barrier of plywood on his lawn. Standing on one side of the barrier with his dowsing rod at the ready and plugs in his ears to deafen him, he asked subjects to approach it silently on the other side from thirty feet away. Many tests

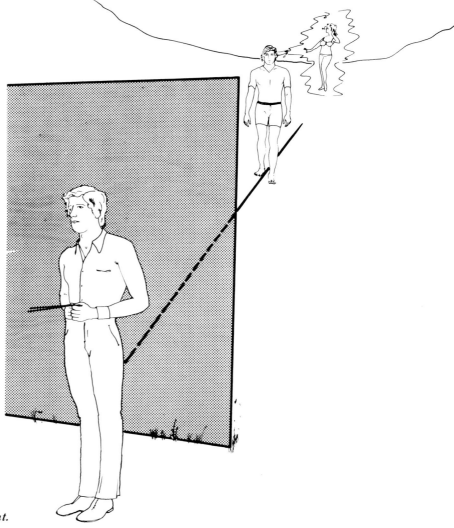

Illustration of Harvalik's experiment.

258

indicated to Harvalik that when he "programmed"—his computer age definition for Christophe's "mental orientation"—for brain waves, his rod would react when the subjects were approximately ten feet from the wall. When he asked the same subjects to repeat their approaches while thinking "exciting thoughts"—sex, fear, annoyance, and pleasant anticipation were examples—the distance nearly doubled.

Harvalik next had subjects conjure up "exciting thoughts" while standing two feet from him and staring at the L-rods in his hands. The rods generally reacted from five to fifty seconds after the subjects had activated their thought trains. This not only suggests that dowsers might serve as crude polygraphs, or lie detectors, but leads to the conjecture, itself an "exciting thought," that mental activity which precedes brain functioning or intent, may be intimately related to a form of magnetism. Harvalik's findings seem to relate that of a French engineer, Voillaume, who many years ago came to discover that with a pendulum he could detect "forces" emanating from the human brain as they radiated into the atmosphere. Voillaume was able to walk around a person thinking concentratedly about an object at some distance and intercept an invisible straight line leading from the thinker to the object itself. "You are thinking about that clock on the mantel piece, Monsieur," Voillaume would say. "Yes, Monsieur, that's it!" the subject would reply.

Search for the Sensors

If minute changes in a magnetic field were responsible for the appearance of the field dowsing signal, then where, Harvalik asked himself, were the "sensors" for such gradients located in the body? One clue came from a Swiss friend who reported that when a dowser had been carried over a water vein on a stretcher in a horizontal position, his rod had reacted only when the dowser's solar plexus, a complex of nerves under the heart, was directly over the vein.

Knowing that the effects of a magnetic field could be blocked by a special alloy called *Mu*-metal, he rolled a sheet of the material into a 10-inch wide cylinder and alternately shielded the head, shoulders, torso, and pelvic areas of the dowsers' bodies. While walking through the magnetic field between the pipes they could easily pick up a signal except when the shield was positioned between the navel and the breast bone. This suggested that the "receiver" of the signal was slightly below the solar plexus, perhaps in the kidney region.

In 1973, Harvalik received a letter from Wilhelm de Boer, a *rutenmeister*—or master dowser—living in Bremen, Germany, who had first been introduced to the art by British officers in a prisoner-of-war camp in Alexandria, Egypt. Having read Harvalik's reports on his work in *The American Dowser,* de Boer asked the researcher whether he would test him during a vacation trip he was planning to the United States.

Harvalik was more than happy that he graciously accepted the Bremener's suggestion because de Boer turned out to be more keenly sensitive to magnetic fields, and accurate in detecting them, than any other dowser he had encountered.

259

During repeated tests de Boer was able unfailingly to sense a magnetic field produced by a current in the ground of only one microampere (1/1000 of 1 milliampere) equivalent to a magnetic field change of 10^{-12} gauss, or far more sensitive than the MIT magnetometer. De Boer's ability seemed roughly comparable to that of cats which can see in the dark or dogs which can hear ultrasonic frequencies inaudible to any human.

Modifying his method for determining the sensitivity of dowsers, Harvalik had de Boer walk between the pipes, now powered by alternating current, which could produce frequency ranges from 1 to 1 million Hertz. When de Boer reacted to all of them, with varying degrees of sensitivity, Harvalik at once realized that dowsers were also potentially sensitive to all kinds of natural or man-made electromagnetic signals, ranging from thunderstorms to radio and television waves, for which they should be able to serve as detectors.

To test this supposition Harvalik took de Boer out into his back lawn next to the river and asked him to program for the 570-kilocycle frequency of WGMS, Washington, D.C.'s "good music" radio station. De Boer rotated in place until, when he was facing an azimuth of about 85 compass degrees, his rod snapped down. To check his finding Harvalik switched on a cheap transistorized radio receiver, turned it to 570 kc, and rotated with it until the sound of the broadcast reached a minimum. At this point the receiver's casing was approximately perpendicular to the azimuth pinpointed by de Boer, thus confirming the accuracy of his dowsing. De Boer proceeded to detect the azimuths for a dozen more radio and TV stations scattered through the Washington, D.C. metropolitan region. Any dowser wishing to check his own ability, says Harvalik, can use this procedure anywhere in the inhabited world.

During several successive annual visits by de Boer to Harvalik's home in Lorton, the innovative scientist and the supersensitive dowser worked together to check whether the magnetic vector actually caused a dowsing response and to seek out exactly where in the body sensors for it might be located. The first problem was solved when Harvalik had de Boer walk in a tight circle in front of electrically activated coils and dipoles while blindfolded, so that he could not know either their location or the axis of their vectorial configuration. Strong dowsing signals

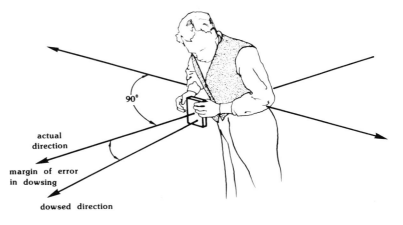

90°

actual
direction

margin of error
in dowsing

dowsed direction

Dowser checking his accuracy with transistor radio.

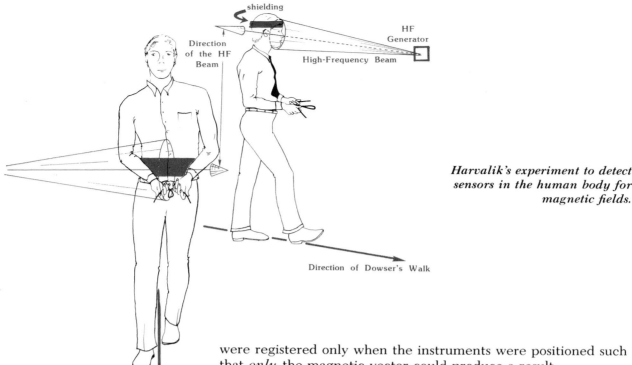

shielding

Direction
of the HF
Beam

HF
Generator

High-Frequency Beam

Harvalik's experiment to detect sensors in the human body for magnetic fields.

Direction of Dowser's Walk

were registered only when the instruments were positioned such that *only* the magnetic vector could produce a result.

Going a step further, Harvalik, who built all his experimental instrumentation in his own cellar-laboratory, created a device that emitted, as from a flashlight, an invisible high-frequency beam in the 5 to 7 meter and 5 centimeter wave bands of the EM spectrum (the wavelengths selected to keep the cost of the device low and its construction simple). He reasoned that if the beam were cut off by a copper screen, which could block it as effectively as a piece of cardboard would block a light beam, any magnetically sensitive bodily sensors should fail to react.

When he proved this assumption, he then circled de Boer's body with a three-inch-wide belt of aluminum sheeting, just as effective a shield as the screen, to confirm not only that the kidney area seemed to contain the sensors he sought but an area in the head as well. This conclusion satisfied the idea that at least two sensors were necessary to pick up "gradiometric configurations." Harvalik knew that the discriminating of dowsing signals from various underground targets would be enhanced if bodily sensors covered both horizontal and vertical fields, the horizontal sensors being located in the torso, the vertical in the head. By "programming," to some extent the dowser would then function like a magnetometer which is able, in geophysical prospecting, to discriminate a different magnetic field signature for objects as different as electric cables, pipes, dry underground cavities, water courses, faults, and other geological anomalies.

To come even closer to the exact location of the sensors he was seeking, Harvalik cut playing card-sized rectangles of aluminum and hung them from de Boer's shoulders down his back and sides to cover from various angles parts of his kidneys. When they screened the adrenal glands at the top of the kidneys, and all dowsing signals ceased, Harvalik seemed to have found

261

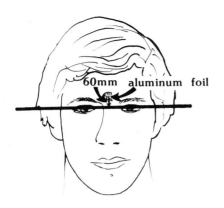

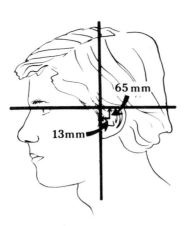

(ABOVE) Pinpointing the sensors in the head.

(RIGHT) Wilhelm de Boer, at Lorton, Virginia, 1977, master dowser from Bremen, West Germany, wearing shields used in experiments by Dr. Zaboj Harvalik.

what he was looking for. This possibility was further strengthened by the medical histories of two experienced dowsers, one, an Australian from Sydney, who had his kidney but not the associated adrenal gland removed by surgery, the other, a Swiss from the Canton of Wallis, who had both organs ablated. Only the Swiss had lost his field dowsing ability.

To exactly pinpoint the sensor in the head, Harvalik experimented with a strip of aluminum wire only an ⅛ of an inch in diameter. When placed like a crown horizontally around the head, 65 mm above the ear orifice, or vertically, like a mast, 13 mm in front of it, all dowsing signals were extinguished. A 2 by 1 inch patch of aluminum foil pasted on the forehead on a line slightly higher than, and midway between, the eyes, also blocked any dowsing signal when the dowser was frontally exposed to the high frequency beam. These measurements indicated to Harvalik that a dowsing sensor might be located in the vicinity of either the pituitary or the pineal gland.

If further research by a team of biomedical experts and physicists can improve and confirm his results, Harvalik may be credited with having discovered that, in addition to sight, hearing, smell, taste, and touch, there is a sixth bodily sense in humans for detecting changes in the geoterrestrial field and that dowsers may be the world's potentially most sensitive magnetometers.

Electromagnetism . . . and Beyond

Harvalik's discovery is of singular importance if only because it lends weight to Malcolm Rae's assertion that physics is approaching the limits of observation achievable with *nonliving* instruments. This is not to imply that hardware far more sensitive than presently available will not one day be invented. In fact, Harvalik's sleuthing in Germany led him to a self-taught genius,

262

Hermann Heidenwolf, who designed a magnetometer that sufficiently impressed Harvalik to spur him to have it patented and assigned to the United States of America through the U.S. Army (see U.S. Patent 3,727,127 dated April 10, 1973). Though, like de Boer, it can pick up magnetic field gradient changes of an order of 10^{-13} gauss and perhaps lower, its drawback lies in its very sensitivity. Unable to "program" like a dowser for a specific target and therefore ignore spurious signals in a virtual cacophony of "magnetic noise," this mindless instrument can easily be "distracted" by random magnetic effects in its environment, even by the thought processes of its user.

It is to Harvalik's credit as a physical scientist that he has not been loath to admit the dowser's "programming ability" into his theoretical conclusions even if he cannot physiologically or physically explain it. In opting for this admission, he has moved further and further along a research track leading away from instrumentally objectifiable phenomena to an acceptance of the act of dowsing itself as an important tool in scientific investigation. Recently he has begun a series of experiments pointing toward a conclusion that dowsers skilled in "programming" may be more sensitive to weak amounts of radioactivity than physical instruments. The equivalent of human Geiger counters, such individuals, he suggests, might well dowse for natural mineral resources especially if radioactive elements in rocky environments are associated with them.

During the ongoing process of his research, Harvalik himself has become so expert in remote, map, and information dowsing, the physics of which he cannot yet begin to explain, that he was able while in Australia to perplex and amaze a Sydney Water Board engineer who, skeptical of dowsing, put him to test. Giving Harvalik the name of one of Sydney's many reservoirs, the engineer asked him in which direction it might lie from where both men were standing and how far away. After dowsing for both answers Harvalik drew an azimuth on a piece of paper fixed to a table and called the distance at 12.6 miles. When the engineer checked his answers on a map, both were correct.

"Can you tell me how deep it is?" he asked.

When Harvalik answered sixty-eight feet, the engineer pulled a booklet from his pocket, flipped a few pages, checked a figure, and said: "Well, you're a little off, but not much. The actual depth is seventy-five feet." The following day, on their way back from a sightseeing tour of the Great Divide, the engineer made a slight detour to show Harvalik the reservoir he had dowsed the day before. When they arrived at its edge he noticed somewhat to his astonishment that the water had dropped from its normal level. Turning to a water board employee he asked: "What's the level of the water today?" "Sixty-eight feet," came the reply.

The persisting question of whether dowsing is a physical or psychic act continues to trouble Harvalik. Particularly puzzling to his physicist's mind are a series of "radionics instruments," black boxes equipped with specially designed electronic circuits and capacitors, resistors, or inductors that can, with the aid of calibrated dials, be set like rheostats to alter values of energy, held to be nonelectromagnetic, coursing through them. The boxes

263

Radionics box designed by the late George De La Warr of Oxford, England. (Photograph by Dr. Harrison E. Lang.)

are tantamount to dowsing devices in that it is asserted they *combine with* their operators to form a *biophysical unit* to search for and identify radiations emanating from both animate and inanimate objects. Facts about human beings, usually relevant to their health, are determined from a sample of blood or hair or even a photograph incorporated into the circuitry.

Harvalik brought one such box back from New Zealand where it was alleged to produce fantastic results. When he opened it to examine the circuitry underneath the dials on the face plate, the box was empty except for a small handwritten note reading: "Ha, ha, there's nothing in this box!" If the dialing mechanism worked at all, it obviously operated only as a function of its operator's belief.

In the eyes of a conventional scientist or engineer, says Harvalik, even the boxes equipped with electronic components are wired nonsensically or in such a manner that no reception of any physically identified radiation is possible. He has therefore come to the conclusion, irritating to some radionics operators, that the devices are merely a form of training aid helping operators to program their minds to react to and recognize stimuli of a given and distinct pattern.

In addition to checking the dial settings with a pendulum, radionics operators also use a rubbing plate attached to their boxes. If, during the rubbing, their fingers move back and forth freely on the plate, the answer to a programmed question is no, if they stick to the plate, yes.

That the rubbing plate, and the box as well, might be completely dispensable came to Harvalik when he met Frances Farrelly, a dowser who, as a trained laboratory technician, had made a prolonged study of radionics devices during the 1950s for Arthur Young's Foundation for the Study of Consciousness in Philadelphia. After mastering the rubbing technique and dial manipulation she was one day introduced by Young to a book, *Witchcraft, Oracles and Magic Among the Azande* by the celebrated English anthropologist Edward Evans-Pritchard. Relating how a Zande witch doctor made a little round disk with a tail attached to it and another disk with a handle, Evans-Pritchard described how the African native sat down and put his foot on the tail of the first disk to steady it, then rubbed the other disk over it while asking, for example, if his neighbor's pig had cholera. If the disk stuck in mid-rubbing, the pig had the disease. If it slid smoothly, the pig was well.

If the act of rubbing alone could provide an answer, concluded Farrelly, perhaps it would work for her. After she tried it, it worked so successfully she has never used a dowsing method other than rubbing the top of a table or a desk to obtain answers.

At the First International Meeting on Psychotronic Research held in Prague, Czechoslovakia, in 1973, Czech scientists who had heard Farrelly lecture asked her on the spot to tell them the age and origin of a small mineral sample that one of them took from his pocket. After sitting at a table and rubbing out answers to a long series of questions, she told the group that the sample was 3,200,000 years old and came from a meteorite. The scientists

(ABOVE, LEFT AND RIGHT) Zande diviner using an iwa, or rubbing board which may be one of the world's earliest "radionics boxes." (From Witchcraft, Oracles and Magic Among the Azande by Edward Evans-Pritchard.)

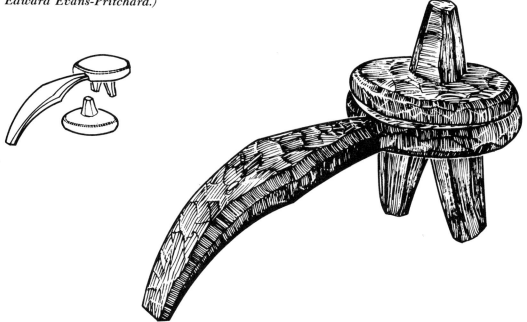

confirmed that, according to the best judgment of their experts, both answers were correct.

When he was introduced to Farrelly at his home in Lorton, Harvalik spent several hours asking her questions of a scientific nature, some of the answers to which were completely unknown to him. As he subsequently wrote in an affidavit:

"From the large number of topics treated during the sessions, I would like to select a few as typical examples.

"Question: 'What is the optimum voltage gradient per meter for beneficial negative ion production?' *Answer:* '2,500 volts DC per meter.'

"At the time this question was asked I did *not* know the answer. However, in subsequent experiments with a variable DC high-voltage power source I measured an optimum value of 1,400 volts per meter when no person is disturbing the electrostatic field. When a person is present in this field the value is 2,500 volts per meter.

"Question: 'Where are the sensors located that trigger the signal in field dowsing?' Her answer, after going over all parts and organs of the human body, was 'yes' when the adrenal glands and the post-pituitary were mentioned. Her answers were correct."

In his affidavit, Harvalik noted that "even now many people, including scientists, believe that field dowsing is grounded on superstition and has no scientific basis. My research establishes a mechanism for it as follows: Small magnetic field gradient changes or electromagnetic radiations stimulate the sensors in the adrenal glands and in the pituitary which form a three-dimensional perception system permitting even pattern recognition. The stimulus is transmitted to the brain which contains a signal processor. The brain gives the arms the command to twist which is accompanied by increased blood flow through the finger capillaries. The twist is very minute but can be made visible with the dowsing rod which is nothing but a mechanical parametric amplifier and can be made of any material. Since the magnetic and electromagnetic field patterns are contingent to their generator-sources, dowsers can program themselves by asking the brain to command the arms to twist *only* if a certain pattern is present in the stimulus reaching the sensors, *i.e.,* attributable to underground water, oil, pipes, etc. The foregoing shows that field dowsing can be explained scientifically and in an understandable manner."

Although he has no such explanation for remote, map, or information dowsing, Harvalik in an essay, "Radionics and Programming," does not close his mind to the idea that they may one day be explained. Since, as he holds, "programming" is a mental act that influences the appearance of a dowsing signal, he concludes that, after mastering the programming method, "one could attempt to program oneself for *energy forms of magnetic and electromagnetic nature and discover structures that would lead to the detection of such esoteric energy forms as postulated by certain radionics practitioners."*

CHAPTER 15

An Electronic Dowser

". . . a book which pulls forward in the hands so strongly it can no longer be held . . ."

Noxious Rays from Underground

In 1975, Herbert Douglas, a businessman living in Shaftsbury, Vermont, drove to a neighboring town on a mission of mercy. Arriving at his destination, he took out a plastic dowsing rod and went over every room in a two-story house, being particularly careful to check the area around and under the bed where a twelve-year old girl with a double curvature of the spine had been sleeping since early childhood.

Douglas found that the house itself had an unusually high number of water veins flowing beneath it and that there were no less than thirty-five intersections of veins under the afflicted child's bed. He immediately suggested to the distraught parents that the bed be moved to a part of the house where no veins would run under it. For the next ten days the child told her parents that the chronic pain in her spine was increasing. Then the pain suddenly began to diminish to the befuddlement of the girl's doctor who noticed, during a visit to fit her for a full body brace, that the curvature had noticeably decreased.

Several months later Douglas received a letter from the child's mother stating that her daughter no longer was suffering any pain at all and that the curvature had diminished sufficiently to obviate any necessity for the brace.

The notion that the onset of disease might be linked to telluric emanations came to Douglas as a persistent theme in observations by English authors. Before World War II, in his book, *Dowsing,* W. M. Trinder had written: "There seems to be very little doubt that rays given off by subterranean water are, if continuous contact is maintained with them, definitely harmful to both human beings and plants. I have known instances of people suffering from nerves and also cases of rheumatism. In all these cases the sufferers were spending a large part of every twenty-four hours right over a subterranean stream and this was slowly having the most deleterious effect on their health."

Echoing Trinder, Marguerite Maury in her own book, *How to Dowse,* stated: "Whatever may be the cause of telluric emissions —sheets of water, subterranean streams or dry faults—the effects produced on the health of animals and human beings is nearly always harmful. If there are several streams superimposed, the emission at the surface will be particularly bad."

267

Herbert Douglas of Shaftsbury, Vermont, dowsing for water veins beneath a bed. (Photograph by David Scribner.)

The French dowsing expert, Abbé Mermet, Douglas found, also insisted that water veins could produce ill effects on human health. He wrote that radiations associated with them were "transmitted from floor to floor in any house situated above them. One may be exposed to them in a workshop, a factory, an office as well as in the flat on the tenth floor of a building. It is in a bedroom that their presence is the most harmful for, in such a case, the affected individual is not only subjected to the bad effects of such radiations but is also deprived of sound and regenerating sleep. Impaired health results in consequence, and the affected person suffers from various ailments which neither he nor the doctor can account for."

Wondering whether there was any substance to the idea, Douglas began checking the beds of people who complained of arthritis to find that his rod *always* detected veins of water beneath them and, more significantly, that two or more veins crossed directly under the part of the body that hurt.

In a two-part article in the Bennington (Vermont) *Banner,* Douglas reported that every one of the patients who had begun sleeping in a new location experienced a substantial reduction or complete disappearance of arthritic pain within periods of time ranging from five days to three months. Forwarding these findings to U.S. health authorities in Washington, D.C., he elicited a reply characterizing his results as "intriguing and seeming to call for additional investigation."

In his newspaper account Douglas concluded that there was no scientifically established relationship between arthritis and underground influences and no logical explanation of why arthritic patients should improve when their beds were moved. However, he added, "it would appear that the research of medical men overseas, coupled with my own experience and that of other dowsers on the matter of underground irritation, is persuasive evidence that some diseases may be related to these underground forces."

By the end of 1976, in an area less than fifty miles from his home, Douglas had found underground veins of water intersecting under the sleeping places of fifty-five patients being treated for arthritis, twenty-five of whom had their beds moved, at Douglas's direction, to areas free from flowing water veins.

The literature he had perused also hinted that sleeping over water veins could cause cancer. When one of his friends, a woman in her thirties, fell ill with breast cancer, Douglas dowsed around her bed to find that his rod produced so many reactions he could not count the veins.

In 1978 Douglas reported: "I have now checked twenty cancer cases of different kinds and in nearly all of them got an almost uncountable number of dowsing signals coming from water veins or, less frequently, clefts or breaks in rocky ledge underground. I thought that the underground veins could be best illustrated if I laid out a series of wooden laths on the bed to show the direction of their flow. When I did this, I asked the person who slept in the bed to lie down in the position they normally assume when falling asleep. Repeatedly, the crossing of the laths indicates precisely where the person is afflicted."

268

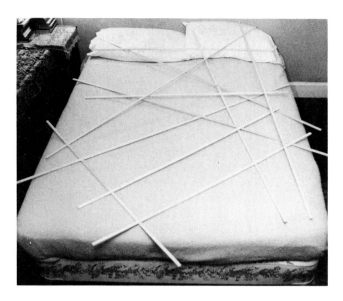

"Over a period of ten years, I've checked sixty cases of arthritis, twenty cases of cancer, and nine cases of cataracts. In every single one of them, I found dowsing reaction lines intersecting under the affected part of the body. In every cancer case but one I found a network of water veins creating anywhere from thirty to fifty crossings."

In 1978, Douglas had a German article translated into English and discovered that his own findings had been paralleled by those of Dr. Joseph Kopp of Ebikon, Switzerland, a consulting geologist who for years had dowsed successfully for water in his country including commercially valuable hot mineral springs for the communities of Zurzach and Eglisau on the shores of Lake Constance.

That radiation from subterranean water veins might be linked to disease came to Kopp's attention in the Swiss Rhine Valley community of Grabs, in Sankt Gallen Canton, where he detected a water vein flowing directly under a new barn. Asked whether there had been cases of animal disease in the barn, a Grabs village official simply swung its door back to reveal it empty. So many animals had become ill when housed in it, he said, that it had been abandoned.

Kopp went on to conduct a personal dowsing survey of 130 barns in which cows confined for considerable periods of time had a high incidence of maladies ranging from severe rheumatism in the joints and uterine deterioration to marked weight loss and repeated miscarriages. Their calves either developed very poorly or died before maturity. He found that one or more strongly flowing veins of water ran under every one of the buildings he surveyed and that, in many cases, the cattle afflicted with disease were tethered at spots directly above them. Learning of his work, one hog farmer assured him that sows confined in particular pens would repeatedly eat their litters, and that all the swine in a pen located directly over a water current suffered from bloody flux while animals in adjacent pens free of such an underground influence were healthy.

269

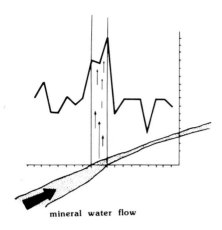

mineral water flow

Graph of ultra high frequency (UHF) waves metered over a vein of mineral water at Eglisau by Dr. Joseph Wüst. Discovered by Joseph Kopp's dowsing, the two meter-wide vein produced water at a rate of over twenty gallons per minute.

In several decades of research Kopp came across hundreds of references on earthly influences and their effects on living organisms. The effect of terrestrial radiation on microorganisms came to light when, in 1897, an Italian dowser in Piacenza traced a current of water under a dairy producing a large quantity of defective cheese. After several days of experimenting he observed that cultures of bacteria necessary to cheesemaking would grow normally or abnormally depending on whether they were located over the current or not. Acting on the clue, Kopp went on to discover that what in German are called "earth rays" could cause potatoes to rot faster, wine or cider to sour, and jams to become mouldy, all of which indicated enhanced activity of microbes.

In 1932, even solider evidence that bacterial growth responded to radiation from veins was put forward by two researchers at the Institute of Biology and Anatomy of the *Technische Hoschschule* in Munich. Mice, inoculated with certain disease-producing bacteria, fell ill more rapidly when the cages in which they were restricted were set over a vein of water, and more slowly when the same cages were installed over an area outside the vein's influence, or vice versa, depending on the type of pathogen used. Similar experiments in the Swiss Canton of Aarau showed that the mice located over perturbed zones were in a constant state of agitation, gnawed at their cages, ate their tails and, though cannibalism is rare among mice, often devoured their offspring.

Strangely, the radiation from the subterranean veins was not harmful to every living thing. Beehives placed over them were attested to produce as much as three times the average amount of honey.

Evelyn Penrose, a British dowser whose prowess won her employment by the government of the Canadian province of British Columbia to locate water for farmers and ranchers during a severe drought, set up a number of hives on the tiny island of Herm in the British Channel. In *Adventure Unlimited*, an account of her life as a dowser, she reported: "After a short time I noticed that some of my hives housed much stronger colonies than others, and I soon discovered that those which did so well were always over a stream of underground water. I then made a minute divining survey of the apiary and put as many hives as possible over the underground streams. The results were invariably good."

Ants appeared to benefit from their effects, since many dowsers discovered that large hills of the insects had been built over water courses. Certain varieties of trees including oaks, elms, ashes, and willows seemed to thrive when rooted over water veins while beeches and various conifers became diseased. One study of 11,000 orchard trees disclosed that, of those planted directly over irritation zones, apples developed cancerous growths on their trunks and cherries an abnormally increased flow of sap. Plums and pears rotted or withered to death.

A crucial finding linked with water vein-associated radiation was first put forward in the 1920s when two German researchers, Winzer and Melzer, divided the city of Stuttgart into districts of

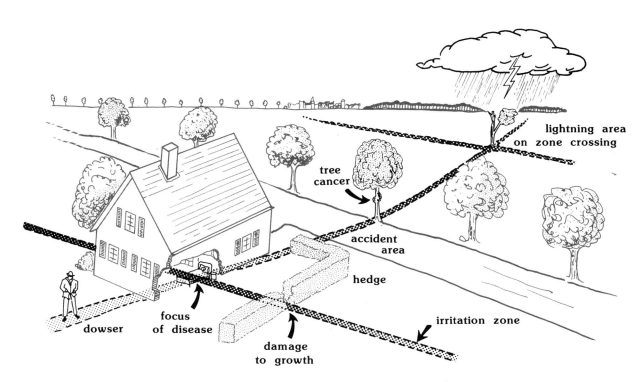

lightning area
on zone crossing

tree
cancer

accident
area

hedge

irritation zone

dowser

focus
of disease

damage
to growth

Various effects of underground water veins as illustrated by Dr. Joseph Kopp. In addition to disease in humans, animals, and plants, it has been observed that auto accidents repeatedly occur at points where veins run under roads and highways. As far back as the turn of the century, the German dowser, Cai von Bülow-Bothkamp discovered that, far from "never striking twice in the same place," as the old folk adage has it, lightning is prone to be attracted to trees growing over an intersection of two water veins. "I would not dare to make such a statement," wrote Bülow-Bothkamp, "had I not been able to confirm it in all cases, of which I have had more than a thousand." (Redrawn from Effects of Harmful Radiations and Noxious Rays, *American Society of Dowsers, Danville, Vermont, 1974.)*

varying cancer incidence only to find that they could in no way be correlated with the overall stratigraphy, or underground rock formations, as they had hoped. When dowsers told them to check the five major geological faults that all of them agreed ran under the city, the researchers were astonished to see that the faults traversed those districts with the highest rates of cancer mortality. They promulgated the theory that some kind of radiation emanating from the faults might be an important cause of cancer that had been completely overlooked.

The Winzer-Melzer survey stimulated the German aristocrat Gustav Freiherr von Pohl who, in 1929, began the first systematic study of human cancer and its possible link to zones of noxious telluric radiation. Selecting the Bavarian community of Vilsbiburg with 8,300 inhabitants, he dowsed its entire confines under the watchful eyes of the mayor and local gendarmes who signed a protocol describing the survey. On a 1:1,000 map of the town, von Pohl traced those veins of water which he considered important enough to play a role in cancer etiology, after which they were compared to the plottings of cancer deaths in houses by one Bernhuber, Vilsbiburg's medical advisor. Precise examinations were next made of those houses only partially affected by the water veins and the beds of cancer patients were confirmed to have actually stood directly above them.

Cancer specialists openly scoffed at the new report which they considered worthless because, as they claimed, the incidence of cancer was so high and Vilsbiburg so small, that von Pohl's conclusions about radiation-produced cancer meant nothing.

Not at all dismayed, von Pohl asked the Bavarian Office of Statistics for the name of the community with the lowest incidence of cancer in the whole province. This turned out to be

271

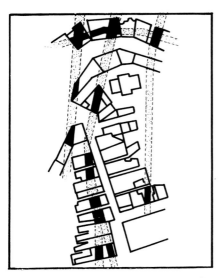

Section of a city map of a German city with indicated irritation zones. In the black-marked dwellings, during a period of twenty years, one to two cancer cases were observed. They are located without exception in irritation zones.

Grafenau, a settlement of 2,000 souls in the Bavarian Forest, where von Pohl made a dowsing survey on May 4 and 5, 1930, to find that each of the persons who had died of cancer during the previous seventeen years had been sleeping over the noxious zones that he had delineated. One and one half years later, a second check determined that ten more cancer victims had succumbed in the interim.

It was the work of French dowsing researchers in the early 1930s that first pointed to a possible physical cause behind harmful radiations. Articles by two authors in the *Cote D'Azur Médicale* detailed how electroscopes, instruments that record the electrical conductivity of the air through the detection of the relative presence of ions (atoms which by gain or loss of an electron acquire an electric charge), revealed a higher degree of conductivity over underground veins than over the area adjacent to them.

The tie between ionizing radiation and the incidence of cancer was made during a seven-year-long study by a French engineer, Pierre Cody, just before the outbreak of World War II. Inspired by dowsers who told him that the inhabitants of many houses in the French port city of Le Havre had died of cancer over several generations, Cody used an Elster and Geitel electrometer to check the concentration of air ions at points in the cellars of houses lying directly under more than 7,000 "cancer

A. A case of morning fatigue and weakness of the eyes of a male; exhaustion; breast cancer modules, operated, recurred after three years. After relocation of the bed a noticeable improvement of state of health. This male writes to the physician, Dr. Blos: "I am glad to be able to tell you that my wife and I feel like newborn after relocation of the beds. Fatigue and extreme tiredness disappeared. Especially striking is the significant reduction of the weakness of my eyes."

B. The woman in the bed, located in the hatched-indicated irritation zone, had attacks of severe neuralgia and gall bladder illness. Six years she was totally bedridden. A gall bladder operation was unsuccessful. Afterward a bed relocation was done. After nine days the woman, who for six years was bed-ridden, was found by her physician doing the laundry. After several months, the pains completely disappeared and the woman was in good health.

C. In this case the physician assumed a terminal sickness. The patient was in a tuberculosis sanatorium and was bedridden because of an ill knee for two months. Six days after bed relocation a noticeable improvement was observed; four days later cough and expectoration disappeared. After two weeks the patient felt better and got up from time to time. After one year he could walk again without aid. (From G. v. Pohl, "Soil Radiations as Causes of Illness," J.E. Huber Publishing House, Hessen, 1932.)

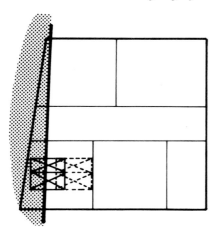

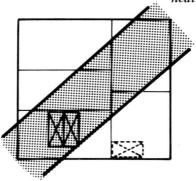

Reproduced from "The Effect of Harmful Radiations and Noxious Rays," pamphlet published by The American Society of Dowsers, Danville, Vermont.

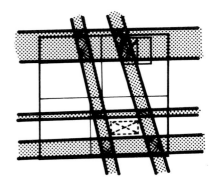

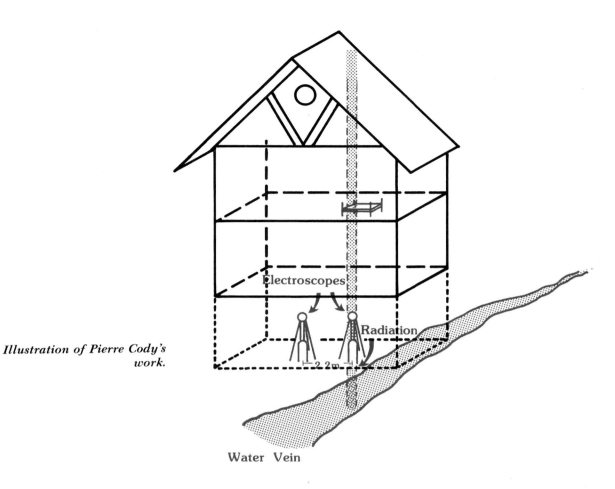

Illustration of Pierre Cody's work.

Water Vein

beds." His procedure in the house of a Monsieur Truffier, whose wife had succumbed to cancer, was typical. He placed an electrometer in its cellar directly below the exact location of her cancerous growth when she was lying in bed and an identical instrument a little more than two meters distant. Ten readings taken during a fourteen-hour period revealed that the first device picked up an ion concentration ten times larger than the second. It was further determined that the band of radiation was no wider than a meter and a half.

The second instrument was then moved to within fifty centimeters of the first. Readings taken over a full year at 8, 10, 12, 14, and 18 hours each day showed exactly the same difference in intensity as when they had been more widely separated, a fact that led to the suspicion that the radiation, whatever it was, rose vertically as it came out of the ground and did not diffuse laterally.

This crucially important conclusion has recently been corroborated by the Swiss nuclear physicist, Angelo Comunetti, of Basel. His experiment, specifically designed to check the claim that the reaction field over water veins or geological discontinuities, or both, is *perpendicular*, was performed with the help of Treadwell and Rupp, the two Hoffman-La Roche executives who so successfully had dowsed water for their

273

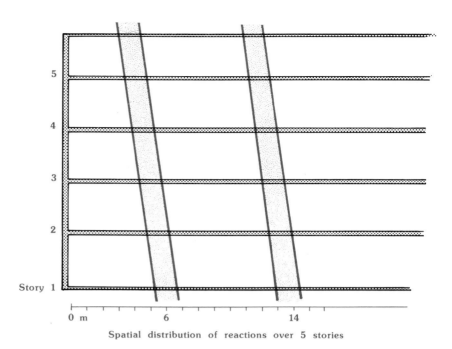

5

4

3

2

Story 1

0 m   6   14

Spatial distribution of reactions over 5 stories

Findings of Dr. Angelo
Comunetti.

company's proposed factory sites. It took place in the corridors of a long multistoried building where a typical dowsing reaction zone had been correlated with a water vein tapped by a successful well that produced large quantities of water.

On five floors about 3½ meters one above the other, two reaction zones each about two meters wide were recorded. In spite of three layers of heavy reinforced concrete that separated the top floor from the bottom, the zones of an unidentified radiation, called the D-agent (D for *dowsing*) by Comunetti, were found to lie on a straight line that, in this case, deviated 15 degrees eastward from the vertical. The rod reaction was equally strong for all five floors indicating no attenuation of the D-agent radiation by the concrete.

His experimentation, said Comunetti, should be repeated in tall buildings and in underground mines as well because it might be of great practical importance for all kinds of geological prospecting.

It occurred to Cody that the telluric emission might be due to radioactivity of some kind. Accordingly, he placed sheets of lead under an electrometer positioned over radiation zones and noted that the time needed for its discharge rose from seven seconds to forty-nine minutes. The normally gray sheets when left in place for more than a month became discolored by peacock-blue or canary-yellow patches, the exact shape and size of the radiation zones presumably causing the discoloration. Both observations indicated the lead was, in fact, blocking a radioactive radiation.

Cody stated in emphatic terms that many cases of physical ailments produced by telluric radiation were ameliorated by moving subjects' beds away from the radiation zone or by screening the zone with lead sheets. In his book, *Experimental Study of Air Ionization by a Certain Radioactivity in the Soil*

274

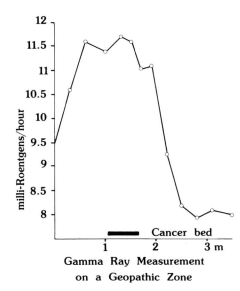

**Pleutersbach
16 September 1955**

milli-Roentgens/hour

Cancer bed

1   2   3 m

**Gamma Ray Measurement
on a Geopathic Zone**

and Its Influence on Human Health, he wrote that in 491 cases of illness, the afflicted persons would experience an increase of pain during the first several weeks following the installation of a lead sheet, after which a marked improvement was to be noticed in their condition. If the lead sheets were *renewed often enough,* a great many cases were healed and, for the rest, progress of the disease was retarded. If the sheet *was not* renewed, after several months maladies took a sudden turn for the worse.

Though Cody's work was supported by the eminent physicist and director of Duke Louis de Broglie's laboratory, Louis le Prince-Ringuet, the engineer's startling conclusions were given no more attention by the medical world than had been paid to the findings of von Pohl and other German researchers more than ten years before.

After World War II dowsing scientists in Germany gathered more evidence that biological effects in humans were being caused by exposure to telluric radiation.

Johann Walther, who later received an honorary medical degree, was the first to coin the term *geopathy* for the study of harmful, or "geopathic" telluric zones. In his booklet *The Mystery of the Divining Rod* Walther urged physicians with patients suffering from degenerative disease to have their homes dowsed. Forcing patients back in bed where they could be exposed to noxious radiation, he said, was like driving horses back into a burning barn.

In 1955, Dr. V. Fritsch, a German geophysicist, underscored the need for combined research by dowsers, medical doctors, geologists, and physicists and stated in his book *The Problem of Geopathic Phenomena from the Viewpoint of Geophysics:* "We must not forget that what has been called the problem of the divining rod is but one of a number of allied problems and that the question of geophysical influences on living beings is one of the greatest importance for biology and, even more significantly, for medicine."

The same year, Dr. Joseph Wüst and others for the first time worked with Geiger counters to prove the emission of gamma radiation, one of the chief results of radioactivity, directly under "cancer beds" in the town of Pleutersbach in September 1955.

From Stängle . . .

As successive studies of this type were taken up, an engineer living near the Würtemberg metropolis of Ulm, Jacob Stängle, was beginning to design a new instrument that, by the early 1970s, seemed not only to settle the gamma ray "connection" once and for all but bid fair to fulfill a long-standing dream of dowsers: the creation of a dowsing machine that could prove beyond the shadow of a doubt their assertions that water flowed in veins.

When gamma rays penetrate a crystalline sensor in Stängle's device, they cause it to scintillate, or throw off extremely weak flashes of light emitted by atoms in the sensor-material as they return to a normal energy state after having been ionized or excited by gamma rays or charged particles passing through the material. These are converted, in turn, to electrical pulses and

275

Photo of Stängle's device.

amplified millions of times by a photomultiplier tube. Since the magnitude of the pulses of light are proportional to the energy lost by particles traversing the scintillator, they can thus provide information about the energy of particles that can be translated and read out on strip chart recorders or electrical meters.

When "soft," or lower frequency, gamma radiation from great depth becomes attenuated by the strata through which it passes, the scintillation counter relies on "hard," or higher frequency, gamma radiation with more penetrating power and especially on neutrons, atomic particles of neutral charge that move at such high speeds they must be slowed down by a special crystal filter before being detected by the phosphor-sensor in which they produce flashes through nuclear collision.

Over any spot on earth there is a weak normal "background" of gamma radiation that is constantly emitted from underground strata. When first switched on, Stängle's machine picks up this background and, as it is wheeled along, registers any variation in the quantity of radiation.

After fifteen years of tinkering with his invention, Stängle, who had no support from private industry or government, was able to report in 1973 that it characteristically revealed a sharp increase in radiation over underground water veins such that reliable conclusions could be made about the depth and even the flow-intensity of any given vein. "Its trustworthiness," wrote the engineer, "has been confirmed by drilling hundreds of wells with such accuracy that one can predict the future possibility of detecting underground water veins precisely."

When medical researchers learned of his new "dowser on wheels," Stängle was asked to check the old von Pohl findings at Vilsbiburg. Provided with some of von Pohl's originally traced results by Dr. Werner Kaufman of Giessen, he trundled his new scintillation counter over three zones in the northern part of the town to find that the pen on his strip chart traced out a sharp increase of radiation similar to that produced by water veins.

Von Pohl's forty-year-old conclusions appeared justified and, as Stängle triumphantly stated: "The principal objection against the existence of pathogenic stimulation zones, namely the inability to objectify them, is no longer valid."

Stängle was invited to France to the town of Moulins near where a physician, Dr. J. Picard, had made his own nine-year study of the incidence of cancer and recorded the dwelling places for 282 cancer victims. Each house in which a cancer death had occurred was located over a water vein or a geological fracture of some kind. In one house a twelve-year old boy sleeping in the same bed night after night had succumbed to a sarcoma in the right side of his body. The nine-year old son in another family, which moved into the dwelling a short time later, also developed a sarcoma in his right side, which proved fatal. He was sleeping in the same bed as the first victim.

Carefully checking his scintillometer readings, Stängle found water courses intersecting below the house in question and many others that had been associated with Moulins cancer deaths but

Measurement of Earth Rays with a Scintillation Counter

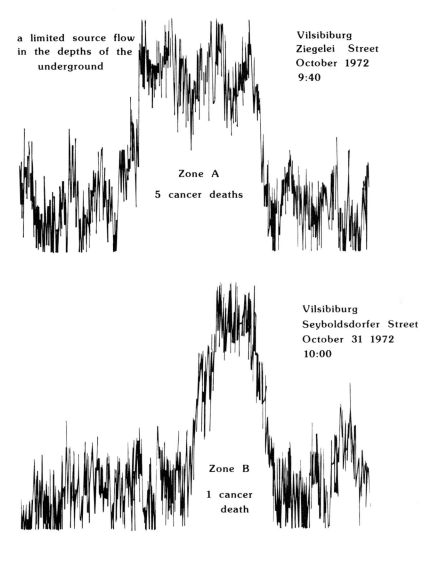

a limited source flow in the depths of the underground

Vilsibiburg
Ziegelei Street
October 1972
9:40

Zone A

5 cancer deaths

Vilsibiburg
Seyboldsdorfer Street
October 31 1972
10:00

Zone B

1 cancer death

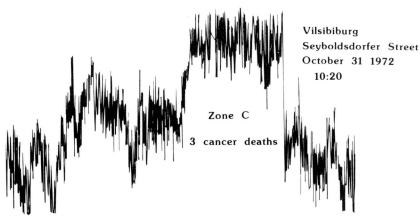

Vilsibiburg
Seyboldsdorfer Street
October 31 1972
10:20

Zone C

3 cancer deaths

Three strip-chart records made by Joseph Stängle with a scintillation counter of his own design in the Ziegeleistrasse and the Seyboldsdorferstrasse, Vilsbiburg, Bavaria, on October 31, 1972. Stängle concluded that the first record indicated a water vein at 80–90 meters depth flowing at a rate of 30–60 gpm, the second at 35–45 meters with 15–30 gpm, and the third at 80–95 meters with 60–80 gpm. By Jakob Stängle.

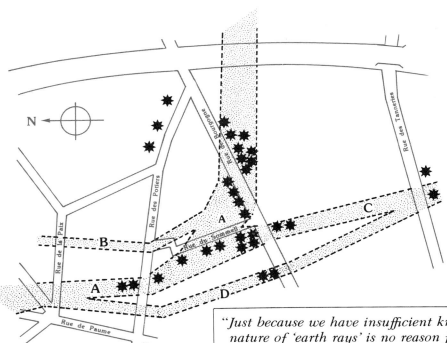

Noxious radiation over veins as correlated with cancer deaths. By Dr. J. Picard, Moulins, France.

"Just because we have insufficient knowledge of the physical nature of 'earth rays' is no reason for us to ignore a phenomenon that is at least a century old for, after all, most therapeutic methods in medicine were developed empirically through practical experience and only theoretically explained in the laboratory much later on."

Dr. Wilhelm Von Gonzenbach
Professor of Hygiene and
Physician-in-Chief for the
City of Zürich, Switzerland

"In the not-too-distant future, it should be possible to draw up regulations making mandatory the examination of existing and future building sites to discover whether they are affected by pathogenic telluric influences. No hospital or school should ever be constructed without checking for subsurface water currents below its prospective foundation. An effort must be made to introduce the concept of geohygienic planning to the world. If this can be accomplished, I believe we shall witness a marked decline in degenerative disease."

Dr. Joseph Kopp
Consulting Geologist
Ebikon, Switzerland, 1975

"If we consider the alarming reports about pathological long-range effects of certain narrowly confined areas such as described by a diviner with a rod, we can but thank the small coterie of hardy researchers who, in spite of attacks from outside, devote themselves to that problem with serious and well-meant intention. More than that, we've reached a point where science has to take on just this kind of problem in order not one day to be exposed to the reproach that it neglected available evidence to the detriment of humanity."

Dr. Herbert Konig
Author of *Unsichtbare Umwelt*
(The Invisible Environment)
Munich, 1975

Picard, fearful of reprisals against his own practice by official medicine unwilling to admit the connection between cancer and noxious radiations, did not publish his data.

Impressed with Stängle's corroboration of von Pohl's and Picard's work, Dr. Dieter Aschoff in the late fall of 1973 published a booklet about it, *Can Official Science Still Deny the Theory that Cancer Can Be Produced by Stimulation Zones?* In it he revealed that as far back as 1960, he had been systematically warning his patients to have dowsers check for noxious radiation under areas where they spent extended periods of time.

... to Bickel   Unknown to Stängle, Dr. Armin Bickel, a German-born research engineer and scientist, who began his career at the German development center in Peenemunde where he worked on the V-2 rocket, and ended it at the NASA's Western Missile Test Range in Lompoc, California, was challenged after his retirement to develop instruments that could be of benefit to geological

"No serious-minded criticism, be it ever so prejudiced, can afford to ignore proofs of the existence of pathogenic telluric influences. Hundreds of cancer institutes all over the world have spent billions without having found any convincing proof of cancer's cause. Why has it not been possible to spend a few million of that huge sum for a thorough investigation of telluric radiation as a prime cause of cancer in human beings. Why has this newly discovered continent of knowledge not been applied to cancer prevention?"

Dr. Paul G. Seeger
Former Chief of Cancer Research
Charité Hospital
Berlin, Germany, 1975

"It is tragic that fruitful new ideas are rejected out of hand or ridiculed, as the history of medicine has clearly shown. Now, in our own time, medical authorities continue intolerantly to oppose the idea that geopathic zones can cause cancer. Is it not weird that while researchers will accept over 300 theories for the etiology of cancer as a basis for research, at the same time they ignore, reject, or snidely attack this finding? Whoever has had direct experience with this problem cannot and must not remain silent even if his credibility as a physician may suffer as a consequence.

"I am prepared to point out cancer-producing geopathic zones to the most confirmed skeptic and let him juggle generations of tragic statistics. I will further introduce patients who have shed ailments and diseases after they were removed from the influence of telluric zones. The health and well-being of human beings is intimately tied to the earth on which they live and to its radiation. Once this is clearly understood, a door will be opened to a healthier, happier existence for everyone and diseases which threaten them like nightmares will disappear."

Ernst Hartmann, M.D.
Founder and Editor, *Wetter, Boden, Mensch*
(Weather, Soil, Man).

Face of Dr. Armin Bickel's instrument. (Photograph courtesy of Dr. Armin Bickel.)

Dr. Armin Bickel and his instrument, Lompoc, California, 1977.

prospecting in the detection of water, oil, and minerals underground.

After two years of experimentation in his laboratory and tests in the field, Bickel came up with a black box, weighing no more than ten pounds, that compares to Stängle's instrument as the latest model Rolls Royce compares to a Model-T Ford. A supersensitive scintillation counter incorporating a built-in computer with more than 1,800 transistors designed by expert William Cunningham, it is assertedly able to pinpoint with uncanny accuracy the length, width, and dip of mineral deposits as well as their approximate quantity at depths as great as 1,000 feet and to detect oil-bearing strata down to 10,000 feet.

280

Two shots of large lemon grown by Dr. Armin Bickel compared with normal lemons. Bickel achieves this growth by treating the lemon tree's roots with a specific frequency of ultrasound. The tree then produces three to four lemon blossoms where only one would normally bloom. When all but one of the group of flowers are plucked, the remaining flower then produces an outsized lemon, the stalk of which is also apparently strengthened such that the lemon will not fall from the tree. Bickel has also produced sunflowers up to eighteen inches in diameter. A palmetto palm he treated ultra-sonically has grown more than twice the height of similar trees planted at the same time.

Hydrogen atom and isotopes.

Normal <u>Hydrogen</u> atom composed of one negatively charged electron and one positively charged proton

Hydrogen stable isotope, <u>Deuterium</u> with chargeless neutron

Hydrogen unstable isotope, <u>Tritium</u>, with additional neutron.

Equipped with a photomultiplier tube with a quantum efficiency of 35 percent, it can register information from an ore sample twenty-five feet distant which ordinary commercial scintillators of 5–10 percent efficiency can pick up only one foot away.

Bickel, who has also been able to perform such miracles as growing six-pound lemons by stimulating the roots of lemon trees with specific ultrasonic frequencies, says that his "Algor Super Scintillation Counter" depends on the fact that constant changes due to crystallization in geological formations that have been going on for half a billion years can, through the proper use of isotope detection, provide clues about what lies below ground.

Before 1913 it was believed that each and every atom of any element was identical in mass. Then it was discovered that an atom could, under certain natural conditions, lose or gain a particle, thereby altering its mass and energy state. These altered atoms, which were later produced artificially in atom-smashers, needed a new name. Called *isotopes,* their nuclei had the same number of protons but different numbers of neutrons.

By 1921 Francis William Aston in England had detected 202 isotopes in seventy-one elements. Today the number has risen to more than 1,500 with an average of four to each element. Only 10 percent of all known isotopes are found in nature where they can be produced by the interaction of radiations from radioactive substances in the interior of the earth or cosmic rays from outer space. The rest are engendered by artificial excitation. Thus, a normal gold atom represented as $_{79}Au^{197}$ (meaning that Au, short for the Latin word *Aurum*—gold—has 197 heavier particles in its nucleus of which 79 are charged protons and 118 uncharged neutrons), can be artificially altered to produce different isotopes from $_{79}Au^{185}$ to $_{79}Au^{203}$, only one of which, $_{79}Au^{196}$ is abundantly found in nature. It is the energy from this single natural isotope which is detectable by the Bickel invention.

In May 1974, Bickel was invited to explore the area around the Paul Isnard gold mine 150 kilometers from Saint Laurent du Maroni in French Guiana. Operating from an airplane, his machine recorded only average to below average readings for gold above the mine site. Above average readings indicated "hot spots" for gold in many places five to twenty kilometers from the mine in two directions. Copper mineralization was also located, says Bickel, near the town of Santonia.

Given the near impossibility of surveying densely wooded terrain normally found in places like French Guiana, Bickel may be correct in stating that his super scintillation detector "is the only tool for exploring South American jungles."

Bickel reported that his scintillators are currently being used by diamond seekers in South Africa to search for undiscovered funnel-shaped bodies of bluish diamond-rich rock called "Kimberlite pipes." Volcanic in origin, Kimberlite ore has subnormally low radioactivity common to the basalt family of which it is a member. Therefore, when Bickel's counter provides a near zero negative reading, it indicates a likely place to find one of the "pipes."

Bickel asserts that he has twice detected a "complete blackout"—a zero negative reading—in California, one of which, he believes, indicates a thirty-foot diameter funnel on Figueroa Mountain fifty miles north of Santa Barbara. The blackouts, he says, can only be caused by Kimberlite ore deposits or pipes of active thermal steam. Intensive aerial search may locate many more of them.

Bickel is confident that his invention's greatest potential lies in its adaptability to oil search. Oil-bearing formations act as buffers to block the normal background radiation issuing from the rocks below them. When directly over a formation's edges, the positive needle on his machine climbs to a much higher reading than for the normal background, due to an anomalous condition in the interface between the oil and the surrounding material.

"While the instrument is carried by car or on foot squarely across an oil formation of a kind known to geologists as a closed

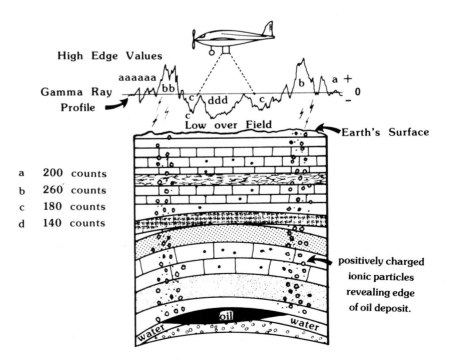

High Edge Values

Gamma Ray Profile

a   200 counts
b   260 counts
c   180 counts
d   140 counts

Low over Field

Earth's Surface

positively charged
ionic particles
revealing edge
of oil deposit.

Aerial survey of Oil Deposit.

Author holding dowsing rod listens for auditory signal as Dr. Z. V. Harvalik turns tube mounted atop tripod. Photo by Lois Pengelly.

The instrument pictured above is one of many contraptions devised to purportedly improve or enhance the art of dowsing while at the same time seeming to heighten its scientific "credibility." Remarkably, not a few of them have managed to win the acceptance of patent examiners.

Invented by Svatopluk Tabara of Lutin, Czechoslovakia, the device consists of a metal tube 5 mm in diameter and at least 150 mm long. The tube is closed at one end with a metal plug with a 0.2 mm. hole pierced through its center, at the other end with a similar plug to which a stethoscope is attached.

A metal sleeve around the tube allows it to be mounted on a goniometer (angle-measuring device) fixed atop a surveyor's tripod. It is claimed that by turning the tube while holding the dowsing rod at the ready and with the stethoscope plugged into the ears, a dowser will obtain a signal only if standing acoustical waves originating from a water vein reach the tube when it is aligned perpendicularly to them. The method is supposed to allow the precise delineation of the water vein, its rate of flow and its depth.

Dr. Harvalik shown here rotating the tube while the author manipulated the rod, comments: "This is the first document I have seen in which it is claimed that a dowsing signal can also be acoustically perceived. The search tube would not seem to constitute a collimator for electromagnetic waves converted in the tube into sonic waves (compressions and expansions of air). If the tube cavity were tuned to the exact frequency of an acoustic signal, it could be a collimator for sonic waves but this does not appear to be the case because the patent reads that the tube can be of any length as long as it is longer than 150mm. I conclude that the gimmick is simply another programming *device, a means to allow dowsers to focus their attention on the problem at hand."*

dome," reports Bickel, "the graph continuously traced on paper looks like a cross section of a volcanic crater. The raised rim corresponds to the halo" of the circle- or ellipse-shaped dome. The central depression, the lowest level of the negative reading on the graph, marks the most likely spot to drill an oil well.

Bickel's device may not entirely replace existing oil

prospecting methods known to trained geologists and field engineers, but he has been told by petroleum experts that, when they first saw the device in action, they felt as if they had been looking for oil blindfolded in the past. According to Bickel, important sources of underground water are also detectable by this new device. Thirty-six producing water wells were located with it during the first three years of experimentation.

Bickel's inventions would have charmed Dr. Armand Viré who over thirty years ago prophetically wrote:

We are not yet endowed with a means of mechanically controlling the dowsing signal, though this has been the dream of so many good-natured souls. But the idea is in the air and it is to be hoped that it will soon be realized. Contrary to what one might think, there are grounds to believe that many dowsers fear such a development. For among dowsers there are two categories: "professionals" and "theoreticians." The latter work and experiment in the laboratory or on the ground with the sole ambition of widening our scientific knowledge and developing our industrial potentials. They thus view the advent of such an apparatus with anticipation.

Among the "professionals," on the contrary, there are those who cannot see beyond an egotistical goal, and a perfectly legitimate one at that, of increasing their own personal resources. These fear that any automatic dowsing apparatus will destroy the dowsing profession and cause its disappearance. In this they are completely wrong, for such an instrument can only increase the reliability of their prognoses and their very ability to furnish geology, engineering, and industry with thenceforth uncontestible and uncontested data.

Has the telescope destroyed the astronomers? The stethoscope or antisepsis the physicians? The automatic calculator the mathematicians?

Today Bickel has developed two closely related models of his instrument. The "Algor Alpha," specially designed for the detection of ore bodies and mineralized zones, can be modified for water finding. The other, "Algor Explorer X," with the same basic specifications as its relative, is adapted for geological study and exploration because it can register any geological fault system or structural change and is therefore useful in checking ground formations prior to building or road construction.

Bickel is presently working on a new machine, the Explorer X100 which, using a 3-inch caesium-antimony photomultiplier tube with a sapphire window and a doped lithium-germanium crystal, will be able to record the whole spectrum of isotopes of precious metals through the use of a special computer. The machine's operator will see the word "gold," "silver," or the name of other elements appear in a "window" built into the instrument whenever considerable quantities of it are indicated underground.

"My new device is nothing short of an atomic age miracle tool for geologists and prospectors," boasts the former rocket engineer. "Perhaps I have created the first electronic dowser."

CHAPTER 16

The Medical Potential

". . . or even a shoulder bar for carrying two buckets."

A Child Saved

Marie-Helène, a little girl of two, was the despair of her mother. For months she had suffered from inflammation of both ears. By August 1963, she could barely stand upright. After trying every remedy he could think of, her family doctor could only counsel the girl's mother to be patient. The child, he said, might grow out of her affliction.

The following April, the same physician was no longer hopeful. An electroencephalogram led him to diagnose a severe disturbance in motor functioning. Impulses from the child's nerve centers to her muscles were retarded and irregular. Blood tests revealed an insufficiency of cholesterol. An X-ray of the head was declared normal.

The doctor could not decide what to do next.

In the fall, Marie-Helène's mother was given the address of a healing practitioner whom she visited in a working-class section of Paris. Her daughter, she told the healer, was in a constant state of agitation day and night, slept fitfully if at all, and could not walk. For six months she had only been able to utter a single word: "Papa." Her doctor believed her to have permanent motor and mental dysfunction which he attributed to microbes contracted by the mother during pregnancy.

The healer filled out a medical dossier, carefully noting all the child's symptoms, including some which did not seem particularly alarming to the mother, all treatments to date, and the medical history of her parents. He then pulled a shiny crystal on a string from his pocket and began to ask a series of questions.

When his dowsing revealed the seat of the child's trouble to be in the spinal cord, the healer was perplexed. The conclusion seemed in no way to accord with the laboratory tests or with the physician's certainty that there was something awry with her brain function.

The dowser then inquired via his pendulum: "Is there something wrong with the girl's brain?" The pendular reply was "No."

The dialogue continued:

"What value should be attributed to the EEG?" Answer: "None."

"What value should be attributed to the blood tests?" Answer: "None."

Father Jean Jurion, in Washington, D.C., 1975.

"What value should be attributed to the head X-ray?" Answer: "None."

Having eliminated the laboratory tests that had seemed so important to the doctor, he next decided to pursue a line of questioning which might indicate what type of treatment could best help Marie-Helène. The answers came back that acupuncture should be gently used on the patient's back to be followed by a course of homeopathic remedies.

Proceeding as directed, the healer first made a pendulum search for acupuncture points along the girl's spine that might benefit from stimulation. To avoid frightening her, instead of piercing them with needles, he massaged them with the tip of his forefinger. He then addressed himself to the homeopathic pharmacopoeia and wrote out a prescription.

Founded in the 1700s by Christian Samuel Hahnemann, a linguistically gifted German chemist and physician, homeopathy is a school of medicine relying on infinitessimally small doses of natural products in solution which, if administered in strong doses, would produce effects *similar* to those of the disease being treated. Today's far more prevalent school of allopathic medicine leans on a therapy whose chemical remedies produce effects *differing* from those of the disease treated. In contrast to homeopathy, which regards symptoms as a means of natural healing—or a form of self-defense to which a doctor should ally his efforts—allopathy views them as an antagonist of nature, or a form of external aggression against which a patient, having no adequate protection, must look for defense to a doctor and his medical armory.

Though Hahnemann was savagely attacked in his day not only by allopaths but by producers of pharmaceuticals, it is a fact that his method was heralded in Europe during a severe epidemic of Asiatic cholera in 1831–33 when in London alone it was able to save the lives of 84 percent of those afflicted, whereas over half of those treated by other means succumbed to the disease.

Allopathic medicine is constantly on the hunt for specific cures: for heart disease, arthritis, cancer, and other as yet unchecked illnesses. Because homeopaths do not think so much in terms of disease itself as the physical, mental, and emotional state of patients that might have permitted its inruption, they look to a wide variety of remedies generally used in conjunction with one another. Seeking them out takes much longer than the rote prescription that is becoming prevalent in an age when mass medicine and even "computerized diagnosis" is in the ascendancy.

As one expert, Dr. Harris Coulter, has it: "Homeopathic prescription, demanding both time and individualized attention, is out of step with the socioeconomic determinants of modern medical practice." It is in the speeding up of the selection of remedies that dowsing has played a commanding role in the practice of homeopathy. Thus, Marie-Helène's prescription took the healer only twenty minutes of his time.

That same evening the mother called the healer to say she had given the first dose of prescribed remedies to her daughter

during lunch, then put her to bed for a nap. The girl had slept until four in the afternoon and upon awakening had climbed out of bed and, for the first time in months, walked without assistance. At supper time, her daughter had clearly uttered a new word, "Mama." At a visit to her doctor two weeks later, when she was beginning to form full sentences, the little girl was pronounced well on the way to full recovery.

Marie-Helène's case is recorded in a book remarkably entitled *Journal of an Outlaw* by the man who prescribed the remedies to her mother, Father Jean Jurion, a Catholic priest of the Oratory who, before his untimely death in 1977, had devoted himself to medical dowsing in Paris for over thirty years.

Born seventy-one years ago at Sedan in the Ardennes, a forested plateau east of the Meuse River which was the scene of heavy fighting in both world wars, Jurion spent the first half of his working life as a teacher and administrator in Catholic colleges in the French capital. He was introduced to the dowsing art in 1930 by a fellow priest in the countryside near his home who used a pierced coin on the end of a string, to find lost objects and missing persons. For some time the young Oratorian looked on the practice only as an amusement until, one afternoon, his sister lost her gold ring while packing apples into baskets between layers of hay.

Entering the shed where the packing was taking place Jurion, driven more by curiosity than purpose, held his own string-suspended nickel-plated coin over several baskets that, filled and covered, were ready for shipment to market and was surprised to see the coin rotate over one of them in the clockwise direction he had established as indicating a positive answer. He opened the basket, removed the top protective layer of hay, then redowsed for the exact position of the lost ring. The pendulum became violently active over one specific apple. When he gingerly lifted it from its resting place, there was the ring lying on the apple beneath.

"Over the next several years," wrote Jurion later, "a mixture of successes and failures made me understand that the dowsing process requires the development of a subtle sensitivity, the creation of a personal method or style, a lot of training and practice and, doubtless, other conditions yet to be discovered."

The Birth of Medical Dowsing

It was only after World War II, during which Father Jurion was awarded the Croix de Guerre for refusing to obey a cowardly officer who had ordered him and his unit to surrender to German forces, that the priest began seriously to consider the use of dowsing in medicine. His inspiration came from the accomplishments of three dowsing priests who had pioneered the art. The first was Abbé Alexis Bouly, curate of Hardelot-Plage, a small seaside village on the English Channel, who became so well known as a water dowser that, after finding commercially important supplies for French manufacturers, he was contracted to do likewise by other industrialists in Belgium, Portugal, Poland, and Romania.

At the end of World War I, Bouly was summoned by a

Abbé Bourdoux. (From Jean-Louis Bourdoux, Notions Pratiques de Radiesthésie pour les Missionnaires, *Desforges, Paris, 1965.)*

Abbé Mermet. (Copied from Jean-Louis Bourdoux, Notions Pratiques de Radiesthésie pour les Missionnaires, *Desforges, Paris, 1965.)*

general at the Camp de Sissone north of Reims to be examined on his alleged ability to locate unexploded shells buried in the ground and to state whether they were of German, Austrian, or French manufacture prior to their unearthing. Impressed with Bouly's faultless performance, the general recommended the dowser's talents to the Ministry of War in Paris.

After the war Bouly founded the Society of Friends of Radiesthesia, based on a new word he coined for dowsing, an amalgam of a Latin root for "radiation" and a greek root for "perception," which he hoped would make the searching art scientifically more acceptable. Seeking new fields to conquer, he finally hit on what he called "the world of microbial vibrations." "I was bold enough to tackle it," he wrote, "but to start with I had to learn about microbes, to study their nature and their influence on the human body."

When word of his new interest spread throughout northern France, those doctors who regarded the prelate as a scientific investigator rather than a competitor were glad to assist him in his experiments, most of which he carried out in the hospitals of Boulogne-sur-Mer, Berck-Plage, Lille, and the Belgian city of Liège. Put to repeated tests, Bouly was able, simply by manipulating a pendulum, to identify cultures of microbes in test tubes just as easily as if he were observing them through a microscope.

In 1950, at the age of eighty-five, in recognition of his accomplishments, the Abbé was made a *Chevalier de La Legion d'Honneur,* the highest decoration his nation could bestow on him. In his acceptance speech the newly knighted priest declared: "This Cross of the Legion of Honor is awarded in my person to all practitioners of dowsing. For my own part, the award represents the crowning of a life I have tried to dedicate to the service of God and the good of humanity."

A second medical dowsing pioneer who inspired Jurion was Father Jean-Louis Bourdoux, who spent sixteen years as a missionary in the jungles of Brazil's Matto Grosso. Of delicate health, he was struck down with a nearly fatal case of galloping consumption and later by a six-week-long fever contracted while on an apostolic mission into the wilderness from which he returned at the point of death on a stretcher. Both times he was brought back to health with saps from local plants prescribed by his Indian parishioners.

His health restored, Bourdoux launched into a study of the medicinal properties of Brazilian plants, extracts of which he took back to France where they were tested in dilution by homeopaths who confirmed their salubrious effects.

Following extended talks with doctors and patients, as well as study of herbals native to France, Bourdoux decided to write a book that might help his fellow missionaries care for the sick in outbacks of the world. The main question bothering him was: "How can they be taught which plants in a particular region would act as specific remedies for specific ailments?"

In the midst of his deliberations, Bourdoux met Father Alexis Mermet who had learned to dowse for water from his grandfather and father in Savoy. As early as 1906, Mermet came

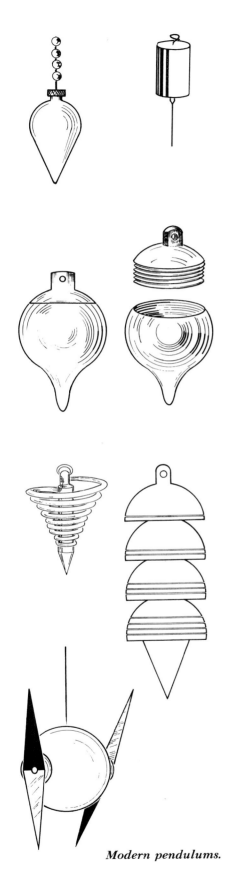

Modern pendulums.

to the conclusion that if what lay hidden in the earth and in inanimate objects could be studied with a pendulum, then why couldn't the same pendulum detect hidden conditions in animals and human beings? In his classic book, *How I Proceed in the Discovery of Near or Distant Water, Metals, Hidden Objects and Illnesses,* that explained a lifetime of research on dowsing, Mermet proudly stated: "I invented the method of 'pendular diagnosis.'"

Mermet's well-publicized results convinced Bourdoux that dowsing was the answer to rapid selection of autochthonous plants. "If the Abbé Mermet can do it, why can't I?" he wrote. "If I had only known about this art when I was in Brazil!"

After years of study and practice, and another visit to the South American jungles, Bourdoux published his *Practical Notions of Radiesthesia for Missionaries,* the preface of which read in part: "If you have the patience to read these pages you shall see how, thanks to a new science called 'radiesthesia,' you will be able, without any medical training and hardly any funds, to succor both believers and pagans. Perhaps you will be amazed at some of the things I have set down and be tempted to say: 'That's impossible.' But are we not living in a time of marvelous discoveries each more disconcerting than the next?"

When Jurion decided to follow in the dowsing steps of his clerical predecessors, he began both a simultaneous study of homeopathy and a survey of the already vast French literature on dowsing that had appeared since 1900. Seeking a concrete explanation for radiesthetic practice, he was met only with a welter of contradictory opinions that, unsupported by experimental proof, had simply to be taken for granted. Numerous precautions filled the pages of dowsing guides: One should never dowse unless one was facing north or while wearing rubber-soled shoes. One should remove metallic objects from one's clothing. The list was endless.

Jurion tried a score of several hundred pendulums differing in size, shape, and substance, each of which was promoted as indispensable to dowsing success. He was finally persuaded by a colleague to choose a black sphere of bakelite whose "antimagnetic properties" were supposed, in the opinion of its progenitor, to somehow assist in the "battle with waves" by "capturing" some of them, "warding off" others.

"That black ball," he later admitted, "I found it depressing. One day I threw it away in favor of a translucent pendulum of rock crystal which cheerily reflected light. My impulse was no different than that of a person who buys an automobile for its color. What of it? The crystal ball rotated no better or worse than any of the other pendulums I had tried, and I liked it."

After liberating himself from what he called a conglomeration of "self-imposed servitudes," Jurion found he could dowse anywhere, any time, under any conditions. When he began his own first attempts at diagnosis, he obtained excellent results confirmed by doctors. His greatest surprise came with the realization that his most spectacular achievements were related to cases which he thought practically impossible to solve because doctors had given up on them.

289

A particularly difficult case concerned a forty-nine-year old Belgian whose wife came to Jurion's Paris office with a lock of hair cut from her husband's head. Weeping, she related that, when X-rays had confirmed two inoperable cancerous tumors in his brain, he had been given over forty cobalt radiation treatments accompanied by doses of X-rays. All of these ministrations had not stopped the spread of cancer which now was blocking the back of his throat to the point where he could barely swallow and causing him acute pain in the nerve ganglia under his armpits. He had lost all hearing and the sight of his right eye and lay in a coma in an oxygen tent.

Permitted to attend to her husband on a round-the-clock basis, the wife was able to get him to swallow a series of homeopathic remedies which Jurion had indicated should help him. The treatment began in May. For a month hardly any change was observable though the patient's condition seemed to have stabilized. At the beginning of August, cancer specialists were astonished to note a daily change for the better. Toward the end of the same month, Jurion redowsed the patient's general condition and prescribed a new series of remedies.

On October 10, in a virtual return from the dead, the patient walked into Jurion's Paris office to thank him. Though still blind in his right eye, the man had completely recovered his hearing and could enjoy a good meal. His doctors, he said, considered his recovery a miracle. None of the hospital staff could in any way account for a turnaround in what they had regarded a "hopeless case." The patient took a third set of remedies recommended by Jurion over the next twelve months, at the end of which cancerologists pronounced him free of disease.

Of the case, Jurion wrote: "This treatment, which most medical specialists could not even hope to be effective, amply justifies the existence of the healing practitioner who is often the patient's 'last chance.' Again, I proclaim it our duty to take on even the seemingly most intractable cases. Certainly, we must avoid 'selling hope' to any ill person. But if we can, we must make them the promise of doing our level best to heal them and everything in our attitudes must translate and express this desire."

The "again" in his statement was a reference to years of harassment by the Order of Physicians, the French medical association that, jealously guarding its monopoly to treat the sick, had hauled Jurion into court six times before the appearance of his book.

"So I became an outlaw," Jurion wrote in his preface. "He who cares for the sick without a medical degree commits an offense that can put him in a cell behind bars next to an embezzler, a con man, or a murderer."

At one of his trials, Jurion was testifying about patients he had cured by dowsing remedies when, suddenly and savagely, the judge turned on him to shout sarcastically: "This tribunal is not objecting to your curing people but to your treating them." When his young defense lawyer found no words to rebut the absurd illogicality of this remark, Jurion almost broke court decorum. "I could hardly restrain myself," he wrote, "from giving that judge a piece of my mind. His statement was an act of cowardice, revealing, as it did, that he refused to study the problem from the human perspective, that of the patient. Abandoning all social responsibility, he took refuge in the life-destroying letter of the law, and it's high time to say so."

During a quarter century Jurion amassed medical records on more than 30,000 patients which he invited anyone to scrutinize using any statistical or computer process to determine whether or not his healing was more than a match for that of any physician. In over 2,000 printed pages he set forth in detail everything he had learned about medical dowsing and homeopathy throughout his career and pointed out that in countries such as the Netherlands, Germany, and Great Britain, no law forbids doctors from working together with unorthodox healers. "If such cooperation were universal," he asked, "how many times would a patient be cared for ever so much more rapidly and effectively?"

Jurion's battle with medical authority in following the Christ's admonition to "heal the sick" has encouraged many laypersons among his compatriots to do likewise. Today, over one hundred medical dowsers, officially recognized as a professional group by the Ministry of Labor, practice their art in France. Their most influential supporter is Robert Felsenhardt, who was introduced to the world of medical dowsing when, over two decades ago, an irate woman appeared at the claims window of *Mutuelle Complementaire,* the Parisian medical insurance firm which he directed.

"For years," she shouted at the embarrassed clerk, "you've been covering fees I've paid to doctors, none of whom has ever relieved my suffering. Now that I've found a man who is healing me, you won't meet the modest forty francs he's charged me. I demand to see the president!"

Interrupted at his work *Mutelle's* chief executive officer was told that though they had tried, several of his underlings could not get rid of the woman who was causing such a commotion that she was upsetting a whole office full of employees.

"All right," said Felsenhardt calmly, "I'll deal with her personally. Send her up."

In his office the woman told Felsenhardt that she had been bedridden for years and that the only reason she was now sitting

291

before him was that she had finally been prescribed a series of medicines that restored her ability to walk. Informing her firmly that his company was not in business to support medically unqualified "charlatans," Felsenhardt politely added that he would look into her case and let her know his final decision when he had studied it.

What he found in her dossier troubled his conscience. On the one hand a group of doctors seemed to have been completely stymied in their attempts to relieve the woman. On the other, a "healer" had effectively and significantly improved her condition. When Felsenhardt saw to his surprise that the healer in question was a Roman Catholic priest he decided to visit him. To his blunt question about why his healing methods were so successful, the priest replied: "The best way to answer that is for you to attend our next assembly."

The meeting to which Father Jurion referred was that of the *Syndicat des Radiesthésistes*, or Union of Medical Dowsers, of which he was president, where Felsenhardt was introduced to fifteen men and women who described to him how they diagnosed medical ills and selected remedies with the aid of a pendulum.

"They were dead serious," remembers Felsenhardt, "and though none of them had any orthodox medical training, they knew a great deal about medicine."

For a month Felsenhardt studied what to him seemed cases of medical treatment that were little short of miraculous. "I then decided that my company could responsibly meet the astonishingly modest fees the dowsers were charging," he recalls, "at least in certain cases. I was so taken with their spirit of service that I became legal counsellor to the Union which I knew to be under constant attack from the *Ordre des Médecins.*"

Felsenhardt who, under Jurion's tutelage, learned to become an expert dowser, today is editor of *Radiesthésie Magazine*, France's most widely circulated dowsing journal and director of the *Centre International de la Radiesthésie* with headquarters in Paris's *La Rue Boétie* which offers dowsing services to anyone seeking them.

The Pattern of Health

In 1938 Aubrey Westlake, a young English physician, was stricken with an attack of food poisoning that none of his colleagues could effectively treat. He was finally introduced to Hector Munro, a doctor reputed to possess extraordinary methods of diagnosis. Lying stripped on Munro's examination table, Westlake was surprised that Munro only passed his hands over that part of the abdomen where he felt pain without touching the flesh itself. When he finished, he told Westlake not to worry. The remedies he would prescribe would make him well.

When Westlake asked how he might learn more about the kind of diagnosis he had just witnessed, Munro suggested that he attend a meeting of doctors and laymen studying under the aegis of a newly formed Medical Society for the Study of Radiesthesia.

At the meeting Westlake, introduced to what he later called an "exciting and fascinating world of healing," met the president and founder of the society, Guyon Richards, who, having acquainted himself with French medical dowsing, published an enormous amount of original research in his book, *The Chain of Life.* He also met a number of other men: Ernest Martin, the first doctor in England to use a pendulum in diagnosis and treatment, who had discovered that the muscles of "sensitives" would twitch reflexively whenever it entered an "etheric" field or "aura" surrounding the human body; Ernest Jensen, an eminent and erudite Harley Street physician, whose recent conversion to dowsing had led him to conclude that the same "aura" grew larger or smaller depending on a patient's health; and a dozen other medical dowsers who were "open-minded, tolerant, sympathetic, and possessed of an excellent sense of humor."

For several years Westlake and his wife, who was far more sensitive with a pendulum than himself, worked with the new diagnostic technique only to be confronted with as many puzzling setbacks as with successes. It seemed to them that the more they learned about medical dowsing, the more they became aware of countless pitfalls on the road leading to true diagnosis and treatment. Westlake finally realized that anyone taking up medical dowsing had to jettison most of the shibboleths of their former medical training and restructure their thinking to approach the whole subject from an entirely new viewpoint.

The central weakness of ordinary medicine, he concluded, was that because it stressed pathology above all else, it dealt mainly with the gross final *results* of disease processes rather than their underlying cause. True diagnosis, he felt, was to be sought in a radiesthetic analysis, not of pathological tissue, but of a harmonious balance of energy patterns constituting health. So many medical men, when first introduced to dowsing, seemed to profit little from it because they thought in terms of pathology instead of function, disease instead of health, and matter instead of energy. What was needed, said Westlake, was a completely different mode of thinking that would allow the recovery in a new and modern form of an age-old integrating philosophy of medicine. Only this could order and simplify the ever-increasing complexity, fragmentation, and specialization of modern medical science that threatened to overwhelm the profession with a plethora of unrelated details.

293

(ABOVE LEFT) Aubrey T. Westlake, B.A., M.B., B. Chir. (Cantab). M.R.C.S., L.R.C.P., F.I. Psi. M. (ABOVE RIGHT) Officers of the Medical Society for the Study of Radiesthésia. Drs. Aubrey Westlake, vice-president; Dr. Watson, president; Dr. Laurence, vice-president. (Photographs courtesy of Dr. Aubrey Westlake.)

Westlake also abhorred the proclivity to explain dowsing purely in terms of modern physics, and maintained that, like the explorers of old, dowsers must forge ahead into undiscovered territory if they were to acquire the vital information they sought. It was by setting sail that Columbus had proved wrong the majority opinion that no land lay beyond the western ocean, he wrote, and dowsers would only progress in their art by transcending equally deep-rooted but misled conceptions as to how it worked.

Westlake's conviction was particularly encouraged by a retired member of the Indian police force who had served in intelligence in the Middle East during World War II, W. O. Wood. Wood had met all leading European exponents of medical dowsing. Keenly aware that for thirty years the art had made no major advance in technique, he was of the opinion that it was being approached from the wrong point of view. He called to Westlake's attention the answer given when someone asked Signore Pareti, the most successful Italian practitioner of medical dowsing, to define the art and its limits. "Radiesthesia," replied Pareti, "is a means of knowledge and of action which is exercised outside the ambit of the five physiological and traditional senses; there are no limits to our art, save those personal to each operator."

Equally impressive to Westlake was a lecture by the Reverend J. A. C. Murray that demonstrated how various nuclear discoveries had shattered supposedly unshatterable concepts in science. "In the process of being dynamited," he declared, "scientists have become more open-minded in regard to certain realms of experience which previously they had ignored. They know that reality is a bigger thing than the facts which they have gathered about it. One department of science, experimenting with the new forces inherent in matter, and with certain powers

294

of radiation which seem to function in a new dimension, independent of space and time, has evolved a healing method so revolutionary in its premises as to threaten all the established ways of medicine and so etherial in its command of vibration and radiation as to knock at the gates of the spiritual. I refer, of course, to radiesthesia which reveals most clearly the fact that there is no hard and fast frontier between matter and spirit."

Westlake's determination to begin a new round of study based on Murray's inspiring statement was further fired by the fact that, with the death of Richards, the Society for Medical Radiesthesia, succumbing to pressure from orthodox medical circles, shed itself of its lay members, thereby dooming itself to virtual inactivity. Disheartened by the evident cowardice of medical men who had turned their backs on loyal associates simply because they did not have a medical degree, he formed, together with Wood, a small private research group.

To clear the decks they started with the assumption that dowsers operated on various levels at the lowest of which, physical radiesthesia, the dowser was only a sensitive instrument for recording physical radiation. This function would one day be taken over by mechanical hardware, said Westlake, in a prediction that anticipated the work of Dr. Armin Bickel fifteen years before it was initiated.

On the next level, dowsers combined the use of physical senses with extrasensory perception and consequently were no longer constrained by physical and geophysical limitations as detailed by Solco Tromp. It was at this level that map dowsing had to work, as well as the question-and-answer method used in information dowsing, provided that several conditions were met: first, an open-hearted quest for truth devoid of any ulterior motive; second, a search carried out with full conscious awareness independent of trance conditions or any type of mediumship or spiritism; third, an above-average grasp of the subject for which information was sought and a line of questioning unanswerable by ordinary intellectual means; and fourth, the exercise of refined sensitivity and common sense.

As their work continued, Westlake discovered that dowsers on his team were catapulted to a third dowsing level, that of a "full mental consciousness," a state akin to that of subjects used in the remote viewing experiments at the Stanford Research Institute and to Peter Harmon's sudden ability to "see" a scene at the other end of the long-distance telephone. Other dowsers have found that, by practicing their art, they have developed considerable powers of clairaudience, as if the "still small voice" of the Bible were talking to them from within.

To Westlake, one could attain the third level not through sensitivity but through a *receptivity* conditioned by a "conscious understanding of the implications of truth." Here was a way of penetrating into a science of the future based not on number, space, time, atomic particles, energies, organisms, conscious or unconscious mind, or statistics, all of which had served well in the past to increase human understanding of the universe, but on *pattern,* itself a combination of a force and a result. Medical dowsers could be successful in seeking "patterns of health" only

295

Medical dowsing has long been practiced in veterinary medicine. Above is a French dowser diagnosing a malady in a huge Percheron draft horse (first published in the magazine La Vie à la Campagne, *April 1, 1933). Below, another French dowser is determining an illness in a little lamb (first published in the journal* La Côte d'Azur Médicale, *Toulon, August 1932).*

by taking into account all aspects of man, including interlinked physical, emotional, mental, and spiritual states. If the linkage were well understood, it would be possible to determine blockages that impeded the flow of forces between them to produce disorder and disease and to measure the quantity and quality of the flow.

What Westlake and his friends found with respect to specific geometric patterns and their relationship to medical problems is set down in a remarkable book, *The Pattern of Health,* one of the best modern treatments on medical dowsing.

Westlake's philosophical journey into the unknown was matched by that of his colleague George Laurence who, after a lifetime of orthodox medical practice, came to the conclusion that he didn't know *why* people were ill and was reduced to treating outward symptoms with no clue as to their fundamental cause. Only when introduced, late in his career, to the medical dowsing society did he find the concepts missing in medicine that he had been seeking.

To develop them, he dowsed out a special diagnostic pattern that permitted him to determine the degree of deviation from a hypothetical point of dynamic balance equivalent to perfect health which, as in Jurion's case, could usually be rectified by homeopathic remedies. He also came to the conclusion that a limited number of primitive maladies gave rise to thousands of chronic ailments. Due to what Hahnemann had somewhat opaquely called "miasms," they were either retained as toxins from acquired infections such as measles, or passed from one generation to another by an "etheric" heredity, a concept based on an ancient pre-Hindu Indian doctrine that man possessed not just a physical body but an etheric nonmaterial one which surrounded it. Because no one since Hahnemann's time had been able to eliminate miasms, Laurence set to work to solve the problem, at last succeeding when he administered his own homeopathic dilutions of RNA and DNA, the two products organic chemists had found so crucial to the transmission of information from genes to cells in embryonic growth.

In 1969 Laurence formed the Psionic Medical Society to propagate his new teachings which, in the eyes of Westlake who became one of its charter members, incorporated four essential features: simple in both theory and practice, it required a minimum of apparatus; assessment of fundamental invisible causes of disease, environmental, internal, or inherited, could be made rapidly and accurately; because the cause of particularly intractable chronic ailments could be pinpointed, these could be eliminated with remedies found to be specific to them; the course and invisible results of therapy could be monitored throughout the treatment.

The pinpointing of invisible causes and results also lies at the heart of a method adopted by an American professional engineer to deal with illnesses not mentioned by French and English dowsers.

Since his retirement from Texas Instruments, Edward Jastram has devoted his time to researching the possession of persons by nonmaterial entities that cause mental and physical disorders of a

Ed Jastram examines a subject for personality problems with pendulum and diagram.

wholly inexplicable nature. According to Jastram's experience, a thorough analysis of any individual's personality may be rapidly and accurately made through communication via the pendulum with his or her "subconscious mind." The foreign presences detected range in influence, he maintains, from minimally harmful to a near complete subjugation of a subject's primary self.

As a typical case Jastram cites a middle-aged woman who had been praised for her reliability and industry as a domestic worker for a group of households on a Caribbean island. Suddenly she became surly and evasive, addicted to drink, and embroiled in fights and "lost weekends" during one of which she broke her leg in a fall from her bicycle. All of her employers and friends were horrified by the dramatic change that had come over her.

When her situation was brought to Jastram's attention, his pendular analysis indicated "the presence of three alien personalities 'on board,' very negative in character. Steps were taken to eliminate them and a recheck of her personality indicated that they proved successful. Within a week her personality had returned to normal. "During my handling of this case there was no personal contact between the patient and myself. The whole situation was worked on in absentia, add Jastrom."

"Visitors" from otherworldly realms affect his clients, says Jastram, by producing confusion, depression, fear, impaired judgment, inability to make decisions, abrupt deterioration of problem-solving ability, loss of a capacity for creativity, and feelings of inferiority. These mental states are often accompanied by a sudden onset of physical symptoms, arthritis, or ulcers for instance.

Another of Jastram's cases involved a young widow who had raised her two children on her own. After they had completed their education and left home, she pursued a life of church activities and committee work in women's groups where she was universally considered tactful and effective. All at once her fellow-workers became aware of a marked change in her character, at first revealed by a propensity to make unjustifiably nasty remarks. Later her language became so coarse and insulting that her friends began avoiding her company.

"When gossip about the situation reached my ears," reported Jastram, "my analysis indicated the presence of an extra personality which I removed that very night. The next day the woman was telephoning her friends in tears to apologize for her 'bitchy' behavior and ever since she has been her normal jolly self. Her recovery was one of the quickest I have ever known. She knew nothing of the work I performed but, after her return to normal, said she felt she had awakened from a bad dream."

Asked how, once having detected alien personalities with his pendulum, he is able to remove them, Jastram explained: "I get into a state in which my brain emits *alpha* waves and identify the dowsed alien personalities to be exercised, suggesting where they are to go and what they are to do. During this process, I usually take three or four deep breaths to accumulate energy, which is "love," for my purpose. I send the energy to what has been called by the Hawaiian *kahunas*, or shaman-priests, my *aumakua* or "higher self," at which point I usually get a distinct impression of what is occurring in the person I am seeking to help. It is important to thank the "higher self" for a job well accomplished and to be absolutely certain of its effective results. The whole process can be equated to a highly efficient prayer mechanism."

Our growing recognition of our spiritual selves in a world foundering under the weight of materialist, scientific, and technological concepts underlies a new surge of interest in dowsing as a key to solving a whole gamut of problems those concepts have spawned. As Westlake, now nearly ninety, expressed it: "I believe that the rediscovery of the dowsing faculty is not fortuitous, but has been vouchsafed to us by Providence to enable us to cope with the difficult and dangerous stage of human development which lies immediately ahead. For it gives indirect access to the supersensible world, thus raising our level of consciousness and extending our awareness and knowledge. The faculty should be regarded as a special and peculiar sense halfway between our ordinary physical senses which apprehend the material world, and our to-be-developed future occult senses which in due course will apprehend the supersensible world directly."

"The Apprehension of the Supersensible World"

Inaccessible Levels of Human Awareness

Aubrey Westlake's timely characterization of dowsing can be fully savored only through a concomitant awareness that our world is poised on the threshold of an upheaval in science as radical as those engendered by Copernicus' realization that the sun, rather than the earth, was at the center of our planetary system and Einstein's perception that reality, far from being absolute, depended upon extraneous factors, not the least of which is an individual's position in curved space, or point of view.

The coming revolution is predicated on the idea that consciousness—or "mind," to use the Anglo-Saxon term—long regarded as intangible and therefore materially suspect, plays a dominant role in the physical universe. What is mind? The ancient Greeks called it *psyche*, meaning not only "soul," "spirit," and "breath" but also "butterfly," a connotation highlighting its capricious and wayward quality. British psychiatrist Alan McGlashan may have come closest to netting the butterfly by defining psyche as "spontaneous, unpredictable, free, its very existence is a challenge to logical thought, the glitter of an executioner's axe to every strutting orthodoxy. The psyche is beautiful and dangerous."

Heedless of any danger, the initiators of the coming revolution are still sequestered in "backrooms" and "garrets" plotting the rupture of complacement attitudes ascendant in materialist science and mechanistic technology. Central to them is the disposition to discount any subtlety of the psyche as "metaphysical" and picture human beings as biological machines that can have no mind beyond one explainable as chemical processes in the brain.

This restriction, a self-imposed imprisonment, came into being during an age when *gnosis*, or intuitively revealed knowledge, began to cede its place to *scientia*, knowledge based on observable events and repeatable experiments. That cession was completed in the sixteenth century, just as dowsing was beginning to flower, with the declaration by Baron Verulam Viscount Saint Albans, better known as Sir Francis Bacon, that "reality *only* presents itself to us when we look upon the world of the senses that *alone* provide us with realities."

Even a century ago, talented researchers and inventors began

301

to put the lie to so dreary and limiting an outlook as Bacon's. In the proceedings of the German Chemical Society (1890), Friedrich August Kekulé von Stradonitz candidly admitted that he had hit on the shape of the benzene ring, a discovery that laid the basis for modern organic chemistry, as a result, not of painstaking work in his Ghent University laboratory, but of a spontaneous vision that came to him while he was asleep. In the conclusion of his report, he urged his fellow scientists: "Let us learn to dream, gentlemen."

A few years later, the inventive genius Nikola Tesla, while strolling late one afternoon in a Budapest park with a friend, was suddenly moved to declaim lines from Goethe's *Faust:*

> The glow retreats.　　　　Ah, that a wing could lift
> Done is the day of toil.　　　me from the soil.
> It yonder hastes, new　　Upon its track to follow,
> 　fields of life exploring.　　　follow soaring.

Hardly were the words out of his mouth than he was struck with a vision of a magnetic whirlwind turning a motor. Excited, he exhorted his friend to watch the machine run, first in one, then in the opposite direction. The companion, who could only see Tesla staring inanely at the setting sun, became so alarmed that he began dragging the inventor toward a park bench. Snapping out of his reverie, Tesla refused to sit down and, pacing back and forth, went on and on with a detailed description of his vision which, over the next several days, he worked up in exact blueprints in his mind, where they remained stored for the next six years. After Tesla's emigration to the United States, the blueprints were retrieved from his mental computer to be elaborated into hardware and become the alternating current generator.

The forces of revelation that gave rise to such creations as those of Kekulé and Tesla have in our century begun to receive recognition and respect for the vital part they can play in shaping human destiny and guiding the future evolution of the species. If *science* means verifiable knowledge integrated by key concepts that render data intelligible, then, as mathematician Charles Musès has it: "The beginnings of such knowledge come from *normally inaccessible levels of human awareness.* In this sense, the genesis of all science lies in noetics—the master science of the knowledge of consciousness and the release of its potentialities."

The Fusion of Physics and Psychology

The extraction of data from "normally inaccesible levels of human awareness" is, as has been repeatedly demonstrated in the foregoing chapters, the quintessence of dowsing. Like telepathy and other "psychic" acts, it arouses hostility in influential counter-revolutionaries intellectually secure within the comforting confines of a philosophy circumscribed by Bacon's edict. Seeking the cause of this hostility, McGlashan rhetorically offers: "Could it be that the psyche, itself the essence of the paradoxical, sees all things in the light of paradox, thereby challenging the stubborn delusion of mankind that somewhere, sometime, a final answer can be found to the riddle of existence?"

In *The Secret Vaults of Time,* an enthralling account of twentieth century archaeological discoveries by psychic methods, Stephan Schwartz, siding with McGlashan, concludes that orthodox science is averse to any anomaly not tailored to a tidy scheme by which it defines the universe. Both writers concur that a series of measures have been repeatedly enlisted to deal with such anomalies.

First, attempts are made to *murder* a disturbingly new idea in its cradle before too many people realize it has been born. If these attempts fail, the idea is *ignored* on the assumption that, if it will not simply "go away," somewhere down the road it can be disposed of either with the development of new laboratory instruments or the better articulation of theory asserting its "impossibility," or both. This reduction of the idea to a "non-subject" may eliminate it for a time by forcing it to conform to acceptable tenets of scientific thinking. Ideas that refuse to conform are then either subject to *ridicule* or, that failing, *consigned to limbo* even though, as Schwartz succinctly puts it, "everyone knows they are out there lurking like hungry wolves around the fort."

A complete analysis of this antagonism to new ideas might have to be assigned to a capable psychopathologist, were one available, had it not already been addressed by an historian of science, Thomas Kuhn, in his classic *The Structure of Scientific Revolutions.* Kuhn's disheartening conclusion is that a "new paradigm" or breakthrough, can be achieved in science only with that kind of massive upheaval in human thought—akin to earthquakes, tidal waves, and other "acts of God"—as the one potentially at hand.

It may come as a surprise that the coming revolution draws inspiration from physics rather than the purported "science of mind," psychology. Without really recognizing its mission as compelling human beings to question their notions of reality, physics has nevertheless spurred a quest for a new role for mind to play in the overall scheme by continuing to open horizons broader than could have been suspected. The theologian and philosopher, Jacob Needleman exults: "Physics places before us *the demand to think in new categories*" about time, space, matter, energy and, above all, causality and freedom.

The advent of a recognition by physics that *mind* must be included in its considerations was anticipated before World War II by Sir Oliver Lodge, whose *Physics and Philosophy* represented a swan song at the end of a long and fruitful professional life. Directly contradicting Bacon's assertion, Lodge heralded a coming sea change in scientific thought by complaining that "our studies can never put us into contact with reality and we can never understand what events are until man becomes endowed with more senses than he presently possesses."

As early as the 1950s, the Nobel Laureate, Eugene Wigner, went even further by his insistence that "before we can usefully speak of universal reality, a much closer integration of our understanding of physical and mental phenomena will be necessary than we can even dream of at present." Pointing to the claim of physics to be an all-embracing discipline because it endeavors to describe *all nature* and the same claim by psychology because it purports to deal with *all mental phenomena,* Wigner suggested that only a fusion of the two could open a portal out of the prison in which man presently seems to be confined.

That fusion is now in the making with the discovery that *mind,* psychology's ward, plays an active role in physical events exactly as Wigner also boldly proposed. Solco Tromp's neologism, "psychical physics," used as the title of his book on dowsing so many years ago finally appears entirely justified.

Mind Over Metal

The Frontiers of Physics Conference in Iceland, mentioned in this book's introduction, could well have been an historic venue in that the four theoretical physicists participating had no trouble agreeing that data put forward by their experimentalist colleagues strongly suggested that the workings of "mind" could and should be integrated into a coherent theory of the cosmos. More importantly, they argued that human mentation can affect large scale physical experimentation. No longer, it seems, can experimenters discount the part played by their psyches in their experiments.

In mathematical equations, this anomaly had been skirted by reference to experimenters as "observers" external to and independent of the objects of their attention ever since Einstein held such observers to clock, or measure, phenomena without in any way interfering with their measurements. It was only with the development of quantum mechanics by Werner Heisenberg in the mid-1920s that Einstein's assertion was slightly amended to admit the possible role of an observer as an *"uncertainty"* and then only at a micro-level state, i.e., in sub-atomic processes, where it was held to be so infinitesimal that it could not be measured. Up to that point, physics seemed to portend a vital role for consciousness without either being aware of or suggesting the need for its development.

At Reykjavik, among scientists presenting theories of how consciousness could affect matter was Dr. Richard Mattuck, a professor at Denmark's University of Copenhagen, who neatly summed up the paradox. After studying philosophy at Harvard, Mattuck was first confronted with the denial of mind's role in the cosmos when, as a doctoral candidate in physics at the Massachusetts Institute of Technology, he was told categorically by his teachers that mind could have no life independent of matter or, if it did, it was only part of the "gray matter" in the brain.

The budding scientist revolted. "How come," wondered Mattuck, "physicists kept using their minds to construct a theory of matter which, in turn they then used to prove that mind did not exist?"

Mattuck's life was revolutionized when he first saw the Israeli psychic, Uri Geller, bend metal objects without applying any

304

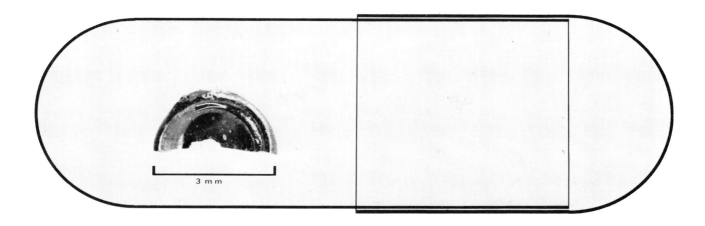

Electron microscope foil fractured by Uri Geller. The missing half vanished. The dimensions of the foil are shown in relationship to the pill capsule in which it was enclosed. The capsule was placed on a metal surfaced plate. Geller only waved his hand above it. (Photograph courtesy of Professor John Hasted, Birkbeck College, University of London, United Kingdom.)

force to them as did another conference participant, Dr. John Hasted, Chairman of the Department of Physics at London University's Birkbeck College. "Until then," says Hasted, "I'd been an experimental physicist and written two books, *The Physics of Atomic Collisions* and *Aqueous Dielectrics,* but had done no work in parapsychology, a subject which had not the slightest interest for me until the appearance of the Geller in London."

In Iceland, Hasted reviewed the highlights of experiments that he made on more than a dozen English children who, inspired by Geller, had discovered that they, too, possessed the ability, when seated at distance from them, to bend keys and other metallic objects as carefully monitored by Hasted's sensitive strain gauges. Ten thousand signals from the gauges appeared on his chart recorder to register what seemed interpretable as actually bending in the metal. Referring to Hasted's experiments, as well as those on distant viewing performed at the Stanford Research Institute, Dr. Olivier Costa de Beauregard, specialist in relativistic and quantum mechanical theory at Paris's *Institut Henri Poincaré,* commented: "Measured by all rigorous criteria of science, the experiments were meticulously performed on the basis of tight protocols and appropriate methods of evaluation. They should reasonably convince anybody."

An extraordinary occurrence with one of his experimental subjects has led Hasted to the belief that the motion of a rod in the hands of a dowser can come about *both* because of involuntary movements by the dowser's muscles, the more usual case, *and* because of an external force independent of the dowser. As he explained in the summer of 1978: "A few months ago, my assistant David Robertson obtained a video-tape recording of a most unexpected character. I was working with a 15-year old girl, Julie Knowles, who lives in Trowbridge, Wiltshire. She's always been a particularly patient subject, scrupulously honest in her work.

"I gave her a thin rod of aluminum measuring 50 cms. long and 0.8 mms. × 0.8 mms. in cross-section, rather flexible, like a dowsing wand, but not something that would bend without considerable force being applied to it. On several occasions, some

305

A collection of aluminum and brass strips decoratively formed by Julie Knowles in fifty minutes flat. Professor John Hasted, Department of Physics, Birkbeck College, University of London. Bowls of dessert spoons reshaped by Julie Knowles. (Photographs courtesy of Professor John Hasted, Birkbeck College, University of London, United Kingdom.)

of my young subjects have been able to cause this kind of rod to collapse at a given point along its axis just by pointing one of their fingers at it. The metal strangely softens at that point and, whoops, the rod bends.

"This time, Julie was holding the rod vertically and being careful to prevent its wobbling or whipping about when, suddenly, the top part of the rod began to arc toward her for a few inches just as if it were being pulled by an invisible thread. Julie wasn't so much surprised by this strange behavior as she was worried that I would think she was trying to trick me, and the video camera, by covertly pulling on it in some manner. She said

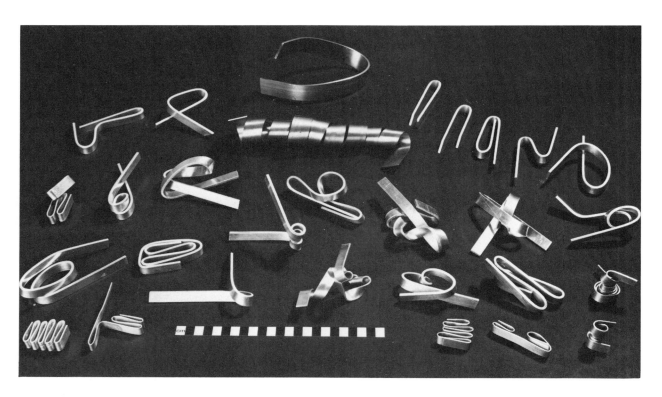

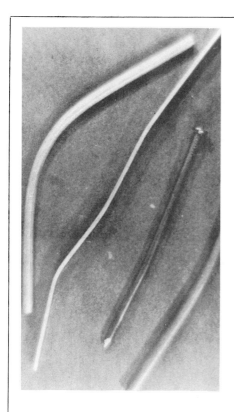

"In this article we have described a certain number of deformations and transformations of metals obtained under unusual conditions. The places where these tests took place and the people who observed them varied. The only constant presence common to all these tests was that of Jean Pierre Girard himself. There was consequently a correlation between his presence and the apparition of the particular effects observed. It would thus seem that we have the right to say that Jean Pierre Girard is part of the "cause" of these effects. But, during these deformations or transformations, we neither observed nor recorded any intervention on his part of muscular force, or physical effects, capable of producing them.

"In this article we have not at all had the intention of imposing our conclusions as complete scientific truths. But we have believed it our duty objectively to set forth the conditions and results of these experiments. We have not found an explanation for the observed effects either in present-day physics or in potential trickery or cheating, but, others, perhaps, may imagine some." C. Crussard, Pechiney-Ugine-Kuhlmann, Paris; and J. Bouvaist, Centre de Recherces Aluminum Pechiney, Voreppe, France. "Etude de Quelques Déformations et Transformations Apparement Anormales de Metaux" (Study of Apparently Abnormal Deformations and Transformations of Metals), *Mémoires Scientifiques Revue Métallurgie*, February 1978.

rather plaintively: 'I can't help it . . . it keeps bending toward me.'

When she pushed against what seemed to be a force, it was as if she were pushing against nothing but the surrounding air. The rod's upper end still kept bending backward and seemed to be held in that position. After it held that way for many seconds, she pressed it hard against the air to see if it would actually reach its yield point and make a permanent bend. That's exactly what happened. It bent into an angle just as if it had been pressed against a solid wall."

Hasted was nonplussed. Until that moment he had attributed all metal bending produced by his subjects either to *dislocations,* well-known in crystal physics, paranormally produced in the metal or to *quasi-viscous creep* caused by an intermelting of a few layers of atoms (an equally "paranormal" event) as could be seen at high magnification in an electron microscope. Now he surmises that a *quasi-force* that he calls a "surface of action" can be extended from a subject as an invisible plane. The details of how this plane functions, to be presented in Hasted's forthcoming book, *The Metal Benders,* may put an end to the age-old controversy among dowsers about the cause of the rod's movement.

The "Waviness" of Things

The latest physical experiments reveal that the *transmitting* mind, as in metal bending, is able to affect the atomic structure of matter as well as to project an undefined force. The *receiving* mind, as in dowsing, apprehends information.

The latest advances in information theory hold that reception is easier than transmission because it is more difficult to *inject* information into a given set of conditions than to *extract* information from it. Here, the term "information" is used not in the ordinary sense of a "gain in knowledge," so much as in the Aristotelian sense of an "organizing power." Aristotle used the example of a sculptor who injects information into a block of marble to create a work of art in order to illustrate his concept.

As French physicist Costa de Beauregard wittily adds: "While the acquisition of random knowledge is cheap, as any recipient of junk mail is aware, the production of specific information is dear, as anyone who has paid for an engineering drawing has discovered. An observer thus pays a bargain price for his admittance to the theater where his consciousness can then become an actor at very high wages."

Even more remarkable is that mind, in its power to organize information, seems able to overcome the *space* barrier, as in map-dowsing or remote viewing. This conclusion goes against the grain of ordinary logic because science has so long instilled in us the idea that physical objects separated in space can only be affected by mechanical forces or the action of an unexplained field such as gravity. Cued by this dictum, psychology maintains that brains, whether those of ants, lizards, whales, or human beings, are *discrete* and thus linkable only by signals such as sounds, (including speech) or symbols (including writing).

Ever since particles so small as to be unobservable have been discovered in microphysics, they have posed gnawing questions about the discreteness of any individual object. Particles also behave as waves, and when they do, they lose a unique property: a *fixed location* in space. They can exist simultaneously *anywhere* in the universe.

308

The *nonlocality* of micro-objects shatters our everyday view of affairs. A "micro-basketball," however bizarre it may seem, can be in the hall closet, the attic, and the cellar all at the same time. Despite our unshakeable certainty that "real" basketballs cannot behave so irrationally, it turns out that they, too, may also have a kind of omnipresence. This is because a new branch of physics known as *holography* reveals that macro-objects have a wave structure allowing them to appear anywhere in the cosmos though in greater or lesser amounts of concentration or definition. The basketball is substantially more "wavy" in the closet than in the cellar or the attic or, say, near one of the moons of Jupiter.

In holography, images of objects can be produced on film that reveals only a pattern of dots or lines having no apparent connection with the object photographed. By beaming laser light on the same film a three-dimensional image of the object is made to appear not on the film itself but *at some distance from it.* The holographically-made film possesses an additional extraordinary property. If divided in two, either of its two *halves* is capable of emitting an image of the *whole* originally photographed object. If the halves are then quartered, each quarter section of film will also reveal the original object as will eighth, sixteenth, and thirty-second parts of the film which, in fact, can be cut into miniscule pieces, all of which can reflect the object *in toto*. The only thing lost in the subdivision is detail. The image of the object becomes fuzzily less distinct, until Miss America may be indistinguishable from her grandmother.

Physics maintains that holographic images that can be seen but not felt are what are known as "standing waves" of light. By extending the holographic principle to the world of macro-objects, one may visualize any of them not only as a mass of solid substance but as a conglomerate of waves. This is the view of some Soviet researchers as reported in a new book, *Parapsychology and Contemporary Science*, written in Russian by a biophysicist, Alexander Dubrov, and a psychologist, Veniamin Pushkin, a work which they hold to represent "the first steps toward the establishment of the science of the future, the science of the twenty-first century, in the understanding of its laws and interconnections, its axioms and postulates."

If one combines this view of the "waviness" of objects with the possible ability of the mind, in its receiving mode, to *tune* to the specific frequencies of an object's wave spectrum, one may be approaching at least one explanation for map dowsing or distant viewing. A sought-for object could be contacted through its omnipresent wave structure and traced back to its actual physical location, the source of the waves' emission. In this sense, every object is a broadcasting station, as the great Bengali scientist, Sir Jagadis Chandra Bose, proposed over seventy years ago with his finding that all things in the universe, animate and inanimate, pulse with life.

The same idea could also help to explain a strange anomaly experienced by dowsers over many decades: *remenence*. After locating an underground object, say, a treasure, dowsers dig down to find it missing, though many physical signs of its former presence at the spot indicated remain. Searches for missing

309

persons also have often ended with the same annoying result, the dowser being informed that, yes, the person sought was in fact at the location pinpointed but has since moved on. It might be that remenence is tied to a concentration of waves from a sought object that remain behind after its displacement, this concentration being much stronger than in other parts of the universe but not as strong as at the site of the object itself.

Beyond Time

Just as the information-organizing mind seems capable of transcending the space barrier, so it also has the apparent power to dispose of time as a reality. Distant viewers at the Stanford Research Institute have been able to "home in" on locations not just where target persons actually *were* but where they *would be* at some precise moment in the future. These locations were determined *before* they were fixed by the experimenters or made known to the subjects of search.

The explanation of this disturbing paradox begins with the astronomer gazing into the infinite through a telescope. When a star or a whole galaxy heaves into view, what he actually sees is *not* what these bodies *are* but what they *used to be*—hundreds, thousands, and even millions of years ago, the time depending on how long it takes light, moving at a speed of 300,000 kilometers per second to travel from the body to the telescope. In this sense, a being looking at the earth from a distant orb, with the help of some light-dependent futuristic telescope capable of focusing accurately on our planet's surface, would see not what is taking place today but historical or prehistorical events: the volcanic explosion that destroyed Minoan civilization or dinosaurs grazing in their Mezozoic swamps. He would be looking backward in time!

We revolt at this notion because we have been taught to think in terms of only three dimensions. Suppose, for a moment, that we lived on an infinitely thin plane of infinite extension, a world limited to only two dimensions. In such a "flatland," creatures, however intelligent, would have only length and breadth. Heightless, they could not even *think* of rising or falling.

If, one day, a sphere were to pass through their world, flatlanders would be able to see it first only as a point as it initially touched their plane, then as a widening circle until it passed halfway through the plane, finally as a circle shrinking back to a point again before it disappeared from the flat world entirely. If they approached the plane base down, a cube would be perceived only as a square, a four-sided pyramid as a square shrinking to a point.

All this is so far easy to visualize if only because it can be illustrated on paper. The *fourth* dimension, like the smell of a rose, the buzzing of a bee, the taste of something sweet or the feel of something slimy, cannot be visually represented but it is nonetheless real. Einstein called it time, or velocity, and it has two important attributes: It cannot travel faster than the speed of light and it contains, along with the other three dimensions, all of modern physics.

310

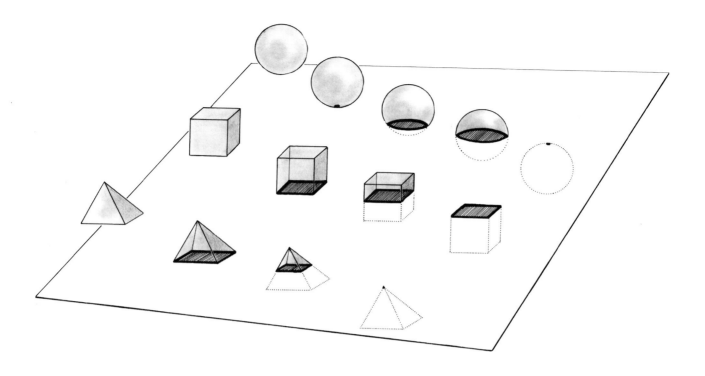

Three-dimensional objects passing through a two-dimensional "flatland" (objects as seen by "flatlanders").

This is why some researchers have resorted to models incorporating *more* than four dimensions to account for such mental acrobatics as map dowsing, clairvoyance, and precognition. These "other universes" are as indescribably strange to the "man in the street" as that same man's comfortable universe of three dimensions would be to "flatlanders." In them, it is proposed that things can happen at speeds faster than that of light and "time" itself can move not only in one, but in any, direction. Consequently, objects no longer have to move from one point to another. They can be at one point, then suddenly at another, without moving. In the process, the need for *causality*—the relationship between cause and effect—disappears.

Proponents of a multidimensional universe believe that only such a medal can provide an explanation for such mysteries as unidentified flying objects (UFOs) and extraterrestrial intelligences (ETIs). Such is the approach of Tom Bearden, a retired U.S. Army officer working at a Huntsville, Alabama, consulting firm, who holds that *mind* may be "an entire universe in itself." Any thought about an object whether present or missing, he declares, is "as physical and solid" in the mind universe as the same objects are in the physical world. Confiding that "dowsers are only detecting their *selves*, entities which include the whole of the known universe, the earth, the sun, the stars, or whatever," he unwittingly harks back to the intuitions of Johann Wilhelm Ritter, the early nineteenth century advocate of *siderism.* Bearden also

311

insists, like Wigner, that a new science must emerge to unite mind with matter and believes dowsing can point the way to this union.

Will the addition of new dimensions help to elucidate the mystery of dowsing and kindred enigmas? Or are they to be seen as unnecessary burdens swelling the baggage train of an expedition into the wilderness? Is a point of view, or an intent really all that is necessary? Two automobilists speeding in opposite directions up and down a winding mountain road cannot see the hairpin turn which will ultimately cause their head-on collision. A person atop the same mountain with full view of the same road and all its bends could predict the fatal accident by *seeing the future before it occurred* or, to put it more concisely, the "potential present."

"Seeing the potential present," an apt definition for the dowsing art, can provide all of us with a view of the future more exhilarating than the scenarios offered by morning headlines. At the practical level, it can help to solve problems as no other method can. Zaboj Harvalik is not the only scientist to avail himself of the talents of a dowser as expert as Frances Farrelly. Another is William Tiller, professor of materials science at California's Stanford University who admits that her answers to his queries received from "God knows where" have been useful to Tiller because, as he admits, "they helped to steer my thinking, sometimes into quite new channels that I haven't sufficiently considered."

To Tiller, the question-and-answer method of information dowsing "became like the scrapings and gougings a sculptor makes in creating a new work of art out of a shapeless mass of clay. In conventional science, one can often obtain this service from one's scientific peers and colleagues. In this new area of science, no commonly accepted model exists that can be used as a basis for discussion and few, if any, scientifically trained colleagues exist who would tolerate such extravagant ideas. Thus, one has few sources of mental nourishment for stimulation and help in the whittling process required to transform a new and vague concept into a precise and effective tool. In such a barren desert, the few Frances Farrelly's of the world function as much needed oases for stumbling explorers. God bless them!"

The tribute is a fitting conclusion for this book. Having long been adept at finding water to create oases on the face of the earth, today dowsers are beginning to open new life-springs into the wasteland of our limited philosophy. Accepting the idea that their psyches have subtleties they do not fully understand, they draw upon ingredients unrecognized, perhaps unrecognizable, by contemporary science. Their acquiescence ranges all the way from the pragmatic to the sublime—from Dr. Peter Treadwell's "we use methods that are profitable whether they are scientifically explainable or not," to Paul Brown's "what I have done is what any man can do with the right spiritual approach, and that approach is the truly scientific one."

No words can more eloquently urge us, as stewards of the earth and its residents, to develop our divining powers.

312

APPENDIX

The accent on the revelation of physical influences may in itself lead to the discovery of undreamed-of physical properties of our planet. More than forty years ago a physician, Dr. Francois Peyre of Bagnoles del Orne, France, reported at an international congress on radio-biology held in Paris that his dowsing had discovered a checkerboard pattern of emanations. Each square measured 4 × 4 meters, rising perpendicularly from the ground. The pattern seemed to cover the earth like a fish-net and was oriented in a magnetic, rather than in a geographic, north-south and east-west direction.

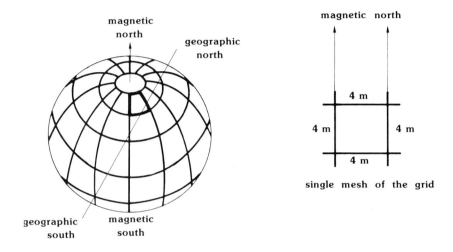

Orientation of universal earth grid according to Peyre.

The grid was later studied by a German factory director, Siegfried Wittman, who concluded from his dowsing that its meshes, which he termed "polarized fields," were oriented NW-SE with respect to the magnetic pole and measured 16 meters on a side.

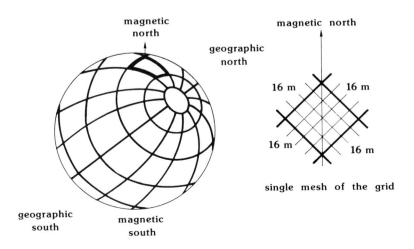

Orientation of universal earth grid according to Wittman.

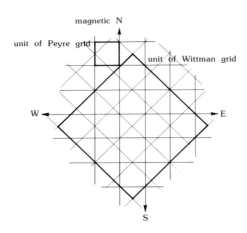

The intersection of the grids.

These findings did not necessarily conflict with Peyre's because the German's grid can be neatly superimposed on the Frenchman's.

Working with Wittman, the German physician, Manfred Curry, Director of the Medical-Bioclimatic Institute in Riederau/Ammersee, came to the conclusion that an unidentified energy radiation was emitted at places where lines of the grid intersect. This radiation could cause as much harm to persons who spent extended periods of time above the intersecting lines as the telluric emanations associated with water veins.

One of the most important figures in the establishment of a link between noxious telluric radiation and disease is a German doctor and balneologist from Eberbach on the Neckar River, Ernst Hartmann, founder of the world's first Society for Geobiological Research, editor of its German-language journal *Weather, Soil Man,* and author of a book *Sickness as a Problem of Location.*

When Hartmann began his own careful study based on the foregoing research, he found that the meshes of his *Globalnetzgitter,* or universal grid, as he christened it, were oriented to magnetic north just as Peyre had claimed but, far from being perfect squares, they measured 2 meters on their N-S axes and 2.5 meters on their E-W axes, at least at the latitude of his home town Eberbach/Neckar, 49.28°N.* Hartmann added that his dowsing indicated the breadth of the same energy-emitting lines to be respectively twenty-five and fifteen centimeters and that, if their intersections coincided with water veins, their potential lethal effect was greatly increased.

Hartman's universal grid.

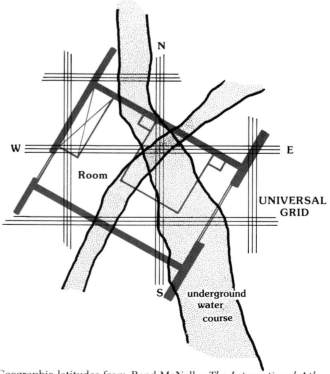

*Geographic latitudes from Rand-McNally: *The International Atlas,* Rand McNally & Co., Chicago, Illinois, 1969.

314

The first American to attack the problem of the grid was Dr. Zaboj Harvalik who, after discussing it with European dowsers, gained the impression that insight into the meaning of its magnetic orientation was lacking. Working over open ground in Ried, Switzerland (42.12°N), and Dornbirn, Austria (46.25°N), he teamed with his brother Vincent, a professional cartographer, and Wilhelm de Boer to dowse out grid dimensions of each location. Using white tape the three dowsers marked out the interlocking meshes of the grid at separate corners of the area they had selected. When they met at the center, all three patterns neatly overlapped, confirming the fact that each dowser had independently measured a similar orientation and a common set

When compared to the geographic latitudes at which they were dowsed, the E-W grid dimensions show no correspondence:

	Reykjavik Iceland	Hårbølle Denmark	Dornbirn Austria	Ried Switzerland	Danville Vermont	Lorton Virginia
Geographic Latitude (Decreasing)	64.09°N	54.49°N	47.25°N	46.12°N	44.25°N	38.50°N
E-W Grid Dimension Measured by Dowsing	0.95 m.	1.26 m.	1.48 m.	1.5 m.	1.5 m.	1.7 m.

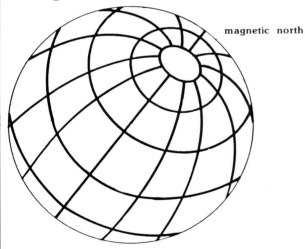

magnetic north

The Universal Grid oriented to magnetic north. It can be seen that as the grid meshes proceed northward, their N-S dimensions could remain constant at 2 meters while their E-W dimensions must necessarily shorten. This suggests some kind of correspondence between the E-W grid dimensions and *magnetic* latitudes at which they were dowsed, as revealed below:

	Reykjavik Iceland	Danville Vermont	Lorton Virginia	Hårbølle Denmark	Dornbirn Austria	Ried Switzerland
Magnetic Latitude (Decreasing)	63.36°N	56.13°N	53.3°N	47.48°N	41.14°N	40.50°N
E-W Grid Dimension Measured by Dowsing (Increasing)	1.2 m.	1.5 m.	1.7 m.	1.84 m.	2.04 m.	2.06 m.

of dimensions which turned out to be 2 meters long in a N-S direction, just like Hartmann's at Eberbach, but 2.3 and 2.25 meters in an E-W direction at Ried and Dornbirn respectively.

Harvalik went on to dowse grids at Hårbølle, Denmark (54.49°N), Reykjavik, Iceland (64.09°N), Danville, Vermont (44.25° N), and at his home in Lorton, Virginia (38.65°N). At each of these sites the dimensions of the N-S axes was still 2 meters but those of the E-W axes, ranging from a maximum of only 1.7 meters at Lorton to a minimum of 1.2 meters at Reykjavik, were further at variance with Hartmann's measurements.

When Harvalik compared the E-W dimensions obtained at the six locations with their *geographic* latitudes, he could see no meaningful correlation between them. By using a relevant spherical trigonometric formula, he then transposed the geographic north pole at 90°N to the *magnetic* north pole on Canada's Bathurst Island at 76.10°N, 100°W, whereupon a rough correlation between the two parameters was evident. As values for the magnetic latitude decreased, so did those for the dimensions measured by dowsing.

	Reykjavik Iceland	Danville Vermont	Hårbølle Denmark	Lorton Virginia	Dornbirn Austria	Ried Switzerland
Magnetic Inclination (Dip Angle)	75.73°	72.8°	69.07°	69.05°	63.11°	61.79°
E-W Grid Dimension Measured by Dowsing	1.2 m.	1.5 m.	1.7 m.	1.7 m.	2.25 m.	2.3 m.

Dip needles have also been used as crude "mechanical dowsers" for more than three centuries. Their most recent application to water location is that of George Jamieson, president of Accurate Water Location in Poughkeepsie, New York. His dip needle, christened an "aquatometer," is swung from an aluminum rack attached like a knapsack on the operator's back such that it hangs directly in front of his nose. With the help of another compass fixed to the rack in the normal horizontal position, the apparatus is carried southeast to northwest along tracks about nine feet apart. When the dip needle, e.g. preset at the 35° point on the 360° face of the compass, comes directly over a water vein, it is deflected by the weak magnetic field associated with it. The various points of deflection along the tracks are linked up to trace the course of the vein itself.

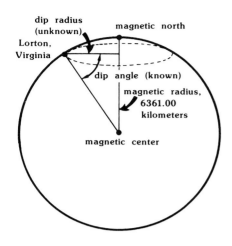

Harvalik's dip needle.

At this point Harvalik recalled that a dip needle, a compass oriented vertically rather than horizontally with respect to the earth's surface, points through the earth to measure the dip angle, or inclination, from its surface to its magnetic center. He therefore consulted a "Magnetic Inclination or Dip, Epoch 1975.0 map published by the U.S. Defense Mapping Agency's Hydrographic Center that records magnetic inclination, updated it to 1978.5 epoch, and charted the dip angle values for the locations at which he had dowsed dimensions for the universal grid. This time an even better correlation appeared between the two sets of data.

If the dip angle is known for any location, a corresponding dip *radius* can be calculated, using a formula in which one side of a right triangle, representing the earth's magnetic radius, is constant at 6361.00 kilometers.

The calculated radius can be used in another equation where the constant is the dimension of the E-W grid mesh at Lorton, 1.7 meters, as repeatedly checked. The dimension of an E-W grid mesh can then be calculated for any place on earth. If, for instance, one wants to know the dimension for Miami, Florida, the simplified equation reads:

$$\text{E-W grid Dimension Miami} = \frac{\cos \text{dip angle, Miami}}{\cos \text{dip angle, Lorton}} \times 1.7 = 2.56 \text{ in.}$$

Using the same equation Harvalik calculated the grid mesh dimensions for the five locations he had dowsed in Switzerland, Austria, Iceland, Vermont, and Denmark and found them to correspond very closely.

	Ried Switzerland	*Dornbirn Austria*	*Reykjavik Iceland*	*Danville Vermont*	*Hårbølle Denmark*
Inclination/ East-West Grid Dimension (calculated)	*2.25*	*2.16*	*1.17*	*1.5*	*1.7*
E-W Grid Dimension Measured by Dowsing	*2.3*	*2.25*	*1.2*	*1.5*	*1.7*
% of error	*2.2*	*4.0*	*2.5*	*0*	*0*

So far there is no explanation for the existence of the universal grid, which may have a cosmic origin dependent or independent of the earth's location in space. It may also be related to certain features of the earth's geosphere, including atmospheric phenomena such as the ionization layers of jet streams and deep or shallow magnetic structures within the earth itself, whether linked to the earth's rotation or not. If the work of Louis Romani, Director of Paris's Eiffel Laboratory, is confirmed, the nodes of the grid are able markedly to slow down the movement of a torsional pendulum in an extremely accurate "Atmos" clock which is perpetually wound by the influence of changes in ambient temperature on the state of a fluid incorporated into its works.

Those fascinated with mathematical regularity will be interested to note that exactly 8,400,000 E-W grid mesh dimensions make up the circumference of a circle, the radius of which is equivalent to the dip radius corresponding to them.*

Dr. Zaboj Harvalik explains features of the universal grid to Malcolm Stewart, English film director.

Dr. Zaboj Harvalik and Wilhelm de Boer laying out a portion of the universal grid at Harvalik's Lorton, Virginia home next to the Potomac River.

*In October, 1978, Dr. Zaboj V. Harvalik added that with the aid of a 12-metric diameter copper wire coil of two turns, inclined 7° (North magnetic-South magnetic direction) to the horizontal thus simulating a geographic latitude of 31.50° (from 38.50°) and energized with a DC electric current, he was able to modify the local dip angle of 69.05° to any dip angle desired by regulating the intensity of the current flow through the coil. The result of this artificially altered dip angle produced a change of the ambient 1.7 meter E-dimension of the Universal Grid, e.g., when the dip angle was 85°, the dimension was 0.4 meters and when the dip angle was 30° the dimension 4.1 meters. The North-South Grid dimension was not changed; it stayed at 2.0 meters. These observations suggest that the Universal Grid is of magnetic nature. Slight dip angle changes owing to increased solar activity, tectonic dislocations, etc., cause a temporary change of the E-W Grid dimensions. These observations would rule out any cosmic origin of the Universal Grid. It is therefore very likely that the grid is of purely terrestrial origin, temporarily influenced by cosmic factors.

318

BIBLIOGRAPHY

(Each reference is listed in the first chapter to which it pertains. If it pertains to additional chapters, it is not relisted.)

Gratitudes

Barrett, William F., "On the So-Called Divining Rod or Virgula Divina," *Proceedings of the Society for Psychical Research,* July, 1894.

Barrett, Sir William Fletcher and Theodore Besterman, *The Divining-Rod, An Experimental and Psychological Investigation,* Methuen and Co., London, 1926.

Klinckowstroem, Count Carl von, *Die Wünschelrute als Wissenschaftliches Problem mit Anhang: Geophysikalische Aufschlussmethoden* (The Divining Rod as a Scientific Problem with Appendix: Interpretive Geophysical Methods), Stuttgart, 1922.

Introduction: The Substance of Dowsing

Borlase, William, *The Natural History of Cornwall,* Oxford, 1758.

Del Rio, Martin, *Disquisitionum Magicarum* (Treatise on Magic), 3 vols., Mainz, 1593.

Encyclopedia of Philosophy, 8 vols., Macmillan and The Free Press, New York, 1967.

Gutierrez, Alfonso, *Physica Speculatio* (Speculative Philosophy), Mexico, 1557.

Hooson, William, *The Miner's Dictionary,* Wrexham, 1747.

Hyman, Ray and Evon Z. Vogt, *Water Witching: U.S.A.,* University of Chicago Press, Chicago, 1959.

Jago, Frederick W. P., *An English-Cornish Dictionary,* Simpkin Marshall and Co., London, 1887.

Lakhovsky, Georges, *La Cabale: Histoire d'une Decouverte (L'Oscillation Cellulaire)* (The Cabal: History of a Discovery [Cellular Oscillation]), G. Doin, Paris, 1934.

Locke, John, *Some Considerations on the Consequences of the Lowering of Interest,* London, 1692.

Mager, Henri, *Les Sourciers et Leurs Procédés* (Dowsers and Their Methods), H. Dunod et Pinat, Paris, 1913.

Ogburn, Charles, *Adventure of Birds,* Morrow, New York, 1976.

Parapsychology Bulletin, Duke University Press.

Pryce, William, *Mineralogia Cornubiensis* (Mineralogy of Cornwall), J. Phillips, London, 1778.

Quarterly Mining Review, 1831.

Rae, Malcolm, "The Scope and Limitation of Radiesthetic Investigation," in Westlake, A. T. and Malcolm Rae, *The Radiesthetic (or Dowsing) Faculty,* Sandy Balls, Godshill, Fordingbridge, Hampshire, 1973.

Targ, Russell and Harold Puthoff, *Mind-Reach,* Delacorte, New York, 1977.

Viré, Armand, *Comment Devenir Sourcier, Ce Que J'ai Vu, Ce Que J'ai Fait* (How to Become a Dowser, What I've Seen and What I've Done), Librairie J-B Baillière, Paris, 1948.

Young, Arthur M., *The Reflexive Universe,* Delacorte, New York, 1976

Chapter 1: Three Professionals

An extended auto trip with Jack Livingston from California's Marin County to the Sierra Nevada in the late spring of 1977 provided a good portion of the substance for this chapter. Also consulted:

Anderson, Jim, "The Dowsers—Those Who Witch for Water Find Business Booming in California," *The Sacramento Bee* (Scene Section, page 1), March 13, 1977.

Ground Water Age, August and October, 1970.

Plimpton, Robert B. "The Millionaires and the Dowser," chapter from an unpublished manuscript, no date.

Chapter 2:
The Non-Subject

Through Jack Livingston I met and had extended and delightful conversations with Francis Lindsay. Also consulted:

Cameron, Verne, *Aquavideo: Locating Underground Water*, El Cariso Publications, Elsinore, California, 1970.

D'Aulaire, Ola, "The Forked Stick Phenomenon," *The Reader's Digest*, May 1976.

"Die erfolgreichen Roche-Wünschelruten-wassersucher" (The Successful Roche Water Dowsers), *Roche-Zeitung*, Hoffman-LaRoche, Basel, December 1972.

Ellis, Arthur J., *The Divining Rod: A History of Water Witching*, Water Supply Paper 416, U.S. Geological Survey, U.S. Government Printing Office, 1917.

Layne, Meade, *The Cameron Aurameter*, Borderland Sciences Research Foundation, Vista, California, 1952.

"Water Dowsing," U.S. Geological Survey brochure, 1977.

"Water Witching," U.S. Geological Survey brochure, 1966.

Chapter 3:
From Divination to Dowsing

Archaeology, Israel Pocket Library, Keter Publishing House, Jerusalem, 1974.

Besterman, Theodore, "The Divining Rod," *The Occult Review*, Vol. 38, 1923.

Callaway, Bishop H., *The Religious System of the Amazulu*, Natal, 1870.

Codrington, R. H., *The Melanesians*, Oxford, 1891.

Conrad of Würzburg, *Engelhard*, Leipzig, 1884.

———, *Goldene Schmiede* (The Golden Smithy), Berlin, 1840.

———, *Lieder und Sprüche* (Songs and Sayings), Vienna, 1871.

———, *Der Trojanische Krieg* (The Trojan War), Literarischer Verein, 1858.

Contenau, Georges, *La Divination chez les Assyrians et Les Babyloniens* (Divination Among the Assyrians and the Babylonians), Payot, Paris, 1940.

Le Dragon Rouge ou L'Art de Commander les Esprits (The Red Dragon or the Art of Commanding Spirits), Célestes, Nismes, 1823.

Flacelière, Robert, *Greek Oracles*, Elek Books, London, 1965.

Hauber, Eberhard David, *Bibliotheka Acta et Scripta Magica* (A Collection of Magical Deeds and Writings), Lemgo, 1738.

Hsü, Chin-hsiung, *The Menzies Collection of Shang Dynasty Oracle Bones*, The Royal Ontario Museum, Toronto, 1972.

Hutchinson, Thomas J., *Two Years in Peru*, London, 1873.

The Living Bible, Paraphrased, Tyndale House Publishers, Wheaton, Illinois, 1971.

Long, Max Freedom, *The Secret Science Behind Miracles*, De Vorss, Los Angeles, 1948.

———, *The Secret Science at Work*, De Vorss, Los Angeles, 1953.

Man, Myth and Magic, an Illustrated Encyclopedia of the Supernatural, Vols. 1–24, Marshall Cavendish Corporation, New York, 1970.

Needham, Joseph, F.R.S., *Science and Civilization in China*, University Press, Cambridge, England, 1959 continuing.

The New American Bible, P. J. Kennedy and Sons, New York, 1970.

Notker, Labeo, *Die Schriften Notkers und seiner Schule* (Notker's Writings and His School), 3 vols., Freiburg/Breisgau, 1882.

Remy, Nicolas, *Demonolatry*, University Books, Secaucus, New Jersey, 1974.

Soymie, Michel, "Sources et Sourciers en Chine" (Water Springs and Water Finders in China), *Bulletin de la Maison Franco-Japonaise*, Nouvelle Série, Vol. VII, No. 1, Tokyo, Paris, 1961.

Swettenham, Sir F. A., *Malay Sketches*, London, 1895.

Valentine, Basil, *Bergwerckschatz* (Mining Treasure), Frankfurt, 1618.

Wu, Jing Nuan, *The I Ching: A New Interpretation and Translation,* unpublished manuscript, no date.

Chapter 4:
The Dawn of Dowsing

Agricola, Georgius, *De Re Metallica* (On Metals), translated by Herbert Clark Hoover and Lou Henry Hoover, Dover Publications, New York, 1950.

Boyle, Robert, *Certain Physiological Essays,* London, 1661.

———, "Articles of Inquiries Touching Mines," *Philosophical Transactions,* Vol. 1, 1665–66.

Del Mar, Alex, *A History of Precious Metals From the Earliest Times to the Present,* G. Bell and Sons, London, 1880.

Dibner, Bern, *Agricola on Metals,* Burndy Library, Norwalk, Connecticut, 1958.

Eglin, Raphael (Heliophilus Percis, pseudonym), *Disquisitio de Helia Artista* (Treatise on the Helian Art), Marpurgi, 1698.

Fludd, Robert, *Philosophia Moysaica* (Mosaic Philosophy), Gouda, 1638.

Gassenid, Pierre, *Opera Omnia* (Complete Works), 1658, 6 volumes.

Harsdorfer, Philipp, *Deliciae physico-mathematicae* (Physico-mathematical Delights), 1636–92.

Kircher, Athanasius, *Magnes sive De Arte Magnetica* (The Magnet or On the Magnetic Art), Cologne, 1643.

———, *Mundus Subterraneus* (The World Below Ground), 2 vols., Amsterdam, 1665.

Krüger, Johann Gottlob, *Geschichte der Erde in den allerältesten Zeiten* (History of the Earth in Most Ancient Times), Halle, 1746.

Löhneyss, George Engelhard, *Bericht vom Bergwerck* (Report on Mines), 1617.

Luther, Martin, *Decem Praecepta* (Ten Precepts), Wittenberg, 1528.

———, *Tischreden* (Table Talks), Eisleben, 1566.

Maksimov, M. M. "Tysyacheletie Otkrytiya" (Thousand-Year-Old Discoveries), *Geologiya Rudnykh Mestorozhdenii* (The Geology of Ore Deposits), No. 5, 1970.

Melanchton, Phillip, *Discours sur la Sympathie* (Discourse on Sympathetic Attraction). No date.

Münster, Sebastian, *Cosmographia Universalis* (Universal Cosmography), Basel, 1550.

Paul, Wolfgang, *Mining Lore,* Morris Printing Company, Portland, Oregon, 1970.

Peucer, Gaspar, *Les Devins* (The Diviners), Antwerp, 1584.

Plattes, Gabriel, *A Discovery of Subterraneall Treasure,* London, 1639.

Praetorius, Johann, *Philogemata Abstrusa de Police* (Hidden Wisdom of the Thumb), Sagani et Lipsiae, 1677.

Reilly, Conor, S.J., *Athanasius Kircher S.J.: Master of a Hundred Arts, 1602–1680,* Band I, Studia Kircheriana, Edizioni del Mondo, Wiesbaden-Rom, 1974.

Rickard, Thomas A., *Man and Metals,* McGraw Hill, New York and London, 1932.

Schott, Gaspar, *Magia Universalis Naturae et Artis, sive recondita naturalium et artificialium rerum scientia* (The Magic of Nature and Art, or Occult Science of Natural and Artificial Things), 4 vols., Wurzburg, 1657–59.

Sperling, Johann and Jacobus Klein, *An Virgula Mercurialis Agat ex Occulta Qualitate?* (Does the Rod of Mercury Act from an Occult Power?), Wittenberg, 1658.

Webster, John, *Metallographia or a History of Metals,* London, 1672.

Willenius, Matthaeus, *De Salis Origine, Tractatus Philosophicus* (On the Origin of Salt, a Philosophic Treatise), Jena, 1671.

Witcombe, Wallace H., *All About Mining*, Longmans, Green, London and New York, 1937.

The Works of the Highly Experienced and Famous Chemist, John Rudolph Glauber: Containing Great Variety of Choice Secrets and Alchemy in the Working of Metallic Mines and the Separation of Metals, translated into English and published for the Publick Good by the Labor, Care and Charge of Christopher Packe, Philochymico-Medicus, London, 1689.

Chapter 5:
Sorciers or Sourciers?

Barba, Alonzo, *Arte de Los Metales* (The Art of Metals), Madrid, 1640.

Bertereau, Martine de, *Véritable Déclaration de la Descouverte des Mines et Minières de France, par le Moyen Desquelles sa Majesté et ses Subjects se Peuvent Passer de Tous les Pays Estrangers; Ensemble des Propriétez d'Aucunes Sources et Eaux Minérales Descouvertes depuis peu de Temps a Chateau-Thierry* (True declaration of the discovery of mines and minerals of France, by means of which his Majesty and his subjects are able to surpass all foreign countries; together with the properties of certain springs and mineral waters discovered a short time ago at Chateau-Thierry), 1632.

————, *La Restitution de Pluton* (The Restitution of Pluto), 1640.

Chauvin, Pierre, *Lettre à Madame la Marquise de Senozan sur les moyens dont on s'est servi pour découvrir les complices d'un assassinat commis à Lyon, le 5 Juillet 1692* (Letter to Madame la Marquise de Senozan on the means employed to discover the accomplices to an assassination committed at Lyons on July 5, 1692), Lyon, 1692.

Comiers, Claude, "La baguette justifiée et ses effets démontrés naturels" (The divining rod justified and its action shown to be natural), *Mercure Galant*, Paris, August 1693.

Galien, Claude, *La Découverte des Eaux Minérales de Chateau-Thierry et de Leurs Propriétés* (The Discovery of the Mineral Waters of Chateau-Thierry and their Properties), Paris, 1630.

Garnier, Pierre, *Dissertation Physique* (Physico-Philosophic Dissertation), Lyon, 1692.

————, *Histoire de la Baguette de Jacques Aymar Pour Faire Toutes Sortes de Découvertes* (History of the Divining Rod of Jacques Aymar for Making all Sorts of Discoveries), Lyon, 1693.

Gobet, Nicolas, *Les Anciens Minéralogistes du Royaume de France* (Former Mineralogists of the French Kingdom), 2 vols., Paris, 1779.

LeBrun, Pierre, *Histoire Critique des Practiques Superstitieuses, qui ont Seduit le Peuple et Embarassé les Scavans* (Critical History of Superstitious Practices which have Seduced the People and Embarrassed the Learned), Rouen, 1701.

————, *Lettres qui Découvrent l'Illusion des Philosophes sur la Baguette, et qui Détruisent Leurs Systemès* (Letters which Expose the Illusion of Philosophers in Regard to the Divining Rod and which Destroy Their Systems), published anonymously, Paris, 1693.

Lettre Sur la Physique Occulte de la Baguette Divinatoire (Letter on the Occult Philosophy of the Divining Rod), *Mercure Galant*, Paris, April 1693.

Menestrier, Claude Francois, *La Philosophie des Images Enigmatiques* (The Philosophy of Enigmatic Appearances), Lyon, 1694.

————, *Réflexions sur les Usages et Les Indications de la Baguette pour Découvrir les Sources d'Eau, les Métaux Cachez, les Vols, les Bornes Déplacés, les Assassinats, etc.* (Reflections on the Uses and Indications of the Rod to Find Underground Water, Hidden Metals, Thefts, Displaced Boundaries, Murders, etc.), Lyon, 1694.

Nicolas, Jean, *La Verge de Jacob ou l'Art de Trouver les Trésors, les Sources,*

322

les Limites, les Métaux, les Mines, les Minéraux et Autres Choses Cachées, par l'Usage du Baton Forché (The Rod of Jacob, or the Art of Finding Treasures, Springs, Boundaries, Metals, Mines, Minerals, and other Hidden Things, by the Use of the Forked Rod), Lyon, 1693.

Panthot, Jean-Baptiste, Traité de la Baguette ou la Recherche des Véritables Usages Auxquels Elle Convient, etc. (Treatise on the Divining Rod, or the Investigation of Genuine Uses to which It is Adapted, etc.), Lyon, 1693.

Porta, G. B. della, Magia Naturalis (Natural Magic), Naples, 1569.

Renaud, André, Critique Sincère de Plusiers Ecrits sur la Fameuse Baguette (Sincere Criticism of Many Writings on the Famous Divining Rod), Lyon, 1693.

Vaginay, Jean, Histoire Merveilleuse d'un Maçon qui, Conduit par la Baguette Divinatoire, a Suivi un Meurtrier pendant Quarante Cinque Heures sur la Terre et Plus de Trente Heures sur l'Eau (Marvelous Story of a Mason who, Led by a Divining Rod, Followed a Murderer for Forty-five Hours over Land and for more than Thirty Hours over Water), Grenoble, 1693.

Vallemont, Abbé de (Pierre Le Lorrain), La Physique Occulte, ou Traité de la Baguette Divinatoire (Occult Philosophy, or Treatise on the Divining Rod), Paris, 1693.

**Chapter 6:
Dowsers Tested—by Skeptics
and Electricity**

Albinus, Theophil, Das entlarvete Idolum der Wünschel-Ruthe (The Exposed Idolatry of the Divining Rod), Leipzig, 1704.

Amoretti, Carlo, "Lettera del Sign Abbé Carlo Amoretti al Prof. Francesco Soave su Alcune Sperienze Electriche" (Letter from Signor Abbé Carlo Amoretti to Prof. Francesco Soave in regard to Certain Electrical Experiments), Opuscoli Scelti sulle Scienze e sulle Arti, Vol. 16, Milan, 1793.

———, "Ricerche Storico-fisiche sulla Raddomanzia ossia sulla Elettrometria Sotteranea" (Historical-physical Researches on Rhabdomancy or on Subterranean Electrometry), Opuscoli Scelti sulle Scienze e sulle Arti, Vol. 20, Milan, 1798.

———, "Ricerche Storiche sulla Raddomanzia" (Historical Researchers on Rhabdomancy), Opuscoli Scelti sulle Scienze e sulle Arti, Vol. 21, Milan, 1801.

———, "Su vari Individui che Hanno la Facolta di Sentire le Sorgenti de Miniere etc." (Concerning Various Individuals who Possess the Faculty of Sensing Springs, Minerals, etc.), Opuscoli Scelti sulle Scienze e sulle Arti, Vol. 19, Milan, 1796.

Bertholon, M. L'Abbé, De L'Eléctricité des Végétaux (On Electricity of Plants), Lyon, 1783.

D'Arcet, J. d' et al., "Observations Faites sur la Vertu de Bléton de Sentir L'Impression des Eaux Souterraines Coulantes" (Observations on the Ability of Bléton to Sense the Impression of Underground Water), in Journal de Paris, June 26, 1782 (see same journal for August 18, 1782, pp. 719–26; September 6, 1782, pp. 1015–17).

Decremps, Henri, La Magie Blanche Dévoilée . . . avec des Réflexions sur la Baguette Divinatoire, etc. (White Magic Exposed . . . with Reflections on the Divining Rod), 3 vols., Paris, 1784–91.

Fabrioni, G. V. M., Vera Vera Verissima Relazione dei Fatti e Detti della Bachetta Divinatoria . . . (A Strictly True Account of the Promises and Performance of the Divining Rod . . .), Florence, 1791.

Feudivirus, H. F., Gebrauch der Berg—und Wünschel-Ruthe (Use of the Ore and Divining Rod), Leipzig, 1763.

Formey, J. H., "Baguette Divinatoire" (The Divining Rod), in *Dictionnaire des Merveilles de la Nature* (Dictionary of Nature's Wonders) by Sigaud de la Fond, 2 vols., Paris, 1781.

Fortis, Abbé Alberto, "Lettera del Abbé Fortis al Sign. Abbé Lazaro Spallanzani sugli Sperimenti di Pennet" (Letter from Abbé Fortis to Signor Abbé Lazaro Spallanzani on the Experiments with Pennet), *Opuscoli Scelti sulle Scienze e sulle Arti,* Vol. 14, Milan, 1791 (see also Spallanzani's reply in same journal).

_____, Abbé Albert, *Mémoires pour Servir a L'Histoire Naturelle et Principalement à l'Oryctographie de l'Italie et des Pays Adjacens* (Memories on the Natural History and Oryctography of Italy and Adjacent Countries), 2 vols., Paris, 1802.

Histoire Véritable et Merveilleuse d'une Jeune Anglaise . . . (The True and Marvelous Story of a Young English Girl . . .), Paris, 1772.

Hooson, William, *The Miners' Dictionary,* Wrexham, 1747.

Jugel, Johann Gottfried, *Geometria subterranea* (Underground Surveying), Leipzig, 1773.

Lalande, J. J., "Lettre sur le Prétendu Hydroscope" (Letter on the So-Called Hydroscope), *Le Mercure de France,* July 2, 1772.

_____, "Lettre sur la Baguette Divinatoire de Bléton" (Letter on Bléton's Divining Rod), *Journal des Scavans,* Paris, 1782.

Ozanam, Jacques and J. E. Montuclo, *Recreations in Mathematics and Natural Philosophy,* translated and edited by Charles Hutton, London, 1803 and 1814.

Rössler, Balthazar, *Speculum Metallurgiae Politissimum* (Mirror of Metallurgy), Dresden, 1700.

Thouvenel, Pierre, *Mémoire Physique et Médicinal montrant des Rapports Evidents entre les Phénomènes de la Baguette Divinatoire, du Magnétisme Animale et de l'Electricité* (Physical and Medical Memoir Showing the Evident Relations between the Phenomena of the Divining Rod and Animal Magnetism and Electricity), Paris, 1781.

_____, *Nuovi Ragguagli dell' Esperienze d' Elettrometria Organica* (New Data on an Experiment in Organic Electrometry), Venice, 1794.

_____, *Second Mémoire Physique et Médicinal* (Second Physical and Medical Memoir), Paris, 1784.

Zeidler, Johann Gottfried, *Pantomysterium, oder das Neue vom Jahre in der Wünschelrute . . .* (All Mystery or News of the Year Contained in the Divining Rod . . .), Magdeburg, 1700.

Chapter 7:
Physical or Sidereal: A
Pendular Question

Amoretti, Carlo, "Dell'azione di Varie Sostanze Sopra Altre Sostenute Pendenti su di Esse Sperimenti del Fu Alberto Fortis" (On the Action of Various Substances Supported Above Others Based on Experiments Made by the late Alberto Fortis), *Soc. Ital. delle Scienze Mem.,* Vol. 13, Modena, 1806.

_____, *Della Raddomanzia ossia Eletrometria Animale* (On Rhabdomancy or Animal Electrometry), Milan, 1808.

Aretin, C. F. von, *Beyträge zur litterarischen Geschichte der Wünschelruthe (Contributions to the Literary History of the Dowsing Rod),* Munich, 1807.

Baader, F. X. von, *Samtliche Werke* (Complete Works), Leipzig 1851, Aalen, 1963.

Bähr, Johann Karl, *Der dynamische Kreis die naturliche Reihenfolge der Elemente und Zusammengesetzten Korper, als Resultat der Beobachtung ihrer dynamischen Wirksamkeit.* (The Dynamic Circle.) The natural sequence of elements and composite bodies as a result of observations of their dynamic activi'y), Verlag von Waldemar Turk, Dresden, 1861.

"Candi," pseudonym for Cunibert Mohlberg, *Radiesthetische Studien—Briefe an Tschü* (Radiesthetic Studies—Letters to Tschü), RGS publishers, Sankt Gallen, 1970.

Chevreul, Michel E., *De la Baguette Divinatoire et du Pendule Dit Explorateur* (On the Divining Rod and the So-Called Exploratory Pendulum), Mallet-Bachelier, Paris, 1854.

Christophe, Emile, *La Téléradiesthésie* (Teleradiesthesia), Editions de la Revue des Independents, Paris, 1933.

————, *Tu Seras Sourcier* (You Will Be a Dowser), Editions Vallot, Paris, 1930.

Fortis, Abbé Albert, "Mémoire sur les Pendules 'Electrometres'" (Memoir on "Electrometric" Pendulums), *Soc. Ital. Sci. Exactes*, Vol. 13, 1806.

Gehlen, Adolph Ferdinand, "Nachrichten von den neuern durch Francesco Campetti wieder rege gewordenen Versuchen über Pendel, Baguette, etc." (News About New Tests Revived by Francesco Campetti on the Pendulum, Divining Rod, etc.), *Journale für die Chemie, Physik und Mineralogie*, Vol. 4, Munich, 1807.

Gerboin, Antoine Clement, *Recherches Expérimentales sur un Nouveau Mode de l'Action Electrique* (Experimental Research on a New Mode of Electrical Action), Strasbourg, 1808.

Gilbert, L. W., *Kritische Aufsätze über die in München wieder erneuten Versuche mit Schwefelkiespendeln und Wünschelruthen* (Critical Essays on Renewed Experiments in Munich with Magic Pendulums and Divining Rods), Halle, 1808.

Klemm, Friederich and Armin Hermann, *Briefe eines Romantischen Physikers . . .* (Letters of a Romantic Physicist . . .), Heinz Moos Verlag, Munich, 1966.

Mermet, Abbé Alexis, *Le Pendule Révélateur ou Moyen de Découvrir les Corps Cachés et les Maladies de Près ou à Distance, sur Plan ou sur Photographie* (The Revealing Pendulum as a means of Discovering Hidden Bodies and Illnesses, Nearby or at Distance, on a Map or a Photograph), Cognac, 1928.

————, *Comment J'Opère* (How I Work), Maison de la Radiesthesie, 1934.

————, *Abrégé de Ma Méthode* (A Short Description of My Method), Alsatia, 1938.

————, *La Radiesthésie* (Radiesthesia), Alsatia, 1938.

Paoli, P., "Sperimenti col Pendolo" (Experiments with the Pendulum), *Nuova Scelta d'Opuscoli Interessanti sulle Scienze e sulle Arti*, Vol. 2, Milan, 1807.

Reichenbach, Karl L. F. Freiherr von, *Physico-Physiological Researches on the Dynamics of Magnetism, Heat, Light, Electricity and Chemism, in their Relations to Vital Force*, J. S. Redfield, New York, 1851.

Resch, Andreas, *Zur Geschichte und Theorie des Siderischen Pendels mit Bericht über Eigene Experimente* (On the History and Theory of the Sidereal Pendulum with a Report about My Own Experiments), Ph.D. dissertation, Leopold-Franzensuniversität, Innsbruck, Austria, January 1967.

Ritter, Johann Wilhelm, *Der Siderismus* (Siderism), Tübingen, 1808.

Tromp, S. W., *Psychical Physics: A Scientific Analysis of Dowsing, Radiesthesia and Kindred Divining Phenomena*, Elsevier Publishing Company, New York etc., 1949.

Wetzels, Walter D., *Johann Wilhelm Ritter: Physik im Wirkungsfeld der Deutschen Romantik* (Johann Wilhelm Ritter: Physics in the Purview of German Romanticism), Walter de Gruyter, Berlin and New York, 1973.

Wüst, Joseph, "Messungen der Polarisationskapazität und Leitfähigkeit am Körper von Rutlern und Pendlern" (Measurements of Polarization Capacity and Conductivity of Bodies by Rod and Pendulum Dowsers), *Zeitschrift für Radiesthesie*, Vol. 12, 1960.

325

**Chapter 8:
Icebergs or "Waters of the
Earth"**

Talks with Stephan Riess both at his home in Ojai, California, and during some 2,000 miles of automobile travel to sites of water wells brought in by him over the years developed a great deal of the material for this chapter and for Chapter 9. Also consulted:

Biswas, Asit K., *History of Hydrology,* North Holland Publishing Company, Amsterdam–London; American Elsevier Publishing Company, New York, 1970.

Kervran, C. Louis, personal communication, 1977–78.

Roberts, Kenneth, *The Seventh Sense,* Doubleday, Garden City, New York, 1953.

Salzman, Michael H., *New Water for a Thirsty World,* Science Foundation Press, Los Angeles, 1960. (Contains a bibliography of 198 references.)

Smith, Grant M., *The History of the Comstock Lode, 1850–1920,* University of Nevada Bulletin, July 1, 1943.

Young, Otis E., *Western Mining,* University of Oklahoma Press, 1970.

**Chapter 9:
The Politics of Water**

Ackerman, William C., "Needed: Three Wise Men," *Transactions,* American Geophysical Union, Vol. 42, No. 1, March 1961.

Arnold, Ralph, "Some Geologic Aspects of the Stephan Riess Concept of Primary Water," copies filed in 1960 at the U.S. Geological Survey and Banner Club of the California Institute of Technology.

California, Department of Public Works, Division of Water Resources, *Memorandum Report on Reconnaissance Investigation of Wells Located by Stephen (sic) Riess,* October 1954.

California, Department of Water Resources, *Information Bulletin,* "Is 'Primary Water' or 'Rock Fissure Water' a Potential Source of Water Supply?", December 1960.

McGuinness, Charles Lee, *The Role of Ground Water in the National Water Situation,* Geological Survey Water-Supply Paper 1800, U.S. Government Printing Office, 1963, 1,121 pp.

**Chapter 10:
Gusher!**

The chapter is based on extensive interviews with Paul Clement Brown and Chet Davis and on documents from their files.

**Chapter 11:
The U.S. Marines Learn
to Dowse**

The chapter is based on extensive interviews with Louis Matacia and on documents loaned from his files.

**Chapter 12:
Ships and People in Trouble**

This chapter is based on correspondence with Vosum both from Saigon, Vietnam, and from California; an interview with Ralph Harris in Glendale, California; several visits with Gordon MacLean in South Portland, Maine; and documents supplied by Robert Ater from Bath, Maine. Also consulted:

Auscher, Jean, *Les Mystérieux Pouvoirs, du Cerveau Humain Démontrés par la Radiesthésie Graphique,* Deforges, Paris, 1974.

**Chapter 13:
Pay Dirt**

Adaykina, E., "Nothing Fantastic," *Vecherniy Tashkent* (Evening Tashkent), June 11, 1969.

Akimov, V. and V. Plotnikov, "Tainy Volshebnoi Lozy" (Secrets of the Magic Rod), *Krasnaya Zvezda* (Red Star) USSR Ministry of Defense newspaper, section on "Science," October 17, 1970.

Bakirov, A. G., "Geologicheskie Vozmozhnosti Biofizicheskogo Metoda" (The Geological Possibilities of the Biophysical Method), *I. Konference o Výzkumu Psychotroniky, sborník referátů* (1st Conference of Psychotronics, collection of abstracts), 2 vols., Prague, June 1973, (Hereafter referred to as First Conference).

Bakirov, A. G., A. A. Malakhov, V. S. Matveyev and N. N. Sochevanov, "Da, Biofizicheskii Metod Sushchestvuet!" (Yes, the Biophysical Method Does Exist!), *Geologiya Rudnykh Mestorozhdenii* (The Geology of Ore Deposits), July-August 1976.

Bazhenov, A.S., "Oprobovanie Biofizicheskogo Metoda s Tselyu Otyskaniya Podzemnykh Pustot" (Testing with the Biophysical Method to Locate Subterranean Cavities), *Vtoroy Nauchno-Tekhnicheskiy Seminar po Biofizicheskomu Effektu* (BFE) (The Second Scientific Technical Seminar on the Biophysical Effect, [BPE]), Moscow, March 1971, (Hereafter referred to as Second Seminar).

Belyshev, B. F., "Approaches to Mystery," *Vechernii Novosibirsk* (Evening Novosibirsk), April 19, 1969.

———, "Gipoteza BFE" (The Hypothesis of the Biophysical Effect), *Sovetskaya Rossiya* (Soviet Russia), August 31, 1974.

Ber, N. V., "Opyt Primeneniya BFM pri Reshenii Zadach Geokartirovaniya i Poiskov Poleznykh Iskopaemykh v Tsentral'nom Kazakhstane" (Experiment on the Use of the Biophysical Method in Solving Problems of Geological Mapping and Prospecting for Mineral Deposits in Central Kazakhstan), (Second Seminar).

Biofizicheskaya Reaktsiya Cheloveka na Nalichie v Zemle Vod i Rud Geofizika, Meditsina i Parapsikholugiya: Vyborochnyi Spisok Otechestvennoi i Inostrannoi Literatury 1950–1971 (The Biophysical Reaction of Man to the Presence of Water and Ores in the Earth—Geophysics Medicine and Parapsychology: a Selected Bibliography of Soviet and Foreign Literature 1950–1971), USSR Academy of Sciences Library, Leningrad, 1972.

Bogolyubov, A. N., N. A. Voroshilov and O. D. Gorbunov, "Opyt Izucheniy Sutochnykh Variatsii Biofizicheskogo Effekta" (Experimental Study of Diurnal Variations of the Biophysical Effect), (Second Seminar).

Bondarev, Boris, "Sushchnost Biofizicheskogo Effekta" (The Nature of the Biophysical Effect), *Geologorazvedchik Uzbekistana* (The Uzbekistan Geological Prospector), June 7, 1969.

———, "O Sushchnosti Primeneniya Biofizicheskogo Effekta pri Poiskakh Mestorozhdenii Poleznykh Iskopaemykh" (On the Essence of the Application of the Biophysical Effect in Prospecting for Minerals), *Geologorazvedchik Uzbekistana* (The Uzbekistan Geological Prospector), June 7, 1969.

———, "O Biofizicheskom Metode v Geologii" (On the Biophysical Method in Geology), *Geologorazvedchik Uzbekistana* (The Uzbekistan Geological Prospector), July 19, 1969.

———, "Gipotezy o Prirode Biofizicheskogo Effekta" (Hypotheses on the Nature of the Biophysical Effect), *Geologorazvedchik Uzbekistana* (The Uzbekistan Geological Prospector), July 29, 1969.

———, "Snova o Volshebnoi Palochke" (More About the Magic Rod),

Geologorazvedchik Uzbekistana (The Uzbekistan Geological Prospector), October 28, 1969.

———, "Effektivnost BFM" (The Effectiveness of the Biophysical Method), *Geologorazvedchik Uzbekistana* (The Uzbekistan Geological Prospector), December 30, 1969.

———, "Biofizicheskaya Reaktsiya Cheloveka na Nalichie v Zemle Rud i Vod" (The Biophysical Reaction in Man to the Presence of Ores and Water in the Ground), Tashkent State University, Alma Ata, issue No. 338, (Mineralogy, Geochemistry, Petrography) 1970.

———, "Biofizicheskiy Effekt i Ego Primenenie pri Poiskakh Poleznykh Iskopaemykh" (The Biophysical Effect and Its Use in Prospecting), Tashkent State University, issue No. 372, (Mineralogy, Geochemistry, Petrography) 1970.

Burova, T. A., "Opyt Primeneniya Biofizicheskogo Metoda pri Izuchenii Struktur Olovorudnykh Mestorozhdenii Kirgizii i Tadzhikstana," (Experiment on the Use of the Biophysical Method in the Study of the Structure of Tin Ore Deposits in Kirgiziya and Tadzhikistan) (Second Seminar).

Chekunov, Anatolii Ya., "Metodika Opredoleniya Glubiny Zaleganiya Mednokolchedanykh Rudnykh Tel" (Methodology for Determining the Depth of Copper Pyrite Bodies), (First Conference).

Frantov, G., "Dowsing: Myth or Reality?" (in Russian), *Komsomolets* (The Komsomol), December 28, 1968.

Frolova, S., " 'Volshebnyi' Prut" (The "Magic" Rod), *Uzbekistan*, no. 10, 1969.

Grigor'yev, A. M., "O Nekotorykh Vozhmozhnostyakh Biofizicheskogo Metoda pri Poiskakh Perekrytykh Zoloto-Rudnykh Mestorozhdeniy i Geologicheskom Kartirovanii v Severnom Kazakhstane" (Certain Possibilities Displayed by the Biophysical Method in Prospecting of Covered Gold Ore Deposits and Geological Mapping in North Kazakhstan), (Second Seminar).

Inyutin, I. P., "Metod Poiskov Podzemnykh Vod i Rud Priborami Ispolzuyushchimi Biofizicheskii Effekt" (A Method for Prospecting for Water and Ores by Test Bores Using the Biophysical Effect), *The Sverdlovsk Mining Institute*, issue No. 104, 1974.

Ivanov, N. I., A. I. Pluzhnikov and N. N. Sveshnikov, "Primenenie Biofizicheskogo Metoda k Issledovaniyu i Restavratsii Pamyatnikov Istorii i Arkitektury" (The Application of the Biophysical Method to Researching and Restoring Historical and Architectural Monuments), *Voprosy Okhrany, Restavratsii i Propagandy Pamyatnikov Istorii i Kultury* (Problems in the Preservation, Restoration, and Publicizing of Historical and Cultural Monuments), Scientific-Research Institute for Culture, RSFSR Ministry of Culture, Moscow, 1975.

Kapachauskas, V. M., "O Nekotorykh Prichinakh Nesootvetstviya Mezhdu Pokazaniyami BFE i Dannymi Bureniya i Gornoprokhodicheskikh Rabot" (Some Reasons for Discrepancies Existing Between BPE Indications and Data from Drilling and Cutting Operations), (Second Seminar).

Komin, M. F., "Opyt Primeneniya Biofizicheskogo Metoda pri Oprcdelenii Treshchinovatosti Gornykh Porod i Slezhenii Razryvnykh Struktur" (Experience in the Use of the Biophysical Method for the Determination of Jointing of Rocks and Tracking of Fractured Structures), (Second Seminar).

Lipetskii, V., "The Magic Wand," *Tekhnika Molodezhi* (Technics for Youth), No. 9, 1944.

Malafeyev, A. A., Effekt 'Biolokatsii' " (The Effect of "Biolocation"), *Sovetskaya Rossiya* (Soviet Russia), March 22, 1974.

Malakhov, A. A., "Sensitiviy i Perspektivy" (Sensitives and Perspectives), *Voprosy i Otvety* (Questions and Answers), No. 12, 1968.

————, "' Volshebnaya Loza,' Chto Eto Takoe?" (The "Magic Rod," What Is It?), *Ural'skii Rabochii* (The Urals Worker), Sverdlovsk, February 3, 1973.

————, "Biofizicheskii Effekt 500 Mineralov" (The Biophysical Effect of 500 Minerals), (First Conference).

————, "O Nekotorykh Zakonomerostyakh Razmeshcheniya Prirodnykh Resursov Srednego i Yuzhnogo Urala—Po Dannym Biofiziki" (On Several Regularities in the Distribution of Natural Resources in the Middle and Southern Urals—according to Biophysical Data), *Razmeshchenie Proizvoditel'nykh Sil* (The Distribution of Productive Forces), Ministry of Higher and Middle Specialized Education of the RSFSR, issue No. 7, Sverdlovsk, 1975.

Matveyev, V. S., "O Biofizicheskom Metode v Geologii" (On the Biophysical Method in Geology), *Izvestiya Akademii Nauk Kazakhskoi SSR* (Izvestiya of the Kazakh SSR Academy of Sciences), Geological Series, No. 3, 1967.

Matveyev, V. S. and G. P. Konovalov, "O Seysmovariatsionnom Yavlenii v Biofizicheskom Metode" (On Seismovariational Phenomena in the Biophysical Method), (Second Seminar).

Mel'nikov, Ye. K., "Nekotorye Rezultaty Primeneniya Aerobiofizicheskoy S'emki pri Geologo-Poiskovykh Rabotakh" (Some Results from the Use of Aerobiophysical Surveys in Geological Prospecting Operations), (Second Seminar).

Morozov, Vyacheslav, "Geometriya Chudes" (The Geometry of Miracles), *Moskovskiy Komsomolets* (The Moscow Komsomol), Interview, April 15, 1975.

Ogil'vi, A. A., "Ispol'zovanie Biofizicheskogo Metoda pri Issledovanii Treshchinno-Karstovogo Vodonosnogo Gorizonta" (Use of the Biophysical Method in Exploring a Fissured Karst Water-Bearing Level), (Second Seminar).

Ogil'vi, A. N., *Geofizicheskie Metody Issledovanii* (Geophysical Methods of Research), Moscow State University Press, 1962.

Pluzhnikov, A. I., "O Biofizicheskikh Poiskakh i Razvedke Podzemykh Aekhitekturno-Arkheologicheskikh i Voenno-Istoricheskikh Ob'ektov Podmoskov'ya" (Biophysical Exploration and Prospecting of Subterranean Architectural-Archaeological and Military-Historical Objects in the Moscow Area), (Second Seminar).

Popovkin, Viktor, "V Rukakh—Neizvestnoe" (In the Hands, Something Unknown), *Komsomol'skaya Pravda*, June 18, 1966.

————, "The Magic Wand: Myth or Problem," *Znaniya Sila* (Knowledge is Power), No. 12, 1967.

Prokhorov, V. G., "Osobennosti Biofizicheskikh Anomalii nad Razlichnymi Ob'ektami" (Special Features of Biophysical Anomalies Over Various Objects) (First Conference).

Pukhovskaya, S., "Vidyashchie Skvoz' Zemlyu" (Those Who Can See Through the Ground), *Leninskoya Znamya* (Lenin Banner), Moscow, July 15, 1973.

Rainey, Froelich, personal communication, 1978.

Scott, Elliot, J. *Dowsing: One Man's Way,* Neville Spearman, Jersey, 1977.

Shmidt, N. G., I. M. Blokh and D. A. Gorelov, "O Primenenii Biofizicheskogo Metoda pri Poiskakh" (On the Application of the Biophysical Method to Prospecting), *Razvedka i Okhrana Nedr* (The Search for and Conservation of Resources), No. 9, 1974.

Shmidt, N. G., A. N. Yeremeyev and A. P. Solorov, "Sushchestvuet li Biofizicheskiy Metod Poiskov Rudnykh Mestorozhdenii?" (Does There Exist a Biophysical Method for Prospecting for Ore Deposits?), *Geologiya Rudnykh Mestorozhdenii* (The Geology of Ore Deposits), September–October, 1975.

Simonov, E. V. and E. M. Tareyev, "Problema 'Volshebnoi Palochki' " (The

Problem of the "Witching" Rod), *Elektrichestvo* (Electricity), No. 1–2, 1944.

"S 'Lozoi' za Poleznymi Iskopaemyi" (Hunting for Minerals with the "Rod"), *Voprosy i Otvety* (Questions and Answers), No. 8, 1973.

Sochevanov, N. N., ". . . Ukazyvaet Na Tainu" (. . . Reveals a Secret), *Vokrug Sveta* (Around the World), No. 12, 1967.

————, "Vliyaniye Nekotorykh Faktorov na Intensivnost' Biofizicheskogo Effekta (Influence of Several Factors on the Intensity of the Biophysical Effect), in *Psikhicheskaya Samoregulyatsiya* (Psychic Self-Regulation), 2 vols., A. S. Romen, editor, Alma Ata, 1974.

————, "Novye Dannye o Biofizicheskom Effekte i Osobennostyakh Biofizicheskikh Polei" (New Data on the Biophysical Effect on the Characteristics of Biophysical Fields), (Second Seminar).

————, and M. F. Komin, "Rezul'taty Primeneniya Biofizicheskogo Metoda pri Glubinnykh Rudnykh Mestorozhdeniy" (Results of Using the Biophysical Method in Deep Prospecting of Ore Deposits), (Second Seminar).

————, and V. P. Kuronov, "Metodika Vyyavleniya Operatorov BFE pri Massovykh Proverkakh" (Method for Detecting Operators in Mass Trials), (Second Seminar).

————, "Nekotorye Osobennosti Proyavleniya Biofyzicheskogo Effekta" (Certain Features of the Manifestation of the Biophysical Effect), (First Conference).

Sochevanov, N. N. and V. S. Matveyev, "Biofizicheskii Metod v Geologicheskikh Issledovaniyakh" (The Biophysical Method in Geological Research), *Geologiya Rudnykh Mestorozhdenii* (The Geology of Ore Deposits), September-October, 1974.

Tareyev, B. M., "Discovery of Subterranean Water as an Electrophysical Manifestation" (in Russian), *Elektrichestvo* (Electricity), No. 3, 1931.

Viktorov, A., "The Magic Rod," (in Russian) *Nauka i Religiya* (Science and Religion), No. 4, 1964.

Volkov, O., "Podzemnye Khody v Kolomenskom" (Underground Passages in Kolomenskii), *Komsomol'skaya Pravda*, September 30, 1970.

Volosyuk, G. K. *et al.*, "O Pryamykh Metodakh Poiskov, i Razvedki Rudnykh Mestorozhdenii" (Direct Methods of Searching and Prospecting for Mineral Deposits), *Razvedka i Okhrana Nedr* (Prospection for and Conservation of Resources), No. 3, 1967.

Yakovlev, B., "Taina 'Volshebnoi Lozy' " (The Secret of the "Magic Rod"), *Vecherniy Chelyabinsk* (Evening Chelyabinsk), April 5, 1975.

Chapter 14:
The Sixth Sense of the
Anthropomagnetometer

Chadwick, Duane G. and Larry Jensen, *The Detection of a Magnetic Field Caused by Ground Water and the Correlation of Such Fields with Water Dowsing*, Utah State University Bulletin PRWG78-1, January 1971.

Evans-Pritchard, Edward, *Witchcraft, Oracles and Magic Among the Azande*, Clarendon Press, Oxford, 1973.

Harvalik, Zaboj V., "Tunnel Detection by Dowsing," unpublished manuscript, February 21, 1968.

————, "A Biophysical Magnetometer-gradiometer," *Journal of the Virginia Academy of Science*, 1970.

————, personal communications.

"The Search for the Magnetic Sensors in Man," (proposed title), *Physiological Chemistry and Physics*, Pacific Press, New York, (in press).

Harvalik, writing alone or with Wilhelm de Boer, has published the following articles relevant to the chapter (plus others) in the quarterly *The American Dowser* from November 1970 to August 1976:

"Signal Sensitivity Determination of Dowsers."

"Signal Sensitivities of Eleven Selected Dowsers."

"Saturation Effects Reduce Sensitivity of Dowsers."

"Fatigue Effects Influence the Signal of the Dowser."

"The Riddle of the Signal Suppression."

"Dowsing Reactions to Polarized Electromagnetic Radiations."

"High Frequency Beams Aid Locating the Dowsing Sensors."

"Dowsing Reactions to Artificial Alternating Magnetic Fields in the Frequency of 1-75 Hertz."

"Dowsing Reactions to Electromagnetic Fields with Frequency Ranges from 1 Hertz to 1 Mega-Hertz."

"Where are the Dowsing Sensors?"

"Locating the Dowsing Sensors by the 'High Frequency Beam' Method."

"Programming by Radio."

"Dowsing Signals Produced by Alternating Electromagnetic Fields in the Frequency Range of 1 Hertz to 500 Hertz."

Maby, J. Cecil and T. Bedford Franklin, *The Physics of the Divining Rod*, Bell, London, 1939.

Rocard, Yves, *Le Signal du Sourcier* (The Dowser's Signal), Dunod, Paris, 1964.

Trefil, James S., "A Consumer's Guide to Pseudoscience," *The Saturday Review*, New York, April 29, 1978. (See reply in a subsequent "Letter to the Editor" by Christopher Bird.)

Chapter 15:
An Electronic Dowser

Aschoff, Dieter, *Kann die offizielle Wissenschaft die Theorie von der Entstehung des Krebses auf Reizzonen Heute noch ablehnen?* (Can Official Science Today Still Reject the Theory of Cancer Incidence in Irritation Zones?), Wuppertal, November 1973. (Privately printed)

————, "Welche Fragen zum Krebs und Reizzonen Problem stellt man uns Heute, 45 Jahre nach der Rutenbegehung in Vilbisburg durch Freiherrn v. Pohl?" (What Questions on Cancer and Irritation Zones Are Posed Today 45 years after Freiherr von Pohl's Dowsing Rod Survey in Vilbisburg?), *Zeitschrift fur Radiesthesie*, No. 4, 1974.

Bachler, Käthe, *Erfahrungen einer Rutengängerin, Geobiologische Einflüsse auf den Menschen* (Experiences of a Dowser, Geobiological Influences on Man), Veritas Verlag, Linz, Austria, 1976.

Bickel, Armin, *Algor Explorer "X"—The Supersensitive Subteranean Isotope Sensor*, privately printed brochure, Lompoc, California, no date.

Brüche, E., "Problematik der Wünschelrute" (Problematics of the Dowsing Rod), *Mensch und Umwelt*, Vol. 5, J. R. Geigy S.A., Basel, 1962.

Cody, Pierre, *Etude Expérimentale de L'Ionisation de L'Air par une Certaine Radioactivité du Sol* (Experimental Study of Air Ionization by a Certain Radiation of the Soil), International Congress on Biophysics, New York, 1939.

Comunetti, Angelo, interviewed with Dr. Peter Treadwell: "Mutungen" (Dowsing), *Roche Magazin*, No. 3, April 1978.

Côte D'Azur Medicale

Douglas, Herbert, "Taking Another Look at the Arthritis Dowsing Link," December 17, 1973; "The Strange Role of Dowsing in Medicine," 2 parts, December 7 and 8, 1976; "Dowsing: Can It Cure Arthritis?" May 5, 1978; *The Banner*, Bennington, Vermont.

Effects of Harmful Radiations and Noxious Rays, American Society of Dowsers, Danville, Vermont, 1974.

Fritsch, Volker, *Das Problem geopathischer Erscheinungen von Standpunkten der Geophysik* (The Problem of Geopathic Phenomena from the Geophysical Point of View), Verlag Lehmann, Munich, 1955.

Gonzenbach, Wilhelm von, *Gesundheit als Recht und Pflicht* (Health as a Right), Basel, 1945.

König, Herbert L., *Unsichtbare Umwelt* (The Invisible Environment), Heinz Moos Verlag, Munich, 1975.

Kopp, J. A., "Which Part of the Body Reacts to Earth Irritation Zones Detected by Dowsing Techniques?" *The American Dowser,* May 1973.

Jenny, E., "Experimental-biologische Untersuchungen zum Erdstrahlen-Problem" (Experimental-Biological Research on the Problem of Earth Rays), *Gesundheit und Wohlfahrt,* No. 1, 1947.

Jenny, E. and A. Ohler, "Krebs and Erdstrahlen" (Cancer and Earth Rays), *Schweiz, Med. Wochenschr,* 1937.

Kopp, Joseph, "Tierkrankheiten und Geophysikalische Bodenreize" (Animal Diseases and Geophysical Earth Irritation), *Archiv für Tierheilkunde,* 1954.

————, "Eigene Erfahrungen über Bodenreize und Krebs" (Personal Experiences with Earth Stimulation and Cancer), *Oncologia,* No. 2, 1955.

————, *Gesundheitsschädliche und bautenschädliche Einflüsse von Bodenreizen* (Harmful Influences of Earth Stimulation on Health and Buildings), Schweizer Verlagshaus, Zurich, 1965.

————, "40 Jahre praktische Reizstreifen Forschung" (40 Years of Practical Research into Irritation Zones), *Wetter-Boden-Mensch,* Vol. 16, 1972.

————, "Die Erdstrahlen-forschung des eidgenossischen Veterinäramtes in Bern" (Research on Earth Rays by the Federal Veterinary Bureau in Bern), *Wetter-Boden-Mensch,* Vol. 14, 1972.

————, "Krebs durch Bodeneinflüsse" (Cancer through Soil Influence), *Umdenken-Umschwenken,* Arbeitsgemeinschaft Umwelt, Zürich, 1975.

Petschke, H., "Der Krebs im Lichte geophysikalischer Strahlung" (Cancer in Light of Geophysical Rays), *Erfahrungsheilkunde* No. 9, 1954.

————, "Krebs und geopatische Zonen" (Cancer and Geopathic Zones), *Gesundheit und Wohlfart,* Vol. 5, Zurich, 1955.

Peyré, Francois, *Radiations Cosmo-Télluriques* (Cosmo-Telluric Radiations), Maison de la Radiesthésie, Paris, 1947.

Prokop, Oskar, *Wünschelrute, Erdstrahlen und Wissenschaft* (The Dowsing Rod, Earth Rays and Science), Ferd. Enke Verlag, Stuttgart, 1955.

Rambeau, H., "Besteht ein Zusammenhang zwischen der Tektonik der Erde und dem Krankheitsproblem?" (Is There a Connection Between the Tectonics of the Earth and the Problem of Illness?), *Biologische Heilkunst,* January 20, 1934.

Ringger, A., "Kritische Bemerkungen zum Reizzonen-Versuch des Eidg. Veterinäramtes und Vorschläge für die Zukunft (Critical Observations on the Irritation Zone Experiment by the Federal Veterinary Bureau and Suggestions for the Future), *Die Gründe,* Vol. 37, 1971.

Seeger, P. G., "Können Standortfaktoren die Verkrebsung von Zellen provozieren oder beeinflussen?" (Can Location Factors Provoke or Influence Cancer in Cells?), *Wetter-Boden-Mensch,* Vol. 1, 1967.

————, "Geopathogene Reizstreifen und Krebs" (Geopathic Irritation Zones and Cancer), *Wetter-Boden-Mensch,* Vol. 4, 1969.

————, "Ist eine Vorbeugung gegen Krebs möglich?" (Can Cancer Be Prevented?), *Wetter-Boden-Mensch,* Vol. 5, 1969.

————, "Die Bedeutung einer unpassenden Prophylaxe des Krebses für die sozialhygienischen Erfordernisse" (The Significance of an Unsuitable Prophylaxis of Cancer for Social Hygienic Requirements), *Wetter, Boden-Mensch,* Vol. 9, 1970.

————, *Krebs—Problem ohne Ausweg* (Cancer—a Problem without Solution), Verlag für Medizin, Heidelberg, 1974.

————, "Radikaler Umweltschutz—letzte Chance zum Überleben" (Radical Environmental Protection—Last Chance for Survival), *Wetter-Boden-Mensch,* No. 22, 1975.

Stängle, Jacob, "Strahlungsmessungen über unterirdischen Quellführungen" (Radiation Measurements over Underground Aquifers), *Bohrtechnik—Brunnenbau—Rohrleitungsbau,* No. 11, 1960.

———, "Sind unterirdische Quellführungen physikalisch messbar?" (Are Underground Water Courses Physically Measurable?) *Zeitschrift fur Radiesthesie,* Vol. 1, 1965.

Von Pohl, Freiherr, "Krankheiten durch Erdausstrahlungen, 1. Mitteilung Krebs" (Illness as a Result of Radiation from the Earth, 1st report: Cancer), *Zeitschrift fur Krebsforschung,* 31 Band, Julius Springer, Berlin, 1930.

———, *Erdstrahlen als Krankheitsreger* (Earth Rays as Initiators of Illness), Jos. Huberts Verlag, Diessen vor München, 1932.

Walther, Johannes, *Das Rätsel der Wünschelrute* (The Riddle of the Dowsing Rod), Verlag von Philip Reclam jun., Leipzig, 1933.

Winzer, H. and W. Melzer, *Cancer in the Light of Geophysical Radiation,* New York, 1927.

Wüst, Joseph, "Zur gegenwärtigen Situation der Geopathie" (On the Present Situation in Geopathy), *Erfahrungsheilkunde,* No. 12, 1954.

———, "Über physikalische Nachweismethoden der sogenannten 'Erdstrahlen' " (On Physical Methods of Proof of the so-called 'Earth Rays'), *Erfahrungsheilkunde,* No. 6, special issue on Geopathy, 1954.

———, "Wünschelrute, Erdstrahlen und Wissenschaft" (The Dowsing Rod, Earth Rays and Science), *Erfahrungsheilkunde,* No. 8, 1955.

———, "Gammastrahlungsmessungen auf geopathischen Zonen" (Gamma-Rays Measurement on Geopathic Zones), *Erfahrungsheilkunde,* No. 2, 1956.

Chapter 16: The Medical Potential

Bouly, Abbé, *La Radiesthésie ou Comment Devenir Expert dans L'Art de Capter les Ondes* (Radiesthesia or How to Become an Expert in the Art of Capturing Waves), M.A. Carpon, Paris (no date).

Bourdoux, Jean-Louis, *Notions Pratiques de Radiesthésie pour les Missionaires* (Practical Notions of Radiesthesia for Missionaries), Desforges, Paris, 1965.

Coulter, Harris, Ph.D., "Homeopathy," *Wholistic Dimensions in Healing, A Resource Guide,* Leslie J. Kaslof, compiler and editor, Doubleday and Co., New York, 1978.

Felsenhardt, Robert, "Des Services Extraordinaires Rendus par la Radiesthésie," Interview in *Psiréalité,* No. 3, December 1977.

Jurion, Jean, R. P. *Journal d'un Hors-la-Loi—Un Prêtre Parmi les Guérisseurs* (Diary of an Outlaw—A Priest Among Healers), Guy Victor, Paris, 1966.

———, *Médicine Naturelle, Médicine de L'Avenir* (Natural Medicine, The Medicine of the Future), self-published, Paris, 1968.

———, *La Radiesthésie, Moyen de Connaissance Universelle, Son Apprentissage, Ses Possibilités, Ses Limites* (Radiesthesia, A Means for Universal Knowledge, Its Apprenticeship, Its Possibilities, Its Limitations), self-published, Paris, 3rd edition, 1970–73.

———, *La Radiesthésie Médicale, Thérapeutiques Naturelles* (Medical Radiesthesia, Natural Therapies), Soprode, Paris, 1973.

———, *Thérapeutiques Naturelles, Homéopathie, Conseils Pratiques* (Natural Therapies, Practical Advice in Homeopathy), Vol. 1, self-published, Paris, 1975.

———, *Thérapeutiques Naturelles, Radiesthésie Médicale, Documentation* (Natural Therapies, Medical Radiesthesia, Documentation), Vol. 2, self-published, Paris, 1975.

———, *La Radiesthésie, Techniques et Applications* (Radiesthesia, Techniques and Applications), Belfond, Paris, 1976.

Notions Générales et Pratiques de Radiesthésie—Sur les Traces d'un Missionaire, le Père J. L. Bourdoux (General and Practical Notions of Radiesthesia—On the Trail of a Missionary, Father J. L. Bourdoux), Maison de la Radiesthésie, Paris, 1964.

Radiesthésie Magazine, International Center for Radiesthesia, 102 Rue La Boetie, Paris, France.

Reyner, J. M., George Laurence and Carl Upton, *Psionic Medicine, The Study and Treatment of the Causative Factors in Illness,* Routledge and Kegan Paul, London, 1974.

Richards, Guyon, *The Chain of Life,* John Bale Sons and Danielsson, London, 1934.

Westlake, Aubrey T., *The Pattern of Health, A Search for a Greater Understanding of the Life Force in Health and Disease,* Devin-Adair, New York, 1961.

————, *Life Threatened, Menace and Way Out,* Stuart and Watkins, London, 1975.

————, "The Contribution of Psionic Medicine to Hahnemann's Miasmic Theory," *Journal of the Psionic Medical Society,* Winter, 1974.

————, "A New Dimension in Medicine (Two Lectures)," *Journal of the Psionic Medical Society,* nos. 11 and 12, 1976–77.

———— *The Origins and History of Psionic Medicine,* Psionic Medical Society, Hindhead, Surrey, 1977.

Conclusion: "The Apprehension of the Supersensible World"

Parts of the conclusion were inspired by informal lectures given by Drs. Olivier Costa de Beauregard and Richard Mattuck and by conversations with Dr. John Hasted, all at Valle de Bravo, Mexico, in the summer of 1978, and by a visit with Arthur Young at his home in Downingtown, Pennsylvania in September 1978. Also consulted:

Bearden, Thomas, *The Excalibur Briefing,* Strawberry Hill, San Francisco, 1978.

Bird, Christopher and Oliver Nichelson, "Great Scientist, Forgotten Genius, Nikola Tesla," *New Age,* February 1977.

Dubrov, Alexander and Veniamin Pushkin, *Parapsykhologiya i Sovremennoe Estestvoznanie* (Parapsychology and Contemporary Science), unpublished manuscript, completed 1978.

Gatland, Kenneth W. and Derek Dempster, *Worlds in Creation,* Henry Regnery Company, Chicago, 1974.

Kuhn, Thomas S., *The Structure of Scientific Revolutions,* Phoenix–University of Chicago Press, 1962.

McGlashan, Alan, *Gravity and Levity,* Houghton Mifflin, Boston, 1976.

Musès, Charles, "The Exploration of Consciousness," in Musès, Charles and Arthur M. Young, *Consciousness and Reality: The Human Pivot Point,* Outerbridge and Lazard, New York, 1972.

Needleman, Jacob, *A Sense of the Cosmos: The Encounter of Modern Science and Ancient Truth,* Doubleday, New York, 1975.

Schwartz, Stephan A., *The Secret Vaults of Time: Psychic Archaeology and the Quest for Man's Beginnings,* Grosset and Dunlap, New York, 1978.

Shepherd, A. P., *A Scientist of the Invisible: An Introduction to the Life and Work of Rudolf Steiner,* Hodder and Stoughton, London, 1954.

Tiller, William A., private communication, 1977-1978.

Wigner, Eugene P., "The Place of Consciousness in Modern Physics," in Musès, Charles and Arthur M. Young, *Consciousness and Reality: The Human Pivot Point,* Outerbridge and Lazard, New York, 1972.

Appendix:

Curry, Manfred, *Bioklimatik* (Bioclimatics), Bioclimatic Research Institute, Riderau, 1946.

————, "Das Reaktionsliniensystem als krankheitauslösender Faktor" (The

Reaction-Line System as a Pathogenic Factor), *Hippokrates,* May 31, 1952.

Gläser, M. and Siegfried Wittmann, "Krebs und Reizzonen," (Cancer and Stimulation Zones), *Erfahrungsheilkunde,* Vol. 4, 1955.

Hartmann, Ernst, "Theorie und Praxis einer geobiologischen Therapie und Prophylaxe" (Theory and Practice of a Geobiological Therapy and Prophylaxis), *Wetter-Boden-Mensch,* No. 4, 1968.

————, *Krankheit als Standortproblem* (Illness as a Problem of Location), Verlag Haug, 1976.

Hartmann, Ernst and Joseph Wüst, "Über physikalische Nachweismethoden der sogenannten 'Erdstrahlen' " (On Physical Methods of Proof of So-Called "Earth Radiation"), *Geopathie /G. Beiheft zur Zeitschift Erfahrungsheilkunde,* Haug Verlag, Ulm, 1954.

Harvalik, Zaboj V. and Wilhelm de Boer, "The Universal Grid," *The American Dowser,* May 1978.

Pakraduny, T., *Die Welt der geheimen Mächte* (The World of Secret Forces), chapter by Siegfried Wittman, p. 257, Wiesbaden, (date).

Wittmann, Siegfried, "Erklärung zu den Polaren Feldern" (Explanation of the Polar Fields), *Zeitschrift für Radiesthesie,* vol. 27, 1975.

INDEX

337

P. 231 Qty